P9-EDE-067

PEARSON CUSTOM LIBRARY

A custom edition of Human Communication in Society
by Jess K. Alberts, Thomas K. Nakayama, and Judith N. Martin
SFSU Comm 150

PEARSON

Cover Art: "Amperstand Stencil" courtesy of Rob Szajkowski/iStockphoto, "Interview Microphones" courtesy of Valerie Loiseleux/iStockphoto, "Telephone Made Out of Cans" courtesy of Photodisc Photography/Veer Images, "Speech Balloon" courtesy of iStockphoto, "Road Markings" courtesy of iStockphoto, "Spotlight on Curtained Stage" courtesy of Infinity/Veer, "Theatre-Interior View" courtesy of Alex Nikada/iStockphoto; "Working with digital tablet" courtesy of hocus-focus/iStockphoto; "Earth Swirls White" courtesy of Joshua Blake/iStockphoto; "Three business people working at modern office cafeteria" courtesy of Clerkenwell Images/iStockphoto; "Social media concept: communication tree" courtesy of Chris Lemmens/iStockphoto; "Four blank speech bubbles hanging from thread" courtesy of Peter Booth/iStockphoto; "Colorful Speech Bubbles" courtesy of Peter Booth/iStockphoto. Additional images courtesy of Photodisc/Getty Images, Digital Vision, Photodisc, Rubberball Productions, Stockbyte/Getty Images, and Pearson Learning Solutions.

Copyright © 2016 by Pearson Learning Solutions

All rights reserved.

Permission in writing must be obtained from the publisher before any part of this work may be reproduced or transmitted in any form or by any means, electronic or mechanical, including photocopying and recording, or by any information storage or retrieval system.

Additional copyright information is included, where applicable, as a footnote at the beginning of each chapter.

Attention bookstores: For permission to return any unsold stock, contact us at *pe-uscustomreturns@pearson.com.*

Pearson Learning Solutions, 501 Boylston Street, Suite 900, Boston, MA 02116
A Pearson Education Company
www.pearsoned.com

ISBN 10: 1-323-35634-7
ISBN 13: 978-1-323-35634-0

24 2019

Table of Contents

1. Introduction to Human Communication
Jess K. Alberts/Thomas K Nakayama/Judith N. Martin   **1**

2. Communicating Identities
Jess K. Alberts/Thomas K Nakayama/Judith N. Martin   **27**

3. Communicating, Perceiving, and Understanding
Jess K. Alberts/Thomas K Nakayama/Judith N. Martin   **61**

4. Verbal Communication
Jess K. Alberts/Thomas K Nakayama/Judith N. Martin   **89**

5. Nonverbal Communication
Jess K. Alberts/Thomas K Nakayama/Judith N. Martin   **119**

6. Listening and Responding
Jess K. Alberts/Thomas K Nakayama/Judith N. Martin   **149**

7. Communication Across Cultures
Jess K. Alberts/Thomas K Nakayama/Judith N. Martin   **173**

8. Communicating Through Social and Other Interactive Media
Jess K. Alberts/Thomas K Nakayama/Judith N. Martin   **203**

Index   **241**

Introduction to Human Communication

CHAPTER TOPICS	Chapter Objectives
The Importance of Studying Human Communication	1 Explain why it is important to study human communication.
What Is Human Communication?	2 Name and describe the seven primary components of communication.
A Model of Human Communication: The Synergetic Model	3 Explain how the Synergetic Model of Communication differs from previous models.
Communication Ethics	4 Formulate your own communication ethic.
Putting It All Together: Communicating Competently	5 Articulate what makes a communicator competent.

From Chapter 1 of *Human Communication in Society*, Fourth Edition. Jess K. Alberts, Thomas K. Nakayama, Judith N. Martin. Copyright © 2016 by Pearson Education, Inc. All rights reserved.

> *"If good communication skills were just common sense, then communication would not so often go awry."*

On her way to class, Charee called her dad to let him know what time she would arrive home; she then texted a friend to arrange to meet for lunch. While she waited for class to begin, she checked Facebook and Tumblr. When the professor arrived, she muted her phone and listened as the class began.

Most people, like Charee, exist in a sea of communication. They phone, email, and text message their friends and family; spend time on Facebook, Instagram, and Twitter; occasionally watch television; attend class lectures; and are inundated by media images as they shop for groceries or use public transportation. Given all of this, it is hard to imagine that just 25 years ago most communication occurred face to face, on landlines, or through the U.S. mail. But in fact, throughout much of human history, individuals lived close to the people they knew. They conducted commerce and maintained relationships primarily with the same small group of people throughout their lives. Today, people maintain relationships with individuals thousands of miles away, and they buy and sell products halfway around the globe on Amazon, eBay, and countless retail sites. This instant and widespread access to the world has its benefits, but it also has its costs.

With so many communication options, people need a wider range of communication knowledge and skills than ever before. Successful communicators must converse effectively face to face; determine what messages to send via email or Twitter; learn with whom it is appropriate to use text messaging; and absorb the norms and etiquette surrounding the use of social media, such as whether to communicate through a Facebook post or a private message. Becoming an effective communicator involves both understanding the components and processes of communication and putting them into practice. As you work in this course to improve your communication knowledge and skills, you may see positive changes in your relationships, your career, your engagement in civic life, and even your identity. How many other courses can claim all that?

1 The Importance of Studying Human Communication

1 Explain why it is important to study human communication.

As you begin this text, several questions may arise. First, you may wonder exactly how the study of human communication differs from other studies of humans, such as psychology. Communication differs from other social science disciplines because it focuses exclusively on the exchange of messages to create meaning. Scholars in communication explore what, when, where, and why humans interact (Emanuel, 2007). They do so to increase our understanding of how people communicate and to help individuals improve their abilities to communicate in a wide variety of contexts. In addition, unlike most social sciences, the study of communication has a long history—reaching back to the classical era of Western civilization when Socrates, Plato, and Aristotle wrote about the important role of communication in politics, the courts, and learning (National Communication Association, 2003; Rogers & Chafee, 1983). However, the ability to speak effectively and persuasively has been valued since the beginning of recorded history. As early as 3200–2800 BCE, the Precepts of Kagemni and Ptah-Hotep commented on communication (NCA, 2003).

Alternative View

Co-rumination: When Too Much Talk Is as Bad as Not Enough

Can you think of other occasions when people talk "too much"?

You have probably heard that to have good relationships, people need to "communicate more." However, sometimes communicating a lot can have negative effects. One type of "over-communication" that can cause harm is co-rumination. Co-rumination occurs when we talk—again—and again—and again—with others about a problem in our lives. It has been linked to negative outcomes such as depression, anxiety, binge eating, binge drinking, and self-harm (Nolen-Hoeksema, Wiscol, & Lyubomirsky, 2008).

Co-rumination often occurs among friends, because that is to whom we turn most often when we encounter problems. In an attempt to console or support each other, such as when a break-up occurs, friends often tolerate or even encourage each other to talk extensively about what happened and how they feel. Individuals are most likely to engage in co-rumination during adolescence and young adulthood. In addition, because women tend to talk more and offer more emotional and verbal support to their friends, they also are more likely to co-ruminate.

Why is co-rumination unhealthy? During co-rumination, participants' communication focuses on the issue and its negative effects rather than on solutions. Repeatedly discussing how bad something is and how horrible one feels about it does nothing to change the problem or to change how the person feels about it. In fact, such discussions may make one feel worse and helpless to do anything about it. Consequently, experts suggest that conversations that focus on solutions and suggest that the problem can be overcome offer a more effective approach.

SOURCE: Nolen-Hoeksema S., Wisco B., & Lyumbomirski S. Rethinking rumination. (2008). *Perspectives on Psychological Science*, 3, 400–424.

Second, you may question why anyone needs to study communication; after all, most people have probably been doing a reasonably good job of it thus far. And isn't most communication knowledge just common sense? Unfortunately, it is not. If good communication skills were just common sense, then communication would not so often go awry. We would live in a world where misunderstandings rarely occurred; conflicts were easily resolved; and public speakers were organized, clear, and engaging. Instead, communication is a complex activity influenced by a variety of factors, including cultural differences, cognitive abilities, and social norms. Good communication is not a cure-all for every relationship and career ill, but it can help attain goals, establish relationships, and develop one's identity.

Now that we have so many ways to communicate and maintain relationships with others, some scholars have begun to ask if it is possible to have too much communication. Do you think this is possible or likely? To learn how some communication scholars answers this question, see Alternative View: Co-rumination: When Too Much Talk Is as Bad as Not Enough.

Finally, you may think of communication as a set of skills that are easily learned and wonder why there is an entire course (even a major!) that focuses on communication. Although it is true that every day people use communication to accomplish practical goals such as inviting a friend to see a movie, resolving a conflict with a colleague, or persuading the city council to install speed bumps in their neighborhood, communication is more than just a set of skills, like baking, that one can use in a variety of contexts and settings with little alteration. Rather, communication is a complex process whose effective performance requires an in-depth understanding of how it works and the ability to apply one's critical thinking skills to communication experiences to learn from and improve them.

Critical Thinking: A Key to Successful Communication

Critical thinking requires that one become a critic of one's own thoughts and behavior. That is, rather than responding automatically or superficially, critical thinkers reflect on their own and others' communication, behavior, and ideas before responding

If your romantic partner doesn't answer a text message, it could be because she is studying and has turned off her phone.

(Paul & Elder, 2008). Scholars have proposed various definitions of critical thinking; the one we advocate describes it as a process that involves the following steps (Passer & Smith, 2004):

1. Identify the assertion or action.
2. Ask, "what is the evidence for and against the assertion or action?"
3. Ask, "what does the bulk of evidence point to?"
4. Ask, "what other explanations or conclusions are possible?"
5. Continue to keep an open mind for new evidence and new ways of evaluating the assertion.

How might one apply this process to communication interactions? Let's explore this with a simple and common example. Imagine that you send a text message to your romantic partner on a Friday evening, but hours later have not heard back (Step 1: Identify the action). How should you interpret the lack of reply, and consequently, how should you respond? If you were thinking non-critically, you might interpret the behavior negatively (my partner is cheating on me!) even though you have little or no evidence to support this interpretation. You then might respond by dashing off an accusatory text.

However, more critical thinkers evaluate their interpretations and beliefs before responding by asking themselves, "What evidence do I have for this belief or interpretation?" (Step 2). Thus, if their first impulse was to doubt their partner, they would ask themselves, "What evidence exists that my partner is cheating?" (Does failing to return a text necessarily mean the partner is intentionally refusing to respond? Even if the partner is purposely refusing to respond to a text, does that mean the reason for refusing is unfaithfulness?)

The critical thinker would then question whether this interpretation is supported by sufficient evidence and experience (Step 3: What does the bulk of the evidence point to—for example has my partner cheated before? Does my partner usually respond quickly to texts? Is my partner normally trustworthy?). Next he or she would consider what other explanations are possible. (Step 4: What other conclusions are possible—for example, my partner's phone battery is dead; my partner fell asleep early and didn't receive my texts; my partner is studying and turned off her or his phone.)

Only after following this process would a critical thinker settle on a likely interpretation and response. Even then, the critical thinker would continue to keep an open mind and evaluate new information as it was presented (Step 5). Thus, even if you decided there was no evidence that your partner was cheating, you might reevaluate your conclusion if your partner repeatedly failed to reply to texts on Friday nights.

Advantages of Studying Human Communication

Now that you have reviewed the steps involved in critical thinking, would you consider yourself high or low in critical thinking skills? What topics or situations are most likely to cause you to use your critical thinking skills? What can you do to improve these skills?

Studying human communication conveys a number of advantages. Individuals use communication to meet people, to develop professional and personal relationships, and to terminate dissatisfying ones. Communication scholar Steve Duck argues that relationships are primarily communicative (1994). Moreover, the relationships we have with others—including how we think and feel about one another—develop as we communicate. Through communication interactions, relationship partners develop shared meanings for events, explanations for their shared past, and a vision of their future together (Alberts, Yoshimura, Rabby, & Loschiavo, 2005; Dixon & Duck, 1993). So, if you tell your romantic partner, "I have never loved anyone as much as I love you, and I never will," you are simultaneously redefining your past romantic relationships, creating shared meaning for the present relationship, and projecting a vision of your romantic future together. Similarly, through communication with friends, coworkers, and acquaintances, we all define and redefine our relationships.

Perhaps most fundamentally, your communication interactions with others allow you to establish who you are to them (Gergen, 1982; Mead, 1934). As you communicate, you attempt to reveal yourself in a particular light. For example, when you are at work, you may try to establish yourself as someone who is pleasant, hardworking, honest, and competent. With a new roommate, you may want your communication behavior to suggest you are responsible, fun, and easygoing. However, at the same time that your communication creates an image of who you are for others, *their* communication shapes your vision of yourself. For example, if your friends laugh at your jokes, compliment you on your sense of humor, and introduce you to others as a funny person, you probably will see yourself as amusing. In these ways, communication helps create both our self-identities and our identities as others perceive them.

Communication has the potential to transform your life—both for the better and for the worse. (To read how one student's communication created a transformation, see *It Happened to Me: Chelsea*.) As many people have discovered, poor or unethical communication can negatively affect lives. How? Communicating poorly during conflict can end relationships, inadequate interviewing skills can result in unemployment, and negative feedback from conversational partners can lessen one's self-esteem. Sometimes communication can have even more significant effects. In 2005, singer Lil' Kim was sent to jail for lying under oath, or perjury (and thereby obstructing justice), when she testified that she had not noticed her manager's presence in the building with her when a gunfight occurred outside of a New York radio station where she gave an interview. However, security cameras revealed her manager opening the door for her as she left the station. Thus, she was imprisoned for a specific unethical (and illegal) communication act (CNN.com, July 7, 2005).

As you can see from Chelsea's story, developing excellent communication skills also can transform your life for the better. The three authors of this text have all had students visit months or years after taking our communication classes to tell us what a difference the classes have made in their lives. A student in a public speaking class reported that, because of her improved presentation skills, she received the raise and promotion she had been pursuing for years; another student in a conflict and negotiation class revealed that her once-troubled marriage became more stable once she learned to express disagreements better. A third student felt more confident after he took a persuasion class that taught him how to influence people.

Studying human communication may also benefit you by opening doors to a new career path. A degree in communication can prepare you for a wide variety of communication careers.

It Happened to Me
Chelsea

When the professor asked us to identify a time when communication was transformative, many examples came to mind. Finally, I settled on one involving a negative relationship. In high school there's usually one person you just don't get along with. Boyfriend drama, bad-mouthing, you name it. I remember dreading seeing this one girl, and I'm sure she felt the same about me. Graduation came and went, and I completely forgot about her. A year later, I came across her Facebook page as I was searching for old classmates online. As I thought about how petty our arguments were and how cruel we were to each other, I felt smaller and smaller. So I decided to end it. After friending her, I sent her a private message to apologize for my bad behavior. A couple days later I received a response from her saying she felt the same way and was also sorry for the way she acted. Next week we're going to have a cup of coffee together to really put the past behind us. Maybe to some people that doesn't seem all that life changing, but after hating this girl for two years, it's an amazing transformation for me.

2   What Is Human Communication?

2   Name and describe the seven primary components of communication.

human communication
a transactional process in which people generate meaning through the exchange of verbal and nonverbal messages in specific contexts, influenced by individual and social forces, and embedded in culture

Even though you have been communicating for your entire life, you probably have not given much thought to the process. You may question why we even need to provide a definition for something so commonplace. Although communication is an everyday occurrence, the term covers a wide variety of behaviors that include talking to friends, broadcasting media messages, and emailing coworkers. Because the term *communication* is complex and can have a variety of definitions, we need to acquaint you with the definition we will use throughout this text.

Broadly speaking, human communication can be defined as a process in which people generate meaning through the exchange of verbal and nonverbal messages. In this text, however, we emphasize the influence of individual and societal forces and the roles of culture and context more than other definitions do. Because we believe these concepts are essential to understanding the communication process completely, we developed a definition of human communication that included them. Accordingly, we define human communication as a *transactional process in which people generate meaning through the exchange of verbal and nonverbal messages in specific contexts, influenced by individual and societal forces and embedded in culture.* In the following sections, we will illustrate our definition of human communication and explore the meaning of each of these concepts and their relationships to one another. To do so, we first look at the basic components of communication as highlighted in current definitions. Then, we examine the way these components serve as the building blocks of our own model of human communication in society, the Synergetic Model. Finally, we explain how individual and societal influences as well as culture and context contribute to an understanding of the communication process.

Components of Human Communication

Consider the following scenario:

> Charee grew up in the United States and needed to talk to her father, Pham, who was reared in Vietnam, about her desire to attend graduate school out of state. She was worried; she was the first member of her family to attend graduate school and would be the first single family member to move so far away. She hoped to convince her father that it was a good idea for her to go away, while also displaying respect for him as her father and the head of the household. To ensure that things went well, she decided that they should meet at his favorite neighborhood café in the early afternoon so they could talk privately. She rehearsed how she would convey information that he might not be happy to hear and practiced responses to the objections she expected him to raise.

messages
the building blocks of communication events

encoding
taking ideas and converting them into messages

decoding
receiving a message and interpreting its meaning

symbol
something that represents something else and conveys meaning.

As this example reveals, communication is a complex process that can require considerable thought and planning. The complexity inherent in communication is a result of the variety of factors that compose and influence it. The seven basic components of communication to consider in planning an interaction are *message creation*, *meaning creation*, *setting*, *participants*, *channels*, *noise*, and *feedback*. Each of these features is central to how a communication interaction unfolds. To help you understand this process, we analyze Charee's experiences with her father.

MESSAGE CREATION   Messages are the building blocks of communication, and the process of taking ideas and converting them into messages is called **encoding**. (Receiving a message and interpreting its meaning is referred to as **decoding**.) Depending on the importance of a message, people are more or less careful in encoding their messages.

In our example, Charee was concerned with how she encoded her messages to her father. She particularly wanted to communicate to her dad that they would remain close, both to persuade him that she should go to graduate school out of state and to assure him that her leaving would not change their relationship. To accomplish this, she decided to encode her idea into this message: "I promise that I will call at least twice a week, I'll text you every day, and I'll come home for all holidays."

When we communicate, we encode and exchange two types of messages—verbal and nonverbal—and most of these messages are symbolic. A **symbol** is something that represents something else and conveys meaning (Buck & VanLear, 2002). For example, a Valentine's Day heart symbolizes the physical heart, it represents romantic love, and it conveys feelings of love and romance when given to a relational partner. The verbal system is composed of linguistic symbols (that is, words), whereas the nonverbal message system is composed of non-linguistic symbols such as smiles, laughter, winks, vocal tones, and hand gestures.

What is the meaning of the kiss (a symbolic message) in this context?

When we say *communication is symbolic*, we are describing the fact that the symbols we use—the words we speak and the gestures we use—are arbitrary, or without any inherent meaning (Dickens, 2003). Rather, their meaning is derived as communicators employ agreed-on definitions. For instance, putting up one's hand palm forward would not mean "stop" unless people in the United States agreed to this meaning, and the word *mother* would not mean a female parent unless speakers of English agreed that it would. Because communicators use symbols to create meaning, different groups often develop distinct words for the same concept. For instance, the common word for a feline house pet is *cat* in English, but *neko* in Japanese. Thus, there is no intrinsic connection between most words and their meanings—or many gestures and their meanings.

What is the meaning of the kiss (a symbolic message) in this context?

Because human communication is predominantly symbolic, humans must agree on the meanings of words. Consequently, words can, and do, change over time. For example, the term *gay* typically meant happy or carefree from the seventeenth century through much of the twentieth century. Although the term was occasionally used to refer to same-sex relationships as early as the 1800s, it has come to be used widely only since the late 1990s, when users agreed to this meaning and usage. Nonetheless, people may have different meanings for specific symbols or words, especially if they come from different ethnic or national cultures. Read about one student's difficulties communicating while on a trip to Europe in *It Happened to Me: Alyssa.*

As Alyssa's experience reveals, though most people recognize that cultures vary in the words they use for specific ideas and items, they don't always

It Happened to Me
Alyssa

Recently I traveled in Europe; I had no idea how difficult it would be to communicate, even in England. I spent the first few days navigating London on my own. It was so hard! People tried to help, but because of the differences in word choice and accents, I couldn't fully understand their directions. After London I went to Italy, where I had an even harder time communicating due to the language barrier. So I resorted to using nonverbal gestures such as pointing, smiling, and thumbs up and down. However, I ran into problems doing this. One night I ordered wine for a friend and myself. The bartender looked uncertain when he brought the two glasses of wine I'd ordered, so I gave him a "thumbs up" to mean okay, that he had it right. However, to him the gesture meant "one," so he thought I only wanted one glass, and he took the other away. It took us a while to get the order straight!

realize that nonverbal gestures can have varied meanings across cultures as well. Creating messages is the most fundamental requirement for communication to occur, but it certainly is not enough. Messages also create shared meanings for everyone involved in the interaction.

MEANING CREATION The goal of exchanging symbols—that is, of communicating—is to create meaning. The messages we send and receive shape meaning beyond the symbols themselves. We also bring to each message a set of experiences, beliefs, and values that help shape specific meanings. This is why people can hear the same message but understand it differently. Charee was aware of this as she planned the conversation with her father. She knew they didn't always have precisely the same meanings for every word. For example, the word "independent" carried positive meanings for her, but she knew it carried more negative and potentially upsetting meanings for her father. Therefore, when talking to her father, she would never argue that going away was good for her because it would make her more independent.

Meaning is made even more complex because, as the example suggests, each message carries with it two types of meaning—content meaning and relationship meaning. **Content meaning** includes denotative and connotative meaning. Denotative meaning is the concrete meaning of the message, such as the definition you would find in a dictionary. Connotative meaning describes the meanings suggested by or associated with the message and the emotions triggered by it. For example, denotatively the word *mother* refers to one's female parent, whereas connotatively it may include meanings such as warmth, nurturance, and intimacy. **Relationship meaning** describes what the message conveys about the relationship between the parties (Robinson-Smith, 2004; Watzlawick, Beavin, & Jackson, 1967). For example, if a colleague at work told you to "run some copies of this report," you might become irritated, but you probably wouldn't mind if your boss told you to do the same thing. In both cases the relationship message may be understood as "I have the right to tell you what to do," which is appropriate if it comes from your supervisor—but not if it comes from a peer.

Finally, communication helps create the shared meanings that shape families, communities, and societies. Specifically, the meanings we have for important issues including politics, civil behavior, family, and spirituality—as well as for less important concerns such as what food is tasty or what type of home is desirable—are created through people's interactions with one another. For example, if you were asked what your family "motto" is (that is, what is important in your family) what would you say? Some people might say it is "family first," whereas others declare it is "do the right thing." How do families come to have these shared beliefs and meanings? They do so through the countless interactions they have with one another; through these conversations and everyday experiences they create a meaning for what is important to their family. What do you think happens when two people marry, one of whom believes "family first" and another who thinks "do the right thing" is more important than even family? Like the families they grew up within, they will interact, live together, and jointly develop shared meanings for their family beliefs. A similar process occurs when people come together to form groups, organizations, communities, and societies. In sum, our relationships, our understanding of the world, and our beliefs about life and death are created through the interactions we have with others.

SETTING The physical surroundings of a communication event make up its setting. **Setting** includes the location where the communication occurs (in a library versus a bar), environmental conditions (including the temperature, noise, and lighting), time of day or day of the week, and the proximity of the communicators. Together these factors create the physical setting, which affects communication interaction.

content meaning
the concrete meaning of the message, and the meanings suggested by or associated with the message as well as the emotions triggered by it

relationship meaning
what a message conveys about the relationship between the parties

setting
the physical surroundings of a communication event

Why do you think Charee chose to meet in mid-afternoon at her father's favorite café as the setting for their conversation? She did so for several reasons. First, her father would be more likely to feel relaxed and in a good mood in a familiar location that he liked. Second, she selected the middle of the afternoon so they would have more privacy and fewer interruptions. Finally, she chose a public setting because she believed her father would remain calmer in public than in a private setting, such as at home. As you can see, Charee carefully selected a comfortable setting that she believed would enhance her chances of being successful.

PARTICIPANTS During communication, **participants**—two or more people—interact. The number of participants, as well as their characteristics, will influence how the interaction unfolds. Typically, the more characteristics participants share (cultural, values, history), the easier they will find it to communicate, because they can rely on their common assumptions about the world.

As Charee planned her conversation, she recognized that she and her father shared a number of important characteristics—respect for elders in the family, a communal approach to relationships, and a desire for harmony. However, she also realized that they differed in important ways. Although she was close to her family, she desired more independence than her father would want for himself or for her. In addition, she believed it was acceptable for young, single women to live away from their families, a belief she was sure her father didn't share.

The type of relationship communicators have and the history they share also affect their communication. Whether communicators are family members, romantic partners, colleagues, friends, or acquaintances affects how they frame, deliver, and interpret a message. Because Charee was talking with her father rather than her boyfriend, she focused on displaying respect for his position as her father and asking (rather than telling) him about wanting to move away for college. As we have suggested already, the moods and emotions that communicators bring to and experience during their interaction influence it as well. Because Charee wanted to increase the likelihood that the conversation with her father would go well, she tried to create a situation in which he would be in a calmer and happier frame of mind.

CHANNELS For a message to be transmitted from one participant to another, it must travel through a channel. A **channel** is the means through which a message is conveyed. Historically, the channels people used to communicate with one another were first face to face, then written (for example, letters and newsprint), and yet later electronic (for example, telephone calls, radio, and television). Today, thanks to technology, we have many more communication channels—email, texting, Twitter, social networks such as Facebook and MySpace, and Facetime, to name just a few.

The channel a person selects to communicate a message can affect how the message is perceived and its impact on the relationship. For example, if your romantic partner broke up with you by changing his or her Facebook relationship status instead of by talking to you face to face, how would you respond? Because Charee was sensitive to the importance of the communication channel she used with her father, she elected to communicate with him face to face because it was a channel her father was familiar with and would find appealing.

NOISE **Noise** refers to any stimulus that can interfere with, or degrade, the quality of a message. Noise includes external signals of all kinds: not only loud music and voices, but also distracting clothing or hairstyles, uncomfortably warm or chilly temperatures, and so on. Noise can also come from internal stimuli, such as hunger or sleepiness. Semantic interference, which occurs when speakers use words you do not know or use a

participants

the people interacting during communication

channel

the means through which a message is transmitted

noise

any stimulus that can interfere with, or degrade, the quality of a message

Text messaging is one channel of communication. What other channels do you often use?

How do you choose which channel to use when you communicate with others? Do you consider who they are, the topic, the importance of the message, or something else? Overall, do you think you pick the best channel most of the time? If not, what do you need to do to select more appropriately?

feedback

the response to a message

familiar word in an unfamiliar way, is another form of noise. If you have ever tried to have a conversation with someone who used highly technical language in a noisy room while you were sleepy, you have experienced a "perfect storm" of noise.

How did the noise factor affect Charee's choices? She chose to meet at a café in the middle of the afternoon, avoiding the crowded lunch and dinner hours. There would be fewer competing voices and sounds, and the wait staff would be less likely to interrupt with meal service, so there would be fewer distractions. By choosing a setting that minimized interference, she improved the chances that her message would be clear.

FEEDBACK Finally, the response to a message is called **feedback**. Feedback lets a sender know if the message was received and how the message was interpreted. For example, if a friend tells you a joke and you laugh heartily, your laughter serves as feedback, indicating that you heard the joke and found it amusing. Similarly, if you fall asleep during a lecture, you provide feedback to your professor that either you are tired or you find the lecture boring. Thus, your feedback serves as a message to the sender, who then uses the information conveyed to help shape his or her next message.

Although Charee wasn't sure what type of feedback her father would provide or what type she would need to give him, she did spend time anticipating what they each would say. She also knew that she would need to be sensitive to his messages and be prepared to offer feedback that was both supportive and persuasive.

3 A Model of Human Communication: The Synergetic Model

3 **Explain how the Synergetic Model of Communication differs from previous models.**

To help people understand complex processes, scientists and engineers, among others, create visual models to show how all components of a process work together. Scholars of human communication have done the same. They have developed models to reveal how the seven components described work together to create a communication interaction.

The first such model of human communication depicted communication as a linear process that primarily involved the transfer of information from one person to another (Eisenberg, Goodall, & Trethewey, 2010; Laswell, 1948; Shannon & Weaver, 1949). In this model, communication occurred when a sender encoded a message (put ideas into words and symbols) that was sent to a receiver who decoded (interpreted) it. Then, the process was believed to reverse: The receiver became the sender, and the sender became the receiver (Laswell, 1948). This model (see Figure 1) also included the components of "noise" and "channel." Since that time other, more complex models, such as our Synergetic Model, have been created to show a greater variety of factors that interact with one another to influence the communication process.

Synergetic Model

a transactional model that emphasizes how individual and societal forces, contexts, and culture interact to affect the communication process

The **Synergetic Model** is a transactional model that, like most previous models, depicts communication as occurring when two or more people create meaning as they respond to each other and their environment. In addition, it is based on a belief in the important roles of individual and societal forces, contexts, and culture in the communication process. We call the model synergetic because synergy describes when two or more elements work together to achieve something either one couldn't have achieved on its own. For example, in the ubiquitous volcano science fair project, "lava" is created by adding vinegar to baking soda. Once the two products interact, something new is created. Our communication model is synergetic in that the different elements of communication work together to create something different, and greater, than just

Figure 1 A Linear Model of Communication

Early models depicted communication as a linear process that primarily involved the transfer of information from one person to another

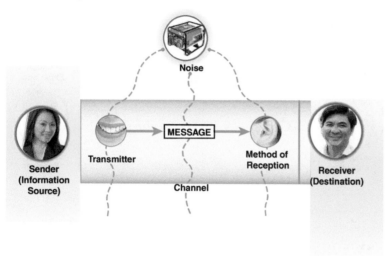

the sum of its parts. We discuss each of these elements, and to help clarify the concepts, we revisit Charee's interaction with her father once again to illustrate how they function during the communication process.

After carefully planning for the interaction with her father about her desire to leave home to go to graduate school, Charee engaged in the following conversation with him:

CHAREE: *Purdue, Illinois, ASU, and Texas all let me in.* (While talking, Charee notices a quizzical look on her father's face.)

CHAREE: *I mean, all of them accepted me for graduate school.*

DAD: *Oh. How many did you apply to?*

CHAREE: *Just four. They all accepted me.*

DAD: (frowning, speaking uncertainly) *So where are you gonna go?*

CHAREE: (looking away, speaking hesitantly) *Uh, Texas, I think.*

DAD: (startled) *Texas?! Why not stay at ASU?*

CHAREE: (speaking patiently) *Because it's better for my career to go and study with other people. I'll be able to get a better job when I graduate if I can say that I studied with 12 people instead of 6, Dad. Plus, Texas is real high up there in the rankings. It's a good school.*

DAD: (shaking his head, speaking firmly) *Oh. Well, I think you can get a better job if you can show that you're loyal. If you stay at ASU, people will think, "Oh, she can stay at one place and do a good job. She has loyalty."*

CHAREE: (nodding her head, speaking carefully) *But I have been loyal to ASU for six years. People here know me and how I work. They also know that I can learn and grow somewhere else.*

DAD: *I guess I can see that. I just wish you didn't have to go.*

Communication Is Transactional

To say that *communication is a transaction* (see Figure 2) captures the fact that (1) each participant is a sender and receiver *at the same time*, (2) meaning is created as people communicate together, (3) communication is an ongoing process, and (4) previous

Figure 2 Communication Is Transactional

Transactional models express the idea that meaning is created as people communicate.

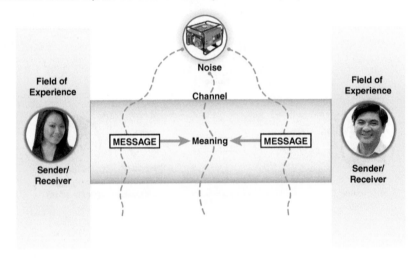

communication events and relationships influence its meaning (Warren & Yoder, 1998; Watzlawick, Beavin, & Jackson, 1967). What does this mean?

First, all participants in a communication event both receive and send messages simultaneously, even if those messages are sent only nonverbally. As you may have noted, as Charee explained that she was "let in" to four universities, she realized from her father's nonverbal behavior that he was confused. That is, she received his message even as she talked, and he sent a message even as he listened.

Second, as the example suggests, meaning is not something one person creates and then sends to another person via a message. If that were true, Charee's father would not have been confused by the expression "let in"; Charee's initial message would have been sufficient. Rather, meaning was created as Charee and her dad communicated together; she made a statement, he showed his lack of understanding, and Charee offered more information until they shared similar understandings or meaning.

Third, describing communication as ongoing highlights the fact that it is a process whose specific beginnings and endings can be difficult to discern. All of the interactions one has had with individuals in the past influence one's communication in the present, just as a person's current communication affects his or her expectations for and experiences of future interactions. For instance, Charee planned her interaction and communicated with her father based on her previous experiences with him. Specifically, she knew he would rather she stay close to home, so she was prepared to offer arguments for why leaving home for graduate school was best. Her experiences with her father, then, affected the messages she crafted for their conversation. In addition, she recognized that their conversation would influence how they communicated with each other in the future. If he became angry, he likely would communicate with her less or more negatively. This, in turn, would influence her future messages to him, and so on.

Finally, because communication is ongoing and interactive, when people communicate, they and their conversational partner(s) reaffirm or alter their identities and relationships. Thus, Charee's conversation with her father is likely to change how they see each other. He might see her as more adult and independent because of her desire to move away, or he may now perceive her as a less loving child. Similarly, she may view him as less of an authority figure and more of a peer, or she might believe he is even more authoritarian and rigid than she previously thought.

Communication Is Influenced by Individual Forces

The individual is a primary focus in communication. Many separate individual forces or characteristics contribute to your identity, and these in turn affect your communication. Individual forces include your demographic characteristics such as age, race, ethnicity, nationality, gender/sex, sexual orientation, regional identity, and socioeconomic class, as well as such factors as personality and cognitive and physical ability. In addition, individual forces include your **field of experience**, such as your education and experiences.

For example, Charee is female, twenty-four, and a college graduate, whereas her father is a male in his late forties who operates an automotive repair shop. Each of these individual factors influences the way they communicate as well the ways others communicate with them and about them. Because of her experiences as a college student, Charee knows what "let in" means and understands that universities often evaluate students who obtain all three degrees at one college negatively when they hire new professors. On the other hand, her father is not aware of this information, and based on his culture and his experiences in the workforce, he understands that loyalty is often an important quality in an employee.

The combination of these individual characteristics is unique for every person, so people communicate in distinctive ways. However, every society places limits on the variations that are deemed acceptable. For example, not all men speak assertively, enjoy talking about sports, or "high five" one another. In mainstream U.S. culture, though, many people consider these behaviors as normal for males. Speaking in a more "female" style, such as speaking quietly or politely, talking about fashion, or using "effeminate" nonverbal gestures, is typically considered inappropriate for men and boys. Those who veer somewhat from the norm may be seen as odd, or they might be shunned; those who veer too far from the norm may be labeled as mentally ill. So although we are each individuals, society places constraints on the range of our individualism.

field of experience
the education and experiences that a communicator possesses

Communication Is Influenced by Societal Forces

As we suggested, individual differences are not value free. They are arranged in a hierarchy in which some individual characteristics are more highly valued than others. For example, being Caucasian is often advantageous in U.S. society, being young has advantages over being old, and being physically able is more advantageous than having a disability. How society evaluates these characteristics affects how we talk to—and about—people who display them.

The political, historical, economic, and social structures of a society influence this value hierarchy and affect how we view specific individual characteristics. The historical conditions under which many U.S. racial and ethnic groups arrived in the United States, for instance, continue to affect their identities. For example, many of the earliest Vietnamese immigrants who moved to the United States during and shortly after the Vietnam War had strong work ethics but were not fluent in English, so they created businesses of their own—as restaurant owners, nail technicians, and other service professionals. Consequently, many people still fail to realize that Vietnamese Americans also work as lawyers, professors, and physicians. Similarly, even though Barack Obama was elected President of the United States, the fact that many African Americans are descendants of people who came to the United States as slaves continues to influence the ways people think and talk about him.

The values attributed to individual characteristics such as age, sexual orientation, and sex also come from these larger societal forces—whether communicated to us through the media, by our friends and family, or by organizations such as schools, religious institutions, or clubs. For example, the teachings of religious groups shape many people's views on sexual orientation, and because most societies historically

Being gay is both an individual and cultural factor.

have been patriarchal, they continue to value women in the public realm less than they do men.

In Charee's case, two societal forces at work in her interaction with her father are how society views women and parent–child interactions. Pham was reared in a culture and time where males held considerably more power than females, and parents were assumed to know what was best for their children even when the children were grown. Consequently, he tends to hold the belief that fathers should have considerable decision-making power over their children, especially their unmarried female children. On the other hand, Charee grew up in a culture and time where men and women are seen as more equal and parents exert less control over their children's lives as the children grow up.

Social hierarchies wherein men are more valued than women, or older people's opinions are considered more worthwhile than younger people's, arise from the meanings that societal structures impose on individual characteristics, and communication maintains these hierarchies. For example, cultures that value maleness over femaleness have many more stereotypes and negative terms for women than they do for men. Moreover, these cultures value certain types of communication over others. Thus, men in leadership positions are expected to communicate decisively and avoid appearing "weak" by apologizing or admitting mistakes, whereas the same is not usually true for women.

Communication Is Influenced by Culture

culture

learned patterns of perceptions, values, and behaviors shared by a group of people

Communication also is embedded in culture. **Culture** refers to the learned patterns of perceptions, values, and behaviors shared by a group of people. Culture is dynamic and heterogeneous (Martin & Nakayama, 2005), meaning that it changes over time and that despite commonalities, members of cultural groups do not all think and behave alike. You probably belong to many cultures, including those of your gender, ethnicity, occupation, and religion, and each of these cultures will have its own communication patterns.

When you identify yourself as a member of a culture defined by age, ethnicity, or gender, this culture-group identity also becomes one of your individual characteristics. For example, as people move from their teen years into young adulthood, middle age, and old age, they generally make a transition from one age-related culture to another. Because each cultural group has a unique set of perceptions, values, and behaviors, each also has its own set of communication principles. As you become an adult, then, you probably stop using language you used as a teenager. And even though changing your language is an individual decision, it is influenced by cultural and societal expectations as well.

Culture affects all or almost all communication interactions (Schirato & Yell, 1996). More specifically, participants bring their beliefs, values, norms, and attitudes to each interaction, and the cultures they belong to shape each of these factors. Cultural beliefs also affect how we expect others to communicate. As we discussed, because he is Vietnamese, Charee's father values family closeness, loyalty, and the role of the father as head of the family. Because she is Vietnamese American, Charee holds many of these same beliefs, but she also values independence and individuality in ways that her father does not.

In addition to participants' cultural backgrounds, the culture in which a communication event takes place influences how participants communicate. In the United States, politicians routinely mention religion in their public addresses and specifically refer to God; however, in France, because of a stricter separation between church and state, politicians typically do not mention religion or deities in their public communication and would be criticized if they did. Regional culture can also affect participants' expectations for appropriate communication behavior. For instance, southerners in the United States tend to be more nonverbally demonstrative and thus might hug others more than do northeasterners (Andersen, Lustig, & Andersen, 1990). Of course, other cultural differences (ethnic background, religious background) might influence these nonverbal behaviors as well.

Communication Is Influenced by Context

Each communication interaction occurs in a specific context. Context includes the setting, or aspects of the physical environment, in which an interaction occurs. It also includes which and how many participants are present, as well as the specific occasion during which the interaction unfolds (for example, a Sunday dinner or a birthday party). Context can exert a strong influence on how people communicate with one another. For example, you could argue with your close friend in private when just the two of you are present, during a social event when you are part of a group, during a staff meeting at work, on a television talk show about feuding friends, or on the sidewalk at campus. Can you imagine how each of these contexts would influence your communication? You might be more open if the two of you are alone and in private; you may try to get others involved if you are with friends; you could be more subdued in public on campus; you might refrain from mentioning anything too negative on television; or you might be more hostile in an email or text. It is because context strongly affects individuals' interactions that Charee arranged to talk with her father at his favorite café in the afternoon.

The tensions that exist among individual forces, societal forces, cultures, and contexts shape communication and meaning. To help clarify this tension, let's return yet again to Charee's conversation with her father. Their conversation was influenced by the context (a restaurant), multiple individual forces (each person's age, sex, cultural background, and education), multiple societal forces (the value placed on education, family, sex, and age) as well as their cultures (the meanings of independence, loyalty, and family). Thus, in the conversation between Charee and her father, the context in which the conversation occurred, their individual experiences with higher education, and the cultural meaning of the parent–child relationship all came together to influence the communication interaction. These components and their relationships to one another are depicted in Figure 3, the Synergetic Model.

As we stated at the beginning of the text, and as is revealed in our model, for us, communication is a transactional process in which people generate meaning through the exchange of verbal and nonverbal messages in specific contexts, influenced by individual and societal forces and embedded in culture. This is the definition and model of communication that we will use in this text. After you complete this course, we recommend that you return to this section to assess how your own understanding of the communication process has changed and deepened.

Our goal in developing this model is to provide a framework for students to organize, read, and understand this complex process we call communication. However, before moving on, we need to discuss one more essential concept that frames and guides all of your communication efforts—ethics.

Figure 3 The Synergetic Model

The Synergetic Model presents communication as a transactional process in which meaning is influenced by cultural, societal, and individual forces.

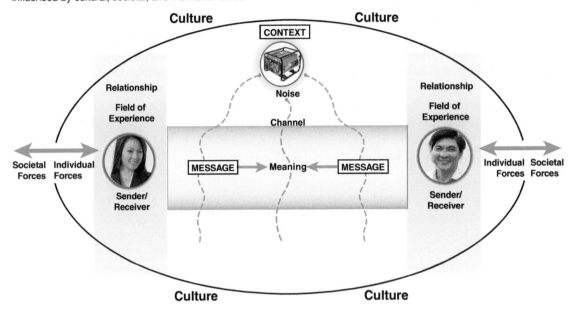

4   Communication Ethics

4   Formulate your own communication ethic.

In the United States, we appear to be in the midst of a crisis with regard to ethical communication. In the business world, Lee Farkas, the founder of what was once one of the nation's largest mortgage lenders, was convicted of fraud for masterminding a scheme that cheated investors and the government out of billions of dollars (Protess, 2011) and in 2014 the leaders of the fallen law firm Dewey and LeBoeuf were indicted on charged of grand larceny, securities fraud, conspiracy, and falsifying business records (Smith & Jones, 2014).The world of politics does not seem to be faring much better: In 2013 Democratic Congressman Jesse Jackson Jr. was sentenced to prison for wire and mail fraud related to his misuse of campaign funds (Schmidt, February 2, 2013), and Republican Congressman Rick Renzi was found guilty of wire fraud, conspiracy, extortion, racketeering, money laundering, and making false statements (Huffington Post, June 11, 2013).

Individuals' personal lives are apparently in a state of ethical disarray as well: A diary study of college students found that college students lied in one out of about every three social interactions, and over the course of a week only 1 percent of students said they told no lies at all. (DePaulo, 2011). In another study 74 percent of students admitted to cheating on exams and 84 percent to cheating on written assignments (McCabe & Trevino, 1996). And it isn't only college students who admit to deceiving others. In a survey conducted by the National Endowment of Financial Education (2011), 31 percent of respondents confessed to lying to their marital and living partners about money, often with disastrous consequences.

Given examples such as these, one may wonder if a communication ethic still exists. We strongly believe that it does. Even if unethical communication is widespread, and some people get away with their misbehavior, most people are still held responsible for the messages they create (Barnlund, 1962; Christians & Traber, 1997; Johannesen, 1990). If you spread gossip about your friends, lie to your employer, or withhold information from your family, justifying your behavior by pointing to the ethical failures of others will not excuse you. Those who know you and are close to you still expect you to meet basic standards for ethical communication.

Why are communication ethics so important? First, they sustain professional success. Yes, unethical people may prosper in the short run, but over time unethical practices catch up with the people who engage in them. To a great extent, your reputation as a person of integrity determines whether others want to hire you, work for you, or conduct business with you. Once that reputation is damaged, it can be difficult if not impossible to regain; consequently, communicating and behaving ethically is just good business.

Communication ethics are vital to personal relationships as well. Maintaining intimate and caring relationships can be difficult, but they become virtually impossible if one communicates unethically by lying, manipulating, or verbally abusing friends and lovers. Intimate relationships are grounded in trust. Without trust, people can't be open and vulnerable with one another, behaviors that are essential to intimacy. When one person abuses that trust by his or her unethical conduct, the other party often is deeply wounded and finds it difficult to ever again be intimate within the relationship. Far too many people have learned the hard way that a lack of ethics destroys relationships.

As a communicator, you will face many ambiguous and difficult choices of both a professional and a personal nature. If you develop your own set of communication ethics you will be better prepared to face these difficult choices. Therefore, in this section we provide some basic principles of ethical communication for you to consider as you critically review your own ethical standard.

What are three specific communication behaviors you believe are unethical? What principles guide your decisions regarding whether a given communication behavior is ethical or unethical?

Fundamentally, individuals, groups, and communities develop ethical codes to reflect their beliefs and values. Clearly the guidelines we offer reflect our own communication ethics. We do not expect you to adopt our beliefs wholesale. Rather, we present this information so that you can analyze it critically to determine to what extent it reflects your own beliefs and behavior, what evidence supports it, and what other guidelines may be as useful or more useful for you. Thus, we want you to use your critical thinking skills specifically to critique our claims here and to use that analysis to form your own ethical code.

Defining Your Communication Ethic

Ethics can be defined in a variety of related ways. Most basically, it refers to a system of moral principles by which actions are judged as good or bad, right or wrong. It also has been defined as the rules of conduct recognized by a group, class, or individual; and as a belief system in which the determination of what is right is based on what promotes the most good or the common good. After reading these definitions, which one do you believe is the best explanation? Which one most closely reflects your current perspective?

ethics
standards of what is right and wrong, good and bad, moral and immoral

Communication ethics describes the standards of right and wrong that one applies to messages that are sent and received. When you hear the term *communication ethics*, you might think we are simply referring to whether messages are truthful. Although truthfulness is one of the most fundamental ethical standards, communicating ethically requires much more than simply being truthful. It also involves deciding what information can and should be disclosed or withheld, and assessing the benefit or harm associated with specific messages. Individuals have a responsibility to evaluate the ethics of their own and others' communication efforts. Similarly, corporations ought to weigh the ethics of sharing or withholding information that might affect the value of their stock shares, and media companies should decide whether it is ethical to report private information about individuals. Let's look at some of the issues you need to reflect on as you develop your code of ethics.

communication ethics
the standards of right and wrong that one applies to messages that are sent and received

TRUTHFULNESS Truthfulness plays a fundamental role in ethical communication for two reasons: First, others expect messages to be truthful, and second, messages have consequences. Because people inherently expect speakers to be truthful, we actually may make it easier for them to deceive us (Buller & Burgoon, 1996). If an audience is not suspicious, they probably won't look for cues that the speaker is lying (McCornack & Parks, 1986). However, because of the implicit contract to be honest, discovery of deception can severely damage relationships. The more intimate the relationship, the greater the expectation people have that their partners will be truthful, and the more damaging any deception will be.

As we've implied, people rely on messages to be truthful because they have consequences. One's communication can influence the beliefs, attitudes, and behaviors of others. For example, an individual's communication could persuade a customer to purchase an item, a friend to lend money, or an acquaintance to become romantically involved with him or her. The more consequential the outcome of your message, the more likely you will be held accountable to the truth. You might not be criticized too harshly for exaggerating your salary during a flirtation with a stranger, but an employer will most likely consider it unethical if you lie about your salary on a job application.

SHARING OR WITHHOLDING INFORMATION A related fundamental principle of ethical communication concerns what information should be divulged and what can be withheld. When is withholding information a matter of legitimate privacy, and when is it a matter of inappropriate secrecy? Thus, you have to determine whether to tell your romantic partner how many sexual partners you have had; media organizations have to decide whether to reveal the identity of confidential news sources; and physicians have to choose how much information to tell patients about the possible side effects of a prescribed drug.

In our view, a message can be considered legitimately private when other parties have no right to expect access to it. Inappropriate secrecy, on the other hand, occurs when other parties might legitimately expect access to a message that is withheld. This distinction is important because it is generally ethical to maintain privacy, but it may be unethical to engage in secrecy.

What's the difference between privacy and secrecy? We believe communicators have an ethical responsibility to share information that other people require to make informed decisions. For example, if you have only dated someone once or twice, you may choose to keep private that you have a sexually transmitted disease. However, if the two of you consider becoming sexually intimate, you probably have an ethical obligation to reveal the information. Without this information, your partner cannot make an informed decision about whether to engage in sexual contact. What will happen to your relationship if you withhold the information and your partner contracts your disease—and finds out later that you withheld the information? Similarly, your friends may not need to know why you were fired from your last job, but your new boss may have a legitimate need for access to this information.

Is it ethical to gossip or share others' private information?

On the other hand, revealing information can sometimes be unethical. For example, if you have agreed to maintain confidentiality about a topic, it could be considered unethical to reveal what you know. However, if you violate a confidence because of a higher ethical principle, most people would likely consider your behavior ethical. For example, if you have a duty of confidentiality to your employer, but your company engages in illegal toxic dumping, it likely would be more ethical to break this confidence. Here, the ethic of protecting the public health likely supersedes the ethic of keeping a confidence. These are not easy decisions, but they reflect the type of complex ethical choices that people have to make.

Now that you have read our guideline for differentiating secrecy and privacy, do you find yourself agreeing or disagreeing with it? Can you think of situations in which it would not apply? Can you think of a better principle one could use to make decisions about whether to withhold or reveal information? Again, it is not important that you adopt our guideline but that you think through and develop one that is in line with your own ethical code.

You can begin to think through your position on this issue by exploring an important trend in job searches—the growing use of Internet searches by corporations to gather information on potential or current employees as well as the practice of potential or current employees hiding Facebook information from employers. When individuals hide information on Facebook, do you believe they are engaging in secrecy or privacy attempts? How would you defend your position to someone who disagrees with you? That is, what evidence and examples would you use to argue for your belief? What arguments might someone make who disagrees with you? To what extent does the context of Facebook communication influence your response?

BENEFIT AND HARM OF MESSAGES   To determine the most ethical choice, you also should consider the benefit or harm associated with your messages. A classic example concerns whether it is right to lie to a potential murderer about the whereabouts of the intended victim. A principle of honesty suggests that you should tell the truth. But in this case, once you evaluate the potential harm of sharing versus withholding the information, you might well decide to withhold the information.

More typically, issues of harm and benefit are less clear. For example, if you discover your best friend's romantic partner is being unfaithful, should you share that information? Will it result in more harm or more benefit? If you know that a relative cheated on her taxes, should you report her to the IRS?

Because many communication events are complex and the underlying ethical principles are not definitive, you will need to gradually develop your own philosophy of ethical communication and apply it on a case-by-case basis. This is one requirement of being an effective communicator. However, just as you develop your own ethical standards and decisions, others will do so as well, which means you and others in your life may not always agree.

ABSOLUTISM VERSUS RELATIVISM   A fundamental decision in communication ethics concerns how **absolute** or **relative** your ethical standards will be. Will you use the same absolute standards for every communication interaction, or will your ethical choices be relative and depend on each situation? The Greek philosopher Plato and the German philosopher Immanuel Kant conceptualized the absolutist perspective (Kant, 1949), and both believed there is a rationally correct, moral standard that holds for everyone, everywhere, every time. Relativists such as French philosopher Jean-Paul Sartre, on the other hand, hold the view that moral behavior varies among individuals, groups, and cultures. They argue that because there is no universal standard of morality, there is no rational way to decide who is correct (Sartre, 1973).

If you hold to the absolutist perspective that lying is always wrong, then in the previous example regarding the potential murderer, you would be obligated not to lie about the whereabouts of the intended victim. But if you adhere to a relativistic position regarding truth and deception, you would decide in the moment what the most ethical choice is based on the specific circumstances. You might tell a lie to save a life.

In reality, few people develop an ethical standard that is completely absolute or relative. Instead, absolutism and relativism are the opposite ends of a continuum, and most people's standards lie somewhere along that continuum.

The issue for you is to decide how absolute or relative your ethical standards will be. If you strongly believe that deception is wrong, you may choose the path of deception only when you believe the truth will cause great harm—a standard that falls

absolutism

the belief that there is a single correct moral standard that holds for everyone, everywhere, every time

relativism

the belief that moral behavior varies among individuals, groups, and cultures and across situations

Should a salesperson admit that a competitor's product might be as good as the product he or she is selling?

toward the absolutist end of the continuum. However, if you favor a more relative view, you will consider a variety of factors, in addition to harm, as you make your decisions.

Communication Ethics in Practice

In this discussion of ethics, we have offered guidelines for creating your own communication ethics. However, in practice, many situations arise that are ambiguous, complex, and multilayered. At times you may not see how you can be ethical and accomplish important goals at the same time. For example, if you know that a friend and classmate has plagiarized a paper, what should you do? Should you keep quiet and maintain your friendship, or should you maintain your personal ethics and tell the instructor? Similarly, if you are a salesperson, how do you respond if a potential client asks whether a competitor's product is as good as yours, and you don't believe it is? Do you tell the truth and thus jeopardize a potential sale? People who tend toward an absolutist view say that you must always tell the truth, so you should only sell a product you truly believe is superior. Others may tell you that no one expects salespeople to be completely truthful in this context; therefore, you are not bound to share your opinion (Diener, 2002; Wokutch & Carson, 1981).

We believe that all communicators need to create an ethical stance based on their own beliefs, values, and moral training. Once *you've* established your ethical stance, you will be prepared to make thoughtful and deliberate communication choices.

For further guidance in creating your own communication ethic, please see *Communication in Society: Making Ethical Decisions.*

5   Putting It All Together: Communicating Competently

5   Articulate what makes a communicator competent.

The goal of this text is to help you improve your communication skills so that you can become a more successful, or competent, communicator. A competent communicator is one who is able to use communication to achieve his or her (realistic and appropriate) goals. More specifically, communicators are competent when they use their understanding of themselves, others, the context, and communication principles to adapt their communication to achieve their goals (Friedrich, 1994).

communication competence

the ability to adapt one's communication to achieve one's goals

appropriateness

following the rules, norms and expectations for specific situations or relationships

effectiveness

achieving one's goals successfully

Communication competence is composed of two elements: **appropriateness**, which is defined as following the relevant rules, norms, and expectations for specific relationships and situations; and **effectiveness**, which involves achieving one's goals successfully. Speakers are competent when they understand the expectations regarding their behavior and are able to behave in a way that fulfills those expectations. For example, a best man offering a wedding toast is expected to be amusing, complimentary, and brief (as well as sober!). Failure to fulfill these expectations not only results in a poor toast, but it often also results in audience members negatively evaluating the speaker. If the toast seriously violates these expectations, the consequences may even include terminated relationships.

Effectiveness refers to the ability to achieve one's goals for an interaction without interfering with other, potentially more important goals. Taking the example above, a person giving a toast may have a goal of being humorous. However, if the best man makes jokes that are in poor taste, he might meet his goal of making the audience laugh, but he may fail another, more important goal of remaining friends with the bride and groom.

Communication in Society

Making Ethical Decisions

Making good ethical decisions requires a trained sensitivity to ethical issues and a practiced method for exploring the ethical aspects of a decision and weighing the considerations that should impact our choice of a course of action. Having a method for ethical decision making is absolutely essential. When practiced regularly, the method becomes so familiar that we work through it automatically without consulting the specific steps.

The more novel and difficult the ethical choice we face, the more we need to rely on discussion and dialogue with others about the dilemma. Only by careful exploration of the problem, aided by the insights and different perspectives of others, can we make good ethical choices in such situations.

We have found the following framework for ethical decision making a useful method for exploring ethical dilemmas and identifying ethical courses of action.

A Framework for Ethical Decision Making

Recognize an Ethical Issue

1. Could this decision or situation be damaging to someone or to some group? Does this decision involve a choice between a good and bad alternative, or perhaps between two "goods" or between two "bads"?
2. Is this issue about more than what is legal or what is most efficient? If so, how?

Get the Facts

3. What are the relevant facts of the case? What facts are not known? Can I learn more about the situation? Do I know enough to make a decision?
4. What individuals and groups have an important stake in the outcome? Are some concerns more important? Why?

5. What are the options for acting? Have all the relevant persons and groups been consulted? Have I identified creative options?

Evaluate Alternative Actions

6. Evaluate the options by asking the following questions:
   - Which option will produce the most good and do the least harm? (The Utilitarian Approach)
   - Which option best respects the rights of all who have a stake? (The Rights Approach)
   - Which option treats people equally or proportionately? (The Justice Approach)
   - Which option best serves the community as a whole, not just some members? (The Common Good Approach)
   - Which option leads me to act as the sort of person I want to be? (The Virtue Approach)

Make a Decision and Test It

7. Considering all these approaches, which option best addresses the situation?
8. If I told someone I respect—or told a television audience—which option I have chosen, what would they say?

Act and Reflect on the Outcome

9. How can my decision be implemented with the greatest care and attention to the concerns of all participants?
10. How did my decision turn out and what have I learned from this specific situation?

SOURCE: Markkula Center for Applied Ethics (2010). A framework for thinking ethically. Retrieved March 9, 2010, from http://scu.edu/ethics/practicing/decision/framework.html

This framework for thinking ethically is the product of dialogue and debate at the Markkula Center for Applied Ethics at Santa Clara University. Primary contributors include Manuel Velasquez, Dennis Moberg, Michael J. Meyer, Thomas Shanks, Margaret R. McLean, David DeCosse, Claire André, and Kirk O. Hanson.

Generally, speakers have three types of goals that are important during an interaction: content, relationship, and identity. *Content* goals describe the concrete outcomes you would like to achieve during an interaction—to receive a job offer, earn a high grade on a speech, or to successfully initiate a new relationship. *Relationship* goals refer to your desire to change or maintain your relationship with another, for example, when you say "I love you" to your romantic partner in hopes of increasing your commitment to one another, or when you apologize so your romantic partner won't leave you. Finally, *identity* goals describe how we would like others to see us or help us see ourselves. When complaining about a grade, for instance, you likely want your grade changed (a content goal) but you probably also want your instructor to see you as deserving the higher grade (an identity goal).

Based on this definition, a communication behavior is judged to be competent only within specific situations or relationships (Cupach, Canary, & Spitzberg, 2009). That is, a behavior that might be appropriate or effective for one situation may not be so for another. For example, although "trash talking" may be competent (that is, appropriate and effective) in a sports context, is not likely to be appropriate during a discussion with one's romantic partner, even if it were effective. Communication competence requires that you understand yourself, your relationships and specific situations well enough that you can pull from your repertoire of communication skills exactly the right ones to use at this time, in this place, with this person, on this topic.

If you think all of this sounds like a lot to do, you are beginning to understand why learning to communicate well is so complex. The good news is that we are here to help you develop the skills you need to be competent in a wide range of interactions.

Summary

Studying human communication can enrich and transform your life professionally and personally. *Critical thinking*, which involves reflection and weighing evidence, is a key to successful communication. Communication skills are crucial in developing relationships, establishing identity, and opening career doors.

The *process of communication* involves seven basic components: message creation, meaning creation, setting, participants, channels, noise, and feedback. Communication has been described in the past as a linear process between sender and receiver; more recently a transactional model was introduced. The *Synergtic Model* views communication as a transactional process; it emphasizes that all communication interactions are influenced by the intersection of individual and societal forces, that they are embedded in culture, and that they occur in specific contexts.

The *ethics* of individual communication choices are another essential feature of communication. Key aspects of communication ethics to consider as you make decisions include truthfulness, decisions regarding sharing or withholding information, and the benefit and harm associated with one's choices. Communicators' ethical choices are affected by their position on the continuum of absolutism versus relativism, which in turn influences their language use and how they receive and how they respond to others' communication efforts. Understanding communication processes and the ethics of your own communication choices is the first step toward you becoming a more *competent communicator*.

Key Terms

human communication	participants	communication ethics
messages	channel	absolutism
encoding	noise	relativism
decoding	feedback	communication
symbol	Synergetic Model	competence
content meaning	field of experience	appropriateness
relationship meaning	culture	effectiveness
setting	ethics	

Apply What You Know

1. **Guidelines for Responding to Electronic Communication**

   Much debate has raged over whether it is appropriate to talk or text on one's cell phone in restaurants, in front of friends, or in the car. The Federal Aviation Administration is considering whether

   to allow airline passengers to use their cell phones during flights—and many people are already complaining about the possibility. The widespread use of instant text messaging and the ability to access our email almost anywhere have made the issues surrounding the appropriate use of electronic communication even more complex. To focus the discussion and guide your own decisions regarding your responses to these types of electronic communication, develop a list of rules for how, when, and with whom it is appropriate to use the various types of electronic communication.

2. **Creating a Communication Ethic**
   Interview three people and ask them to describe the underlying ethic(s) that guide their communication choices. Then write a brief statement that describes your own communication ethic.

Explore

1. Make a list of all of the careers that you believe require good communication skills. Then, locate a list of careers from a university career center, such as North Carolina Wilmington's Career Center or Western Washington University Department of Communication's Career Information page, and examine the site's list of careers for which a communication degree prepares students. What careers did you list that are not listed on a university's career Web site? Why do you think the differences exist? Finally, create a list of careers you would post if you were responsible for creating such a site for your university.

2. Locate a Web site that discusses how to develop authentic communication skills, such as the site Authentic Communication or Hodu.com. After reading the suggestions and strategies described on the Web site, answer the following questions: When are you most likely to lie? What benefits do you think you will accrue if you lie? What can you do to increase how authentic you are when you communicate with others?

Glossary

absolutism the belief that there is a single correct moral standard that holds for everyone, everywhere, every time

appropriateness following the rules, norms and expectations for specific situations or relationships

channel the means through which a message is transmitted

communication competence the ability to adapt one's communication to achieve one's goals

communication ethics the standards of right and wrong that one applies to messages that are sent and received

content meaning the concrete meaning of the message, and the meanings suggested by or associated with the message and the emotions triggered by it

culture learned patterns of perceptions, values, and behaviors shared by a group of people

decoding receiving a message and interpreting its meaning

effectiveness achieving one's goals successfully

encoding taking ideas and converting them into messages

ethics standards of what is right and wrong, good and bad, moral and immoral

feedback the response to a message

field of experience the education, life events, and cultural background that a communicator possesses

human communication a process in which people generate meaning through the exchange of verbal and nonverbal messages

messages the building blocks of communication events

noise any stimulus that can interfere with, or degrade, the quality of a message

participants the people interacting during communication

relationship meaning what a message conveys about the relationship between the parties

relativism the belief that moral behavior varies among individuals, groups, and cultures and across situations

setting the physical surroundings of a communication event

symbol something that represents something else and conveys meaning

Synergetic Model of communication a transactional model based on the roles of individual and societal forces, contexts, and culture in the communication process

References

Alberts, J. K., Yoshimura, C. G., Rabby, M. K., & Loschiavo, R. (2005). Mapping the topography of couples' daily interaction. *Journal of Social and Personal Relationships, 22*, 299–323.

Andersen, P. A., Lustig, M. W., & Andersen, J. F. (1990). Changes in latitude, changes in attitude: The relationship between climate and interpersonal communication predispositions. *Communication Quarterly, 38*, 291–311.

A year and a day for Lil' Kim. (July 7, 2005). CNN.com. Retrieved March 10, 2014, from: http://www.cnn.com/2005/LAW/07/07/ctv.lilkim/.

Barnlund, D. C. (1962). Consistency of emergent leadership in groups with changing tasks and members. *Speech Monographs, 29*, 45–52.

Buck, R., & VanLear, C. A. (2002). Verbal and nonverbal communication: Distinguishing symbolic, spontaneous and pseudo-spontaneous nonverbal behavior. *Journal of Communication, 52*, 522–541.

Christians, C., & Traber, M. (Eds.), (1997). *Communication ethics and universal values*. Thousand Oaks, CA: Sage.

Cupach, W., Canary, D., & Spitzberg, B. (2009). *Competence in interpersonal conflict*. Prospect Heights, IL: Waveland Press.

DePaulo, B. (September 6, 2011). Who lies? Frequent liars. What kinds of people lie most often? *Psychology Today*. Retrieved March 11, 2014, from: http://www.psychologytoday.com/blog/living-single/201109/who-lies.

Dickens, T. E. (2003). General symbol machines: The first stage in the evolution of symbolic communication. *Evolutionary Psychology, 1*, 192–209.

Diener, M. (2002, January). Fair enough: To be a better negotiator, learn to tell the difference between a lie and a *lie*. *Entrepreneur Magazine*. Retrieved March 16, 2006, from: http://www.Entrepreneurmagazine.com.

Dixon, M., & Duck, S. W. (1993). Understanding relationship processes: Uncovering the human search for meaning. In S. W. Duck (Ed.), *Understanding relationship processes, Vol. 1: Individuals in relationships* (pp. 175–206). Newbury Park, CA: Sage.

Duck, S. (1994). *Meaningful relationships: Talking, sense and relating*. Newbury Park, CA: Sage.

Eisenberg, E. M., Goodall, H. L., Jr., & Trethewey, A. (2010). *Organizational communication: Balancing creativity and constraints*. New York: St. Martin's.

Emanuel, R. (2007). Humanities: Communication's core discipline. *American Communication Journal, 9*(2). Retrieved March 11, 2009, from: http://www.acjournal.org/holdings/vol9/summer/articles/discipline.html.

Friedrich, G. W. (1994). Essentials of speech communication. *In SCA Rationale Kit: Information supporting the speech communication discipline and its programs* (pp. 9–12). Annandale, VA: Speech Communication Association.

Gergen, K. J. (1982). *Toward transformation in social knowledge*. New York: Springer.

Johannesen, R. (1990). *Ethics in human communication*. Prospect Heights, IL: Waveland.

Kant, I. (1949). *Fundamental principles of the metaphysic of morals* (tr. by T. K. Abbott, Trans.). Indianapolis: Bobbs-Merrill. (Original work published 1785.)

Laswell, H. D. (1948). The structure and function of communication in society. In L. Bryson (Ed.), *The Communication of Ideas*. New York: Harper.

Markkula Center for Applied Ethics (2010). A framework for thinking ethically. Retrieved March 9, 2010, from: http://scu.edu/ethics/practicing/decision/framework.html.

Martin, J. N., & Nakayama, T. K. (2005). *Experiencing intercultural communication* (2nd ed.). Boston: McGraw-Hill.

McCabe, D. L., & Trevino, L. K. (1996). What we know about cheating in college: Longitudinal trends and recent developments. *Change, 28*, 28–33.

McCornack, S. A., & Parks, M. R. (1986). Deception detection and relationship development: The other side of trust. In M. L. McLaughlin (Ed.), *Communication Yearbook 9* (pp. 377–389). Newbury Park, CA: Sage. Retrieved March 16, 2006, from: http://www.natcom.org/policies/External/EthicalComm.

Mead, G. H. (1934). *Mind, self, and society*. Chicago: University of Chicago Press.

National Communication Association, (2003). What is communication? *Pathways*. Retrieved October 24, 2008, from: http://www.natcom.org/nca/Template2.asp?bid=339.

Nolen-Hoeksema S., Wisco B., & Lyumbomirski S. Rethinking rumination. (2008). Perspectives on Psychological Science, 3, 400–424.

Passer, M. W., & Smith, R. E. (2004). *Psychology: The science of mind and behavior* (2nd ed.). New York: McGraw-Hill.

Paul, R., & Elder, L. (2008). *The miniature guide to critical thinking concepts and tools*. Dillon Beach, CA: Foundation for Critical Thinking Press.

Protess, B. (April 19, 2011). Leader of big mortgage lender guilty of $2.9 billion fraud. *New York Times*. Retrieved March 11, 2014, from: http://www.nytimes.com/2011/04/20/business/20fraud.html?_r=0.

Rick Renzi, Former Congressman, Convicted on 17 of 32 Counts in Corruption Case. (June 11, 2013). *Huffington Post*. Retrieved March 11, 2014, from http://www.huffingtonpost.com/2013/06/11/rick-renzi-convicted_n_3424403.html.

Robinson-Smith, G. (2004). Verbal indicators of depression in conversations with stroke survivors. *Perspectives in Psychiatric Care, 40*, 61–69.

Rogers, E. M., & Chafee, S. H. (1983). Communication as an academic discipline: A dialogue. *Journal of Communication, 3*, 18–30.

Sartre, J. P. (1973). *Existentialism and humanism* (P. Mairet, Trans.) London: Methuen Ltd. (Original work published 1946.)

Schirato, T., & Yell, S. (1996). *Communication & cultural literacy: An introduction*. St. Leonards, Australia: Allen & Unwin.

Schmidt, M. S. (February 2, 2013). Jesse Jackson Jr. Pleads Guilty: "I Lived Off My Campaign." *New York Times*. Retrieved March 11, 2014, from: http://www.nytimes.com/2013/02/21/us/politics/jesse-l-jackson-jr-pleads-guilty-to-wire-and-mail-fraud.html.

Shannon, C. E., & Weaver, W. (1949). *A mathematical model of communication*. Urbana: University of Illinois Press.

Smith, J., & Jones, A. (March 6, 2014). Fallen law firm's leaders charged with fraud. *Wall Street Journal*. Retrieved March 11, 2014, from: http://online.wsj.com/news/articles/SB10001424052 7023045540045794230822663432 04?mg=reno64-wsj&url=http%3A%2F%2Fonline.wsj.com%2Farticle%2FSB10001424052702304554004579423082266343204.html.

Warren, S. F., & Yoder, P. J. (1998). Facilitating the transition to intentional communication. In A. Wetherby, S. Warren, & J. Reichle (Eds.), *Transitions in Prelinguistic Communication*, (pp. 39–58). Baltimore: Brookes Publishing.

Watzlawick, P., Beavin, J., & Jackson, D. D. (1967). *Pragmatics of human communication*. New York: W. W. Norton.

Wokutch, R. E., & Carson, T. L. (1981). The ethics and profitability of bluffing in business. In Lewickis, Saunders, & Minton (Eds.), *Negotiation: Readings, exercises, and cases* (pp. 341–353). Boston: Irwin/McGraw-Hill.

Credits

Photo Credits

Credits are listed in order of appearance.

Photo 1: Ian Shaw/Alamy

Photo 2: Greenstockcreative/Fotolia

Photo 3: Igor Mojzes/Fotolia

Photo 4: Hugo Félix/Fotolia

Photo 5: Andres Rodriguez/Fotolia

Photo 6: Geo Martinez/Fotolia

Photo 7: DragonImages/Fotolia

Photo 8: Nobilior/Fotolia

Photo 9: Piotr Marcinski/Fotolia

Photo 10: yevgeniy11/Fotolia

Photo 11: Geo Martinez/Fotolia

Photo 12: DragonImages/Fotolia

Photo 13: yevgeniy11/Fotolia

Photo 14: Eric Audras/Onoky- Photononstop/Alamy

Photo 15: Geo Martinez/Fotolia

Photo 16: DragonImages/Fotolia

Photo 17: yevgeniy11/Fotolia

Photo 18: George Dolgikh/Fotolia

Photo 19: Robert Stainforth/Alamy

Text and Art Credits

Based on Nolen-Hoeksema S., Wisco B., & Lyumbomirski S. Rethinking rumination. (2008). Perspectives on Psychological Science, 3, 400–424.

Michael W Passer, Ronald Edward Smith, Psychology: the science of mind and behaviour, Boston, Mass: McGraw-Hill, 2004.

Chelsea

Alyssa

Markkula Center for Applied Ethics (2010). A framework for thinking ethically. Retrieved March 9, 2010, from http://scu.edu/ethics/practicing/decision/framework.html This framework for thinking ethically is the product of dialogue and debate at the Markkula Center for Applied Ethics at Santa Clara University. Primary contributors include Manuel Velasquez, Dennis Moberg, Michael J. Meyer, Thomas Shanks, Margaret R. McLean, David De-Cosse, Claire André, and Kirk O. Hanson

Communicating Identities

CHAPTER TOPICS

The Importance of Identity

What Is Identity?

The Individual and Identity

The Individual, Identity, and Society

Ethics and Identity

Skills for Communicating About Identities

⌄ Chapter Objectives

1 Identify five reasons identity is important to communication.

2 Define *identity*.

3 Clarify how reflected appraisals, social comparisons, self-fulfilling prophecies, and self-concept contribute to identity development.

4 Identify examples of racial, national, ethnic, gender, sexual, age, social class, disability, and religious identities.

5 Discuss three ethical considerations for communicating in a sensitive manner to and about others' identities.

6 Explain three ways to communicate more effectively about identities.

From Chapter 3 of *Human Communication in Society*, Fourth Edition. Jess K. Alberts, Thomas K. Nakayama, Judith N. Martin.
Copyright © 2016 by Pearson Education, Inc. All rights reserved.

"We cannot separate our identities—as individuals or as members of society—from our communication experiences."

When you think about identity, you may be pondering who you "really" are and how you got to be that way. When Charee thinks about her identity, sometimes she thinks about her national identity as a U.S. citizen when she applies for jobs and is asked if she is eligible to work in the United States. Other times she thinks about her ethnic identity as an Asian American from an immigrant family. Her father is an immigrant from Vietnam and she sees herself as a Vietnamese-American. Sometimes she thinks about her gender identity in other contexts. Can you choose to be whomever you want, or do your background and social environment determine who you are? In this text, we address these identity questions as well as the important role communication plays in them.

Communication is a deeply cultural process. In this text, we explore how individual characteristics, such as gender and age and the societal meanings associated with them, interact to create cultural identities—and the important role communication plays in that development. Within cultures, communication patterns, habits, values, and practices develop around specific individual characteristics such as race, gender, sexuality, age, social class, and religion. For example, in the United States, people commonly understand that it is not acceptable to tell racist or sexist jokes, particularly in the workplace, at job interviews, and in other formal settings. This understanding exists because people are aware of the impact of this type of communication on people's identities. We all possess many cultural identities because we identify with genders, races, ethnicities, religions, organizational affiliations, schools, and so on. Some of these identities affect our communication experiences more than others. We explain which identities are most influential and why. We also examine how societal forces influence identity and discuss ethical issues associated with communication and identities. We conclude by looking at some skills for communicating about identities.

1 The Importance of Identity

1 Identify five reasons identity is important to communication.

Identity has a tremendous impact on the communication process in a number of ways. How we communicate, as well as how our communication is received by others, can be shaped by our identities and the identities of others. Let's look at some of the ways that identity influences communication. First, because individuals bring their self-images or identities to each communicative encounter, every communication interaction is affected by their identities. For example, when elderly people converse with teenagers, both groups may have to accommodate for differences in their experiences and language use.

Second, communication interactions create and shape identities (Hecht, 1993). If older adults treat teenagers with respect and admiration during their conversations, these young people may view themselves as more mature and more valuable than they did previously. Conversely, communication can also be used to denigrate other identities and create tension between groups. It is always important to think about the impact of communication on various identity groups.

Third, identity plays an important role in intercultural communication, which is something that has become increasingly common in our global, technology-based world. As more and more businesses have international branches and subsidiaries, workers are increasingly likely to have contact with people from other cultures. The more familiar they are with the values related to identity in these cultures, the better prepared they will be to succeed in today's society.

Fourth, understanding identity is useful because so much of U.S. life is organized around and geared toward specific identities (Allen, 2004). In the United States we have television stations such as *Black Entertainment Television* and *Telemundo* and magazines like *Ebony* and *Out*, which are targeted to groups based on their race, age, gender, or sexuality. We also have entertainment venues such as Disneyland and Club Med that are developed specifically for families, romantic couples, and singles. In this identity-based climate, individuals often communicate primarily with others who share their identities. Consequently, learning how to communicate effectively with individuals whose identities vary from yours may require considerable thought and effort.

Finally, identity is a key site in which individual and societal forces come together to shape communication experiences. Although we each possess identity characteristics such as social class or nationality, the society where our communication takes place will define the meanings of those characteristics. For example, depending on whether you are in the United States or visiting a country where anti-American sentiment is common, what it means to be an "American" can have different nuances. Moreover, we cannot separate our identities—as individuals or as members of society—from our communication experiences. Identity is vital to how meaning is created in communication (Hecht, 1993). We explain this interaction more fully throughout this text.

2   What is Identity?

2   *Define* identity.

When you enrolled in college, you were most likely required to provide a piece of identification, such as a birth certificate, passport, or driver's license. Identity is tied closely to identification; it refers to who you are and the specific characteristics that make you different from other individuals. In communication studies, *identity* includes not only who you are but also the social categories you identify yourself with and the categories that others identify with you. Society creates social categories such as *middle aged* or *college student*, but they only become part of one's identity when one identifies with them or others identify you in these categories. For example, you may think of yourself as short, but others may classify you as being of average height. Many young people in their late teens and early twenties identify with the category *college student*, but a growing number of people in their thirties, forties, and even older are also returning to school and identifying with this category. The many social categories that exist can be divided into two types: *primary* and *secondary identities* (Loden & Rosener, 1991; Ting-Toomey, 1999). Primary identities are those that have the most consistent and enduring impact on our lives, such as race, gender, and nationality. Secondary identities, such as college major, occupation, and marital status, are more fluid and more dependent on situation.

To help define the term **identity**, let's examine its essential characteristics. The first characteristic is that identities exist at the individual and the societal levels. Jake Harwood (2006) explains this concept: "At the individual (personal identity) level, we are concerned with our difference from other individuals, and the things that make us unique as people. At the collective (social identity) level, we are concerned with our group's differences from other groups, and the things that make our group unique" (pp. 84–85). For example, if you are an athlete, and you are

identity

who a person is; composed of individual and social categories a person identifies with, as well as the categories that others identify with that person thinking about how you are different and unique from others who are not athletic, then you are focusing on part of your individual identity. If you are focusing on how your sports team is different and unique from other sports teams, then you are focusing on your social identity.

We should note that identities are not necessarily only individual or social; they can be both, depending on the situation. How is this contradiction possible? Let's look at an example. Many readers of this text are U.S. Americans, and their national identity is part of their social identity. Because they are surrounded by others from the United States, they may not be conscious of this as being part of their individual identity. But if they travel abroad, their national identity becomes part of their individual identity because this significant characteristic will differentiate them from others.

A second important aspect of identity is that it is both fixed and dynamic. Again, this seems like a contradiction. If you think about it, however, you will realize that certain aspects of our identities, although stable to some extent, actually do change over time. For instance, a person may be born male, but as he grows from an infant to a boy to a teenager to a young man to a middle-aged man and then to an old man, the meanings of his male identity change. He is still a male and still identifies as a male, but what it means to be male alters as he ages, and social expectations change regarding what a boy or a man should be (Kimmel, 2005).

A third characteristic of identity is that individual and social identities are created through interaction with others. The relationships, experiences, and communication interactions we share with others shape how we see ourselves. For example, people who travel abroad and then return home may experience stress, but they also experience growth and change—and communication with those they meet as they travel plays a key role in both (Martin & Harrell, 1996). As another example, in the 1960s and 1970s, many U.S. women became more aware of, and dissatisfied with, their social identity as wives and mothers. This prompted them to become involved in a larger social movement known as feminism, in which women organized and attended "consciousness raising" groups designed to alter how they perceived and performed their identities as females. Women in these groups were encouraged to think of themselves not primarily as wives and mothers but as the professional and social equivalents of men. This type of mobilization of women also occurred previously in history, when they organized to gain the right to vote. It also happened for others—both women and men—who organized to protest against racial discrimination. In these instances a common social identity brought people together into communities, and these communities in turn acted to improve the position of the particular social identity in society.

A fourth consideration is that identities need to be understood in relation to historical, social, and cultural environments. The meaning of any identity is tied to how it has been viewed historically and how people with that identity are situated in a given culture and society (Hecht, Jackson, & Ribeau, 2003; Johnson, 2001). For instance, throughout history, we have had varied notions of what it means to be female (Bock, 1989).

Although Cleopatra was an Egyptian Pharaoh and Joan of Arc led the French army into battle in the fifteenth century, these individual women were significant exceptions to the rule. In their times and for much of history, women have been perceived as intellectually inferior, physically delicate, or morally weak when compared to men. Because of these beliefs, in many cultures women were denied voting and property rights and even custody

Our relationships with others help us understand who we are and how others perceive us.

of their children in the event of divorce. For example, until 1881, upon marriage, English women's legal identities were subsumed by their husbands such that all of their property and wealth transferred to their spouses as well as their right to enter into any contracts (Erickson, 1993). In the United States, women didn't win the right to vote until 1920—and, more recently, Supreme Court Justice Antonin Scalia has argued that the U.S. Constitution "does not, in fact, bar sex discrimination" (Cohen, 2010).

Contemporary U.S. women have all of the legal rights of men, yet historical conceptions of women still affect how they are positioned in society today. For example, "Women earned 76.5 cents for every dollar that men did last year, moving no closer to narrowing a gender pay gap that has barely budged in almost a decade" (Cronin, 2013). The value of women's work can vary from Nevada where women earn about 85 cents for every dollar that men earn to Wyoming where women earn only 64 cents for every dollar that men earn (Casserly, 2013). Moreover, a number of religions still remain opposed to women serving as ministers and priests. The situation for women in other cultures can be even more challenging. In Saudi Arabia, although women make up 70 percent of those enrolled in universities, they compose just 5 percent of the workforce; their testimony in court is treated as presumption rather than fact; and they live mostly segregated lives (Azuri, 2006). Thus, a hierarchy exists across cultures in which one identity (male) is preferentially treated over another (female). You can probably think of other examples in which preferential treatment was given—or denied—based on race, sexuality, religion, social class, or age (Allen, 2004).

In sum, identity is key to understanding communication, and communication is key to understanding identity. As Abrams, O'Connor, and Giles have stated, "identity and communication are mutually reinforcing" (2002, p. 237).

3 The Individual and Identity

3 Clarify how reflected appraisals, social comparisons, self-fulfilling prophecies, and self-concept contribute to identity development.

Although it can be tempting to boil a person's identity down to one word—say, *nerd*, *jock*, or *sorority girl*—in reality, everyone is more complex than that. If you had to pick only one word to describe yourself and you had to use it in every situation—personal and professional—what word would you choose? For most people this task is impossible, for we all see ourselves as multidimensional, complex, and unique. People in the United States, especially, are invested in the notion that they are unique. Twins often go to great lengths to assure people that they are *not* the same. Perhaps the most famous example of this is the Olsen twins, Mary-Kate and Ashley. Mary-Kate dyed her hair dark so she would look less like her sister, and when the sisters received a star on Hollywood's Walk of Fame, they requested that they be given separate stars (a request that was denied). Like almost everyone, they recognize and value their uniqueness—and they would like others to do so as well (see *Did You Know? Famous Twins Just Want to Be Individuals*).

How is it possible that people who are as much alike as twins can still have distinct identities? It is possible because of the ways in which identities are created and how these identities are "performed" in daily life—the topics we take up in the next section.

Identity Development Through Communication

In communication, our understanding of identity development arises out of a theory called symbolic interactionism (Blumer, 1969; Mead, 1934). According to this theory, individuals' meanings for the objects, actions, and people around them

Alternative View

Census in India Includes a Third Gender Choice

As the official record of a nation's population, what information should any census seek? What categories should the census use?

The United States is just one of many countries that conduct a census at regular intervals. Census forms typically ask for basic personal data such as age, race, and gender. In 2000, the U.S. census made history by allowing respondents to check multiple race/ethnicity categories. In the 2010 census, the form was designed to "give the nation's more than 308 million people the opportunity to define their racial makeup as one race or more" (El Nasser, 2010).

The 2011 census in India also made history because its new census form gave respondents the option of answering the question about their gender identity with either "Male," "Female," or "Other." In India, individuals who are biologically male and adopt female gender identity are considered a third gender known as *hijra*; they face severe discrimination in mainstream Indian society (Venkat, 2008). The 2011 census "[gave] India a firm count for its 'third-gender' hijra community—the origins of which go back millennia to a time when transsexuals, eunuchs and gays held a special place in society backed by Hindu myths of their power to grant fertility" (Daigle, 2011).

In Europe, Germany was the first country to give legal status to intersex persons by allowing parents to choose X, instead of M or F on the birth certificate, as of November 1, 2013. In Australia, "individuals can select the third category irrespective of whether or not they have undergone sex reassignment surgery or hormone therapy" (Heine, 2013).

To view a copy of the 2011 census form for India, see: http://www.censusindia.gov.in/2011-Schedule/Shedules/English_Household_schedule.pdf.

To view a copy of the 2010 census form for the United States, see: http://2010.census.gov/2010census/about/interactive-form.php.

---

arise out of social, or symbolic, interaction with others. What you define as beautiful, ethical, and even edible is based on what you have heard and experienced during your interactions with others. You likely learned through observing and communicating with others that eating lobster is a luxury but that eating bugs is disgusting. We develop and reveal identities through communication interactions in much the same way. In this section we describe three communication processes involved in identity development—*reflected appraisals, social comparison,* and *self-fulfilling prophecies*—and explore how they shape one's sense of self, or self-concept.

REFLECTED APPRAISALS A primary influence on identity development is a communication process called **reflected appraisals** (Sullivan, 1953). The term describes the idea that people's self-images arise primarily from the ways that others view them and from the many messages they have received from others about who they are. This concept is also often referred to as the **looking-glass self** (Cooley, 1902; Edwards, 1990), a term that highlights the idea that your self-image results from the images others reflect back to you.

The process of identity development begins at birth. Although newborns do not at first have a sense of self (Manczak, 1999; Rosenblith, 1992), as they interact with others, their identities develop. How others act toward and respond to them influences how infants build their identities. For example, as infants assert their personalities or temperaments, others respond to those characteristics. Parents of a calm and cheerful baby are strongly drawn to hold and play with the infant, and they describe the child to others as a "wonderful" baby. On the other hand, parents who have a tense and irritable baby may feel frustrated if they cannot calm their child and might respond more negatively to the infant. They may engage in fewer positive interactions with their baby and describe the child as "difficult." These interactions shape the baby's identity for himself or herself and for the parents, as well as for others who have contact with the family (Papalia, Olds, & Feldman, 2002).

reflected appraisals

the idea that people's self-images arise primarily from the ways that others view them and from the many messages they have received from others about who they are

looking-glass self

the idea that self-image results from the images others reflect back to an individual

Did You Know?

Famous Twins Just Want to Be Individuals

As identical twins, how are you most alike? Different?

Drew: It is true that twins share a brain. Ha! Well, at least we can complete each other's sentences. We are extremely driven and also share a huge enthusiasm for using our voices to bring awareness to charities we are passionate about. As for differences, Jonathan is an illusionist; that's not my forte. However, I am a total fitness and health junky. I spend a lot of time playing sports and working out. Feel free to ask Jonathan how he likes my protein shakes.

Jonathan: Drew and I have the same drive and passion in everything we do. The reason we work so well together is because we have a "no B.S." policy and always get everything out on the table. As far as differences, well, everybody knows I have much better hair (Chareunsy, 2013).

Most twins strive to differentiate themselves from one another (Prainsack & Spector, 2006), whether that means dressing differently or pursuing disparate hobbies and careers. However for famous twins, developing separate identities is a greater challenge than for most. Jonathan and Drew Scott of *Property Brothers* became celebrities through the shows they make together on HGTV. Celebrity twins Mary-Kate and Ashley Olsen, James and Oliver Phelps (who play the Weasley twins in the *Harry Potter* movies), and Dylan and Cole Sprouse (of Disney's *The Suite Life of Zack and Cody*) all became famous either playing twins or playing the same character on television and in movies. Because their professional identities are so closely connected, people often forget that they have the same needs as "singletons" to be seen as unique and individual. Consequently, they have to remind us—and remind us again—that they are.

Twins often go to great lengths to assure people they are *not* the same.

SOURCE: Chareunsy, D. (2013, July 21). Q+A: Jonathan and Drew Scott of Las Vegas face off on HGTV's 'Brother vs. Brother'. *Las Vegas Sun*. Retrieved March 2, 2014, from: http://www.lasvegassun.com/vegasdeluxe/2013/jul/21/jonathan-drew-scott-las-vegas-face-off-hgtv-brothe/.

The reflected appraisal process is repeated with family, friends, teachers, acquaintances, and strangers as the individual grows. If as a child you heard your parents tell their friends that you were gifted, your teachers praised your classroom performance, and acquaintances commented on how verbal you were, you probably came to see yourself those ways. However, if family, friends, and acquaintances commented on how you couldn't "carry a tune in a bucket" and held their ears when you sang, then over time you likely came to view yourself as someone who couldn't sing. Through numerous interactions with other people about your appearance, your abilities, your personality, and your character, you developed your identities as a student, friend, male or female, or singer, among others. To read about one student's experiences with reflected appraisals, see *It Happened to Me: Bianca*.

Children's self-images are affected by their teachers' reflected appraisals.

particular others

the important people in an individual's life whose opinions and behavior influence the various aspects of identity

generalized other

the collection of roles, rules, norms, beliefs, and attitudes endorsed by the community in which a person lives

Interaction with two types of "others" influences this process of identity development. George Herbert Mead (1934) described them as *particular others* and the *generalized other*. **Particular others** are the important people in your life whose opinions and behavior influence the various aspects of your identity. Parents, caregivers, siblings, and close friends are obvious particular others who influence your identity. Some particular others may strongly influence just one of your identities or one aspect of an identity. If you perceive that your soccer coach believes you have no talent, then you may see yourself as a poor soccer player even if friends and family tell you otherwise.

Your sense of yourself is also influenced, however, by your understanding of the **generalized other**, or the collection of roles, rules, norms, beliefs, and attitudes endorsed by the community in which you live. You come to understand what is valued and important in your community via your interactions with significant others, strangers, acquaintances, various media such as movies, books, and television, and the social institutions that surround you. For example, if you notice that your family, friends, and even strangers comment on people's appearances, that the media focus on people's attractiveness, that certain characteristics consistently are associated with attractiveness, and that people who look a certain way seem to get lighter sentences in criminal proceedings, get more attention at school, and are hired for the best jobs, then you develop an internalized view of what the generalized other values and rewards with regard to appearance. You then will compare yourself to others within your community to see if you fulfill the norms for attractiveness, which then affects how this aspect of your identity develops.

Gradually, you begin to see yourself in specific ways, which in turn influences your communication behavior, which further shapes others' views of you, and so on. Thus, individual identities are created and re-created by communication interactions throughout one's life. (See *Communication in Society: Reflected Appraisals Affect All of Us—Even the Rich and Famous*.)

However, reflected appraisals aren't the only type of communication interaction that shapes identity. Each of us also engages in a process called *social comparison*, which influences how we see and value our identities.

SOCIAL COMPARISONS Not only do we see ourselves as possessing specific characteristics, we also evaluate how desirable those characteristics are. As we discussed, the generalized other becomes the basis for our understanding of which characteristics are valued. For example, Amish children learn through their interactions with family, friends, the church, and their community that aggression is a negative trait that one should minimize or eliminate (Kraybill, 1989). In contrast, in gangs, aggression is valued and encouraged, and community members learn this as well (Sanders, 1994).

Once we understand what characteristics are valued (or disdained) in our communities,

It Happened to Me

Bianca

I really relate to the concept of reflected appraisals. I was born in Brazil with an Italian mother and a Brazilian father. When I attended an all-girls private school in Cleveland, Ohio, I had a very difficult time blending in. After spending so much time with these other students, however, I gradually began feeling like one of them. I was speaking English all the time, even at home with my parents (whose first language is not English). I felt like I was an American. People communicated to me as an American. In my junior year, I moved back to Brazil. Being Brazilian and speaking Portuguese fluently, their reflections of me made me feel completely Brazilian and I began to lose my sense of American identity. Even today, at a U.S. college, I feel confused about my selfhood because of the different ways I am reflected off of people depending on which nationality group I am hanging out with.

Communication in Society

Reflected Appraisals Affect All of Us—Even the Rich and Famous

How does the looking-glass self explain successful people's low self-esteem and poor self-concepts? Why do you think their significant success does not change how they feel about themselves? How do the concepts particular other and generalized other apply in the examples discussed in the article?

Though it may seem unlikely, many famous, beautiful, or talented people suffer from negative self-concepts. Kate Winslet has admitted that before going off to a movie shoot, she sometimes thinks, "I'm a fraud, and they're going to fire me … I'm fat; I'm ugly …" (Eby, 2009). When Bradley Cooper was named the "Sexiest Man Alive" in *People* Magazine in 2011, even he did not seem to think that he was sexy. He said he felt that as he ages, he is not really that focused on his sexiness anymore.

He said he doesn't feel sexy and not feeling sexy is not a problem for him.

What accounts for the negative self-concepts of these talented and attractive people? Although Winslet has never spoken about the causes of her feelings, she has remarked on the fact that magazines and reporters at times have commented unfavorably on her body size and weight. Bradley Cooper said that Ryan Gosling should have won.

As these examples suggest, success, wealth and fame are no guarantee that individuals will feel happy and satisfied with who they are.

SOURCE: Eby, D. (2009, April 6). Actors and self-esteem-boosting self confidence. Retrieved from: ezinearticles.com/?id=2199637.

we assess whether we individually possess more, or less, of them than do others in our communities. We compare ourselves to others to determine how we measure up, and through this social comparison, we evaluate ourselves. In this way, the groups we compare ourselves to—our reference groups—play an important role in shaping how we view ourselves.

We compare ourselves to others in our identity group and decide how we rate. A woman might say, "I look good for my age," comparing herself to others in her reference group, which in this case is other women her age. Similarly, classmates often want to know each other's test scores and grades so that they can decide how to view their own performances. For example, how would you feel if you earned a 78 on an exam and your grade was the highest in the class? What if 78 were the lowest grade in the class? Thus, your evaluation of yourself and your abilities is shaped not only by a specific trait but also by how it compares to the traits of others in your reference group. However, your self-evaluation can vary depending on what you use as a reference group. If you compare your appearance to that of your friends, colleagues, and classmates, you may feel pretty good. However, if you use the idealized images of actors and models in magazines and movies, you may not feel as positively about your attractiveness.

The Web site and app "Hot or Not" allows you to upload photos of yourself to be judged by others. You can then post your rating to Facebook or other social media sites (Creighton, 2014). This kind of new media experience adds to the way that social comparison works because you are rated on a scale of 1 to 10 and can see where others place your appearance. Is this technological development a positive or negative influence on our identities?

SELF-FULFILLING PROPHECY Communication interactions can also influence one's identity through a process known as the **self-fulfilling prophecy**, meaning that when an individual expects something to occur, the expectation increases the likelihood that it will because the expectation influences behavior. For example, if you believe you can perform well on an exam, you are likely to study and prepare for the exam, which typically results in your doing well. Others also have expectations for you that can influence your behavior. For example, if your sales manager believes you are a poor salesperson, she may assign you to a territory where you won't have

self-fulfilling prophecy
when an individual expects something to occur, the expectation increases the likelihood that it will, as the expectation influences behavior

We compare ourselves with others in our reference group and decide how we measure up.

access to big accounts, and she may refuse to send you to sales conferences where your skills could be honed. If you still succeed, she may believe that you just got lucky. However, because you have a poor territory, don't have the opportunity to enhance your sales skills, and receive no rewards for your successes, you probably will not be a very good salesperson.

Thus, the belief in a particular outcome influences people to act and communicate in ways that will make the outcome more likely; in turn, the outcome influences how we perceive ourselves. For example, parents often unwittingly influence how their children perform in math and how their children perceive themselves as mathematicians. If a child hears her mother complain about her own poor math skills and how unlikely it is that her child will do better, the child is unlikely to succeed in math classes. When the child encounters difficulty with math, the messages she heard from her mother may increase the likelihood that she will give up and say, "Well, I'm just not good at math." On the other hand, if a child hears messages that she is good at math, she is more likely to keep trying and work harder when faced with a difficult math problem. This, in turn, will influence her to see herself as a competent mathematician.

Self-fulfilling prophecies can have a powerful effect on an individual's performance, especially when they are grounded in stereotypes of one's identity. For example, stereotypes exist that Asian students excel at math, that African American students are less verbally competent than white students, and that females are worse at math and spatial reasoning than males. Studies have shown that even subtly or implicitly reminding individuals of these stereotypical expectations can impact their performance, a concept called **stereotype threat**.

stereotype threat

process in which reminding individuals of stereotypical expectations regarding important identities can impact their performance

In one study, African Americans who were simply reminded of race performed significantly worse on a verbal exam than when the issue of race was not mentioned (Steele & Aronson, 1995); and in another study, Asian American students performed better on a math test when reminded of their race (Shih, Pittinsky & Ambady, 1999). In a similar study, females who were cued to think about gender performed worse on math and spatial ability tests than when the issue of gender was not raised (McGlone & Aronson, 2006). Yet another study found that white male engineering students solved significantly fewer problems when told that they were part of a study to examine why Asian Americans perform better in math than when told it was simply a timed test (Smith & White, 2002).

These studies reveal that individuals' performances can be enhanced or hampered when they are reminded, even implicitly, of expectations related to important identities. This is true not only of sex and gender but also has been shown to be true of socioeconomic status (Croizet & Claire, 1998) and age. These findings remind us that we need to be careful about creating self-fulfilling prophecies for others and allowing others' expectations to become self-fulfilling prophecies for us.

Through repeated communication interactions such as reflected appraisals, social comparisons, and self-fulfilling prophecies, we come to have a sense of who we are. This sense of who we are is referred to as one's *self-concept*.

SELF-CONCEPT As we have suggested, identity generally continues to evolve, as people age and mature, and, at the same time, individuals also have some fairly stable perceptions about themselves. These stable perceptions are referred to as self-concept. **Self-concept** includes your understanding about your unique characteristics as well as your similarities to, and differences from, others. Your self-concept is based on your reflected appraisals and social comparisons. However, reflected appraisals only go so far. When someone describes you in a way that you reject, they have violated your self-concept. For example, if you think of yourself as open and outgoing, but a friend calls you "a very private person," you are likely to think the friend doesn't know you very well. Thus, your self-concept is an internal image you

self-concept

the understanding of one's unique characteristics as well as the similarities to, and differences from, others hold of yourself. It affects the external image you project to others, and in turn, your self-concept influences your communication behavior. If you think of yourself as ethical, you may correct others or assert your views when they behave in ways you believe are unethical.

Self-esteem is part of an individual's self-concept. It describes how you evaluate yourself overall. It arises out of how you perceive and interpret reflected appraisals and social comparisons. Like identity, self-esteem can alter over time. It functions as a lens through which we interpret reflected appraisals and social comparisons, which may make it hard to change. For example, if you have relatively high self-esteem, you may discount negative reflected appraisals and overgeneralize positive ones. So, if a student with high self-esteem fails an exam, he may attribute the failure to external factors (e.g., the test was unfair) rather than to himself. On the other hand, a person with low self-esteem may see negative reflected appraisals where none exist and may consistently compare herself to unrealistic reference groups. In addition, this person is more likely to attribute a failure to the self (I'm not smart enough) than to external factors.

self-esteem

part of one's self-concept; arises out of how one perceives and interprets reflected appraisals and social comparisons

Because self-esteem is such a powerful lens through which you see the world, your self-concept may not be entirely consistent with how others see you. Several additional factors can create a mismatch between how you see yourself and how others do. First, your self-image and the feedback you receive may be out of sync because others don't want to hurt your feelings or because you respond negatively when faced with information that contradicts your self-image. Few people tell their friends and loved ones that they are not as attractive, talented, smart, or popular as they themselves think they are. Why? They don't want make others feel bad or they don't want to deal with the recipient's feelings of anger or sadness.

Second, if you hold onto an image of yourself that is no longer accurate, you may have a distorted self-image—or one that doesn't match how others see you. For example, if you were chubby in grade school, you may still think of yourself as overweight, even if you are now slim. Similarly, if you were one of the brightest students in your high school, you may continue to see yourself as among the brightest students at your college, even if your GPA slips.

Finally, people may not recognize or accept their positive qualities because of modesty or because they value self-effacement. If your social or cultural group discourages people from viewing themselves as better than others, you may feel uncomfortable hearing praise. In such cases, the individual may only compare himself to exceptionally attractive or talented people or may refuse to acknowledge his strengths in public settings. In Japanese culture the appearance of modesty (*kenkyo*) is highly valued (Davies & Ikeno, 2002). A similar trait of "yieldedness to others" (*glassenheit*) leads the Amish to downplay their accomplishments (Kraybill, 1989). As you can see, both culture and identity are deeply embedded in our communication.

self-respect

treating others, and expecting to be treated, with respect and dignity

Communication plays an important role in how we develop our self-concept.

Yet another aspect of self-concept is self-respect. Whereas self-esteem generally refers to feeling good about one's self, **self-respect** describes a person who treats others—and expects themselves to be treated—with respect (Rawls, 1995). Self-respect demands that individuals protest the violation of their rights and that they do so within the boundaries of dignity and respect for others. However, people with high self-esteem may not necessarily have self-respect (Roland & Foxx, 2003). For example, some people with high self-esteem may not treat others with respect or respond to violations of the self with dignity. Many atrocities, such as those committed by Saddam Hussein against his people, have

been waged by those who, because of their sense of superiority, thought they had the right to dominate and harm others.

Throughout this discussion of identity development we have focused on four separate constructs: reflected appraisals, social comparison, self-fulfilling prophecy, and self-concept. However, identity development is a circular process in which these constructs are interrelated. For example, reflected appraisals influence your self-concept, which affects your communication behavior, which in turn shapes how others see you and, ultimately, what they reflect back to you. Then the process starts all over again. The issue of identity goes beyond this complex process of development, however. In everyday life we enact or "perform" these identities. Let's see how this process works.

Performance of Individual Identity

performance of identity

the process or means by which we show the world who we think we are

self-presentation

influencing others' impressions by creating an image that is consistent with one's personal identity

The **performance of identity** refers to the process or means by which we show the world who we think we are and is related to **self-presentation**—the notion that in performing identity we try to influence others' impressions of us, by creating an image that is consistent with our personal identity. For example, many Green Bay Packers fans express their identity by wearing team colors, calling themselves Cheeseheads, and wearing plastic cheese wedges on their heads. In contrast, Pittsburgh Steelers fans often wave "the terrible towel" to cheer on their team. People also perform their identities in more subtle ways every day—with the type of clothing or jewelry (including wedding rings) that they choose to wear or the name they use. Some celebrities have taken stage names that the public is more familiar with than their legal, birth names. For example, Charlie Sheen's name is Carlos Estevez. Lady Gaga's real name is Steffani Germanotta. What do these different names communicate to the public? How do these names help these celebrities perform their public identities?

Communication style is another way people perform, or enact, their identities. For example, do you speak to your mother in the same way that you speak with your friends? If you bring a friend home, do you feel like a different person as he watches you communicate with your family? If so, you're not alone. Most people adapt their communication to the identity they wish to perform in a given context.

enacting identities

performing scripts deemed proper for particular identities

We show the world who we think we are through the performance of identity—in this case, identity as Green Bay Packers fans.

In fact, the branch of communication studies called performance studies focuses on the ways people perform, or communicate, their various roles. In other words, people **enact identities** by performing scripts that are proper for those identities. In their analysis of how men use body size as a positive identity, communication scholars Tony Adams and Keith Berry (2013) analyze the performance of a heavy size as a positive identity on FatClub.com. On the one hand, "members explicitly reframe weight gains and bigger bodies as desirable and erotic," but they also know that "affirming performances and relationships do not proceed without the possibility for criticism" (p. 321). Here the question of identity and what that identity means is answered through communication. The members of this Web site use communication to recreate different meanings about what a large size body means, but they also recognize that they are open to negative criticism of their body size by others in a culture that generally looks down on large bodies. Their performances reject dominant images of attractiveness and perform different identities as their "orientations toward and uses of bigger bodies are creative, and the community

offers a pedagogical space in which to imagine distinct and often-devalued ways of relating" (p. 322). Performing their identities becomes a way to resist the dominant negative view of large bodies.

Nadene Vevea (2008) analyzed how people use tattoos and body piercing to perform their identities. In her interviews, she found that people use body art for many different reasons, to communicate many different feelings. For example, "some of the fraternity brothers who responded to my survey all got matching tattoos to signify their membership but use body art as a positive connection between friends to show loyalty to one another" (p. 22).

Sometimes we enact family roles; other times we enact occupational roles. The enactment of identity is closely tied to one's movements into and out of different cultural communities and one's expectations regarding particular roles. Police officers, physicians, and teachers also enact particular roles in performing their occupations. If one of these professionals—say, a teacher—steps out of the appropriate role and tries to be the best friend of her students, problems can arise. In Minnesota, a physician "has been reprimanded for allegedly touching 21 female patients inappropriately during what were described as 'unconventional' medical exams" (Lerner, 2008). In this case, "Dr. Jed E. Downs, 51, reportedly would close his eyes and make 'unusual sounds or facial expressions' while examining female patients, according to an investigation by the Minnesota Board of Medical Practice" (Lerner, 2008). In this case, we expect physicians to communicate—verbally and nonverbally—in professionally appropriate ways. When the physician does not do this, problems can arise.

Thus, we perform various roles and communicate with others based on **role expectations**. If you are pulled over for a traffic violation, you expect the police officer to perform in a particular way. In turn, you communicate with the officer based on a prescribed script. If you do not enact the expected role or if the police officer does not enact the prescribed role, then confusion—or worse—can occur. Everyone carries many scripts with them into all kinds of interactions. For example, the authors of this text are all pet owners. When we speak to our pets, we sometimes repeat communication patterns that our parents used with us when we were children. Pets are not children, yet we often communicate to them as if they were because the script is familiar to us.

role expectations
the expectation that one will perform in a particular way because of the social role occupied

As we noted previously, identities are **mutable**, or subject to change. When people change identities, they also change the way they perform them. For example, as people age, if they perform the "grown-up" role appropriately, they hope others will treat them more like adults. If they don't change the way they behave, then they might be told to "stop acting like a child."

mutable
subject to change

Because identities are not fixed, sometimes you see mismatches between the performance of identity and any single identity category. Sometimes the difference between identity performance and identity category can be rather benign. For example, if we say that someone is young at heart, we are saying that we perceive that person's identity performance to resemble that of someone much younger in years. Thus, two people may be the same chronological age, but one may listen to contemporary music, watch current films and television shows, and dress according to the latest fashion trends. The other may listen to oldies radio stations and dress as he or she did years ago.

Sometimes this disconnect is viewed much more negatively. When people enact a gender identity at odds with the cultural identity category, such as when males perform identity scripts that are typically female, they may be ridiculed, ostracized, or worse. Still, how do particular identity categories, or ways of performing them, acquire meaning? How do you know what a particular category is supposed to "look like" or how it is to be performed? The answer has to do with societal forces, the subject we take up next.

4 The Individual, Identity, and Society

4 Identify examples of racial, national, ethnic, gender, sexual, age, social class, disability, and religious identities.

The development of individual identities is influenced by societal forces. Therefore, you cannot understand yourself or others without understanding how society constructs or defines characteristics such as gender, sexuality, race, religion, social class, and nationality. For example, as a child, you were probably told (some of) the differences between boys and girls. Some messages came from your parents, such as how boys' and girls' clothing differs or how girls should behave as compared with boys. Other messages came from your schoolmates, who may have told you that "they" (either boys or girls) had "cooties." You may also have picked up messages about gender differences, or about any of the identity categories mentioned, from television or other media. By combining messages from these various sources you began to construct images of what is considered normal for each identity category.

Communication scholars are particularly interested in how identities are communicated, and created, through communication. For example, in his work focusing on communication interactions, Donal Carbaugh (2007) is particularly interested in studying intercultural encounters, and he focuses on how communication interaction reveals insights into cultural identities.

When people enact identities that are contrary to social expectations, they may be pressured to change their performance. Thus, boys and girls who do not perform their gender identities in ways prescribed by society can be called "sissies" or "tomboys." People who do not perform their racial identities in ways that are expected are sometimes called "oreos," "apples," "coconuts," "bananas," or "race traitors." Although the Church of Jesus Christ of Latter Day Saints has banned the use of alcohol, those Mormons who do drink are sometimes called "Jack Mormons." Similarly, a person who does not perform heterosexuality as expected might be seen as gay or lesbian. Chaz Bono, son of Cher and Sonny Bono, has spoken publicly about his decision to transition from female to male starting in 2009. In 2011, the film, *Becoming Chaz*, and the book, *Transitions*, both were released and tell Chaz's story of gender change from Chastity Bono.

Those who do not conform to expected social communication or performance patterns may become victims of threats, name calling, violence, and even murder (Sloop, 2004). These aggressive responses are meant to ensure that everyone behaves in ways that clearly communicate appropriate identity categories. For example, after a lengthy lawsuit, Shannon Faulkner became the first woman to enroll at the Citadel, South Carolina's formerly all-male military college. During the time she attended the school, she received death threats and had to be accompanied by federal marshals (Bennett-Haigney, 1995). Thus, some groups in society have strong feelings regarding how identities should be performed, and they may act to ensure that identities are performed according to societal expectations.

In this section of the text, we will look at a range of primary identity categories. Note that each is a product of both individual and societal forces. Thus, whatever you think your individual identity might be, you have to negotiate that identity within the larger society and the meanings society ascribes to it.

Many parents choose clothes that communicate the gender of their babies.

Did You Know?

Performing Identity

What difference does it make who you think you are and who others think you are? How much of your identity is a feeling that you have about who you are?

Some people who are born into female bodies feel that they feel more like a male. Chaz Bono transitioned from female to male and now identifies as a man. In contrast, Laverne Cox from *Orange is the New Black* was born into a male body but identifies as a female. Today, she lives her life as a woman. Yet, some people do not have a fixed notion of their gender identity. Chris Crocker, who became famous from his "Leave Brittany Alone" YouTube video, has lived his life moving between male and female identities. He is more content changing gender identities rather than living as either a man or a woman.

SOURCE: Marikar, S. (2009, October 29). Chaz Bono opens up about becoming a man, taking hormones. ABC News. Retrieved August 12, 2014 from: http://abcnews.go.com/Entertainment/chaz-bono-talks-man-hormones-gender-reassignment/story?id=8946932.

Racial Identity

Despite its frequent use, the term *race* is difficult to define. Historically, races were distinguished predominantly by physical aspects of appearance that are generally hereditary. A race was defined as a group with gene frequencies differing from those of other groups. However, many physical anthropologists and other scholars now argue that because there is as much genetic variation among the members of any given race as between racial groups, the concept of race has lost its usefulness (Hirschman, 2003). For more on this contemporary view of race, based on the new tools of DNA analysis, refer to *Alternative View: DNA and Racial Identity*.

Despite the difficulty in accurately delineating the various races, race is still a relevant concept in most societies, and individuals still align themselves with specific racial groups, which we discuss next.

Racial identity, the identification with a particular racial group, develops as a result of societal forces—because society defines what a race is and what it is called. This means that racial categories are not necessarily the same from country to country. For example, the 2001 census in the United Kingdom did not include Chinese in the "Asian/Asian British" category, but the 2011 census "re-positioning of the 'Chinese' tick box from 'Any other ethnic group' to Asian/Asian British" shows that these racial categories are fluid (Office for National Statistics, 2012). Their census includes the "Irish Traveller" category that the U.S. census does not.

racial identity
identification with a particular racial group

Even within the United States the categorization of racial groups has varied over time. The category *Hispanic* first appeared on the U.S. census form as a racial category in 1980. In the 2000 census, however, Hispanic was categorized as an ethnicity, which one could select in addition to selecting a racial identity. Therefore, one could be both *Asian* (a race) and *Hispanic* (an ethnicity), or one could be both *white* (a race) and *Hispanic* (again, an ethnicity). Similarly, as Susan Koshy (2004) has noted, people from India were once labeled "non-white Caucasians," but today are categorized with Asian Americans on the U.S. census. These categorizations are important because historically they have affected the way people are treated. Although discrimination based on race is no longer legal, we continue to live with its consequences. For example, although slavery ended almost 150 years ago in the United States, many churches, schools, and other social institutions remain racially segregated (Hacker, 2003).

What do you think you would do if a total stranger began making racist or other bigoted comments to you? How would you react?

Alternative View

DNA and Racial Identity

Craig Cobb began buying properties in Leith, North Dakota, in 2011. His goal is to create a refuge for white supremacists where "white nationalists to take control of the town government" (Eligon, 2013). He has since bought a dozen properties:

It is difficult to tell whether Mr. Cobb wants or expects his vision for Leith to succeed.

Although he said that four fellow white nationalists have bought or acquired some of his plots, he said he did not know if or when they would be moving to the town, nor would he push the issue on them.

He gave the community's run-down former meat locker and creamery to the National Socialist Movement. Jeff Schoep, the movement's leader, said he was unsure how easy it would be for people, in a tough economy, to pack up and head to Leith. But he said he thought it was a fantastic idea to establish a community for white nationalists so they could have a safe place to land in a crisis—say, a civil war. (Eligon, 2013).

Mr. Cobb's vision ran into some trouble when a DNA test on the Trisha Goddard Show revealed that he is not all-white.

When Goddard revealed that, according to a DNA analysis, Cobb is not 100% European, but has some sub-Saharan African ancestry, he immediately rejected the validity of the results. Although he was not ready to accept publicly any results that indicated that he might have some black ancestors, many others might view his racial identity differently. It will be interesting to see if his appearance on this television show will affect his ability to establish an all-white city. It may change how other residents in Leith view him, as well as other members of the white nationalist movement. (Pearce, 2013).

Since then, Cobb has wondered "if he'll be target of discrimination against octoroons in Leith."

Octoroons are people with one African American great-grandparent. (Donovan, 2013).

SOURCES: Donovan, L. (2013, November 11). DNA finds Craig Cobb part black. *The Bismarck Tribune.* Retrieved March 2, 2014, from: http://bismarcktribune .com/news/state-and-regional/dna-finds-craig-cobb-part-black/article_ bfcbf59e-4b23-11e3-a44c-001a4bcf887a.html.

Eligon, J. (2013, August 29). New neighbor's agenda: White power take-over. *New York Times.* Retrieved March 3, 2014, from: http://www.nytimes. com/2013/08/30/us/white-supremacists-plan-angers-a-north-dakota-town. html?pagewanted=1&_r=1.

Pearce, M. (2013, November 12). White supremacist takes test, find out he's part black. *Los Angeles Times.* Retrieved March 2, 2014, from: http://articles.latimes.com/2013/nov/12/nation/la-na-nn-white-supremacist-dna-20131112.

Although people often think of racial categories as scientifically or biologically based, the ways they have changed over time and differ across cultures highlight their cultural rather than their biological basis. How cultures describe and define specific races affects who is considered to belong to a given race and, consequently, how those individuals are treated. As anthropologist Gloria Marshall explains: "Comparative studies of these popular racial typologies show them to vary from place to place; studies of these popular racial classifications also show them to vary from one historical period to another" (1993, p 117). Moreover, communication is a strong factor in furthering, affecting, or altering racial categories and identities to serve different social needs. For example, Guzman and Valdivia (2004) studied the media images of three Latinas—Salma Hayek, Frida Kahlo, and Jennifer Lopez—to see how gender and Latinidad are reinforced through the media. Face-to-face communication also influences peoples' ideas about racial identities. If individuals have little contact with people of a different racial group, it is especially likely that one or two encounters may lead them to draw conclusions about the entire group.

Beginning with the 2000 census, the U.S. government has allowed people to claim a **multiracial identity** (Jones & Smith, 2001). This category recognizes that some people self-identify as having more than one racial identity. So, how should we categorize Barack Obama? Although "there is much to celebrate in seeing Obama's victory as a victory for African Americans," writer Marie Arana (2008) also thinks that "Obama's ascent to the presidency is more than a triumph for blacks." She feels that "Barack Obama is not our first black president. He is our first biracial, bicultural president."

multiracial identity

one who self-identifies as having more than one racial identity

What difference does it make if we see Obama as our first African American president or as our first biracial president? As you think through this issue, you can see the complexities of race and racial politics within a culture.

Multiracial identities have arisen as a result of history as well. The Dutch colonization of Indonesia led to many mixed race children who were known as "Indische Nederlanders," or Dutch Indonesians. The actor Mark-Paul Gosselaar is an example of a Dutch Indonesian. There is even a Facebook page devoted to the Dutch Indonesian community. What other multiracial identities have resulted from the many ways that people have migrated around the world (e.g., through colonization, slavery, wars, invasions, and so on)?

National Identity

Racial identity can often be confused and conflated with **national identity**. We often misuse the notion of nationality when we ask someone "What's your nationality?" but what we really want to know is their ancestry or ethnic background. *Nationality* or national identity refers to a person's citizenship. In other words, Lady Gaga's nationality is not Italian, but U.S. American because she holds U.S. citizenship. John F. Kennedy's nationality was not Irish; he was a U.S. citizen. Many U.S. Americans did not actively choose their national identity; they simply acquired it by being born in the United States. Although many of us have not actively chosen our national identity, most of us are content with—or even proud—of it.

Like our other identities, the importance placed on national identity can vary, depending on many factors. At the 2014 Winter Olympics in Sochi, Russia, the U.S. women's hockey team came up with the hashtag #dawnsearlylight to promote the U.S. men's hockey game against Russia which aired at an early hour in the United States. As *Sporting Times* noted, "Sound familiar? Hopefully, since it's the second line of the national anthem." (Negley, 2014). The Olympics are one context that tends to draw on national identities.

In a recent study on Iranian-American and Iranian-Canadian children, M. Razavi found that they use the Internet in developing what she calls "New National Identities" (2013). These youths use the Internet to gather information about the United States or Canada and incorporate this new information into their sense of their national identity. She distinguishes this new national identity from local co-ethnic cultures to highlight the role of the Internet.

national identity

a person's citizenship

Ethnic Identity

Although race and ethnicity are related concepts, the concept of ethnicity is based on the idea of social (rather than genetic) groups. Ethnic groups typically share a national or tribal affiliation, religious beliefs, language, or cultural and traditional origins and background. A person's **ethnic identity** comes from identification with a particular group with which they share some or all of these characteristics. Thus, some U.S. citizens say that they are Irish because they feel a close relationship with Irish heritage and custom, even though they are no longer Irish citizens—or perhaps never were. Likewise, in the United States many U.S. Americans think of themselves as Italian, Greek, German, Japanese, Chinese, or Swedish even though they do not hold passports from those countries. Nonetheless, they feel a strong affinity for these places because of their ancestry. Unlike national identity, ethnic identity does not require that some nation's government recognizes you as a member of its country. It is also unlike racial identity, in that any racial group may contain a number of ethnic identities. For example, people who are categorized racially as white identify with a range of ethnic groups, including Swedish, Polish, Dutch, French, Italian, and Greek.

ethnic identity

identification with a particular group with which one shares some or all of these characteristics: national or tribal affiliation, religious beliefs, language, and/or cultural and traditional origins and background

When people enact a gender identity at odds with the cultural identity category, they may be ridiculed, ostracized, or worse.

gender identity

how and to what extent one identifies with the social construction of masculinity and femininity

In other parts of the world, ethnic identities are sometimes called *tribal identities*. For example, "in Kenya, there are 50 tribes, or ethnic groups, with members sharing similar physical traits and cultural traditions, as well as roughly the same language and economic class" (Wax, 2005, p. 18). Tribal identities are important not only across Africa, but also in many nations around the world, including Afghanistan (Lagarde, 2005). In some societies, tribal or ethnic identity can determine who is elected to office, who is hired for particular jobs, and who is likely to marry whom. In Malaysia the three major ethnic groups are Malay, Indian, and Chinese. Because the Malay are in power and make decisions that influence all three groups, being Malay gives one an important advantage. In the United States, however, the ethnic identities of many white Americans are primarily symbolic because they have minimal influence in everyday life (Waters, 1990). Even if ethnic identity does not play an important role in your life, it can carry great significance in other parts of the world.

Gender Identity

Similar to race, gender is a concept constructed through communication. *Gender* refers to the cultural differences between masculinity and femininity, whereas *sex* refers to the biological differences between males and females. Gender describes the set of expectations cultures develop regarding how men and women are expected to look, behave, communicate, and live. For example, in U.S. culture women (who are biologically female) are expected to perform femininity (a cultural construction) through activities such as nurturing, crossing their legs and not taking up too much room when sitting, speaking with vocal variety and expressivity, and wearing makeup. How do people respond to women who cut their hair in a flattop, sit sprawled across the couch, speak in an aggressive manner, and refuse to wear makeup? Often, they call them names or ridicule them; occasionally they even mistake them for males because these behaviors are so culturally attached to notions of masculinity.

Gender identity refers to how and to what extent one identifies with the social construction of masculinity and femininity. Gender roles and expectations have changed enormously over the centuries, and cultural groups around the world differ in their gender expectations. How do we develop our notions of gender, or what it means to be masculine or feminine? We learn through communication: through the ways that people talk about gender, through the media images we see, and through observing the ways people communicate to males and females. For example, although crying is acceptable for girls, young boys receive many messages that they are not supposed to cry.

A leading scholar on gender, Judith Butler (1990, 1993) was one of the first to argue that gender identity is not biological but based on performance. She asserted that people's identities flow from the ways they have seen them performed in the past. In other words, a man's performance of male identity rests on previous performances of masculinity. Because the performances of traditional masculinity have been repeated for so long, individuals come to believe that masculine identity and behaviors are natural. However, some people choose to enact their identity in non-traditional ways, and their performances will be interpreted against the backdrop of what is considered acceptable and appropriate.

Table 1 Statistics on Intersex Births, 2000

People whose chromosomal pattern is neither XX nor XY	1 in 1,666 births
People whose bodies differ from standard male or female	1 in 100 births
People receiving surgery to "normalize" genital appearance	1 or 2 in 1,000 births
Discussion of the statistical approach	For a discussion of the significance of stats like these, go to this link: http://www.isna.org/node/972.

SOURCE: Intersex Society of North America (2005). How common is intersex? Retrieved June 12, 2006, from www.isna.org/faq/frequency.

A woman taking the last name of the man she marries is a traditional enactment of gender identity. What do you think of this tradition?

The case of South African runner Caster Semenya underscores the complexity of gender. After Semenya achieved some very fast running times, accusations about her gender arose. If she was not a woman, then she could not compete in women's track events. The International Association of Athletics Federations (IAAF), the governing body of track and field events, decided to examine her gender through a series of tests. Although the "details of the medical testing that Semenya underwent will remain confidential" (Zinzer, 2010), the difficulty in knowing Semenya's gender highlights the complexity of categorizing people. After 11 months in limbo, the IAAF finally cleared her to compete in women's track events again. The issue of identifying males and females can be problematic (see Table 1 for the relative numbers of people who are intersex).

The complexity of how people identify with gender is reflected in Facebook's 2014 change to the gender options. "Facebook offers 56 options. You can use up to 10 of them on your profile." (Weber, 2014). Yet, even this array of choices may not capture the diversity of gender identifications possible in people's everyday lives.

Sexual Identity

sexual identity
which of the various categories of sexuality one identifies with

Sexual identity refers to which of the various categories of sexuality one identifies with. Because our culture is dynamic, it has no set number of sexual identity categories, but perhaps the most prominent are heterosexual, gay or lesbian, and bisexual. Although most people in our culture recognize these categories today, they have not always been acknowledged or viewed in the same ways. In his *History of Sexuality*, French historian and theorist Michel Foucault (1988) notes that over the course of history, notions of sexuality and sexual identities changed. In certain eras and cultures, when children were born with both male and female sexual organs, a condition referred to as *intersexuality*, they were not necessarily operated on or forced to be either male or female.

Not everyone chooses to enact gender in the same way, as evidenced by Conchita Wurst, the 2014 winner of the Eurovision contest.

Many people think of sexuality or sexual identity as private, but it frequently makes its way into the public arena. In everyday life, we often encounter people who will personally introduce us to their husbands or wives, a gesture that shares a particular aspect of their sexual identity. However, our society often exposes an individual's sexual identity to public scrutiny. For example, Brian Boitano, the 1988 gold medalist from the Olympics, revealed that he is gay when he was chosen by President Obama to attend the 2014 Winter

Olympics in Sochi, Russia. He said, "I don't feel that I can represent the country without revealing this incredible side of myself" (qtd in "Brian Boitano," 2014). In contrast, former congressman Anthony Weiner sending a link to a sexually explicit photo to a twenty-one-year-old woman led to other issues about his sexuality and his need to engage in sexting: "I went from not really thinking through very much to having everything just blow up in such a monumental way, that you'd have to be really blind to not realize there must be some things that I need to resolve here and understand a little better. Therapy wasn't something that came naturally to me. I am this middle-class guy from Brooklyn, the men in our family don't hug each other, we don't talk about our feelings" (qtd. in Van Meter, 2013).

Because identity categories are social constructions, there is not always agreement about what they mean. Clearly, in the public arena, people manipulate these identity categories to help retrieve their reputations when their sexual activities become public.

In daily life, a person's sexual identity plays a role in such mundane matters as selecting which magazines to read and which television shows and movies to watch, as well as choosing places to socialize, people to associate with, and types of products to purchase. Television shows, magazines, books, Internet sites, and other cultural products are targeted toward particular sexual identities, or they assume a certain level of public knowledge about sexual identities and groups. For example, *The Bachelor/Bachelorette*, *Millionaire Matchmaker*, and *Real Housewives of Orange County* presume an understanding of U.S. heterosexual culture. In contrast, the Logo cable channel is specifically geared to gay and lesbian viewers. *Modern Family* includes gay characters, whereas *Looking* centers gay characters in its storyline. *Glee* and *Orange is the New Black* include transgender characters. These communication texts can reinforce, confirm, or challenge our notions of various categories of sexual identity.

Age Identity

age identity

a combination of self-perception of age along with what others understand that age to mean

Age, when thought of strictly as the number of years you've been alive, is an important identity for everyone. But your **age identity** is a combination of how you feel about your age as well as what others understand that age to mean. How old is "old"? How young is "young"? Have you noticed how your own notions of age have changed over the years? When you were in first grade, did high school students seem old to you? Although *age* is a relative term, so are the categories we use for age groups. Today, for example, we use the terms *teenager*, *senior citizen*, *adult*, and *minor*, but these terms have meaning only within our social and legal system. For example, the voting age is eighteen, but people have to wait until they are 21 to buy liquor. Someone who commits a heinous crime can be charged as an adult, even if he or she is not yet 18. Still, whether a person feels like an adult goes beyond what the law decrees and comes from some set of factors that is far more complex.

Other age-related concepts are culturally determined as well. For example, the notion of "teenager" has come into use only relatively recently in the United States, and it is certainly not a universal category (Palladino, 1996). The notion that people have "midlife" crises is not a universal cultural phenomenon, either. Moreover, these age categories are relatively fluid, meaning that there are no strict guidelines about where they begin and end, even though they do influence how we think about ourselves (Trethewey, 2001). For example, because people today generally live longer, the span of years thought of as middle age comes later in our lives. These changes all illustrate the dynamic nature of age identity and the categories we have for it.

You probably feel your age identity when you shop for clothes. How do you decide what is "too young" for you? Or what is "too old"? Do you consciously consider the messages your clothing communicates about your age? As you reflect on your shopping experiences, think about the tensions between what you like (the individual forces) and what others might think (societal forces). Here you see the tension that drives all social identities, including age.

Social Class Identity

Social class identity refers to an informal ranking of people in a culture based on their income, occupation, education, dwelling, child-rearing habits, and other factors (Online Glossary, 2005). Examples of social classes in this country include working class, middle class, upper-middle class, and upper class. Most people in the United States identify themselves as middle class (Baker, 2003). However, there is no single agreed-on definition for each of the classes. For example, "the "middle class" income range has been described as between $32,900 and $64,000 a year (a Pew Charitable Trusts study), between $50,800 and $122,000 (a U.S. Department of Commerce study), and between $20,600 and $102,000 (the U.S. Census Bureau's middle 60% of incomes)" (Horn, 2013).

For Ken Eisold, social class "is really more about identity" (qtd. in Horn, 2013). In other words, the amount of money that people earn is only one part of identifying as middle class.

In his work on social class, French sociologist Pierre Bourdieu (1984) found that people of the same social class tended to view the world similarly: They defined art in similar ways, and they enjoyed similar sports and other aspects of everyday life. Moreover, based on his study of social class, Paul Fussell (1992) noted that U.S. Americans communicate their social class in a wide variety of ways, some verbal and some nonverbal. For example, middle-class people tend to say "tuxedo," whereas upper-class people are more apt to say "dinner jacket." In the category of nonverbal elements that express social class identity, he included the clothes we wear, the way we decorate our homes, the magazines we read, the kinds of drinks we imbibe, and the ways we decorate our automobiles.

Those in occupations such as nursing, teaching, and policing soon may no longer be considered middle class. What other occupations have fallen or might fall from middle-class status? In their study *The Fragile Middle Class*, Teresa Sullivan and her colleagues noted the increasing numbers of bankruptcy filings (2001), especially among those in occupations that we consider securely middle class, such as teachers, dentists, accountants, and computer engineers. In the wake of the recent recession, there has been increasing public discussion about income inequality and its toll on the middle class. The recession has drawn attention to the very wealthy and the increasing wealth they are amassing while unemployment remains stubbornly high. These discussions may portend a new focus on social class identity.

One reason people in the United States avoid discussing social class is because they tend to believe that their country is based on *meritocracy*, meaning that people succeed or fail based on their own merit. This idea leads to claims such as "anyone can grow up to be president." However, this has not proven to be true. For example, until the election of Barack Obama in 2008, every president in the United States has been white, male, and, in all cases but one, Protestant. Social identity and class have a powerful impact on one's life because they can determine where you go to school (and what quality of education you receive), where you shop (and what quality of resources you have access to), which leisure activities you participate in (on a scale from constructive and enriching to destructive and self-defeating), and who you are most likely to meet and with whom you are mostly likely to socialize. In this way, social class identity tends to reproduce itself; the social class one is born into is often

social class identity

an informal ranking of people in a culture based on their income, occupation, education, dwelling, child-rearing habits, and other factors

How does your own speech reveal your social class background and identity? Can you identify aspects of your family's home, yard, interior decorating, and clothing that reveal social class identity?

Social class identity is an important influence in the ways that people socialize and engage in leisure activities.

the same as the social class one dies in. People who are working class tend to live around other working-class people, make friends with working-class people (who influence their expectations and behavior), and attend schools that reinforce working-class values. In an early study that showed how communication was used to perform social class identity in conjunction with gender and race, Gerry Philipsen (1992) noted that men tended to speak much less than women and rarely socialized outside their working-class community, which he called "Teamsterville." More recently, Kristen Lucas (2011) studied how family is an important site for communication messages that "both encourage and discourage social mobility" (p. 95). By examining how families reproduce their working-class identity, we can see how there are contradictory messages sent to the children about social class and moving toward white-collar occupations.

It Happened to Me
Melinda

My parents went through a divorce when I was two, and my mother has worked hard so we could have a comfortable life. Throughout my life, I've gone to private schools and universities with other students whose families had much more money than mine. I've always tried to fit in with the other students. Recently my mother has gone into debt, and I am having trouble adjusting to this change. I haven't told any of my upper-class friends because I am afraid they won't understand my situation. It can be a struggle to be honest with people you don't think will understand your situation, but it is a struggle that I have to overcome. People should accept each other for who they are, not what social class they fit into.

In our previous example of the 2011 census in India, the census form does not ask people about their caste. In that cultural context, "census officials worried the sensitive subject of caste in multicultural and secular India could upset the results of the population count" (Daigle, 2011). Social class can be a sensitive topic in many cultures.

Disability Identity

disability identity

identification with physical or mental impairment that substantially impact everyday life

People can identify with or be identified as disabled for many different reasons. **Disability identity** is often defined as having an impairment of some kind. Some people experience differences in hearing, sight, or mobility. Not all disabilities are visible or evident to others. In 1990, the United States passed the Americans with Disabilities Act, which recognized disability as an important identity that needed federal protection from discrimination. This act also defines "disability" in Section 12102:

The term "disability" means, with respect to an individual

(A) a physical or mental impairment that substantially limits one or more major life activities of such individual;

(B) a record of such an impairment; or

(C) being regarded as having such an impairment (Americans with Disabilities Act, 1990, 2008).

Although this legal definition may be helpful to some, it does not tell us what this identity means and how it is performed by those who identify as disabled, nor does it tell us how disability is viewed by others.

It is through communication that "disability" as an identity gains its meaning in our society. As Deanna Fassett and Dana L. Morella explain,

> while someone might have a medical or physical condition that structures her/his experience, it is in her/his interactions with others that that condition takes on meaning and becomes what our collective social environment would consider disability, with all the punishments and privilege that entails. We build this social environment in our own mundane communication, in classrooms and faculty meetings; we learn and reiterate, often unknowingly, as institutional members, what is normal and what is not and what that means (p. 144).

If we are swimming in a sea of communication, the many meanings that we generate in everyday communication give meaning to disability.

Like other identities, disability is performed; it is "always in the process of becoming, then disability is something we do, rather than something we are" (Henderson and Ostrander, 2008, p. 2). Disability, in this view, is about how it is enacted and lived; it is not about a fixed state of being. For example, in his study on disabled athletes who play wheelchair rugby, Kurt Lindemann found that "performances of disability, especially in a sport context, can subvert the stigma associated with physical disability in surprisingly effective ways" (2008, p. 113). By focusing on athletic activities, disabled people attempt to challenge stereotypical views of those with disabilities. More recently, disabled actors have complained about media productions that feature able-bodied actors portraying disabled characters, such as Kevin McHale's portrayal of Artie Abrams in *Glee*. Some question whether there is a stereotype that disabled actors can't perform and work as well on studio sets as able-bodied actors.

People who are not disabled can become disabled and then develop this new identity as a part of their larger configuration of identities. For example, many people, as they grow older, may experience increasing hearing loss, reduced visual acuity, or other physical or mental impairments that can render them disabled. But disability, of course, is not limited to older people. How we talk about disability, see it in media images, and experience it in everyday life are all part of how we communicate about and construct the meanings of disability as an identity. In her study on autobiographical narratives of those growing up with chronic illness or disability, Linda Wheeler Cardillo found that "communication at all levels has a powerful impact on these persons and their experiences of difference. A deeper understanding of this experience and how it is shaped by communication can lead to more sensitive, respectful, affirming, and empowering communication on the part of health-care providers, parents, teachers, and others" (2010, p. 539).

Religious Identity

In the United States today, **religious identity** is becoming increasingly important. Religious identity is defined by one's spiritual beliefs. For example, although Jim hasn't been to a Catholic church in decades, he still identifies himself as Catholic because of his upbringing and the impact the religion has had on his outlook. Most researchers and writers agree that "religion is certainly one of the most complex and powerful cultural discourses in contemporary society, and religion continues to be a source of conflict between nations, among communities, within families, and ... within one's self" (Corey, 2004, p. 189). Although you may believe that your religious identity is part of your private life and irrelevant outside your family, this is not true. For example, in the aftermath of the 2001 September 11 attacks, Muslim identity has been viewed with particular suspicion. A 2004 study done by researchers in the Department of Communication at Cornell University found the following attitudes about Muslim Americans:

About 27 percent of respondents said that all Muslim Americans should be required to register their location with the federal government, and 26 percent said they think that mosques should be closely monitored by U.S. law enforcement agencies. Twenty-nine percent agreed that undercover law enforcement agents should infiltrate Muslim civic and volunteer organizations to keep tabs on their activities and fund-raising. About 22 percent said the federal government should profile citizens as potential threats based on the fact that they are Muslim or have Middle Eastern heritage. In all, about 44 percent said they believe that some curtailment of civil liberties is necessary for Muslim Americans (Cornell University, 2004).

religious identity
aspect of identity defined by one's spiritual beliefs

Alternative View

Respecting Religious Differences

Should Americans care about the religious identity of their elected leaders, or is someone's religion a private matter? Should elected leaders be guided by their religious beliefs to a greater or lesser extent than ordinary citizens? Explain your answers.

When any society has multiple religions, difficult issues can arise. As we look back on the media coverage of the 2008 U.S. presidential election, "much of the coverage related to false yet persistent rumors that Obama is a Muslim" (Pew Forum on Religion and Public Life, 2008). Concerns about John F. Kennedy's religion (Catholicism) also circulated when he ran for the presidency. In a society that values religious freedom, what difference does it make what religion (if any) a political candidate follows? How should we deal with these claims in a society that wants to respect and tolerate different religious beliefs? Although, some people in the U.S. still believe that President Obama is a Muslim. The fact is he is not a Muslim; he is a Christian. We must ask ourselves what difference does his religious identity make in how we see him? Does it mean that Muslims should not be elected to political offices? Does it mean that somehow Muslims are inferior to non-Muslims? Or is it used simply to attack President Obama for his various policies and political decisions?

Religious identity also takes on public significance because it correlates with various political views and attitudes (Corey & Nakayama, 2004). For example, the 2004 Cornell study found that Christians who actively attend church were much more likely to support differential treatment of Muslim Americans. In contrast, the nonreligious, or those less active in their churches, were less likely to support restrictions on civil liberties of Muslim Americans.

However one responds to other people's religious beliefs, most U.S. Americans feel a strong need to embrace and enact personal religious identities (Corey & Nakayama, 2004). In 2000, for example, 46 percent of U.S. Americans belonged to religious groups, and approximately 40 percent of U.S. Americans claimed to attend religious services regularly (Taylor, 2005). Thus, in their article on "Religion and Performance," Frederick Corey and Thomas Nakayama (2004) write that individuals feel a "tremendous need to embody religious identities and reinforce those identities through spirited, vernacular performances" (p. 211). To understand how one student's religious identity affects her life, read *It Happened to Me: Elizabeth*.

The virtual environment has also been influenced by, and influences, religious identity. Sometimes people find religious communities online, and some people even use their iPhones for prayer and other religious purposes. Others resist the Internet for fear it would compromise or challenge their religious beliefs. Communication scholar Heidi Campbell notes: "Digital religion as a concept acknowledges not only how the unique character of digital technology and culture shapes religious practice and beliefs, but also how religions seek to culture new media contexts with established ways of being and convictions about the nature of reality and the larger world" (p. 4).

We've shown throughout this text that aspects of our personal identity such as race, nationality, ethnicity, gender, age, social class, and religion develop through the tension between individual and societal forces. Although we may assert a particular identity or view of ourselves, these views must be

It Happened to Me

Elizabeth

If I meet someone in a college class, I don't tell them that I'm involved in a church or that I'm a Christian unless they bring it up or it's obvious they are, too. I do not want to appear to be a religious nut waiting to shove my belief system down their throat. My belief in Christ is really at the core of who I am, though. When I meet people through work who are in churches, I am open with them about my work, my life, and even my challenges. This is because they are my brothers/sisters in Christ, and that's the culture of what we do—care for, and about, one another.

negotiated within the larger society and the meanings that the larger society communicates about that identity. See *Alternative View: Respecting Religious Differences* for an example of how one individual's religious identity became a public issue whose meaning was discussed and negotiated within the larger society. In the next section, we discuss the role of ethics in communication about identity.

How would you describe your religious identity? How do you communicate it to others? Do you ever conceal it? If so, when and why?

5   Ethics and Identity

5   Discuss three ethical considerations for communicating in a sensitive manner to and about others' identities.

As you are probably aware, a person's sense of identity is central to how he or she functions in the world. Moreover, because identities derive their meanings from society, every identity comes with values attached to it. The ways we communicate may reflect these values. If you wish to be sensitive to other people's identities, you should be aware of at least three key ethical issues that can impact your communication with others.

One issue you might consider is how you communicate with people whose identities are more, or less, valued. What do we mean by more or less valued? You probably already know. In the United States, for example, which of the following identities is more highly valued: White or multiracial? Male or female? Lawyer or school bus driver? Still, these rankings are not necessarily consistent across cultures. In Denmark, for example, work identities do not follow the same hierarchical pattern as those in the United States (Mikkelsen & Einarsen, 2001). Thus, Danes are more likely to view street sweepers and doctors as social equals because they don't place as high a value on the medical profession nor as low a value on service jobs as many U.S. Americans do. In the United States, in contrast, many service workers complain that most of the people they serve either ignore them or treat them rudely—even with contempt. Consequently, you might ask yourself, "Do I communicate more politely and respectfully with high- versus low-status people?" If you find yourself exhibiting more respect when you communicate with your boss than you do with the employees you manage, then you might want to consider the impact of your communication on your subordinates' identities.

The second ethical point to reflect on involves language that denigrates or puts down others based on their identities. Such language debases their humanity and shuts down open communication. Examples of unethical communication and behavior related to identity occur if men yell sexual slurs at women on the street, or straight people harass individuals they believe are gay, or when white people are disrespectful to people of color. Although you probably don't engage in such obvious insults to people's identities, do you denigrate them in other, more subtle ways? For example, have you ever referred to someone as "just a homemaker" or "only a dental assistant"?

Third, think about whether you tend to reduce others to a single identity category. As we pointed out previously, each of us is composed of multiple identities, and even within a specific identity group, individuals may differ widely from one another. Thus, individuals may be offended when others respond to them based on only one of their identities, especially one that is not relevant to the situation at hand. For example, managers in some organizations will not promote mothers of small children to highly demanding positions. They justify this by claiming the women won't be able to fulfill both their family and their professional roles competently. Although these women may be mothers, their identities as mothers likely are not relevant to their workplace identities and performances—just as men's identities as fathers are rarely seen as relevant to their jobs. Each person is a complex of identities, and each person desires others to recognize his or her multiple identities. You are more likely to communicate ethically if you keep this fact in mind.

Alternative View

Catfishing

Sometimes people invoke identities that are not their own to gain something from others. Sometimes called "catfishing," people will engage others into their fabricated network of identities and social relationships to get them into a relationship. Manti Te'o, who played football at Notre Dame, and Thomas Gibson, an actor on "Criminal Minds," were both purported to have been snared in catfishing games. Both are believed to have been in lengthy online relationships with women that they had never met.

In *Digital Trends*, Molly McHugh identifies five different types of catfish:

There's the Revenge Catfish: This catfish feels he or she was wronged by you (or someone or something you're tied to) and is pathologically creating this online romance simply to get back at you.

There's the Bored Catfish. This catfish has an Internet connection and too much time on his or her hands

There's the Secretly-in-love-with-you Catfish. This catfish harbors an unrequited crush on you, and for some reason doesn't find him- or herself good enough in real life to go for it

There's the Scary Catfish. This catfish is simply out to break hearts and cause chaos.

There's the Lonely Catfish. This catfish usually has some sort of sob story and needs someone to talk too, and with a pretty picture and a Facebook profile, you've become that person.

Although the motives for engaging in catfshing may be even more complex than these five categories, what are the ethics of catfishing? McHugh raises an important challenge for all of us when she asks:

Really, we're all catfish. Have you ever edited your profile picture to look a little better? Do you untag? Have you ever faked a location check-in? We're all guilty of bending the truth with our profiles to some degree—hell, it's what all these platforms want us to do. Social media is a very aspirational beast and it's not very surprising that it's led to a catfishing epidemic.

SOURCE: McHugh, M. (2013, August 23) It's catfishing season! How to tell lovers from liars online, and more. *Digital Trends*. Retrieved March 3, 2014, from: http://www.digitaltrends.com/web/its-catfishing-season-how-to-tell-lovers-from-liars-online-and-more/#ixzz2uvnrrkOx. Read more: http://www.digitaltrends.com/web/its-catfishing-season-how-to-tell-lovers-from-liars-online-and-more/#ixzz2uvnL1KoP.

6 Skills For Communicating About Identities

6   Explain three ways to communicate more effectively about identities.

Related to our discussion about ethical issues, we offer three guidelines for communicating more effectively about identities. The first guideline concerns the self-fulfilling prophecy we discussed previously: How you communicate *to* someone and *about* someone can influence how they perform their identity or how it develops. If a parent continually communicates with the child as if she were irresponsible, then the child is likely to act irresponsibly. To communicate effectively, be aware of the ways you create self-fulfilling prophecies through your own communication.

Second, there are many ways to perform a particular identity. You can improve your ability to communicate if you are tolerant of the many variations. For example, even if you believe that "real men" should act in certain ways, you are likely to communicate more effectively if you do not impose your beliefs on others. For example, you should not assume that because someone is male, he enjoys watching football, baseball, and other sports; wants to get married and have children; or eats only meat and potatoes. If you do, you are likely to communicate with some men in ways they will find less interesting than you intend.

Third, remember that people change over time. If you have been out of touch with friends for a period of time, when you encounter them again you may find that they have embraced new identities. Sometimes people change religious identities, or sometimes they change occupations. You can increase your communication effectiveness if you recognize that people change and that their new identities may be unfamiliar to you.

Summary

Learning about identities and communication is important for at least five reasons: (1) we bring our identities to each communication interaction, (2) communication interactions create and shape identities, (3) identity plays a key role in intercultural communication, (4) much of our life is organized around specific identities, and (5) identity is a key site in which individual and societal forces come together.

Identities are defined social categories, and each of us is made up of many of them. They may be primary or secondary. Primary identities (race, ethnicity, age) are the focus in this text and have the most consistent and enduring impact on our lives; secondary identities, such as occupation and marital status, are more changeable over the life span and from situation to situation. Our identities exist at both the individual and social level, are both fixed and dynamic, and are created through interaction. Furthermore, identities must be understood within larger historical, social, and cultural environments. Important communication processes that influence personal identity development include reflected appraisals, self-concept, and self-fulfilling prophecies.

The primary identity categories—race, nationality, ethnicity, gender, sexuality, age, social class, disability, and religion—are constructed between individual and social forces and what society communicates about those identities. Individuals perform their identities, and these performances are subject to social commentary. Straying too far from social expectations in these performances can lead to disciplinary action.

Ethical concerns center on how people are treated based on their identities. Guidelines to ethical communication include learning to value and respect people within all identity groups, to avoid using denigrating language or reducing people to a single identity category. Guidelines for more effective communication about identities involve being aware of the ways you create self-fulfilling prophecies through your communication and being tolerant of different ways of enacting various identities.

Key Terms

identity	self-respect	ethnic identity
reflected appraisals	self-presentation	gender identity
looking-glass self	performance of identity	sexual identity
particular others	enacting identities	age identity
generalized other	role expectations	social class identity
self-fulfilling prophecy	mutable	disability identity
stereotype threat	racial identity	religious identity
self-concept	multiracial identity	
self-esteem	national identity	

Apply What You Know

1. List the identities that are most important to you. Some of these identities may not have been discussed in this text. Note some situations in which the identities not discussed in the text become most relevant and some situations in which other identities dominate.

2. Which of your identities are shared by a majority of people in society? What are some of the stereotypes of those identities? To answer this question, you may need to ask people who do not share that identity.

Glossary

age identity a combination of self-perception of age along with what others understand that age to mean

disability identity identification with physical or mental impairment that substantially impact everyday life

enacting identities performing scripts deemed proper for particular identities

ethnic identity identification with a particular group with which one shares some or all of these characteristics: national or tribal affiliation, religious beliefs, language, and/or cultural and traditional origins and background

gender identity how and to what extent one identifies with the social construction of masculinity and femininity

generalized other the collection of roles, rules, norms, beliefs, and attitudes endorsed by the community in which a person lives

identity who a person is; composed of individual and social categories a person identifies with, as well as the categories that others identify with that person

looking-glass self the idea that self-image results from the images others reflect back to an individual

multiracial identity one who self-identifies as having more than one racial identity

mutable subject to change

national identity a person's citizenship

particular others the important people in an individual's life whose opinions and behavior influence the various aspects of identity

performance of identity the process or means by which we show the world who we think we are

racial identity identification with a particular racial group

reflected appraisals the idea that people's self-images arise primarily from the ways that others view them and from the many messages they have received from others about who they are

religious identity aspect of identity defined by one's spiritual beliefs

role expectations the expectation that one will perform in a particular way because of the social role occupied

self-concept the understanding of one's unique characteristics as well as the similarities to, and differences from, others

self-esteem part of one's self-concept; arises out of how one perceives and interprets reflected appraisals and social comparisons

self-fulfilling prophecy when an individual expects something to occur, the expectation increases the likelihood that it will

self-presentation influencing others' impressions by creating an image that is consistent with one's personal identity

self-respect treating others, and expecting to be treated, with respect and dignity

sexual identity which of the various categories of sexuality one identifies with

social class identity an informal ranking of people in a culture based on their income, occupation, education, dwelling, child-rearing habits, and other factors

stereotype threat process in which reminding individuals of stereotypical expectations regarding important identities can impact their performance

References

Abrams, J., O'Connor, J., & Giles, H. (2002). Identity and intergroup communication. In W. B. Gudykunst & B. Mody (Eds.), *Handbook of international and intercultural communication* (2nd ed., pp. 225–240). Thousand Oaks, CA: Sage.

Adams, T. E., & Berry, K. (2013). Size matters: Performing (il)logical male bodies on *FatClub.com*. *Text and Performance Quarterly, 33* (4): 308–325.

Allen, B. (2004). *Difference matters: Communicating social identity*. Long Grove, IL: Waveland.

Americans with Disabilities Act of 1990, as amended with Amendments of 2008. Retrieved May 13, 2011, from: http://www.ada.gov/pubs/adastatute08.htm.

Arana, M. (2008, November 30). He's not black. *Washington Post*, p. B1. Retrieved December 31, 2008, from: www.washingtonpost.com/wp-dyn/content/article/2008/11/28/AR2008112802219.html.

Azuri, L. (2006, November 17). Public debate in Saudi Arabia on employment opportunities for women. *Inquiry and Analysis 300*. Retrieved March 16, 2009, from: www.memri.org/bin/articles.cgi?Area=ia&ID=IA30006&Page=archives.

Baker, C. (2003, November 30). What is middle class? *The Washington Times*. Retrieved January 16, 2005, from: www.washtimes.com/specialreport/200311291058557412r.htm.

Bennett-Haigney, B. (1995, August). Faulkner makes history at the Citadel. *NOW Newsletter*. Retrieved March 1, 2006, from: www.now.org/nnt/08-95/citadel.html.

Blumer, H. (1969). *Symbolic interactionism: Perspective and method*. Englewood Cliffs, NJ: Prentice Hall.

Bock, G. (1989), Women's history and gender history: Aspects of an international debate. *Gender & History, 1*: 7–30.

"Brian Boitano: I never intended to reveal I'm gay." (2014, January 10). *CBS News*. Retrieved March 3, 2014, from: http://www.cbsnews.com/news/brian-boitano-i-never-intended-to-reveal-im-gay/.

Bourdieu, P. (1984). *Distinction: A social critique of the judgment of taste*. (R. Nice, Trans.). London: Routledge & Kegan Paul.

Butler, J. (1990). *Gender trouble: Feminism and the subversion of identity*. New York: Routledge.

Butler, J. (1993). *Bodies that matter: On the discursive limits of "sex."* New York: Routledge.

Campbell, H. A., (Ed.). (2013). *Digital religion: Understanding religious practice in new media worlds*. New York: Routledge.

Carbaugh, D. (2007). Cultural discourse analysis: Communication practices and intercultural encounters. *Journal of Intercultural Communication Research, 36*, 167–182.

Cardillo, L. W. (2010). Empowering narratives: Making sense of the experience of growing up with chronic illness or disability. *Western Journal of Communication, 74*(5), 525–546.

Casserly, M. (2013, September 19). The geography of the gender pay gap: Women's earnings by state. *Forbes*. Retrieved March 2, 2014, from: http://www.forbes.com/sites/meghancasserly/2013/09/19/the-geography-of-the-gender-pay-gap-womens-earnings-by-state/.

Chareunsy, D. (2013, July 21). Q+A: Jonathan and Drew Scott of Las Vegas face off on HGTV's 'Brother vs. Brother'. *Las Vegas Sun*. Retrieved March 2, 2014, from: http://www.lasvegassun.com/vegasdeluxe/2013/jul/21/jonathan-drew-scott-las-vegas-face-off-hgtv-brother/.

Cohen, A. (2010, September 22). Justice Scalia Mouths Off on Sex Discrimination. *Time*. Retrieved May 12, 2011, from: http://www.time.com/time/nation/article/0,8599,2020667,00.html.

Cooley, C. H. (1902). *Human nature and the social order*. New York: Scribner's.

Corey, F. C. (2004). A letter to Paul. *Text and Performance Quarterly, 24*, 185–190.

Corey, F. C., & Nakayama, T. K. (2004). Introduction. Special issue "Religion and Performance." *Text and Performance Quarterly, 24*, 209–211.

Cornell University. (2004). Fear factor: 44 percent of Americans queried in Cornell national poll favor curtailing some liberties for Muslim Americans. *Cornell News*. Retrieved December 6, 2006, from: www.news.cornell.edu/releases/Dec04/Muslim.Poll.bpf.html.

Creighton, J. (2014, January 30). Digging into the "Hot or Not" App: What's It All About? *Information Space*, Syracuse University. Retrieved March 2, 2014, from: http://infospace.ischool.syr.edu/2014/01/30/digging-into-the-hot-or-not-app-whats-it-all-about/.

Croizet, J., & Claire, T. (1998). Extending the concept of stereotype threat to social class: The intellectual underperformance of students from low socioeconomic backgrounds. *Personality and Social Psychology, 24*(5), 588–594.

Cronin, B. (2013, September 17). Women's wage gap stays stuck in place. *Wall Sreet Journal*. Retrieved March 3, 2014, from: http://online.wsj.com/news/articles/SB20001424127887323981304579081371718549100.

Daigle, K. (2011, February 12). India's census counts 'third gender.' *Edge Boston*. Retrieved March 22, 2011, from: http://www.edgeboston.com/?116206.

Davies, R., & Ikeno, O. (Eds.). (2002). *The Japanese mind: Understanding contemporary culture*. Boston: Tuttleman.

Donovan, L. (2013, November 11). DNA finds Craig Cobb part black. *The Bismarck Tribune*. Retrieved March 2, 2014, from: http://bismarcktribune.com/news/state-and-regional/dna-finds-craig-cobb-part-black/article_bfcb-f59e-4b23-11e3-a44c-001a4bcf887a.html.

Eby, D. (2009, April 6). Actors and self-esteem-boosting self confidence. Retrieved from: ezinearticles.com/?id=2199637.

Edwards, R. (1990). Sensitivity to feedback and the development of the self. *Communication Quarterly, 38*, 101–111.

El Nasser, H. (2010, March 15). Multiracial no longer boxed in by the Census, *USA Today*. Retrieved May 12, 2011, from: http://www.usatoday.com/news/nation/census/2010-03-02-census-multi-race_N.htm.

Eligon, J. (2013, August 29). New neighbor's agenda: White power takeover. *New York Times*. Retrieved March 3, 2014, from: http://www.nytimes.com/2013/08/30/us/white-supremacists-plan-angers-a-north-dakota-town.html?pagewanted=1&_r=1.

Erickson, A. L. (1993). *Women and property in early modern England*. London: Routlege.

Everett, C. (2011, December 5). Bradley Cooper admits Ryan Gosling should have been named People's 'Sexiest Man Alive'." *New York Daily News*. Retrieved March 2, 2014, from: http://www.nydailynews.com/entertainment/gossip/bradley-cooper-admits-ryan-gosling-named-people-sexiest-man-alive-article-1.987083#ixzz2uxHR0wF3

Fassett, D. L., & Morella, D. L. (2008). Remaking (the) discipline: Marking the performative accomplishment of (dis)ability. *Text and Performance Quarterly, 28*(1–2), 139–156.

Foucault, M. (1988). *History of sexuality* (R. Hurley, Trans.). New York: Vintage Books.

Fussell, P. (1992). *Class: A guide through the American status system*. New York: Touchstone.

Guzmán, I. M., & Valdivia, A. N. (2004). Brain, brow, and booty: Latina iconicity in U.S. popular culture. *Communication Review, 7*, 205–221.

Hacker, A. (2003). *Two nations: Black and White, separate, hostile, unequal.* New York: Scribner.

Harwood, J. (2006). Communication as social identity. In G. J. Shepherd, J. St. John, & T. Striphas (Eds.), *Communication as … : Perspectives on theory* (pp. 84–90). Thousand Oaks, CA: Sage.

Hecht, M. L. (1993). 2002—A research odyssey. *Communication Monographs, 60,* 76–82.

Hecht, M. L., Jackson R. L., III, & Ribeau, S. A. (2003). *African American communication: Exploring identity and culture.* (2nd ed). Mahwah, NJ: Lawrence Erlbaum Associates.

Heine, F. (2013, August 16). M, F, or Blank: 'Third Gender' official in Germany from November. *Der Spiegel.* Retrieved May 15, 2014, from: http://www.spiegel.de/international/germany/third-gender-option-to-become-available-on-german-birth-certificates-a-916940.html.

Henderson, B., & Ostrander, R. N. (2008). Introduction to special issue on disability studies/performance studies. *Text and Performance Quarterly, 28*(1–2), 1–5.

Hirschman, C. (2003, May). The rise and fall of the concept of race. Paper presented at the Annual Meeting of the Population Association of America, Minneapolis, MN.

Horn, D. (2013, April 14). Middle class a matter of income, attitude. *USA Today.* Retrieved March 2, 2014, from: http://www.usatoday.com/story/money/business/2013/04/14/middle-class-hard-define/2080565/.

Intersex Society of North America (2005). How common is intersex? Retrieved June 12, 2006, from: www.isna.org/faq/frequency.

Johnson, A. G. (2001). *Privilege, power and difference.* Boston: McGraw-Hill.

Jones, N. A., & Smith, A. S. (2001). The two or more races population. *Census 2000 Brief (U.S. Census Bureau Publication No. C2KBR/01-6).* Washington, DC: U.S. Government Printing Office.

Kimmel, M. S. (2005). *The history of men: Essays in the history of American and British masculinities.* Albany: State University of New York Press.

Koshy, S. (2004). *Sexual naturalization: Asian Americans and miscegenation.* Stanford, CA: Stanford University Press.

Kraybill, D. B. (1989). *The riddle of Amish culture.* Baltimore: Johns Hopkins University Press.

Lagarde, D. (2005, September 22–28). Afghanistan: La loi des tribus. *L'Express International,* 30–37.

Lindemann, K. (2008). "I can't be standing up out there": Communicative performances of (dis)ability in wheelchair rugby. *Text and Performance Quarterly, 28*(1–2), 98–115.

Lerner, M. (2008, November 18). Minnesota disciplines four doctors, two for inappropriate contact. *Star-Tribune.* Retrieved May 3, 2011, from: http://www.startribune.com/lifestyle/34691559.html?page=all&prepage=1&c=y#continue.

Loden, M., & Rosener, J. B. (1991). *Workforce America: Managing workforce diversity as a vital resource.* Homewood, IL: Business One Irwin.

Lucas, K. (2011). Socializing messages in blue-collar families: Communication pathways to social mobility and reproduction. *Western Journal of Communication, 75*(1), 95–121.

Manczak, D. W. (1999, July 1). Raising your child's self-esteem. *Clinical Reference Systems,* 1242.

Marikar, S. (2009, October 29). Chaz Bono opens up about becoming a man, taking hormones. *ABC News.* Retrieved August 12, 2014 from: http://abcnews.go.com/Entertainment/chaz-bono-talks-man-hormones-gender-reassignment/story?id=8946932

Marshall, G. A. (1993). Racial classification: Popular and Scientific. In S. G. Harding (Ed.), *The "racial" economy of science: Toward a democratic future* (pp. 116–127). Bloomington: Indiana University Press.

Martin, J. N., & Harrell, T. (1996). Reentry training for intercultural sojourners. In D. Landis & R. S. Bhagat (Eds.), *Handbook of intercultural training* (2nd ed., pp. 307–326). Thousand Oaks, CA: Sage.

McGlone, M. S., & Aronson, J. (2006). Stereotype threat, identity salience, and spatial reasoning. *Journal of Applied Development Psychology, 27*(5), 486–493.

McHugh, M. (2013, August 23). It's catfishing season! How to tell lovers from liars online, and more. *Digital Trends.* Retrieved March 3, 2014, from: http://www.digitaltrends.com/web/its-catfishing-season-how-to-tell-lovers-from-liars-online-and-more/#ixzz2uvnrrkOx

Mead, G. H. (1934). *Mind, self, and society.* Chicago: University of Chicago Press.

Mikkelsen, E. G., & Einarsen, S. (2001). Bullying in Danish work-life: Prevalence and health correlates. *European Journal of Work and Organizational Psychology, 10,* 393–413.

Negley, C. (2014, February 17). Hockey creates patriotic hashtag. *Sporting News.* Retrieved March 2, 2014, from: http://www.sportingnews.com/olympics/story/2014-02-17/2014-sochi-olympics-usa-hockey-creates-patriotic-hashtag-america-dawnsearlylight,

Office for National Statistics, (2012, December 11). *Ethnicity and national identity in England and Wales.* Retrieved March 2, 2014, from: http://www.ons.gov.uk/ons/dcp171776_290558.pdf.

Online Glossary. (2005, January). Prentice Hall. Retrieved January 16, 2005, from: www.prenhall.com/rm_student/html/glossary/a_gloss.html.

Palladino, G. (1996). *Teenagers: An American history.* New York: Basic Books.

Papalia, D. E., Olds, S. W., & Feldman, R. D. (2002). *A child's world: Infancy through adolescence.* New York: McGraw-Hill.

Pew Forum on Religion and Public Life. (2008, November 20). *How the News Media Covered Religion in the General Election.* Retrieved December 31, 2008, from http://pewforum.org/docs/?DocID=372.

Philipsen, G. (1992). *Speaking culturally: Explorations in social communication.* Albany: State University of New York Press.

Prainsack, B. & Spector, T. D. (2006). Twins: A cloning experiment. *Social Science & Medicine, 63* (10): 2739-2752.

Rawls, J. (1995). Self-respect, excellence, and shame. In R. S. Dillon (Ed.), *Dignity, character, and self-respect* (pp. 125–131). New York: Routledge.

Razavi, M. (2013). Navigating new national identity online: On immigrant children, identity & the internet. M. A. Thesis. Georgetown University. Retrieved March 2, 2014, from: https://repository.library.georgetown.edu/bitstream/handle/10822/558243/Razavi_georgetown_0076M_12273.pdf?sequence=1.

Roland, C. E., & Foxx, R. M. (2003). Self-respect: A neglected concept. *Philosophical Psychology. 16*(2) 247–288.

Rosenblith, J. F. (1992). *In the beginning: Development from conception to age two.* Newbury Park, CA: Sage.

Sanders, W. B. (1994). *Gangbangs and drive-bys: Grounded culture and juvenile gang violence.* New York: Aldine de Gruyter.

Shih, M., Pittinsky, T. L., & Ambady, N. (1999). Stereotype susceptibility: Identity salience and shifts in quantitative performance. *Psychological Science. 10*(1), 80–83.

Sloop, J. M. (2004). *Disciplining gender: Rhetoric of sex identity in contemporary U.S. culture.* Amherst: University of Massachusetts Press.

Smith, J. L., & White, P. H. (2002). An examination of implicitly activated, explicitly activated, and nullified stereotypes on mathematical performance: It's not just a women's issue. *Sex Roles, 47*(3–4), 179–191.

Steele, C. M., & Aronson, J. (1995). Stereotype threat and intellectual test performance of African Americans. *Journal of Personality and Social Psychology, 69*(5), 797–811.

Sullivan, H. S. (1953). *The interpersonal theory of psychology.* New York: Norton.

Sullivan, T. A., Warren, E., & Westbrook, J. (2001). *The fragile middle class: Americans in debt.* New Haven: Yale University Press.

Taylor, J. (2005, June 6). *Between two worlds.* How many Americans really attend church each week? Retrieved January 30, 2006, from http://theologica.blogspot.com/2005/06/how-many-americans-really-attend.html.

Ting-Toomey, S. (1999). *Communicating across cultures.* New York: Guilford.

Trethewey, A. (2001). Reproducing and resisting the master narrative of decline: Midlife professional women's experiences of aging. *Management Communication Quarterly, 15*, 183–226.

Van Meter, J. (2013, April 10). Anthony Weiner and Huma Abedin's post-scandal playbook. *New York Times.* Retrieved March 3, 2014, from: http://www.nytimes.com/2013/04/14/magazine/anthony-weiner-and-huma-abedins-post-scandal-playbook.html?pagewanted=all&_r=0.

Venkat, V. (2008, Feb. 16–29). Gender issues: From the shadows. *Frontline, India's National Magazine, 25*(4). Retrieved March 3, 2011, from: http://www.frontlineonnet.com/Fl2504/Stories/20080229607610000.htm/.

Vevea, N. (2008) "Body Art: Performing Identity Through Tattoos and Piercing," *Paper presented at the annual meeting of the NCA 94th Annual Convention, TBA, San Diego, CA Online.* Retrieved March 11, 2011, from: http://www.allacademic.com/meta/p258244_index.html.

Waters, M. C. (1990). *Ethnic options: Choosing identities in America.* Berkeley: University of California Press.

Wax, E. (2005, September 26–October 2). Beyond the pull of the tribe: In Kenya, some teens find unity in contemporary culture. *Washington Post*, National Weekly Edition, 22(49), 8.

Weber, P. (2014, February 21). Confused by all the new Facebook genders? Here's what they mean. *Slate.* Retrieved March 2, 2014, from: http://www.slate.com/blogs/lexicon_valley/2014/02/21/gender_facebook_now_has_56_categories_to_choose_from_including_cisgender.html.

Zinzer, L. (2010, July 7). South African cleared to compete as a woman. *New York Times.* Retrieved May 13, 2011, from: http://query.nytimes.com/gst/fullpage.html?res=9803E2DE1430F934A35754C0A9669D8B63&ref=castersemenya.

Credits

Photo Credits

Credits are listed in order of appearance.

Photo 1: Michelle Gilders Canada West/Alamy

Photo 2: infusny-146/Roger Wong/INFphoto.com/Newscom

Photo 3: Michaeljung/Fotolia

Photo 4: Pathdoc/Fotolia

Photo 5: Ian Waldie/Getty Images

Photo 6: Wavebreakmedia/Shutterstock

Photo 7: Bill Greenblatt/UPI/Newscom

Photo 8: Frank Naylor/Alamy

Photo 9: Helga Esteb/Shutterstock

Photo 10: Frank Jansky/ZUMAPRESS/Newscom

Photo 11: Flindt Mogens/ZUMA Press/Newscom

Photo 12: Stockbroker/Alamy

Photo 13: Elenathewise/Fotolia

Photo 14: icsnaps/Fotolia

Text and Art Credits

03 Harwood, J. (2006). Communication as social identity. In G. J. Shepherd, J. St. John, & T. Striphas (Eds.), Communication as …: Perspectives on theory (pp. 84–90). Thousand Oaks, CA: Sage.

Cohen, A. (2010, September 22). Justice Scalia Mouths Off on Sex Determination. Time. Retrieved May 12, 2011, from: http://www.time.com/time/nation/article/0,8599,2020667,00.html

Source: Cronin, B. (2013, September 17). Women's wage gap stays stuck in place. Wall Sreet Journal. Retrieved March 3, 2014, from: http://online.wsj.com/news/articles/SB20001424127887323981304579081371718549100.

Abrams, J., O'Connor, J., & Giles, H. (2002). Identity and intergroup communication. In W. B. Gudykunst & B. Mody (Eds.), Handbook of international and intercultural communication (2nd ed., pp. 225–240). Thousand Oaks, CA: Sage.

El Nasser, H. (2010, March 15). Multiracial no longer boxed in by the census, USA today. Retrieved May 12, 2011, from: http://www.usatoday.com/news/nation/census/2010-03-02-census-multi-race_N.htm

Daigle, K. (2011, February 12). India's census counts 'third gender.' Edge Boston. Retreived March 22, 2011, from http://www.edgeboston.com/?116206

Heine, F. (2013, August 16). M, F, or Blank: 'Third Gender' official in Germany from November. Der Spiegel. Retrieved May 15, 2014, from: http://www.spiegel.de/international/germany/ third-gender-option-to-become-available-on-german-birthcertificates- a-916940.html.

Chareunsy, D. (2013, July 21). Q+A: Jonathan and Drew Scott of Las Vegas face off on HGTV's 'Brother vs. Brother'. Las Vegas Sun. Retrieved March 2, 2014, from: http://www.lasvegassun.com/ vegasdeluxe/2013/jul/21/jonathan-drew-scott-las-vegas-face-offhgtv- brothe/; Prainsack, B. & Spector, T. D. (2006). Twins: A cloning experiment. Social Science & Medicine, 63 (10): 2739-2752.

Bianca

Based on Eby, D. (2009, April 6). Actors and self-esteem-boosting self confidence. Retrieved from: ezinearticles.com/?id=2199637.

Eby, D. (2009, April 6). Actors and self-esteem-boosting self confidence. Retrieved from ezinear-ticles.com/?id=2199637

Lerner, M(2008, November 18). Minnesota disciplines four doctors, two for inappropriate contact. Star-Tribune. Retreived May 3, 2011, from: http://www.startribune.com/life-sytle/34691559.html?page=all&prepage=1&c=y#continue

Adams, T. E., & Berry, K. (2013). Size matters: Performing (il)logical male bodies on FatClub.com. Text and Performance Quarterly, 33 (4): 308–325.

Vevea, N. (2008) "Body Art: Performing Identity Through Tattoos and Piercing," Paper presented at the annual meeting of the NCA 94th Annual Convention, TBA, San Diego, CA Online. Retrieved March 11, 2011, from: http://www.allacademic.com/meta/p258244_index.html. (p. 22).

Based on Marikar, S. (2009, October 29). Chaz Bono opens up about becoming a man, taking hormones. ABC News. Retrieved August 12, 2014 from: http://abcnews.go.com/Entertainment/chaz-bono-talksman-hormones-gender-reassignment/story?id=8946932

Based on Pearce, M. (2013, November 12). White supremacist takes DNA test, finds out he's part black. Los Angeles Times. Retrieved March 2, 2014, from: http://articles.latimes.com/2013/nov/12/nation/la-na-nn-white-supremacist-dna-20131112

Based on Donovan, L. (2013, November 11). DNA finds Craig Cobb part black. The Bismarck Tribune. Retrieved March 2, 2014 from: http://bismarcktribune.com/news/state-and-regional/dna-finds-craig-cobb-part-black/article_bfcbf59e-4b23-11e3-a44c-001a4bcf887a.html Eligon, J. (2013, August 29). New neighbor's agenda: White power takeover. New York Times. Retrieved March 3, 2014 from: http://www.nytimes.com/2013/08/30/us/white-supremacists-plan-angers-a-north-dakota-town.html?pagewanted=1&_r=1 Pearce, M. (2013, November 12). White supremacist takes test, find out he's part black. Los Angeles Times. Re-trieved March 2, 2014, from: http://articles.latimes.com/2013/nov/12/nation/la-na-nn-white-supremacist-dna-20131112

Eligon, J. (2013, August 29). New neighbor's agenda: White power takeover. New York Times. Retrieved March 3, 2014, from: http://www.nytimes.com/2013/08/30/us/white-supremacists-plan-angers-a-north-dakota-town.html?pagewanted=1&_r=1.

Tbl03-01, Society of North America (2005). How common is intersex? Retrieved June 12, 2006, from www.isna.org/faq/frequency. p. 63, Source: Melinda p. 56, Adams, T. E., & Berry, K. (2013). Size matters: Performing (il)logical male bodies on FatClub.com. Text and Performance Quarterly, 33 (4): 308–325

Marshall, G. A. (1993). Racial classification: Popular and Scientific. In S. G. Harding (Ed.), The "racial" economy of science: Toward a democratic future (pp. 116–127). Bloomington: Indiana University Press.

Arana, M. (2008, November 30). He's not black. Washington Post, p. B1. Retrieved December 31, 2008, from: www.washingtonpost.com/wp-dyn/content/article/2008/11/28/AR2008112802219.html.

Negley, C. (2014, February 17). Hockey creates patriotic hashtag. Sporting News. Retrieved March 2, 2014, from: http://www.sportingnews.com/olympics/story/2014-02-17/2014-sochiolympics-usa-hockey-creates-patriotic-hashtag-americadawnsearlylight

Wax, E. (2005, September 26-October 2). Beyond the pull of the tribe: In Kenya, some teens find unity in contemporary culture. Washington Post, National Weekly Edition, 22(49), 8. p. 18.

Zinzer, L. (2010, July 7), South African cleared to compete as a woman. New York Times. Retrieved May 13, 2011, from: http://query.nytimes.com/gst/fullpage.html?res=9803E2DE1430F934A35754C0A9669DbB63&ref=csaterse menya.

Weber, P. (2014, February 21). Confused by all the new Facebook genders? Here's what they mean. Slate. Retrieved March 2, 2014, from: http://www.slate.com/blogs/lexicon_valley/2014/02/21/gender_facebook_now_has_56_categories_to_choose_from_including_cisgender.html.

Brian Boitano: I never intended to reveal I'm gay, CBS/AP, January 10, 2014, http://www.cbsnews.com/news/brian-boitano-i-never-intended-to-reveal-im-gay/

Van Meter, J. (2013, April 10). Anthony Weiner and Huma Abedin's post-scandal playbook. New York Times. Retrieved March 3, 2014, from: http://www.nytimes.com/2013/04/14/magazine/anthony-weiner-and-huma-abedins-post-scandal-playbook.html?pagewanted=all&_r=0.

Horn, D. (2013, April 14). Middle class a matter of income, attitude. USA Today. Retrieved March 2, 2014, from: http://www.usatoday.com/story/money/business/2013/04/14/middle-class-harddefine/2080565/.

Lucas, K. (2011). Socializing messages in blue-collar families: Communication pathways to social mobility and reproduction. Western Journal of Communication, 75(1), 95-121. p. 95.

Daigle, K. (2011, February 12). India's census coun ts 'third gender.' Edge Boston. Retrieved March 22, 2011, from: http://www.edgeboston.com/?116206

Fassett, D. L., & Morella, D. L. (2008). Remarking (the) discipline: Marking the performative accomplishment of (dis)ability. Text and Performance Quarterly, 28(1-2), 139-156. p. 144.

Henderson, B., & Ostrander, R. N. (2008). Introduction to special issue on disability studies/performance studies. Text and Performance Quarterly, 28(1-2), 1-5. p. 2

Lindemann, K. (2008). "I can't be standing up out there": Communicative performances of (dis)ability in wheelchair rugby. Text and Performance Quarterly, 28(1-2), 98-115

Cardillo, L. W. (2010). Empowering narratives: Making sense of the experience of growing up with chronic illness or disability. Western Journal of Communication, 74(5), 525-546. p. 539.

Corey, F. C. (2004). A letter to Paul. Text and Performance Quarterly, 24, 185-190. p. 189.

Pew Forum on Religion and Public Life. (2008, November 20). How the News Media Covered Religion in the General Election. Retrieved December 31, 2008, from http://pewforum.org/docs/?DocID=372

Corey, F. C., & Nakayama, T. K. (2004). Introduction. Special issue "Religion and Performance." Text and Performance Quarterly, 24, 209–211.

Campbell, H. A., ed. (2013). Digital religion: Understanding religious practice in new media worlds. New York: Routledge.

Based on Robinson, E. (2007, August 29). The power of Powell's rebuke, p. A17. Retrieved December 31, 2000, from www.washingtonpost.com/wp-dyn/content/article/2008/10/20/AR2008102002393.html.

Based on Robinson, E. (2007, August 29). The power of Powell's rebuke, p. A17. Retrieved December 31, 2000, from www.washingtonpost.com/wp-dyn/content/article/2008/10/20/AR2008102002393.html.

Elizabeth

McHugh, M. (2013, August 23) It's catfishing season! How to tell lovers from liars online, and more. Digital Trends. Retrieved March 3, 2014, from: http://www.digitaltrends.com/web/its-catfishing-season-how-totell-lovers-from-liars-online-and-more/#ixzz2uvnrrkOx. Read more: http://www.digitaltrends.com/web/its-catfishing-season-how-to-tell-lovers-fromliars-online-and-more/#ixzz2uvnL1KoP

Communicating, Perceiving, and Understanding

From Chapter 4 of *Human Communication in Society*, Fourth Edition. Jess K. Alberts, Thomas K. Nakayama, Judith N. Martin.
Copyright © 2016 by Pearson Education, Inc. All rights reserved.

Communicating, Perceiving, and Understanding

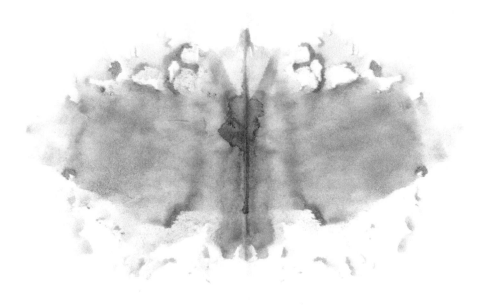

CHAPTER TOPICS	Chapter Objectives
The Importance of Perception	1 Explain why understanding perception is important.
What Is Perception?	2 Describe the three processes people use to understand information collected through the senses.
Perception and the Individual	3 Name three individual factors that affect one's perceptual processes.
The Individual, Perception, and Society	4 Articulate how power, culture, and historical time period influence perception.
Ethics and Perception	5 Explain why ethics is relevant to the perception process.
Improving Your Perception Skills	6 Identify three ways to improve one's perception skills.

> *"No one should assume that what he or she perceives is the same as what others perceive."*

After the first meeting of their research methods class, Charee and Mateo went out for coffee. They soon found themselves sharing their impressions of the instructor.

CHAREE: What did you think of Professor Wolfe?

MATEO: I suppose she's okay. She made the class seem kind of hard, and I am worried she will be difficult to talk to if I need help.

CHAREE: Really? I liked her a lot. I thought she was funny and would be really easy to talk to. I think I am going enjoy taking this class.

MATEO: She seemed kind of unapproachable to me. I guess we'll have plenty of chances to find out what she is really like during the semester.

As the conversation between Cheree and Mateo illustrates, our perceptions of others strongly influence how we respond to and communicate about them. If we perceive people as friendly and similar to ourselves, we tend to be drawn toward them and want to communicate with them. If we view individuals as distant and quite unlike ourselves, we may try to minimize contact. However, not everyone perceives and responds to people and events the same way. Our perceptions are affected by individual factors, such as age, gender, genetics, and experience, as well as by societal forces including culture, historical events, and social roles.

For instance, on average, females experience pain more intensely than do males (Hurley & Adams, 2008), so a touch that feels uncomfortable to a man may feel painful to a woman. (It can be helpful to remember this difference when we are shaking hands with others.) But how can societal forces affect perception? Among other things, societies teach us what foods and beverages are tasty and how they should be served. One example of this is the difference in how soft drinks are served in the United Kingdom versus how they are served in the United States. In most parts of the United Kingdom, cold beverages include a few pieces of ice, whereas in the United States a glass of soda may be half ice. Because of this, people in the two cultures have different perceptions of what a "good" cold drink should taste like.

In this text, we will first explore the importance of perception and the perception process. Next we'll examine how individuals' attributes and experiences affect their perceptions, and we will consider societal influences on perception. We also will discuss how people can evaluate their perceptions through an ethical lens. Finally, we will end with suggestions for sharpening your perception skills.

4   The Importance of Perception

1   **Explain why understanding perception is important.**

How individuals respond to people, objects, and environments depends largely on the perceptions they have about them. For example, when we perceive people as being polite, we are more likely to agree to their requests (Kellerman, 2004). When we communicate, we don't just respond to others' words; we respond to our perceptions of the way they look, sound, smell, and sometimes how they feel. For example, considerable research has established that when people perceive others as attractive, they treat them better than those viewed as less attractive (Chaiken, 1986; Wilson & Nias, 1999).

In addition, research suggests that sexual attraction is influenced by the body odor of a potential partner (McCoy & Pitino, 2002; Singh & Bronstad, 2001). Some studies indicate that people are sexually attracted to others whose body odor they find most attractive and that this attraction serves to help them locate mates likely to be a good genetic match.

So, the next time someone breaks off a relationship by saying, "It's not you; it's me," they may be telling the truth. You just may not smell right to that person! Interestingly, women may be more likely to make this statement than are men because a variety of research has found that on average women have a keener sense of smell than do men (Estroff, 2004; Herz & Inzlicht, 2002). Overall, women may be more positively influenced by smells they find attractive and negatively by smells they dislike. For more information on the influence of smell on perception, see *Communication in Society: Sex Difference in Smell.*

Identities play an important role in communication. They also influence and are influenced by perception. Thus, just as our perceptions of others impact how we communicate with them, our perceptions and communication impact how they see themselves. Let's take our previous scenario as a case in point. How might Mateo's or Charee's perceptions affect Professor Wolfe's perception of herself? If most people perceive Professor Wolfe as Charee does—as amusing and open—and, therefore, respond to her by laughing and spending time with her, then she probably sees herself positively. On the other hand, if most people respond as Mateo did, and consequently choose to have little contact with her, Professor Wolfe may perceive herself more negatively.

As you might expect, then, perception and identity are powerfully intertwined. On the one hand, Mateo's perceptions of Professor Wolfe affect her identity. At the same time, how the professor views herself and others impacts how she perceives and responds to the world around her. If she has a positive self-image, Professor Wolfe may perceive that others like her, she might be more optimistic and see the

Research reveals that when people perceive others as attractive, they treat them better than those viewed as less attractive.

Communication in Society

Sex Differences in Smell

Have you noticed a difference in sense of smell between the sexes? Why do you think women typically have a keener sense of smell?

Did you know that scientists often use all-female panels when they look for objective descriptions of food based on sensory perception, such as taste, smell, and appearance? They do so because on standard tests of smelling ability—including odor detection, discrimination, and identification—women consistently outscore men. One researcher has claimed that this difference is evident even in newborn babies.

Age also influences an individual's sense of smell. A study that tested 3,282 participants found that, overall, one's sense of smell was most acute between the ages of 19 and 35 and was the least acute when one is older than 55. However, in all of the three tests conducted, women out-performed men. Other studies have shown that women also rate the sense of smell as being more important to them than do men.

Experiments that have examined men's and women's scent ability reveal that both sexes are able to recognize others from their body odor alone. In an experiment at Hebrew University, Jerusalem, childless women held an unrelated baby in their arms for an hour. When tested later to see if they could recognize the baby they had held by scent, most of them were successful. This study did not test men, so it isn't clear if men possess similar smell recognition ability for unfamiliar others. However, other tests have determined that men and women both can recognize their own children or spouses by their scent. Typically in these studies, participants' children or spouses wore a T-shirt for several days, and then the participants were asked to use scent to recognize the T-shirt belonging to their family member.

SOURCES: Croy I., Buschhüter D., Seo H. S., Negoias S., & Hummel T. (2010) Individual significance of olfaction: Development of a questionnaire. *Eur Arch Otorhinolaryngol*, 267(1), 67–71. doi: 10.1007/s00405-009-1054-0.

Hummel T., Kobal G., Gudziol H., Mackay-Sim, A. (2007). Normative data for the "Sniffin' Sticks" including tests of odor identification, odor discrimination, and olfactory thresholds: An upgrade based on a group of more than 3,000 subjects. *Eur Arch Otorhinolaryngol, 264*(3), 237–243.

Korneliussen, I. (2012). Women smell better than men. *Science Nordic.* Retrieved May 14, 2014, from: http://sciencenordic.com/women-smell-better-men.

Maccaby, E. E., & Jacklin, C. N. (1978). *The psychology of sex differences.* Palo Alto, CA: Stanford University Press.

positive aspects of a situation more readily, and she could be less aware of others' negative reactions to her.

As you read this text, you are receiving considerable sensory input. An air conditioner or heater might be running, people may be moving past you, and the temperature where you sit likely fluctuates over time. In addition, you may feel hungry or tired, you might detect the scent of cleaning products, and the chair you are sitting on could be uncomfortable. How are you able to manage all the information your senses bring to you so that you can focus on your reading? How are you able to make sense of all this sensory input? The answer is that you continuously engage in a variety of processes that limit and structure everything you perceive (Kanizsa, 1979; Morgan, 1977). Let's look at how this works.

2   What Is Perception?

2   Describe the three processes people use to understand information collected through the senses.

Perception refers to the processes of **selection**, **organization**, and **interpretation** that we use to understand the information we collect through our senses: what we see, hear, taste, smell, and touch. The sensory data we select, the ways we organize them, and the interpretations we assign to them affect the ways we communicate (Manusov & Spitzberg, 2008). Although these processes tend to happen concurrently and unconsciously, researchers separate them to better explain how they function.

Selection

Because people experience more sensory information than they can process, they selectively focus on and remember only part of it. In every interaction, each communicator has a field of perception. In this field, some objects, symbols, or words are at the center, others are on the periphery, and still others are outside the field altogether. Consciously or unconsciously, we attend to just a narrow range of the full array of sensory information available and ignore the remainder. This process is called **selective attention**.

Suppose your friend is telling you an interesting story about a mutual acquaintance while the two of you are seated in a crowded restaurant. Most likely, your friend will have your full attention. Peripherally you may notice the sights and sounds of the other people in the room, the smells of food, and the glare of sunlight coming through the window; however, none of this will distract your focus. You probably will not even notice who is sitting at the table next to you, the color of the walls, or the storm clouds gathering in the sky. Your attention will be devoted to the center of your field: your friend.

The sensory input we select, however, is not random (Goldstein, 2010; Greenough, Black, & Wallace, 1987). When a range of sensory experiences accost you, various factors affect your selection, including your identity, features of the person or object you have encountered, and your experiences and values. For example, at large social events you are likely to attend to only one or a few people because you cannot focus on everyone at once. Who captures your focus depends on:

- aspects of your identity (e.g., if you are Native American, you may find your attention drawn more to participants who also are Native American)

- features of the person (e.g., someone dressed differently from everyone else will likely attract your attention)

selection
the process of choosing which sensory information to focus on

organization
the process by which one recognizes what sensory input represents

interpretation
the act of assigning meaning to sensory information

selective attention
consciously or unconsciously attending to just a narrow range of the full array of sensory information available

- your goals (e.g., if you would like to meet a potential romantic partner, you may pay special attention to attractive men or women in your age range)

Researchers have also found that people are most likely to pay attention to and remember comments that are negative, violate their expectations, and are made in situations that are important to them (Siu & Finnegan, 2004). For example, a comment like "What on earth did you do to your hair?" is more likely to remain prominent in your mind than "Nice haircut." Similarly, when an instructor says, "This will be on the test," students usually pay close attention to what the instructor says next. Comments that violate our expectations also become more salient and gain more attention. Suppose you meet someone new and ask "How are you?" Instead of the expected, "Fine, thanks," the person explains in detail all the misfortunes that have befallen him or her in the past year. You not only will be surprised, you will remember the event. You may even decide that this new person is highly negative, or strange, and that you should avoid future interactions with him or her.

Organization

After selecting the sensory input we will attend to, we need to be able to recognize *what* it represents. To do this, we must organize the information into a recognizable picture that has meaning. If you are awakened in the middle of the night by a loud noise, you will certainly attend to that noise and little else. However, you also must be able to make sense of the sound to respond. Is it a mechanical sound or an animal one? Is it human? You can make judgments such as these because you possess organizational structures or templates that tell you what information belongs together and how to "read" or understand what you perceive (Kanizsa, 1979). How does this work? In this section we examine two primary cognitive principles—cognitive representation and categorization—which help people organize and respond to their perceptions.

cognitive representation

the ability to form mental models of the world

Schools and workplaces have fire drills to help people create cognitive maps that are familiar and enable them to act appropriately in an emergency.

COGNITIVE REPRESENTATION The term **cognitive representation** describes the human ability to form mental models, or cognitive maps, of the world we live in (Levinthal & Gavetti, 2000; Weick, 1995). We create these maps and then refer to them later when circumstances call for them. For example, people know that a fire alarm communicates danger; furthermore, they know how to respond to a fire alarm because they have a cognitive map for alarms. Schools and workplaces have fire drills, in fact, to help people create cognitive maps that are familiar and enable them to act appropriately in an emergency. And research has shown that people who rehearse a plan—or develop a cognitive map—for specific crises are more likely to survive (Sherwood, 2009).

People also develop and use cognitive maps when they communicate. As we grow up, we learn cognitive maps or models for engaging in many types of communication acts, such as complaining, apologizing, and asking for a favor. Many people learn quite early that it is useful to be nice to someone before asking them for a favor, and this information becomes part of the map for requesting favors. Remember that maps are *representations* of things, not the things themselves. Thus cognitive maps consist of general outlines; they are not fixed sets of utterances that are memorized.

Two specific types of cognitive representations, or maps, that individuals use to organize their perceptions about people and communication are called prototypes and interpersonal scripts.

Communication behavior is strongly influenced by idealized maps called prototypes. A **prototype** is the most representative example of a person or concept. For example, many people's prototypical idea of a professor is a person who is male, has white hair (and perhaps a beard), and wears a tweed jacket with leather patches. Although a few professors fulfill this prototype, many more do not. (Just look around your campus.) Nonetheless, this prototype persists, in part because of how media depict college professors. We also possess prototypes for "ideal" best friends, romantic partners, and family members. Many people, for instance, have a specific prototype of what a good spouse should do and be. How their spouses compare to the prototype may influence how satisfied they are with their partners.

prototype
a representative or idealized version of a concept.

Prototypes are important because people compare specific individuals to their prototypes and then respond to them based on the degree to which they perceive that the individual conforms to that prototype. This often happens when it comes to the issue of gender. People have prototypical ideas of what a "man" or a "woman" is. These prototypes represent idealized versions of masculinity and femininity. The degree to which an individual resembles one's prototype influences how one perceives and communicates with that person. One study found that for conservative voters, how feminine a female political candidate appears is associated with how likely she is to win an election (Hehman, Carpinella, Johnson, Leitner, & Freeman, 2014). For these voters, then, women who display traditionally feminine characteristics reflect their idealized version or prototype of women and they, therefore, favor them. Sarah Palin and Michele Bachmann are both conservative politicians who display feminine characteristics and have been successfully elected to public office.

script
a relatively fixed sequence of events that functions as a guide or template for communication or behavior

An interpersonal **script** is a relatively fixed sequence of events expected to occur; it functions as a guide or template for how to act in particular situations (Burgoon, Berger, & Waldron, 2000; Pearce, 1994). We develop scripts for activities we engage in frequently (Fehr, Baldwin, Collins, Patterson, & Benditt, 1999). Most people have a script for how to meet a new person. For example, when you first encounter a student you'd like to get to know, you probably introduce yourself, tell the person a basic fact about yourself such as "I live across the hall from you," and then ask a question such as "How do you like living on campus?" "What is your major?" or "Where is your home town?" Thus, you follow a routine of sorts.

categorization
a cognitive process used to organize information by placing it into larger groupings of information

We enact scripts because we find them comfortable, they are efficient, and they keep us from making too many social mistakes. Although many of the scripts we use will be familiar to others, we also tailor them to fit our own expectations for a situation. Our choice of script or the way we alter a script depends on our perceptions of others. We may use a different script to initiate a conversation with someone we perceive as friendly, attractive, and fun than with someone we perceive as shy, quiet, and withdrawn.

How does the script for obtaining food in a fast-food restaurant differ from scripts for obtaining food in other situations?

As this discussion suggests, cognitive representations help people navigate through the physical and social world. These maps provide guidelines that shape how we communicate with others through the prototypes and interpersonal scripts we develop as we grow up and mature.

CATEGORIZATION Another type of cognitive process we use to organize information is **categorization**. Categorization is inherent to all languages. The linguistic symbols (or words) we use represent the groupings we see around us. Because it is impossible to remember everything, we use groupings that represent larger categories of information or objects (Goldstein, 2010; Lakoff, 1987).

How do you perceive these two males? Do any stereotypes come to mind?

label

a name assigned to a category based on one's perception of the category

stereotyping

creating schemas that overgeneralize attributes of a specific group

For example, we lump a lot of information under the category of *restaurant*. What did you think of when you read the word *restaurant*? You probably envisioned a subcategory, such as a café or a pancake house. However, the concept of *restaurant* has certain features that apply to all subcategories, so that you know what is meant and what to expect when you go to one. You understand that *restaurant* refers to a place to eat and not a place to worship or attend classes. Forming and using categories allows us to understand and store information and makes us more efficient communicators.

Although grouping is a natural cognitive and perceptual process, it also can lead to misperceptions. Categorizing can cause one to reduce complex individuals to a single category or to expect them to behave in ways consistent with the category, regardless of the circumstance. For instance, you might categorize an individual based on your perception that the person is either smart and interesting or dull and boring. Once you reduce people to a category, you may communicate with them as if they possess no other characteristics. For example, if you categorize one of your coworkers as dull and boring, you may only interact with her over tasks and never invite her to join you after work, where she might be able to show you that she actually is interesting and fun.

When people categorize others, they typically also assign them a **label**. The two activities tend to go hand in hand. Thus, groups of people and the individuals within those groups may be labeled or described as jocks, sorority girls, hipsters, or nerds. Although labeling others can function as a useful shortcut, it also can lead to negative outcomes (Link & Phelan, 2001). When we label people, we run the risk of viewing them only through the lens of the label. The label also influences our expectations, evaluations, and responses to them. Labeling can cause problems even when the labels are positive, as was the case in *It Happened to Me: Lin Sue.*

When you were growing up, did your family have a label they used to describe you? Were you the smart one, the well-behaved one, or the goof-up? If you were labeled the goof-up, you may not have been given many opportunities to disprove the label, and your ideas may have been discounted even when they were valid. Because of such a label, you may have come to discount the value of your own ideas. This effect can be magnified when entire groups of people are labeled in ways that create problems, such as the labeling of British people as snobbish or Muslims as terrorists.

As you may have guessed, labeling is related to stereotyping. **Stereotyping** occurs when schemas overgeneralize attributes of a group to which others belong (Cox, Abraham, Devine & Hollon, 2012; Operario & Fiske, 2003). A stereotype is an assumption that every member of the group possesses certain characteristics. For example, you may assume that most females enjoy talking about fashion trends, so, you initiate a conversation with an unfamiliar woman by discussing the Style Network. But not every member of a group fits the stereotype—if you use the fashion opener with every woman you meet, you may encounter some women who give you a blank stare in response.

Although grouping individuals makes it easy to remember information about them, it often leads to inaccurate beliefs and assumptions. Overgeneralizing a group's attributes makes it difficult to see the individuality of the people we encounter. Thus, a reliance on stereotypes can get those who use them into trouble.

It Happened to Me
Lin Sue

Because I am Chinese American, people often assume that I am some kind of whiz kid in academics. Well, I'm not. I was hit by a car when I was little, and I have residual brain impairment because of it. I have to study hard just to make passing grades. I get both angry and embarrassed when people assume I am this great student and imply that I will surely go to graduate school. I will feel fortunate if I just get out of undergraduate school. I really wish people wouldn't do this to me. They think they are being nice and complimentary, but they are still stereotyping me.

Interpretation

After we perceive and organize sensory information, we assign meaning to it (Goldstein, 2010). Returning to our previous example, imagine that you are awakened late at night. You hear a loud noise, which you determine is caused by a banging on your bedroom window. You now have to interpret what this means. Is it a tree branch? A loose shutter? Is it someone trying to break in?

We all assign meaning to the information we perceive, but we do not all necessarily assign the same meaning to similar information. One of the factors that influences how we interpret information is the frame through which we view it.

FRAMES Structures that shape how people interpret their perceptions are called **frames**. An individual's understanding of an event depends on the frame used to interpret it (Dillard, Solomon, & Samp, 1996). For example, if you are someone who frames the world as a dangerous place rife with criminals, you are likely to interpret that banging on your window as an indication of someone trying to break in. Similarly, if your friend frames the world as a place full of rude people, he may interpret your failure to say hello as a deliberate snub, whereas if his view is that people are nice, he may interpret your behavior as a failure to see him. In essence, individuals view the world through interpretive frames that then guide how they make sense of events (Dijk, 1977; Durfeel, 2006).

Individuals' frames develop over time, based on experience, interaction with others, and innate personality (Neale & Bazerman, 1991; Putnam & Holmer, 1992). Because we cannot perceive every aspect of an experience, frames also direct our attention toward some features of an episode and away from others. A bad mood, for example, directs attention to the negative aspects of an event. Usually, people don't become aware of frames until something happens to force them to replace one frame with another. If a friend points out that you are focusing only on the negative, you will become more aware of how your mood is framing, or focusing, your perceptions and interpretations. Your frame can change, then, as new information is introduced.

How should you use this information about framing? Now that you are aware that interpretations of people, events, and objects are influenced by an individual's specific frames, you should be more critical of your own interpretations. It is helpful to recognize that your interpretations (as well as others') do not necessarily represent the "truth"—but simply represent a particular way of viewing the world.

Frames are important elements of interpretation because they function as lenses that shape how observers understand people and events. But bear in mind that interpretation involves more than just framing; when individuals interpret events, they also offer explanations for them. When we develop explanations for our own and others' behaviors, we are engaged in making attributions. Let's see how this process works.

ATTRIBUTION How often do you wonder "why did she (or he) do that?" As we observe and interact with others, we spend considerable energy attempting to determine the causes of the behavior. For example, if your friend ignores you before class, you try to figure out why. At heart, most of us are amateur psychologists who search for the reasons people behave as they do. How confident are you regarding your attributions about specific others, such as your best friend or one of your parents?

Attribution theory explains the cognitive and verbal processes we use to judge our own and others' behavior (Manusov & Spitzberg, 2008). Fritz Heider (1958, 2013), a psychologist and professor, said that attribution is the process of drawing inferences. When individuals observe others, they immediately draw conclusions that go beyond mere sensory information. When someone cuts you off in traffic, what conclusion do

frame
a structure that shapes how people interpret their perceptions

Are you an optimist or a pessimist? Do you think people are inherently generous or self-serving? The answers to these questions, and others like them, reveal how your beliefs help shape the frames you use and how, in turn, those frames influence the way you see—and respond to—the world. What other frames do you use that influence your perceptions?

attribution theory
explanation of the processes we use to judge our own and others' behavior

you usually draw? What attribution would you make if you called your romantic partner at 3 a.m. and he or she wasn't home? Although we're constantly being told we shouldn't judge others, attribution theory says we can't help it (Griffin, 1994).

One attribution we often make is whether the cause of an individual's behavior is internal or external. An *internal* cause would be a personality characteristic, whereas an *external* cause would be situational.

We are particularly likely to make internal attributions when the behavior is unexpected—that is, when it is something that most other people would not do (Kelley, 1973). For instance, if someone laughs during a sad scene in a movie, people are more likely to attribute this unexpected reaction to a personality trait—for example, rudeness or insensitivity. But when the behavior fits our expectations, we are likely to attribute it to external causes. Therefore, if someone cries during a sad movie scene, people are likely to attribute the behavior to the movie.

Besides expectations, attributions may also depend on whether we are the actor or observer of the behavior. We are more likely to attribute our own negative behavior to external causes and our positive actions to internal states (Harvey & Martinko, 2010). This is referred to as an **attributional bias**. If you are polite, it is because you have good manners; if you are rude, it is because others mistreated you. These attributions are examples of a **self-serving bias**. Operating under this bias, we tend to give ourselves more credit than is due when good things happen, and we accept too little responsibility for those things that go wrong.

Most individuals are harsher judges of other people's behavior than they are of their own. We tend to attribute others' negative behavior to *internal* causes (such as their personality) and their positive behavior to *external* causes (such as the situation). This tendency is referred to as the **fundamental attribution error** (Schwarz, 2006). For example, when you are driving during rush hour traffic and someone cuts in front of you abruptly as two lanes merge, what attribution do you make about the other driver? According to fundamental attribution error, people are more likely to attribute the behavior to some trait internal to the other driver ("That driver is a jerk and is deliberately trying to get ahead of me") rather than to something external ("That driver is distracted by a child in the car and doesn't realize the lane is merging"). But if the other driver slows down to let you enter the merged lane first, most people might assume the driver was simply following the rules of the road rather than deliberately attempting to be thoughtful.

A third type of attribution error people engage in is called over-attribution. Over-attribution occurs when you select one or two obvious characteristic (such as an individual's sex, ethnicity, or age) and use it to explain almost anything that person does (Olivier, Leyens, Yzerbyt & Walther, 1999). If your professor forgets a meeting with you and you attribute it to the fact that he is an "absent-minded professor," you likely are engaging in over-attribution. Over-attribution occurs because we use mental "shortcuts" to understand events around us. However, doing so has consequences. For example, you may remember that in 2012 George Zimmerman shot and killed teenager Trayvon Martin as he was walking back from a convenience store. What you may not remember is that Zimmerman saw Martin, an African American youth wearing a hoodie, and made an attribution that likely contributed significantly to what happened later. Before he confronted Martin, Zimmerman called 911 and said that Martin looked like "a real suspicious guy;" then he said "This guy looks like he's up to no good, or he's on drugs or

attributional bias

the tendency to attribute one's own negative behavior to external causes and one's positive actions to internal state

self-serving bias

the tendency to give one's self more credit than is due when good things happen and to accept too little responsibility for those things that go wrong

fundamental attribution error

the tendency to attribute others' negative behavior to internal causes and their positive behaviors to external causes

You are likely to attribute an internal cause to unexpected behavior—such as laughter during a sad movie.

something. It's raining, and he's just walking around." This utterance exemplifies how the over-attribution operates—we see a person, we select one characteristic and make attributions about that person based on our preconceived, often stereotyped, beliefs about that characteristic. In this case, it appears that Zimmerman's attribution, or more properly his over-attribution, about a young African American man wearing a hoodie, led to an encounter that ended with Zimmerman injured and Martin dead.

Typically our attributions don't result in such dire consequences. However, when people who have power make over-attributions about people of color, women, or those with disabilities, among others, it can result in unemployment, housing discrimination, and even violence for members of those groups. When we make over-attributions about others, we can hurt others even if we don't intend to.

Attributional biases have implications for the way people communicate and conduct relationships. For example, the types of attributions spouses make are linked to their feelings of marital satisfaction (Sillars, Roberts, Leonard, & Dun, 2000; 2002). Those in unhappy relationships tend to assume the spouse's negative behaviors are internal, or personality-based, and difficult to change. Unfortunately, they also tend to view their spouse's positive behaviors as situational and temporary (Bradbury & Fincham, 1988). Thus, unhappy spouses often feel helpless to change their partner's negative characteristics. This pessimistic outlook can then increase negative communication within the relationship.

Interestingly, when people make attributions about others, they tend to trust the negative information they hear more than the positive information (Lupfer, Weeks, & Dupuis, 2000). If you hear both positive and negative information about a classmate, you tend to remember and rely on the negative rather than the positive information to formulate your attributions. However, you are not confined to these faulty attributional processes; you can work to overcome them.

First, remember that none of us is a mind reader and that the attributions we make are not always accurate. Remain aware that attributions are really just guesses (even if they are educated guesses). It also helps if one remains aware of the self-serving bias and works to minimize it. Recognize that we all have a tendency to attribute our own positive actions to ourselves and others' negative actions to themselves. Look for alternative explanations for your own and others' behavior. Last, avoid overemphasizing the negative. People have a tendency to remember and to highlight the negative, so try to avoid the negative in your own comments and balance the positive against the negative in your evaluations of others. For an example of a mistaken attribution, see *It Happened to Me: Danika.*

It Happened to Me
Danika

I was at a party recently when I went up to this attractive guy and stood next to him. When he didn't seem to notice me, I introduced myself and tried talking to him. But he completely ignored me! I was so put off that I stomped away and started complaining to my friend Amira. I told her that the guy might be good looking, but he sure was full of himself. She looked puzzled. "Oh, were you standing on his left side?" she asked. When I told her yeah, she explained that he was deaf in his left ear and probably hadn't heard me. I felt bad that I had jumped to a negative attribution so quickly. Later, I approached him on his right side and talked to him; I found out he was a really nice guy.

3   Perception and the Individual

3   **Name three individual factors that affect one's perceptual processes.**

Thus far we have explained how perceptions are formed: Individuals engage in selective attention, use a variety of organizational processes, and assign meaning to their perceptions. Thus, if you hear a loud noise in the street, you will turn your attention to the street; and if you see a car stopped and a person lying in the road with her motorcycle, you will categorize the event as an accident. Finally, you likely will decide (interpret) that the car hit the motorcycle rider. However, a variety of individual factors influence people's perceptual processes and affect their selection, organization, and interpretation of sensory input. For example, those who often ride motorcycles may attribute fault for the accident to the car driver (because they have frequently experienced inattentive auto drivers), whereas people who only drive cars may attribute blame to the motorcyclist (because they observed cyclists driving between lanes of cars on the road). The individual factors that influence our perceptual processes generally fall into three categories: physical, cognitive, and personality characteristics. Let's begin with the physical factors.

Physical Differences

Each person's unique physical capabilities affect what they perceive and how they understand it. Some people have more acute hearing than others, whereas some have more acute sight or taste. For example, professional wine tasters have a highly developed sense of taste, pilots are required to have 40/40 vision, and musicians must possess the ability to identify various pitches and notes. As mentioned previously, age can influence perception, and an individual's sex can affect the sensory input they notice.

Synesthesia is another individual physical difference that affects perception, which has only recently been recognized and studied. Synesthesia is a rare cognitive and physical trait that influences people's perception and, to some extent, their communication. To learn what synesthesia is (and whether you have it!), refer to *Alternative View: Hearing Colors, Tasting Shapes.*

Personality and Individual Characteristics

Each person's unique mix of personality, temperament, and experience also influences how they interpret and respond to sensory information. Elements that make up this mix include emotional state, outlook, and knowledge.

EMOTIONAL STATE If you are feeling happy or optimistic, you will tend to interpret and respond to sensory input differently than if you are feeling depressed, angry, or sad (Planalp, 1993). For instance, if you feel angry, you may perceive music, other people's voices, or background noise as irritating. On the other hand, if you are in a positive mood, you may behave more helpfully toward others. In one experiment, researchers tested 800 passersby (Gueguen & De Gail, 2003). In half the cases, researchers smiled at the passersby, and in half they did not. A few seconds after this interaction, the passersby had the opportunity to help another researcher who dropped his

Did You Know?

The Ringtone Adults Cannot Hear

Are you familiar with Mosquito Ringtones? What are the implications of the Mosquito Teen Repellent and Mosquito Ringtone for communicating, perceiving, and understanding?

The Mosquito Ringtone is based on technology created by Britain Howard Stapleton, who developed a device described as the Mosquito Teen Repellent. The device emitted a high-pitched frequency tone that adults could not hear but that teenagers found annoying. It was used by shopkeepers to disperse teenagers from public spaces where they congregated.

Later, inventive students converted the same technology into a ringtone that adults could not hear. This allowed them to receive phone calls and text messages while in class without their teachers being aware of it—that is, provided their teachers were old enough.

To test your ability to hear Mosquito Ringtones at different frequency levels, go to http://www.freemosquitoringtone.org.

Alternative View

Hearing Colors, Tasting Shapes

People with synesthesia provide valuable clues to understanding the organization and functions of the human brain.

What does synesthesia reveal about how the brain affects perception? How can these differences in perceptual abilities affect how individuals interact with one another?

Across the world, a small percentage of people experience the sensory world in unique ways. They may be able to see colors when they look at specific letters, taste flavors when they feel shapes, or experience strong emotions when they hear particular sounds. All of these individuals have a neurological condition called synesthesia.

Synesthesia arises from Greek and means "a coming together or blending of the senses." Researchers have only recently begun to study synesthesia, and they still aren't sure what causes it to occur. One theory suggests that the creation of unexpected neural connections can cross boundaries in the brain between the senses to cause synesthesia, while another proposes that we are all born with synesthesia, but as we develop, the body "prunes" these connections.

Estimates of how many people are synesthetes range from 4% to .0005% (1 in 2000). The condition runs in families, and women are more likely than men to experience it. But not everyone experiences synesthesia in the same way. Researchers estimate that between 50 and 150 types of synesthesia exist. Five of those types are

- *Lexical-gustatory* occurs when an individual experiences a particular taste when saying a specific word. For example,

the word *pretty* might be associated with a warm, buttery flavor like toast.

- *Mirror-touch* describes occasions when a synesthete feels the same physical sensation as does the person she is observing. When she sees another touch his nose, for example, she can feel the pressure on her own nose.
- *Misophonia* refers to when an individual feels a strong negative emotion when he hears certain sounds. For instance, the sound of someone chewing gum might give rise to feelings of anger or rage.
- *Personification* occurs when ordered sequences, such as days of the week or numbers, have individual personalities and characteristics. Friday, for instance, might be experienced as lively young girl.
- *Cromesthesia* describes when an individual experiences a color when he hears a sound. For example, hearing a violin may cause one to experience pale lavender.

SOURCES: Than, K. (2005). Rare but real: People who feel, taste and hear color. *LiveScience.* http://www.livescience.com/169-rare-real-people-feel-taste-hear-color.html Retrieved December 15, 2014.

Everyday fantasia: The world of synesthesia. *American Psychological Association* http://www.apa.org/monitor/mar01/synesthesia.aspx. Retrieved December 15, 2014

Dean, J. (2014). Intriguing types of synesthesia: Tasting words, seeing sounds and hearing colors. *PsyBlog.* http://www.spring.org.uk/2014/05/6-intriguing-types-of-synesthesia-tasting-words-seeing-sounds-hearing-colours-and-more.php Retrieved December 15, 2014.

or her belongings on the ground. Those who were exposed to the smile in the first encounter were more likely to be helpful in the second. Thus, even a small impact on your emotional state can influence how you perceive and interact with others.

OUTLOOK One's outlook refers to a tendency to view and interpret the world in consistent ways. Research shows that people tend to have a natural predisposition to either optimism or pessimism, based on genetics and experience (Seligman, 1998). People who are optimistic by nature may expect more positive experiences and make fewer negative attributions. These positive expectations can have an influence on their behavior—but not always for the best. For example, young people with an optimistic bias tend to believe that they are less likely than others to experience negative consequences from health behaviors. Therefore, they may be more likely than others to engage in sexual risk-taking (Chapin, 2001).

KNOWLEDGE People frequently interpret what they perceive based on what they know of an event. If you know that your friend has a big exam coming up, you may interpret his or her irritability as the result of nervousness. Our knowledge of specific topics also influences our perceptions, communication, and decision making. For instance, a study on organ donation revealed that members of families that discussed the subject were twice as likely to donate their organs as were members of other families (Smith, Kopfman, Lindsey, Massi, & Morrison, 2004). The researchers concluded that once people communicate and know more about the topic of organ donation, they perceive it in a more positive light.

Cognitive Complexity

constructs

categories people develop to help them organize information

cognitive complexity

the degree to which a person's constructs are detailed, involved, or numerous

As we discussed previously, the process of categorization helps us to organize information. Scientists refer to the categories we form as **constructs**. **Cognitive complexity** refers to how detailed, involved, or numerous a person's constructs are (Burleson & Caplan, 1998; Granello, 2010). But how does cognitive complexity affect perception?

First, people tend to be more cognitively complex about—and have more constructs for—those things that interest them or with which they have had experience. If you enjoy music, you likely have a wide range of constructs regarding types of music, such as rap, hip hop, alternative, progressive, and neocountry, and these are constructs that others may not possess at all. This high number of constructs affects your perceptions of music. As you listen, you can distinguish between multiple forms of music, and you recognize when an artist is employing a specific form or fusing two or more.

Do you wonder how cognitively complex your interpersonal constructs are? To find out, think of a person you know well. Then for the next sixty seconds, write down as many terms as you can think of to describe that person. How many terms were you able to generate? How many different categories of terms were you able to list? (For example, nice, kind, thoughtful would group into one category as would athletic, physically fit, sporty.) Typically, the more terms and categories of terms you can generate, the more cognitively complex your interpersonal constructs are believed to be.

One important purpose of education is to help you expand your constructs related to specific topics. As you progress through this text and attend to your instructor's lectures and discussions, you will develop more constructs for communication. When you began this course, you made have just had one broad construct that you labeled "communication" that included all types of communication in which you engaged. By the time you finish this course, you will have many categories or constructs to describe different types of communication, such as rhetoric, small group communication, interpersonal communication, and intercultural communication. Once you have these constructs, you will then be able to more easily develop them and increase your understanding of them and, ultimately, the communication process as whole. As you acquire new information about each of these constructs, you will have a structure in which to place and organize new information, which in turn will help you understand and remember that information. It might be helpful for you to think of constructs as folders that you use to organize information and to which you refer later to help you understand a topic better.

In addition to these sets of personal constructs that help you interpret the world, you also possess *interpersonal constructs* that you use to make decisions and inferences about other people (Deutsch, Sullivan, Sage, & Basile, 1991). From an early age, everyone possesses simple constructs that help them explain their perceptions of others. These constructs tend to be bipolar, or based on opposing categories of characteristics, such as funny or serious, warm or cold, and responsible or careless. One's age, intellectual ability, and experiences influence how complex or detailed such constructs are. For example, very young children typically describe others with only a few constructs, such as nice or mean; most adults, however, have a much more involved set of constructs that allows them to describe others in more varied and specific ways, such as thoughtful, amusing, argumentative, or kind.

In addition, when you have cognitively complex construct systems, you tend to have many ways of explaining and understanding interpersonal interactions. Suppose, for example, that your friend Laura was almost an hour late meeting you for a dinner date. If you are cognitively complex, you might come up with a number of reasons to explain this behavior: Laura (a) was in a traffic accident, (b) forgot about the date, (c) was detained by an unforeseen event, (d) decided not to keep the date, and so on. These are all plausible explanations; without further information you will not know which one is correct. The point is that cognitively complex individuals can develop a large set of alternative explanations while they wait for more information to clarify the situation.

In turn, your degree of cognitive complexity influences your perceptions and thus your communication behavior. For example, if you can only explain Laura's lateness by deciding that she is thoughtless, you will likely perceive her negatively and use a hostile communication style when you meet. Individuals' levels of complexity influence a broad range of communicative issues, such as how many persuasive messages they can generate (Applegate, 1982) and how well they can comfort others (Holmstrom, & Burleson, 2010; Samter & Burleson, 1984).

Your perceptions strongly shape your communication and your actions. If you strike up a conversation with someone new who looks physically attractive but whose voice reminds you of someone you dislike, you may choose to end the conversation and move on. However, if you meet someone who reminds you of someone you like, you might invest energy in getting to know that person. If you interpret a new friend's teasing as a sign of affection, you may decide to increase your involvement with her. In these ways, your perceptual processes influence your interactions and relationships. In addition, broader societal factors also play a role in what you perceive, how you organize it, and the meanings you attach to it.

Cognitively complex individuals can develop a large number of explanations for the late arrival of a dinner date.

4 The Individual, Perception, and Society

4 Articulate how power, culture, and historical time period influence perception.

How do societal factors affect perception? As we will explain in this section, the position individuals hold in society and the cultures in which they live affect what they perceive and how they interpret these perceptions. As you read this section, we encourage you to consider the societal forces that affect your perceptions as well as how they might affect the perceptions of others.

The Role of Power

Every society has a hierarchy, and in a hierarchy some people have more power than others. Your relative position of power or lack of power influences how others perceive you, how you perceive others, and how you interpret events in the world. Moreover, those in power largely determine a society's understandings of reality.

Power differences affect people's perceptions of how easy or difficult it is to attain financial success.

For example, in the United States, the dominant perception is that everyone can move up in society through hard work and education ("Middle of the Class," 2005). However, individuals who are born poor and who live in deprived areas with few resources can find upward mobility to be difficult, no matter how hard they try to follow the path to "success" as defined by mainstream U.S. culture. Thus, the perceptual reality of these people is likely to differ from that of those higher in the power hierarchy. Nonetheless, a specific view of reality dominates U.S. culture because it is communicated both explicitly and implicitly through media messages, public speeches, schools, and other social institutions.

One's individual experiences within that hierarchy may lead one to accept or reject that dominant perception. For example, middle-class people may believe that if they work hard they will get ahead in society, whereas poor people may perceive that it takes a lot more than hard work and education (Ehrenreich, 2001).

Similarly, if a you grew up relatively wealthy, you may believe that your admission to a highly selective college is largely as a result of your intelligence, hard work, and skills, whereas someone who grew up relatively poor may believe that social connections and family money better explain this achievement (Douthat, 2005).

Your position in the racial hierarchy also influences your perceptions, such as about the reality of racial bias. It is well documented that white Americans and African Americans have different perceptions regarding the role of race in the United States (Hacker, 2003). A study conducted after Hurricane Katrina devastated the Gulf Coast revealed a broad divergence in perceptions: When asked whether racial inequality remains a major problem, 71 percent of African Americans replied yes, compared to only 32 percent of whites (Pew Research Center for the People and the Press, 2005).

The Role of Culture

Culture strongly influences individual perception. One way it does so is through its *sensory model*. Every culture has its own sensory model, which means that each culture emphasizes a few of the five senses (Classen, 1990). Moreover, what a culture empha-sizes affects what its members pay attention to and prefer. People in the United States, for example, tend to give primacy to the visual; thus, we have sayings such as "seeing is believing," and students almost demand that professors use PowerPoint slides in the classroom. On the other hand, people living in the Andes Mountains of South America tend to place more emphasis on what they hear than on what they see. In their culture, important ideas are transmitted through characters in stories and narra-tives (Classen, 1990). Knowing this, how do you think students in the Andes prefer to learn? You might imagine that they would prefer elaborate stories rather than a list of brief terms and concepts on PowerPoint slides.

A culture is composed of a set of shared practices, norms, values, and beliefs beliefs (Brislin, 2000; Shore, 1996), which in turn helps shape individuals' thoughts, feelings, perceptions, and behaviors. For example, individuals in East Asian cul-tures often are highly interdependent and emphasize the group over the individual. Consequently, they don't approve of bragging and encourage greater self-criticism than some other cultures. By encouraging self-criticism (and then working on self-improvement), the thinking goes, they are contributing to the overall strength of the group (Heine & Lehman, 2004; Markus, Mullally, & Kitayama, 1997). In the United States, however, the emphasis is often on the individual, and most people are encour-aged to distinguish themselves from others. For example, current books on dating and work success teach U.S. Americans how to "brand" themselves like a product. The dominant culture in the United States also encourages people to talk about their success and to refrain from self-criticism. As a result, someone from East Asia may see U.S. Americans as braggarts, whereas a person from the United States may see East Asians as overly modest (Kim, 2002).

Cultural background also influences how people expect to talk to one another (Scollon & Wong-Scollon, 1990). In some Native American cultures, for example, in-dividuals perceive strangers as potentially unpredictable, so they may talk little—if at all—until they have established familiarity and trust with the newcomer (Braithwaite, 1990). This approach differs considerably from the customs of some European American cultures, in which people view strangers as potential friends and strike up conversations to become acquainted with them (Krivonos & Knapp, 1975).

Now imagine a Native American and a European American from these dif-ferent communication cultures meeting for the first time. How is each likely to behave? The Native American may remain relatively quiet while observing the new person. The European American will most likely try to engage in a lively conversa-tion and may ask a number of questions to draw the other person out. As a result, the Native American may view the European American as nosy, pushy, and overly familiar, whereas the European American may see the Native American as unfriendly or shy (Braithwaite, 1990). Each perceives or evaluates the other based on expectations that were shaped by his or her own cultural perceptions, values, and the meanings typical for his or her own culture (Scollon & Wong-Scollon, 1990).

Cultural norms, values, and expectations provide a backdrop of familiarity. When we travel or when we meet people from other cultures close to home, we can learn from exposure to our differences. However, sometimes these differences are upsetting, frustrating, or baffling. For example, one of our students, Simone, was taken aback when she was offered *chapulines* (fried grasshoppers) during her trip to Oaxaca, Mexico. Take a look at some foods common in other parts of the world that most people in the United States likely consider strange, if not simply disgusting, such as haggis or head cheese. How much does your own ethnocentrism factor into your personal reaction to each of these foods? Interestingly, most of us not only value the ways of our own culture, we often feel that others' cultural norms are less desirable—or even wrong—an issue we discuss next.

Some travelers become upset when their cultural expectations about what is "food" are not fulfilled.

The Role of Social Comparison

As we discussed previously, categorizing groups of objects, information, or people is a basic quality of perception. *Social* categorization—or categorizing people—leads us to specific expectations about how others should or should not behave. These social categories and the expectations associated with them typically arise out of our culture and where we are positioned in the culture. For example, in the United States, middle- and upper-middle-class people often perceive individuals who receive government subsidies for food or housing as people who do not want to work hard, and they may therefore categorize them as lazy or dependent. However, people who are in the working class or among the working poor may have a different perception, asserting that those who rely on these government subsidies work hard but are underemployed or have to live on a salary that is not a living wage ("Middle of the Class," 2005; Ehrenreich, 2001). As you can see, the perceptions and categories that we develop tend to be tied to stereotypes and prejudice, which both flow from ethnocentrism, the perceptual concept at the core of social comparison.

ETHNOCENTRISM Most people view their own group as the standard against which they evaluate others. Thus, one's own ethnic, regional, or class group is the one that seems right, correct, or normal. This tendency to view one's own group as the standard against which all others are judged is described as **ethnocentrism**. It comes from the Greek words *ethnos*, which means nation, and *kentron*, which refers to the center of a circle (Ting-Toomey, 1999). People behave ethnocentrically when they view their own values, norms, or modes of belief and behavior as better than those of other groups.

ethnocentrism

the tendency to view one's own group as the standard against which all other groups are judged

Although it is normal to be proud of one's national, cultural, racial, or ethnic group, one becomes ethnocentric when he or she engages in polarized thinking and behavior. This occurs when people believe that if "we" are right, correct, normal, and even superior, then "they" must be wrong, incorrect, abnormal, and inferior. Such thinking can seriously interfere with our ability to communicate effectively with those outside our group.

STEREOTYPES Previously we described stereotypes as broad generalizations about an entire class of objects or people, based on some knowledge of some aspects of some members of the class (Brislin, 2000; Stephan & Stephan, 1992). When you stereotype computer programmers as smart but socially inept, you likely are basing your beliefs on your interactions with a few programmers—or perhaps on no interactions at all.

Stereotypes may be based on what you have read, images in the media, or information you have obtained from others, as you'll see was the case with one college student in *It Happened to Me: Damien.*

If you develop a stereotype, it tends to influence what you expect from the stereotyped group. If you believe that someone is a lesbian, you may also believe she engages in specific types of communication behavior, dress, or interests. When you hold these types of beliefs and expectations, they tend to erase the stereotyped person's individual characteristics. In addition, you are likely to communicate with her as if your stereotypes were accurate rather than basing your messages on her actual interests and behavior (Snyder, 1998).

It Happened to Me

Damien

Shortly after school started, I decided to join a fraternity and began going to parties on the weekends. Often when people heard me mention that I was a part-time computer programmer, they would first look shocked and then crack some kind of joke about it, like, "Bill Gates, Jr., eh?" I guess it surprises people that I don't have glasses, that I venture out into the sunlight once in a while, and that I engage in some social activities! I realize that their preconceived notions about "techies" have come from somewhere, but, since at least half of my fellow "computer geeks" are far from the nerdy stereotype, it would be nice if people would recognize that we aren't all pale, glasses-wearing, socially awkward nerds!

Stereotyping is an understandable and natural cognitive activity; in fact, stereotypes can serve as useful shorthand to help us understand the world. If you are interviewing for a job in the southern United States, it may be helpful for you to know that many Southerners prefer to engage in social interaction before getting down to business (though this is certainly not always true). However, when stereotyping leads to polarized understandings of the world as "between me and you, us and them, females and males, blacks and whites," then it can cause problems (Ting-Toomey, 1999, p. 149). In turn, polarized thinking frequently leads to a rigid, intolerant view of certain behavior as correct or incorrect (Ting-Toomey, 1999). For example, do you believe it is more appropriate for adult children to live on their own than with their parents before they marry? People with polarized thinking assume that their own cultural beliefs regarding this issue are right or correct instead of recognizing that cultures differ in what is considered appropriate.

PREJUDICE Stereotypes and feelings of ethnocentrism often lead to prejudice. **Prejudice** occurs when people experience aversive or negative feelings toward a group as a whole or toward an individual because she or he belongs to a group (Rothenberg, 1992). People can experience prejudice against a person or group because of his or her physical characteristics, perceived ethnicity, age, national origin, religious practices, and a number of other identity categories.

prejudice

experiencing aversive or negative feelings toward a group as a whole or toward an individual because she or he belongs to a group

Given the negative associations most people have with the concept of prejudice, you may wonder why it persists. Researchers believe that prejudice is common and pervasive because it serves specific functions, the two most important of which are *ego-defensive functions* and *value-expressive functions* (Brislin, 2000). Let's explore these concepts.

ego-defensive function

the role prejudice plays in protecting individuals' sense of self-worth

The **ego-defensive function** of prejudice describes the role it plays in protecting individuals' sense of self-worth. For example, an individual who is not financially successful and whose group members tend not to be financially successful may attribute blame to other groups for hoarding resources and preventing him or her from becoming successful. The less financially successful individual may also look down on groups that are even less financially successful as a way to protect his or her own ego. These attitudes may make people feel better, but they also prevent them from analyzing reasons for their own failure. Moreover, they negatively affect the ways people talk to and about the targeted groups. People who look down on groups that are less financially successful may describe them and talk to them as if they were lazy, incompetent, or not very bright.

Prejudice serves its **value-expressive function** by allowing people to view their own values, norms, and cultural practices as appropriate and correct. By devaluing other groups' behavior and beliefs, these people maintain a solid sense that they are right. Unfortunately, this same function causes group members to denigrate the cultural practices of others. You may have seen many examples of the value-expressive function of prejudice, as when individuals engage in uncivil arguments and personal attacks over issues such as men's and women's roles, abortion, and politics.

value-expressive function
the role played by prejudice in allowing people to view their own values, norms, and cultural practices as appropriate and correct

The Role of Historical Time Period

In addition to a person's place in the power hierarchy, his or her culture, and his or her awareness of social comparison, the historical period in which one grows up and lives influences perception and communication (U.S. National Research Council, 1989). For example, anyone living in the United States who was older than five or six on September 11, 2001, likely has had their perceptions altered by events of that day. They may feel less safe, perceive air travel as riskier, and feel more patriotic than they did before the terrorist attacks on that day. These perceptions may in turn influence how they talk about the United States, or how they communicate, for example, with individuals who are Muslim.

Other historical events have affected the perceptions of individuals who lived through them. For instance, people who lived through the Great Depression may perceive resources as being scarcer than others do; those who were young during the Vietnam War likely believe that collective action can influence political policy; and those who grew up watching "The Real World" and other reality TV programs probably view privacy differently than do prior generations. As you might expect, these perceptions influence how, and about what, the various generations communicate, a process called the **cohort effect**. Thus, those who came of age after 2000 may feel comfortable discussing a wide range of topics previously considered taboo, such as sexual conduct or family dysfunction. Similarly, women who grew up when sexual discrimination was more prevalent might object to the use of "girls" when referring to women.

cohort effect
the process by which historical events influence the perceptions of people who grew up in a given generation and time period

Social Roles

The roles one plays socially also influence one's perception, and consequently, communication. **Social role** refers to the specific position or positions an individual holds in a society. Social roles include job positions, familial roles (such as mother or father), and positions in society. For example, Teri holds a variety of roles, including mother, religious leader, soccer coach, and community activist. The fact that she holds these social roles affects how people perceive and communicate with her in several ways. First, society defines specific expectations for her various social roles (Kirouac & Hess, 1999). Many people, for example, expect that religious leaders will be especially moral, selfless, and well intentioned. In turn, these expectations affect the ways that religious leaders interact with others. If you expect Teri, as a religious leader, to be highly moral, she may work to communicate with you in ways that fulfill your expectations.

social role
the specific position or positions one holds in a society

Second, the education, training, and socialization Teri undergoes for her social roles influence her perceptions. In much of U.S. culture, it is expected that women will become mothers and that they will behave in specific ways as they fulfill that role. As they grow up, girls are socialized and taught—by both word and example—how mothers are supposed to communicate. Because Teri is a parent, she may perceive different issues as important. For example, she may be more concerned with the quality of schools, the safety of her neighborhood, and access to health care than a nonparent might. Similarly, when individuals receive education and training, their perceptions of the world around them are affected. A person trained as a police officer, for example, may perceive the world as populated with more criminals than the average person does; whereas a person trained as a nurse may be more aware of how to prevent illnesses and injuries.

Each individual's perceptions are unique, based on his or her own roles and characteristics. However, individuals also share certain perceptual realities with others in their power position in society's hierarchy as well as with others in their cultures and social role groups. Because of these differing realities and power positions, your perceptions may lead you into prejudicial and intolerant thinking and communication. In the concluding section of this text, we suggest strategies for improving your perception processes and communication.

Ethics and Perception

5   Explain why ethics is a relevant to the perception process.

As we've discussed throughout this text, the ways people communicate to and about others are connected to their perceptions and cognitions about them. That is, what we select to attend to, what categories we put people in, and the attributions we make about them all strongly influence what we believe, say, and do. For example, Tara was driving home late one night and stopped at a traffic light when she noticed a young man of color in the car next to hers. She reached over and locked her door. As she looked up, she saw the man smile slightly then lean over and lock *his* door. In this case, Tara was responding based on stereotypical perceptions and cognitions, and the other driver was gently reminding her of that fact.

A common example of a time when perception, ethics, and communication intersect occurs when speakers perceive and label other groups of people negatively and then use derogatory terms to refer to them. Unfortunately, using such terms can reinforce and even intensify one's own as well as others' negative responses to these groups. In addition, if what individuals attend to and perceive about people first is their skin color, their sex, or their relative affluence, they may find themselves communicating with those people stereotypically and failing to recognize other roles they fulfill. Doing so may lead one to assume and communicate as if all adult women are mothers (or there is something wrong with them if they are not) or to refer to a physician as nurse because she happens to be female. Each of these behaviors is problematic in that it denies others their right to legitimate identities. Consequently such behaviors are ones that are usefully examined through an ethical lens. That is, when tempted to create stereotypes of others and to communicate with them based on that stereotype, it helps to ask yourself if doing so fits within your own ethical framework.

Although social factors such as power and position can impact many aspects of your life, you do have control of, and responsibility for, your perceptions and cognitions. Even though your social circle and your family may engage in problematic perceptual, cognitive, and communicative processes, once you become an adult you are responsible for how you interpret the world. To help you think about your perceptions and cognitive processes through an ethical lens, we discuss some guidelines to assist you in this process.

6   Improving Your Perception Skills

6   Identify three ways you can improve your perception skills

You probably realize now that perceptions are subject to variance and error because of the variety of steps one goes through in forming them (selection, organization, and interpretation) and the range of factors that influence the perception process (individual characteristics, cognitive complexity, power, culture, historical time period, and social roles). However, certain cognitive and communication behaviors can improve one's ability to perceive and understand the world.

First, one can engage in *mindfulness* to improve perception and understanding. Mindfulness refers to a clear focus on the activity one is engaged in, with attention to as many specifics of the event as possible (Langer, 1978). People tend to be most mindful when they are engaged in a new or unusual activity. Once an activity becomes habitual, they are likely to overlook its details. Mindfulness requires that one bring the same level of attention and involvement to routine activities as one does to novel ones.

In addition, before assuming your perceptions are accurate, you might ask yourself a few questions to help you check those perceptions:

- Have you focused too narrowly and missed relevant information as a result of selective attention? For example, did you focus on what the person was wearing rather than what he or she was saying?

- What type of organizational pattern did you use? For example, just because two people are standing next to one another does not mean they are together.

- To what extent have you considered all possible interpretations for the information you perceived, using the full range of your cognitive complexity? For example, if you did poorly on a test, was it as a result of poor test construction, your lack of sleep, the teacher's failure to prepare you, or your own failure to study sufficiently?

- How might your physical condition have influenced your perceptions? For example, are you tired, hungry, or frightened?

- How has your cultural background influenced your perceptions? For example, are you perceiving politeness as deception?

- How has your social role influenced your perception? For example, have you begun to perceive all elderly people as infirm because you work in a nursing home?

- How has your social position influenced your perception? For example, have you considered how others with different positions might perceive the same issue?

Another way to improve one's perception and understanding is to clearly separate *facts* from *inferences*. Facts are truths that are verifiable based on observation. Inferences are conclusions that we draw or interpretations we make based on the facts. Thus, it may be a fact that Southerners speak more slowly than do people from other regions of the United States, but it is an inference if you conclude that their slow speech indicates slow thought processes.

Finally, one communication act in particular will greatly improve anyone's perception skills: perception checking. That is, checking with others to determine if their perceptions match your own. If they do not, you may need to alter your perceptions. For example, Rosario once had an extremely negative reaction to a job candidate who interviewed at her company. She perceived him as arrogant and sexist. However, when she talked with her colleagues she discovered that no one else had a similarly strong negative response to the candidate. She decided that her perceptions must have been influenced by something in her own background; for example, he may have reminded her of someone she had once known who did display those negative traits. In revising her opinion of the candidate, Rosario demonstrated a well-developed sensitivity to the perception side of communication. All of us can benefit from greater awareness of the assumptions and attributions we make.

One communication act that can improve your perception skills is checking with others to see if their perceptions of others are similar to yours.

Summary

Perception plays an important role in everyday communication. People use three perceptual processes to manage the vast array of sensory data in their environments: selection, organization, and interpretation. From all the sounds, sights, smells, tastes, and textures available, people choose only a few to focus on. Once we attend to particular sensory information, we organize it to make sense of it. Two of the cognitive processes we use to organize information are cognitive representations and categorization. Finally, after we perceive and organize sensory information, we assign meaning to it using frames and attributions.

In addition, the sensory data we select to attend to, how we organize it, and the interpretations we assign are all influenced by our individual characteristics, such as physical abilities and differences, cognitive complexity, and any personality and individual differences. In addition, perception processes are affected by one's position in the power hierarchy, culture, historical events during one's lifetime, and social roles.

Because people vary so much in their perceptions, no one should assume that what he or she perceives is the same as what others perceive. Instead, we all must carefully check our perceptions on a regular basis and expend energy to overcome errors in processing as well as any attributional biases.

Key Terms

selection
organization
interpretation
selective attention
cognitive representation
prototype
script
categorization

label
stereotyping
frame
attribution theory
attributional bias
self-serving bias
fundamental attribution error
constructs

cognitive complexity
ethnocentrism
prejudice
ego-defensive function
value-expressive function
cohort effect
social role

Apply What You Know

1. **Examining Stereotypes** For each of the words, write down your beliefs about the group represented. In other words, provide a list of specific characteristics you believe are typically displayed by members of these groups.

   a. fraternity members
   b. politicians
   c. models
   d. rap stars
   e. body builders
   f. religious leaders

   After you have done so, compare your list to the lists created by other members of your class. What characteristics for each group did you have in common? What characteristics differed? Can you think of at least one person from each group who does not display the characteristics you listed? What information and perceptions helped shaped your stereotypes? How valid do you think your stereotypes are?

2. **Attributional Biases** As this text explains, people have a tendency to attribute their own positive behavior to internal traits and their negative behavior to external factors. However, they are also more likely to attribute others' positive behavior to external conditions and others' negative behavior to internal traits. In this exercise we want you to indicate how the attributional bias would cause you to describe each of the following behaviors, depending on who had performed it.

   Example: Forgetting to make a phone call
   I'm busy. You're thoughtless.

   Example: Earning a good grade
   I'm intelligent. You were lucky.

   Do the exercise for each of the following behaviors/ events:

   a. Receiving a raise
   b. Breaking a vase
   c. Arriving late

d. Winning an award
e. Burning a meal
f. Making a group laugh

Compare your responses with those of others in your class. What terms were used to describe one's own experiences? What terms were used to describe others' experiences? What is it about the perception process that makes attribution bias so common?

Although this is just an exercise, remember that the attributional bias is quite common. Pay attention to your own thoughts and comments the next time something bad happens to you or others.

3. **Ethics and Perception** The authors argue that ethics is relevant to our perceptual processes. To what extent do you agree or disagree with this statement? Provide three arguments for each position. Now that you have considered arguments for both positions, is your opinion the same as it was before or has it altered?

Explore

1. Go to a Web site that features perception exercises and information, such as the Hanover College Sensation and Perception Tutorials or the Encyclopedia of Psychology's Sensation and Perception tutorial. After experiencing at least two of the tutorials, write a paragraph in which you explain what you have learned about perception.

2. Go to a Web site such as Gestalt Laws or Perceptual Grouping and read the information regarding the Gestalts laws of grouping. In a brief paper, provide an explanation of the Gestalt laws then describe how these laws might influence how we view and communicate with others.

Glossary

attribution theory explanation of the processes we use to judge our own and others' behavior

attributional bias the tendency to attribute one's own negative behavior to external causes and one's positive actions to internal state

categorization a cognitive process used to organize information by placing it into larger groupings of information

cognitive complexity the degree to which a person's constructs are detailed, involved, or numerous

cognitive representation the ability to form mental models of the world

cohort effect the influenc e of shared characteristics of a group that was born and reared in the same general period; the process by which historical events influence the perceptions of people who grew up in a given generation and time period

constructs categories people develop to help them organize information

ego-defensive function the role prejudice plays in protecting individuals' sense of self-worth

ethnocentrism the tendency to view one's own group as the standard against which all other groups are judged

frame a structure that shapes how people interpret their perceptions

fundamental attribution error the tendency to attribute others' negative behavior to internal causes and their positive behaviors to external causes

interpretation the act of assigning meaning to sensory information

label a name assigned to a category based on one's perception of the category

organization the process by which one recognizes what sensory input represents

prejudice experiencing aversive or negative feelings toward a group as a whole or toward an individual because she or he belongs to a group

prototype an idealized schema

script a relatively fixed sequence of events that functions as a guide or template for communication or behavior

selection the process of choosing which sensory information to focus on

selective attention consciously or unconsciously attending to just a narrow range of the full array of sensory information available

self-serving bias the tendency to give one's self more credit than is due when good things happen and to accept too little responsibility for those things that go wrong

social role the specific position or positions one holds in a society

stereotyping creating schemas that overgeneralize attributes of a specific group

value-expressive function the role played by prejudice in allowing people to view their own values, norms, and cultural practices as appropriate and correct

References

Applegate, J. (1982). The impact of construct system development on communication and impression formation in persuasive contexts. *Communication Monographs, 49*, 277–289.

Bradbury, T. N., & Fincham, F. D. (1988). Individual difference variables in close relationships: A contextual model of marriage as an integrative framework. *Journal of Personality and Social Psychology, 54*, 713–721.

Braithwaite, C. (1990). Communicative silence: A cross-cultural study of Basso's hypothesis. In D. Carbaugh (Ed.), *Cultural communication and intercultural contact* (pp. 321–327). Hillsdale NJ: Lawrence Erlbaum Associates.

Brislin, R. (2000). *Understanding culture's influence on behavior* (2nd ed.). Belmont, CA: Wadsworth.

Burgoon, J. K., Berger, C. R., & Waldron, V. R. (2000). Mindfulness and interpersonal communication. *Journal of Social Issues, 56*, 105–127.

Burleson, B. R., & Caplan, S. E. (1998). Cognitive complexity. In J. C. McCroskey, J. Daly, & M. M. Martin (Eds.), *Communication and personality: Trait perspectives.* Cresskill, NJ: Hampton.

Chaiken, S. (1986). Physical appearance and social influence. In C. P. Herman, M. P. Zanna, & E. T. Higgins (Eds.), *Physical appearance, stigma, and social behavior: The Ontario Symposium* (Vol. 3, pp. 143–144). Hillsdale, NJ: Erlbaum.

Chapin, J. (2001). It won't happen to me: The role of optimistic bias in African American teens' risky sexual practices. *Howard Journal of Communication, 12*, 49–59.

Classen, C. (1990). Sweet colors, fragrant songs: Sensory models of the Andes and the Amazon. *American Ethnologist, 14*, 722–735.

Cox, W. T. L., Abramson, L. Y., Devine, P. G.; & Hollon, S. D. (2012). "Stereotypes, prejudice, and depression: The integrated perspective." *Perspectives on Psychological Science 7*(5), 427–449. doi:10.1177/1745691612455204.

Croy, I., Buschhüter, D., Seo, H S., Negoias S., & Hummel T. (2010). Individual significance of olfaction: Development of a questionnaire. *Eur Arch Otorhinolaryngol, 267*(1), 67–71. doi: 10.1007/s00405-009-1054-0.

Dean, J. (2014). Intriguing types of synesthesia: Tasting words, seeing sounds and hearing colors. *PsyBlog*. http://www.spring.org.uk/2014/05/ 6-intriguing-types-of-synesthesia-tasting-words-seeing-sounds-hearing-colours-and-more.php Retrieved December 15, 2014

Deutsch, F. M., Sullivan, L., Sage, C., & Basile, N. (1991). The relations among talking, liking, and similarity between friends *Personality and Social Psychology Bulletin, 17*, 406–411.

Dijk, T. A., van (1977). *Text and context: Explorations in the semantics and pragmatics of discourse.* London: Longman.

Dillard, J. P., Solomon, D. H., & Samp, J. A. (1996). Framing social reality: The relevance of relational judgments. *Communication Research, 23*, 703–723.

Douthat, R. (2005, November). Does meritocracy work? *Atlantic*, 120–126.

Durfeel, J. (2006). "Social change" and "status quo" framing effects on risk perception: An exploratory experiment. *Science Communication 27*(4), 459–495. doi: 10.1177/1075547005285334

Ehrenreich, B. (2001). *Nickel and dimed: On (not) getting by in America.* New York: Metropolitan Books.

Estroff, H. (2004, September/October). Cupid's comeuppance. *Psychology Today.* Retrieved March 15, 2006, from www.psychologytoday.com/articles/pto-20040921-000001.html

Everyday fantasia: The world of synesthesia. *American Psychological Association.* http://www.apa.org/monitor/mar01/synesthesia.aspx. Retrieved December 15, 2014.

Fehr, B., Baldwin, M., Collins, L., Patterson, S., & Benditt, R. (1999). Anger in close relationships: An interpersonal script analysis. *Personality and Social Psychology, 25*(3), 299–312. doi: 10.1177/01461672990025003003.

Goldstein, E. B., (2010). *Encyclopedia of perception.* (8th ed.) Thousand Oaks, CA: Sage Publications.

Granello, D. H. (2010). Cognitive complexity among practicing counselors: How thinking changes with experience. *Journal of Counseling and Development, 88*(1). 92–100. doi: 10.1002/j.1556-6678.2010.tb00155.

Greenough, W. T., Black, J. E., & Wallace, C. S. (1987). Experience and brain development. *Child Development, 58*, 539–559.

Griffin, E. (1994). *A first look at communication theory.* New York: McGraw-Hill.

Goldstein, E. B. (2010). Sensation and Perception. (9th ed.) Belmont, CA: Wadsworth.

Gueguen, N., & De Gail, M. (2003). The effect of smiling on helping behavior: Smiling and good Samaritan behavior. *Communication Reports, 16*(2), 133–140.

Hacker, A. (2003). *Two nations: Black and White, separate, hostile, unequal.* New York: Scribner.

Harvey, P., & Martinko, M. J. (2010). Attribution theory and motivation. In N. Borkowski (Ed.), *Organizational behavior in health care,* (2nd ed.,) (pp. 147–164). Boston: Jones and Bartlett.

Hehman, E., Carpinella, C. M., Johnson, K. L., Leitner, J. B., & Freeman, J. B. (2014). Early processing of gendered facial cues predicts the electoral success of female politicians. *Social Psychology and Personality Science, 5*(7), 815–824.

Heider, F. (1958, 2013). *The psychology of interpersonal relations,* New York: Wiley.

Heine, S. J., & Lehman, D. R. (2004). Move the body, change the self: Acculturative effects on self-concept. In A. Schaller & C. Crandall (Eds.), *The psychological foundations of culture* (pp. 305–31). Hillsdale, NJ: Erlbaum.

Herz, R. S., & Inzlicht, M. (2002). Sex differences in response to physical and social factors involved in human mate selection: The importance of smell for women. *Evolution and Human Behavior, 23,* 359–364.

Holmstrom, A. J., & Burleson, B. R. (2010). An Initial test of a cognitive-emotional theory of esteem support messages. *Journal of Counseling and Development, 88*(1), 92–100.

Hummel T., Kobal G., Gudziol H., Mackay-Sim, A. (2007). Normative data for the "Sniffin' Sticks" including tests of odor identification, odor discrimination, and olfactory thresholds: An upgrade based on a group of more than 3,000 subjects. *Eur Arch Otorhinolaryngol, 264*(3), 237–43.

Hurley R. W., & Adams, M. C. B. (2008). Sex, gender and pain: An overview of a complex field. *Anesthesia and Analgesia. 107,* 309–17

Kanizsa, G. (1979). *Organization in vision.* New York: Praeger.

Kellerman, K. (2004). A goal-direct approach to compliance-gaining: Relating differences among goals to differences in behavior. *Communication Research, 31,* 345–347.

Kelley, H. H. (1973). The processes of causal attribution. *American Psychologist, 28,* 107–128.

Kim, M. S. (2002). *Non-Western perspectives on human communication.* Thousand Oaks, CA: Sage.

Korneliussen, I. (2012). Women smell better than men. *Science Nordic.* http://sciencenordic.com/women-smell-better-men. Located on May 14, 2014.

Kirouac, G., & Hess, U. (1999). Group membership and the decoding of nonverbal behavior. In R. S. Feldman & P. Philippot (Eds.), *The social context of nonverbal behavior* (pp. 182–210). New York: Cambridge University Press.

Krivonos, P. D., & Knapp, M. L. (1975). Initiating communication: What do you say when you say hello? *Central States Speech Journal, 26,* 115–125.

Lakoff, G. (1987). *Women, fire, and dangerous things: What categories reveal about the mind.* Chicago: University of Chicago Press.

Langer, E. J. (1978). Rethinking the role of thought in social interaction. In J. H. Harvey, W. Ickes, & R. F. Kidd (Eds.), *New directions in attribution research* (Vol. 2, pp. 3–58). New York: Wiley.

Levinthal, D., & Gavetti, G. (2000, March). Looking forward and looking backward: Cognition and experiential search. *Administrative Science Quarterly,* 1–9.

Link, B. G., & Phelan, J. C. (2001, August). Conceptualizing stigma. *Annual Review of Sociology, 27,* 363–385.

Lupfer, M. B., Weeks, M., & Dupuis, S. (2000). How pervasive is the negativity bias in judgments based on character appraisal? *Personality and Social Psychology Bulletin, 26,* 1353–1366.

Maccaby, E. E., & Jacklin, C. N. (1978). *The psychology of sex differences.* Palo Alto, CA: Stanford University Press.

Manusov, V., & Spitzberg, B. (2008). Attributes of attribution theory: Finding good cause in the search for a theory. In D. O. Braithwaite & L. A. Baxter (Eds.), *Engaging theories in interpersonal* (pp. 37–49). Thousand Oaks, CA: Sage.

Markus, H. R., Mullally, P. R., & Kitayama, S. (1997). Selfways: Diversity in modes of cultural participation. In U. Neisser & D. A. Jopling (Eds.), *The conceptual self in context* (pp. 13–59). Cambridge, UK: Cambridge University Press.

McCoy, N. L., & Pitino, L. (2002). Pheromonal influences onsociosexual behavior in young women. *Physiology and Behavior, 75,* 367–375.

"Middle of the Class" (2005, July 14). Survey: America. *Economist.* Retrieved March 10, 2006, from: www.economist.com/displayStory.cfm?Story_id=4148885.

Morgan, M. J. (1977). *Molyneux's question : Vision, touch and the philosophy of perception.* Cambridge, NY: Cambridge University Press.

Neale, M. A., & Bazerman, M. H. (1991). *Cognition and rationality in negotiation.* New York: Free Press.

Olivier, C., Leyens, J-P, Yzerbyt, V. Y., & Walther, E. (1999). Judgeability concerns: The interplay of information, applicability, and accountability in the over-attribution bias. *Journal of Personality and Social Psychology, 76*(3), 377-387. doi: 10.1037/0022-3514.76.3.377.

Operario, D., & Fiske, S. T. (2003). "Stereotypes: Content, structures, processes, and contexts". In R. Brown & S. L. Gaertner, (Eds.) *Blackwell Handbook of Social Psychology: Intergroup Processes* (pp. 22–44). Malden, MA: Blackwell. ISBN 978-1-4051-0654-2.

Pearce, W. B. (1994). *Interpersonal communication: Making social worlds.* New York: HarperCollins.

Pew Research Center for People and the Press. (2005, September 8). Huge racial divide over Katrina and its consequences. Retrieved June 1, 2006, from: http://people-press.org/reports/pdf/255.pdf

Planalp, S. (1993). Communication, cognition, and emotion. *Communication Monographs, 60,* 3–9.

Putnam, L. L., & Holmer, M. (1992). Framing, reframing and issue development. In L. L. Putnam & M. E. Roloff (Eds.), *Communication and negotiation* (pp. 128–155). Newbury Park, CA: Sage.

Rothenberg, P. S. (1992). *Race, class, and gender in the United States.* New York: St. Martin's Press.

Samter, W., & Burleson, B. R. (1984). Cognitive and motivational influences on spontaneous comforting behavior. *Human Communication Research, 11,* 231–260.

Schwarz, N. (2006). Attitude research: Between ockham's razor and the fundamental attribution error. *Journal of Consumer Research, 33,* 19-21

Scollon, R., & Wong-Scollon, S. (1990). Athabaskan-English interethnic communication. In D. Carbaugh (Ed.), *Cultural communication and intercultural contact* (pp. 259–287). Hillsdale, NJ: Erlbaum.

Seligman, M. (1998). *Learned optimism.* New York: Simon & Schuster.

Sherwood, B. (2009). *The survivor's club.* NY: Grand Central Publishing.

Shore, B. (1996). *Culture in mind: Cognition, culture and the problem of meaning.* New York: Oxford University Press.

Sillars, A. L, Roberts, L. J., Leonard, K. E., & Dun, T. (2000). Cognition during marital conflict: The relationship of thought and talk. *Journal of Social and Personal Relationships, 17,* 479–502.

Sillars, A. L, Roberts, L. J., Leonard, K. E., & Dun, T. (2002). Cognition and communication during marital conflicts: How alcohol affects subjective coding of interaction in aggressive and nonaggressive couples.

In P. Noller & J. A. Feeney (Eds.), *Understanding marriage: Developments in the study of couples' interaction* (p. 85–112). Cambridge, U.K.: Cambridge University Press.

Singh, D., & Bronstad, P. M. (2001). Female body odour is a potential cue to ovulation. *Proceedings of the Royal Society: Biological Science, 268,* 797–801.

Siu, W. L. W., & Finnegan, J. R. (2004, May). An exploratory study of the interaction of affect and cognition in message evaluation. Paper presented at the International Communication Association Convention, San Francisco, CA.

Smith, S. W., Kopfman, J. E., Lindsey, L., Massi, Y. J., & Morrison, K. (2004). Encouraging family discussion on the decision to donate organs: The role of the willingness to communicate scale. *Health Communication. 16,* 333–346.

Snyder, M. (1998). Self-fulfilling stereotypes. In P. S. Rothenberg (Ed.), *Race, class and gender in the U.S.: An integrated study* (pp. 452–457). New York: St. Martin's Press.

Stephan, C., & Stephan, W. (1992). Reducing intercultural anxiety through intercultural contact. *International Journal of Intercultural Relations, 16,* 89–106.

Than, K. (2005). Rare but real: People who feel, taste and hear color. *LiveScience.* http://www.livescience.com/169-rare-real-people-feel-taste-hear-color.html Retrieved December 15, 2014.

Ting-Toomey, S. (1999). *Communicating across cultures.* New York: Guilford.

U.S. National Research Council. (1989). *Improving risk communication.* Committee on risk perception and communication. Washington, DC: National Academy Press.

Weick, K. (1995). *Sensemaking in organizations.* Thousand Oaks, CA: Sage.

Wilson, G., & Nias, D. (1999). Beauty can't be beat. In J. A. DeVito & L. Guerrero, (Eds.), *The nonverbal communication reader: Classic and contemporary readings* (2nd ed., pp. 92–132). Prospect Heights, IL: Waveland Press.

Credits

Photo Credits

Credits are listed in order of appearance.

Photo 1: Dinis Tolipov/123RF

Photo 2: Shout/Alamy

Photo 3: Pete Marovich/ZUMA Press, Inc./Alamy

Photo 4: Taka/Fotolia

Photo 5: SW Productions/Stockbyte/Getty Images

Photo 6: Image 100/Alamy

Photo 7: Auremar/Fotolia

Photo 8: Fancy/Alamy

Photo 9: Berc/Fotolia

Photo 10: Mark Ralstona/AFP/Getty Images/Newscom

Photo 11: Hugo Félix/Fotolia

Photo 12: Radius Images/Alamy

Text and Art Credits

Based on Croy I., Buschhüter D., Seo H. S., Negoias S., & Hummel T. (2010) Individual significance of olfaction: Development of a questionnaire. Eur Arch Otorhinolaryngol, 267(1), 67–71. doi: 10.1007/s00405-009-1054-0. Hummel T., Kobal G., Gudziol H., Mackay-Sim, A. (2007). Normative data for the "Sniffin' Sticks" including tests of odor identification, odor discrimination, and olfactory thresholds:

An upgrade based on a group of more than 3,000 subjects. Eur Arch Otorhinolaryngol, 264(3), 237–243. Korneliussen, I. (2012). Women smell better than men. Science Nordic. Retrieved May 14, 2014, from: http://sciencenordic.com/women-smellbetter-men. Maccaby, E. E., & Jacklin, C. N. (1978).). The psychology of sex differences. Palo Alto, CA: Stanford University Press.

Lin Sue

Danika; pp. 83, Based on Than, K. (2005). Rare but real: People who feel, taste and hear color. LiveScience. http://www.livescience.com/169-rare-real-people-feel-taste-hear-color.html Retrieved December 15, 2014; Everyday fantasia: The world of synesthesia. American Psychological Association, http://www.apa.org/monitor/mar01/synesthesia.aspx. Retrieved December 15, 2014; Dean, J. (2014). Intriguing types of synesthesia: Tasting words, seeing sounds and hearing colors. PsyBlog. http://www.spring.org.uk/2014/05/6-intriguing-types-of-synesthesia-tasting-words-seeing-sounds-hearing-colours-and-more.php Retrieved December 15, 2014.

Damien

Ting-Toomey, S. (1999). Communicating across cultures. New York: Guilford. p. 149.

Verbal
Communication

From Chapter 5 of *Human Communication in Society*, Fourth Edition. Jess K. Alberts, Thomas K. Nakayama, Judith N. Martin.
Copyright © 2016 by Pearson Education, Inc. All rights reserved.

Verbal Communication

CHAPTER TOPICS	Chapter Objectives
The Importance of Verbal Communication	1 Identify three reasons for learning about verbal communication.
What Is Verbal Communication? Functions and Components	2 Describe the functions and components of language.
The Individual and Verbal Communication: Influences	3 Identify and give examples of several major influences on verbal communication.
The Individual, Verbal Communication, and Society: Language, Perception, and Power	4 Describe the relationships between language, perception, and power.
Ethics and Verbal Communication	5 Identify and give examples of confirming communication, disconfirming communication, and hate speech.
Improving Your Verbal Communication Skills	6 Discuss ways to improve your own verbal communication skills.

> *The verbal elements of communication are the foundation on which meaning is created.*

When Charee texts her friends, she knows that her verbal communication changes from when she speaks to them face to face. She uses "lol" and other such "Netspeak" abbreviations, and she makes sure that she doesn't use complete sentences. This is true as well when she is using Twitter, which limits her to 140 characters. Even with other social media sites, she keeps her messages brief. But when she writes a paper for class, she knows that she needs to change the way she uses her verbal communication skills. She needs to use complete sentences and formal language, without using Netspeak.

When we think of "communication," we tend to think about the verbal elements of communication: the words people choose, the accents they speak with, and the meanings they convey through language. We frequently don't consider the ways in which verbal communication assists or hinders relationship development, the technology we use, or its effect on the creation of identities.

We will explore the verbal elements of communication and how people use verbal communication to accomplish various goals. First we discuss the importance of verbal communication and its value as a topic of study. We then describe how individuals use verbal communication, including the functions it serves and the components of language that make it possible. Next we explore individual characteristics that influence verbal communication, such as gender, age, regionality, ethnicity and race, and education and occupation. We investigate the societal forces that influence verbal communication by examining the relationships among language, perception, and power. Finally, we provide suggestions for communicating more ethically and more effectively.

1   The Importance of Verbal Communication

1   Identify three reasons for learning about verbal communication.

Although the nonverbal aspects of communication are important, the verbal elements of communication are the foundation on which meaning is created. If you doubt that this is the case, try this simple test. Using only nonverbal communication, convey this message to a friend or roommate: "I failed my exam because I locked my keys in my car and couldn't get my textbook until well after midnight." How well was your nonverbal message understood? If you have ever traveled in a country where you

Children from families who converse and eat meals together on a regular basis have higher self-esteem and interact better with their peers.

didn't speak the language, no doubt you already knew before trying this experiment that nonverbal communication can only get you so far. Similarly, although you may try to incorporate emoticons or other devices to mimic nonverbals, the verbal elements of messages are vital in texting, email, and many social networking sites. We will touch on the importance of nonverbal communication here. In this section we propose that to be a highly effective communicator you need to understand the verbal elements of communication.

Verbal communication is also important because of the role it plays in identity and relationship development. Individuals develop a sense of self through communication

with others. More specifically, the labels used to describe individuals can influence their self-concepts and increase or decrease their self-esteem. People's verbal communication practices also can impede or improve their relationships. Research by four psychology professors at Emory University supports our claims about the relationship between verbal communication and an individual's identity development and relationship skills. These scholars found that families that converse and eat meals together on a regular basis have children who not only are more familiar with their family histories but also tend to have higher self-esteem, interact better with their peers, and are better able to recover from tragedy and negative events (Duke, Fivush, Lazarus, & Bohanek, 2003).

In addition, the very language people speak is tied to their identities. Studies of bilingual and multilingual speakers show that their perceptions, behaviors, and even personalities alter when they change languages (Ramírez-Esparza, Gosling, Benet-Martínez, Potter, & Pennebaker, 2006). Why does this occur? The answer is that every language is embedded in a specific cultural context, and when people learn a language, they also learn the beliefs, values, and norms of its culture (Edwards, 2004). So speaking a language evokes its culture as well as a sense of who we are within that culture. Thus the language you use to communicate verbally shapes who you are, as you will see in *It Happened to Me: Cristina.*

2   What Is Verbal Communication? Functions and Components of Language

2   Describe the functions and components of language.

Verbal communication generally refers to the written or oral words we exchange; however, as our opening example shows, verbal communication has to do with more than just the words people speak. It includes pronunciation or accent, the meanings of the words used, and a range of variations in the way people speak a language, which depend on their regional backgrounds and other factors.

Language, of course, plays a central role in communication. Some argue that it is our use of language that makes us human. Unlike other mammals, humans use symbols that they can string together to create new words and with which they can form infinite sets of never-before-heard, -thought, or -read sentences.

This ability allows people to be creative and expressive, such as when they take ordinary words and use them in new ways. For example, the word robo sapiens—nominated by the American Dialect Society as one of the most creative words for 2013—refers to a class of robots with human intelligence. This is a play on the words homo sapiens for humans and robo for robot. Even small children who are unschooled in grammar create their own rules of language by using innate linguistic ability together with linguistic information they glean from the people around them. For example, young children often say "mouses" instead of "mice" because they first learn, and apply broadly, the most common rule for pluralizing—adding an *s*.

It Happened to Me

Cristina

I was teaching an adult education class composed primarily of Mexican immigrants when I first noticed that the language people speak affects how they behave. I'm bilingual, so even though we normally spoke English in my class, sometimes we switched to Spanish. Over time, I noticed that several male students were respectful and deferential when we spoke English; however, when we switched to Spanish, they became more flirtatious and seemed less willing to treat me as an authority figure. Now I understand that these differences probably were related to how men and women interact in the two cultures.

To help you better understand the role of language in the communication process, the next section explores seven communicative functions of language as well as four components of language use.

Functions of Language

We all use language so automatically that we usually don't think about the many roles it plays. However, language helps us do everything from ordering lunch to giving directions to writing love poems. Moreover, a single utterance can function in a variety of ways. For example, a simple "thank you" not only expresses gratitude, it also can increase feelings of intimacy and liking. Consequently, understanding the ways language functions can help you communicate more effectively. As we discuss next, language can serve at least seven functions: instrumental, regulatory, informative, heuristic, interactional, personal, and imaginative.

- The most basic function of language is **instrumental**. This means we can use it to obtain what we need or desire. For instance, when you send an e-vite to your friends to a party to celebrate a birthday, the invitation is instrumental in that you want your friends to come to the party and the invitation helps make that happen.

- A second (and closely related) language function is **regulatory**, meaning that we can use it to control or regulate the behaviors of others. In your invitation, you may ask your friends to bring a bottle of wine or a dessert to the party, as a way of regulating their behavior.

- Another basic function of language is to **inform**—to communicate information or report facts. When you invite your friends to the party, you usually include the date and time to inform them of when you want them to come.

- We also use language to acquire knowledge and understanding, which is referred to as a **heuristic** use. When you want to invite friends, you may ask them to respond to indicate if they are available at that date and time to learn if your party is going to occur as scheduled or if you need to make some changes.

- When language is used in an **interactional** fashion, it establishes and defines social relationships in both interpersonal and group settings. Thus, when you invite your friends to a celebration, you engage in a behavior that helps maintain your relationship with them as friends.

- **Personal language** expresses individuality and personality and is more common in private than in public settings. When you invite your friends to the party, you might jokingly add a private message to one, "Don't bring a cheap bottle of wine, like you did last time." In this way, you use language to express your sense of humor.

- A final way you can use language is **imaginatively**. Imaginative language is used to express oneself artistically or creatively, as in drama, poetry, or stories. Thus, if your e-vite says "Screw cake, let's drink!" or "Let Them Eat Cake," you would be using the imaginative function of language.

As our discussion thus far indicates, language has seven basic functions, and speakers use them to accomplish specific goals or tasks. Note that these functions overlap and that one utterance can accomplish more than one function at the same time. For example, when inviting your friends to a party, if you jokingly said, "James, our butler, will be serving bubbly and cake promptly at eight, so don't be late!" your utterance would both be imaginative (unless you actually have a butler named James) and regulatory. That is, you would be using language creatively while also attempting to regulate your guests' behavior to ensure they arrived on time.

instrumental
use of language to obtain what you need or desire

regulatory
use of language to control or regulate the behaviors of others

informative
use of language to communicate information or report facts

heuristic
use of language to acquire knowledge and understanding

interactional
use of language to establish and define social relationships

personal language
use of language to express individuality and personality

imaginative
use of language to express oneself artistically or creatively

As a student, which functions of language do you use most frequently? Which do you use most often in your professional life? If you use different functions in each of these roles, why do you think this is true?

Now that we have summarized the essential functions that language can serve, let's examine the basic components that allow us to use language as a flexible and creative tool of communication.

Components of Language

Scholars describe language use as being made up of four components: *phonology* (sounds), *syntax* (structure or rules), *semantics* (meaning), and *pragmatics* (use). Every language has its own rules of **grammar**—the structural rules that govern the generation of meaning in that language. See *Did You Know? Prescriptive vs. Descriptive Language* to read about the different ways that French and German deal with these issues. In this section, we examine the role each plays in the communication process.

PHONOLOGY: SOUNDS   **Phonology** is the study of the sounds that compose individual languages and how those sounds communicate meaning. Basic sound units are called *phonemes*. They include vowels, consonants, and diphthongs (pairs of letters that operate as one, such as *th*). Different languages can use different phonemes. For example, French does not have the *th* sound. As a result, many native French speakers find it difficult to pronounce "this" or "that." Similarly, in Japanese, a phoneme that is between *r* and *l* is the closest equivalent to the English *r* sound. For more information about phonology, see **www.langsci.ucl.ac.uk/ipa/**, the home page of the International Phonetic Association.

SYNTAX: RULES   **Syntax** refers to the rules that govern word order. Because of the English rules of syntax, the sentences "The young boy hit the old man" and "The old man hit the young boy" have different meanings, even though they contain identical words. Syntax also governs how words of various categories (nouns, adjectives, verbs) are combined into clauses, which in turn combine into sentences. Whether or not we are conscious of them, most of us regularly follow certain rules about combining words—for example, that the verb and subject in a sentence have to agree, so people say "the pencil *is* on the table," not "the pencil *are* on the table." Because of these rules, people combine words consistently in ways that make sense and make communication possible.

SEMANTICS: MEANING   **Semantics** is the study of meaning, which is an important component of communication. To illustrate the effect of syntax compared with the effect of meaning, Noam Chomsky (1957), an important scholar in the field of linguistics, devised this famous sentence: "Colorless green ideas sleep furiously" (p. 15). This sentence is acceptable in terms of English grammar, but on the semantic level it is nonsensical: Ideas logically cannot be either colorless or green (and certainly not both!), ideas don't sleep, and nothing sleeps furiously (does it?).

A central part of our definition of communication is the creation of shared meaning. For any given message, a number of factors contribute to the creation of its meaning. Perhaps most important are the words the speaker chooses. For example, did you have a friend in high school who always gave the right answer in class, got excellent grades, and always seemed to have a wealth of information at his fingertips? What word would you use to describe this friend: *smart, intelligent, clever, wise,* or *brilliant*? Because each word has a slightly different meaning, you try to choose the one that most accurately characterizes your friend. However, in choosing the "right" words, you have to consider the two types of meaning that words convey: *denotative* and *connotative*.

The **denotative meaning** refers to the dictionary, or literal, meaning of a word and is usually the agreed-on meaning for most speakers of the language. Referring back to our description of your friend: The dictionary defines *wise* as "Having the

grammar

the structural rules that govern the generation of meaning in a language

phonology

the study of the sounds that compose individual languages and how those sounds communicate meaning

syntax

the rules that govern word order

semantics

the study of meaning

denotative meaning

the dictionary, or literal, meaning of a word

Did You Know?

Prescriptive versus Descriptive Approaches to Language

As you read the following description of how different languages approach the question of how to properly use each language, decide what you think of each approach. Do you prefer the prescriptive or descriptive approach? Can the approaches be combined?

French and German require different approaches to understanding the proper use of each language. A prescriptive approach guides the use of French in France. This means that the rules for correct usage are prescribed, or rigidly formalized and dictated.

In France, the French language is guided by the Académie française (or French Academy). This institution is the authority on the French language and determines what is and is not proper French. For example, when a minister is a female, sometimes she is referred to as "la ministre" (feminine form) as opposed to "le ministre" (masculine). This may be considered proper in Belgium, Canada, and Switzerland, but not in France, as the French Academy has determined that all ministers are to be referred to as "le ministre" regardless of gender.

Despite the rules of the Academy, however, Cécile Duflot asked to be addressed as "Madame la ministre" after a deputy addressed her as "Madame le ministre" (Duflot, 2012).

Part of their charge is to guard the French language against the intrusion of other languages, especially English, but also Arabic, German, Tahitian, and others. So instead of saying, "un replay" (a replay), the correct French is "une rediffusion," as posted on March 6, 2014.

In contrast, German in Germany takes a *descriptive approach* to language. The Duden dictionary is published every four or five years and describes the changes to the German language as it has been changed by German speakers. Thus, Duden has added "blog" to their dictionary as German speakers use that word, instead of the more German equivalent: digitale Netztagebücher. Although the German Language Society was upset that so many new words borrowed from English appeared in Duden, others see the German language changing as it incorporates these new terms. For Duden, how German speakers use language should determine which terms it includes. Duden takes a descriptive approach because it attempts to describe common usage instead of dictating what usage is correct. German speakers prefer to say "apps" rather than "Anwendungen für mobile Endgeräte," and so Duden recognizes this difference by including the English word.

SOURCES: Académie française. Exemples de remarques normatives, 9th edition. Retrieved March 6, 2014 from: http://www.academie-francaise.fr/le-dictionnaire-la-9e-edition/exemples-de-remarques-normatives.

Académie française. (2014, March 6). Replay. Retrieved March 6, 2014, from: http://www.academie-francaise.fr/dire-ne-pas-dire.

Sauerbrey A. (2013, September 25). How do you say "blog" in German? New York Times. Retrieved March 6, 2014, from: http://www.nytimes.com/2013/09/26/opinion/how-do-you-say-blog-in-german.html?_r=0.

ability to discern or judge what is true, right, or lasting; sagacious" and *intelligent* as "Showing sound judgment and rationality" (American Heritage Dictionary, 2011). Does either word exactly capture how you would describe your friend? If not, which word does?

Words also carry **connotative meanings**, which are the affective or interpretive meanings attached to them. Using the previous example, the connotative meaning of the word *wise* implies an older person with long experience, so it might not be the best choice to describe your young friend.

connotative meaning
the affective or interpretive meanings attached to a word

PRAGMATICS: LANGUAGE IN USE Just like phonology, syntax, and semantics, the field of **pragmatics** seeks to identify patterns or rules people follow when they use language appropriately. In the case of pragmatics, however, the emphasis is on how language is used in specific situations to accomplish goals (Nofsinger, 1999). For example, scholars who study pragmatics might seek to understand the rules for communicating appropriately in a sorority, a faculty meeting, or an evangelical church. They would do this by examining communication that is successful and unsuccessful in each setting. The three units of study for scholars of pragmatics are *speech acts, conversational rules,* and *contextual rules.* Let's examine what each contributes to communication.

pragmatics
field of study that emphasizes how language is used in specific situations to accomplish goals

Speech Acts One branch of pragmatics, **speech act theory**, looks closely at the seven language functions described previously and suggests that when people

speech act theory
branch of pragmatics that suggests that when people communicate, they do not just say things, they also *do* things with their words

communicate, they do not just say things, they also *do* things with their words. For example, speech act theorists argue that when you say, "I bet you ten dollars the Yankees win the World Series," you aren't just saying something, you actually are doing something. That something you are doing is making a bet, or entering into an agreement that will result in an exchange of money.

One common speech act is the request. A recent study examined one type of request that occurs primarily in U.S. family contexts—the common practice of "nagging" (Boxer, 2002). Nagging (repeated requests by one family member to another) often concerns household chores and is usually a source of conflict. The researcher found that nagging requires several sequential acts. First, there is an initial request, which is usually given in the form of a command ("Please take out the garbage") or a hedged request ("Do you think you can take out the garbage this evening?"). If the request is not granted, it is repeated as a reminder (after some lapse of time), which often includes an allusion to the first request. ("Did you hear me? Can you please take out the garbage?") When a reminder is repeated (the third stage), it becomes nagging and usually involves a scolding or a threat, depending on the relationship—for example, whether the exchange is between parent and child ("This is the last time I'm going to ask you, take out the garbage!") or between relational partners ("Never mind, I'll do it myself!").

The researcher found that men were rarely involved in nagging, and she suggests that this is because men are perceived as having more power and are therefore able to successfully request and gain compliance from another family member without resorting to nagging. She also notes that children can have power (if they refuse to comply with a request despite their lack of status) and a parent can lack power despite having status. The researcher also found that nagging mostly occurs in our intimate relationships. She concludes that, by nagging, we lose power—but without power, we are forced into nagging; thus it seems to be a vicious cycle! The study shows that what we *do* with words affects our relationships.

Understanding the meaning of various speech acts often requires understanding context and culture (Sbisa, 2002). For this reason, people may agree on what is *said* but disagree on what is *meant*. For example, the other day Katy said to her roommate Hiroshi, "I have been so busy I haven't even had time to do the dishes." He replied, "Well, I'm sorry, but I have been busy, too." What did he think Katy was "doing" with her utterance? When they discussed this interaction, Katy explained that she was making an excuse, whereas Hiroshi said he heard a criticism—that because *she* hadn't had time to do the dishes, *he* should have. Thus, messages may have different meanings or "do" different things, from different persons' viewpoints. This difference lies in the sender's and receiver's interpretations of the statement. Most misunderstandings arise not around what was said—but around what was done or meant.

As we have seen, speech acts may be direct or indirect. That is, speech acts such as requests can be framed more (or less) clearly and directly. Let's suppose that you want your partner to feed the dog. You may directly ask: "Would you feed the dog?" Or you could state an order: "Feed the dog!" On the other hand, you may communicate the same information indirectly: "Do you know if the dog was fed?" or "I wonder if the dog was fed." Finally, you may make your request indirectly: "It would be nice if someone fed the dog," or "Do you think the dog looks hungry?"

Which do you think is better—to communicate directly or indirectly? This is actually a trick question. The answer is: It depends—on the situation and the cultural context. Although direct requests and questions may be clearer, they also can be less polite. Ordering someone to feed the dog makes one's desire clearly and unequivocally known, but at the same time, it can be seen as rude and domineering.

Recent research shows that U.S. Americans tend to be more indirect in their requests, when compared to Mexicans (Pinto & Raschio, 2007), but probably not as

Nagging is one common type of speech act that occurs in U.S. family contexts.

indirect as many Asians (Kim, 2002). However, when expressing disagreement, most U.S. Americans tend to be more direct than most Asians. A recent study investigated how Malaysians handled disagreements in business negotiation and concluded that the Malays' opposition was never direct or on record, but always indirect and implied. Despite their disagreements with the other party, they honored the other, always balancing power with politeness (Paramasivam, 2007). A pragmatic approach reminds us that how language is used always depends on the situation and cultural context.

Conversational Rules Conversational rules govern the ways in which communicators organize conversation. For example, one rule of conversation in U.S. English is that if someone asks

Conversational rules—such as turn-taking—govern the way we communicate and vary somewhat from context to context.

you a question, you should provide an answer. If you do not know the answer, others expect you to at least reply, "I don't know" or "Let me think about it." However, in some cultures and languages, answers to questions are not obligatory. For example, in some Native American cultures, such as that of the Warm Spring Indians of Oregon, questions may be answered at a later time (with little reference to the previous conversation) or not answered at all (Philips, 1990).

Perhaps the most researched conversational rules involve turn-taking. The most basic rule for English language speakers, and many others, is that only one person speaks at a time. People may tolerate some overlap between their talk and another's, but typically they expect to be able to have their say without too much interruption (Schegloff, 2000). Still, as a refinement of this point, Susanna Kohonen (2004) found in her cross-cultural study of turn-taking that conversationalists were more tolerant of overlaps in social settings, such as at parties or when hanging out with friends, than in more formal settings. Also, in computer-mediated communication, turn-taking is influenced by face-to-face interactions, but uses strategic pauses more to regulate speech (Anderson Beard, & Walther, 2010). In other words, although computer-mediated communication is not face to face, the communication interaction rules mimic face-to-face interactions; however, the different context results in slightly different rules. Thus, sometimes the context influences conversational rules. We discuss contextual rules next.

Other rules for turn-taking determine who is allowed to speak (Sacks, Schegloff, & Jefferson, 1978). For example, if you "have the floor" you can generally continue to speak. When you are finished, you can select someone else. You can do this either by asking a question, "So Sue, what is your opinion?" or by looking at another person as you finish talking. If you don't have the floor but wish to speak, you can begin speaking just as the current speaker completes a turn.

Pragmatics involves understanding the implicit communication rules that apply in one setting or another.

The turn-allocation system works amazingly well most of the time. Occasionally, however, people do not follow these implicit rules. For example, the current speaker could select the next speaker by directing a question to her, but someone else could interrupt and "steal" the floor. Also, some speakers are quicker to grab the talk turn, which allows them more opportunities to speak. Then, speakers who are slower to begin a turn or take the floor have fewer opportunities to contribute to the conversation. They may feel left out or resent the other speakers for monopolizing the conversation.

Contextual Rules No matter what language or dialect you speak, your use of language varies depending on the communication situation (Mey, 2001). For example, you probably wouldn't discuss the same topics in the same way at a funeral as you would in a meeting at your

workplace, in a courtroom, or at a party. What would happen if you did? For example, telling jokes and laughing at a party is typically acceptable, whereas those same jokes and laughing might be interpreted negatively in a courtroom or at a funeral. One challenge for pragmatics scholars, then, is uncovering the implicit communication rules that govern different settings. As noted previously, communication pragmatics also vary by culture. For example, in some houses of worship, appropriate verbal behavior involves talking quietly or not all, acting subdued, and listening without responding—but in others, people applaud, sing exuberantly, and respond loudly with exclamations like "Amen!" Neither set of communication rules is "right"; each is appropriate to its own setting and cultural context.

As you can see, verbal language is far more than the words people use; it also includes the sounds and meanings of those words, and the rules individuals use for arranging words and for communicating in particular settings. Moreover, speakers differ in the ways they use language to communicate. They also differ in the ways they enunciate their words and how they present their ideas. For example, Southerners "drawl" their vowels, whereas New Englanders drop the *r* after theirs; some speakers are extremely direct, and others are not. What accounts for these differences? We explore the answers in the next section.

3 The Individual and Verbal Communication: Influences

3 **Identify and give examples of several major influences on verbal communication.**

Our communication is influenced by our identities and the various cultures to which we belong. In turn, our communication helps shape these identities. When identities influence several aspects of language, we say that speakers have a distinct **dialect**, a variation of a language distinguished by its **lexical choice** (vocabulary), grammar, and pronunciation. In other instances, the influence of identity is less dramatic, and speakers vary only in some pronunciations or word choices. In this section we examine how identities related to gender, age, regionality, ethnicity and race, and education and occupation shape language use.

dialect

a variation of a language distinguished by its vocabulary, grammar, and pronunciation

lexical choice

vocabulary

Gender

Growing up male or female may influence the way you communicate in some situations, because men and women are socialized to communicate in specific ways. In fact—as exemplified in the popularity of books like *Men Are from Mars, Women Are from Venus* (Gray, 2012)—many people believe that English-speaking men and women in the United States speak different dialects. These beliefs are reinforced by media depictions that tend to present stereotypical depictions of men and women in magazines, on television, and in movies. For example, one team of researchers reviewed how journal articles talked about gender differences in the past fifty years and found that because people are more interested in hearing about differences than similarities, shows and books that emphasize these differences tend to sell better and receive wider recognition (Sagrestano, Heavey, & Christensen, 1998).

Even scholarly research tends to focus on, and sometimes exaggerate, the importance of sex differences; some researchers have reported that women's verbal style is often described as supportive, egalitarian, personal, and disclosive, whereas men's is

Televisions shows, such as *The Real Housewives of Orange County*, tend to present stereotypical depictions of men and women.

characterized as instrumental, competitive, and assertive (Mulac, Bradac, & Gibbons, 2001; Wood, 2002), and there is some evidence that differences exist in social media "talk." But other research refutes this claim. A recent review of studies comparing males and females on a large array of psychological and communication differences, including self-disclosure and interruptions, revealed few significant differences (Hyde, 2006). How can these contradictory findings be explained? To begin, many studies of gender differences ask participants to report on their perceptions or ask them to recall men's and women's conversational styles (e.g., Aylor & Dainton, 2004). This approach can be problematic because people's perceptions are not always accurate. For example, Nancy Burrell and her colleagues (1988) argue that persistent, stereotypical, gender-based expectations likely influence people's perceptions that men and women behave or communicate differently even when few behavioral differences exist. More recently, Heilman, Caleo, and Halim (2010) found that gender stereotypes were invoked even more strongly when workers were told they would communicate using computer-mediated communication rather than face to face.

How do these faulty perceptions arise about communication differences between men and women? Two important contributors are a person's perceptions of his or her own gendered communication and media representations of men's and women's communication. Experts assert that gender-based perceptions are hard to change, whether or not the perceptions are true. For example, the negative stereotype of the talkative woman is persistent. In one recent study, students were shown a videotaped conflict between a man and a woman and were asked to rate the two on likability and competence. In different versions of the video, the researchers varied how much the man and woman each talked. As the researchers expected, viewers rated the couple as less likable when they saw the woman doing more of the talking. And the man who talked more was rated as most competent (Sellers, Woolsey, & Swann, 2007). Even though this negative stereotype persists, many studies have shown that not only do women generally *not* talk more than men, actually the opposite is true—men tend to be more talkative in many situations (Leaper & Ayres, 2007). In addition, the stereotype persists that women are more "kind, helpful, sympathetic, and concerned about others," whereas men are seen as "aggressive, forceful, independent, and decisive" (Heilman, 2001, p. 658). Furthermore, these gender stereotypes can create differential treatment in the workplace and in social situations.

When people adapt to a specific audience, they are often adjusting to the communication style of the more powerful members of that audience. Thus, if powerful members of the audience use more direct or task-focused language, so might the speaker. In addition to adapting their communication style, people also often use more deferential or tentative language when communicating with more powerful people. Both men and women adapt to these power differences; thus both groups are more likely to use tentative language with their bosses than with their siblings. Women use language that is more tentative overall because generally they have lower status, and people with lower status are not typically expected to make strong, assertive statements (Reid, Keerie, & Palomares, 2003). Similarly, women tend to use more "filler words" (such as *like* or *well*) and more conditional words (*would, should, could*) (Mehl & Pennebaker, 2003).

Researchers have wondered whether gender differences in conversations are a consequence of interacting with a partner who uses a particular style of communication. For example, if you encourage another person to talk by nodding your head in agreement, asking questions, or giving supportive linguistic cues (such as "uh-huh," or "yes…"), you are using a facilitative style of communication. To explore this question, social psychologists Annette Hannah and Tamar Murachver assigned male and female partners who were strangers to each other to meet and talk several times. After the first conversation, their communication styles were judged by outside observers to be either facilitative or nonfacilitative; and the researchers found that, regardless of gender, participants responded to each other in ways that mirrored their partner's style (Hannah & Murachver, 2007).

Over time, however, in subsequent conversations, the women and men shifted their speech toward more stereotypically gendered patterns; that is, the men talked more, for longer times, whereas women increased their use of minimal responses, reduced the amount they spoke, and asked more questions. In other words, the women increased their facilitative style of speech while the men decreased theirs. Discussing their findings, the researchers pose several questions: Why are women more facilitative in their speech? Why do they talk less when talking with men? Do they feel threatened or insecure? Are they less comfortable in talking more than men? Perhaps women feel that dominating conversations with men has negative social consequences and, therefore, they encourage men to do the talking—an explanation that would be confirmed by the previous study we mentioned, where students negatively evaluated couples in which the women talked more than the men. The researchers provide no definitive explanation, but note, as do we, that gender differences are complicated (Hannah & Murachver, 2007).

In conclusion, women and men do show differences in their communication styles, and much of this difference likely is attributable to differences in power, status, and expectations in communication situations.

Age

You may not think of age as affecting language use, but it does, particularly when it comes to word choice. For example, you might have talked about "the cooties" when you were a child, but you probably don't now. Moreover, children have a whole vocabulary to describe "naughty topics," especially related to bodily functions. Yet, most adults do not use those words. Adolescents also develop vocabulary that they use throughout their teenage years and then drop during early adulthood. Adolescents have described highly valued people and things as "cool," "righteous," "bad," "hot," and "phat," depending on the generation and context. This distinct vocabulary helps teenagers feel connected to their peers and separate from their parents and other adults. For other examples of teen slang terms, see *Did You Know? Contemporary Slang*.

cohort effect

the influence of shared characteristics of a group that was born and reared in the same general period

The era in which you grew up also influences your vocabulary. As you age, you continue to use certain words that were common when you were growing up, even if they have fallen out of use. This is called the **cohort effect** and refers to common denominators of a group that was born and reared in the same general period. For example, your grandparents and their contemporaries may say "cool" or "neat" and your parents may say "awesome" when referring to something they really like. What do you say? Recent research suggests that young girls (particularly young, urban, upwardly mobile) are the trendsetters in language use both for their own and other cohorts. The most recent examples are their use of "I can't even..." and the "vocal fry" or "creaky voice" (made by compressing the vocal chords and reducing the airflow through the larynx, makes speech to sound rattled or "creaky"). Zooey Deschanel and Kim Kardashian slip in and out of this register, as does Britney Spears, but it has been observed in college-aged women across the country. Women have long tended to be the linguistic innovators. Linguists say that if you want to see the future of a language find a young, urban woman. We have women to thank for "up-talk"—the rising intonation at the end of a sentence that has spread into mainstream speech—the discourse marker "like," and now, vocal fry (Arana, 2013; Cohen, 2014).

People's communication skills and the meanings they attribute to concepts also vary because of their age. Why? Older people are more cognitively developed and have had more experiences; therefore they tend to view concepts differently than

Did You Know?

Contemporary Slang

While we are familiar with many of the new slang words that appear as abbreviations in texting and other Internet usage, there are many others that that we might not be as familiar with. For example, you are probably familiar with bff or "best friends forever. Or "kk" for "okay" or "it's cool." But have you ever seen 770880? In Chinese, this is equivalent to XOXO. What about AMHA? This is the French equivalent to IMHO or "in my humble opinion." Different languages have developed different slang to communicate with others, and these slang terms may not be familiar beyond their language group. Other languages have adapted to new technological environments, just as English has.

do younger people, especially children (Pennebaker & Stone, 2003). For example, children typically engage in egocentric speech patterns (Piaget, 1952). This means that they cannot adapt their communication to their conversational partners nor understand that others may feel or view the world differently. Children lack the number of constructs adults have. For example, young children have little concept of future or past time, so understanding what might happen next week or month is difficult for them. Consequently, parents usually adapt their communication when trying to help children understand some event in the future.

Regionality

Geographical location also strongly influences people's language use. The most common influence is on pronunciation. For example, how do you pronounce the word "oil"? In parts of New York it is pronounced somewhat like "earl," whereas in areas of the South it is pronounced more like "awl," and in the West it is often pronounced "oyl" as in "Olive Oyl." Sometimes regionality affects more than just accent, leading to regional dialects. Why do these differences arise?

Historically, verbal differences developed wherever people were separated by a geographical boundary—whether it was mountains, lakes, rivers, deserts, oceans— or some social boundary, such as race, class, or religion (Fromkin & Rodman, 1983). Moreover, people tended to speak similarly to those around them. For example, in the eighteenth century, residents of Australia, North America, and England had relatively little contact with one another; consequently, they developed recognizably different dialects even though they all spoke the same language. Typically, the more isolated a group, the more distinctive their dialect.

In the United States, dialectical differences in English originally arose because two groups of English colonists settled along the East Coast. The colonists who settled in the South, near present-day Virginia, primarily came from Somerset and Gloucestershire—both western counties in England—and they brought with them an accent with strongly voiced s sounds and with the r strongly pronounced after vowels. In contrast, the colonists who settled in the north, what we now call New England, came from midland counties such as Essex, Kent, and London, where people spoke a dialect that did not pronounce the r after vowels, a feature still common to many New England dialects (Crystal, 2003). See Figure 1 for an interesting outgrowth of U.S. local dialects

Other waves of immigration have occurred over the past four hundred years, increasing dialectical diversity in the United States. Each group of immigrants brings a distinctive way of speaking and culture-specific communication rules. Some groups, especially those who have remained somewhat isolated since their arrival, maintain much of their original dialect; an example is the inhabitants of Tangier Island in the Chesapeake Bay (Crystal, 2003). Other groups' dialects have assimilated with

Figure 1

The terms we use to refer to soft drinks also vary by region in the United States.

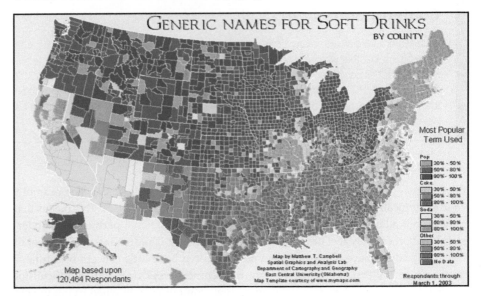

the dialects of their neighbors to form new dialects. Thus, the seventeenth-century "western" English dialect of Virginia has become the southern drawl of the twenty-first century.

Today the world is a global village, so people all over the country (and, for that matter, all over the world) are able to speak frequently with one another and have access to similar media. Nonetheless, according to a recent comprehensive study, local dialects are stronger than ever (Labov, 2005; Preston, 2003). Language professor Julie Sedivy (2012) notes that: "It may seem surprising, but in this age where geographic mobility and instant communication have increased our exposure to people outside of our neighborhoods or towns, American regional dialects are pulling further apart from each other, rather than moving closer together." Do you have a recognizable regional linguistic dialect? Take the *New York Times* quiz and see if it accurately maps you: http://www.nytimes.com/interactive/2013/12/20/sunday-review/dialect-quiz-map.html?_r=0.

Ethnicity and Race

One's ethnicity can influence one's verbal style in a number of ways. In the United States, English is a second or colanguage for many citizens. This, of course, influences syntax, accent, and word choice. For example, if one is Latino or Latina and learns Spanish either before or at the same time as one learns English, one may use the same syntax for both. Thus, Spanish speakers may place adjectives after nouns (*the house little*) when they are speaking English because that is the rule for Spanish. The reverse can also occur: When English speakers speak Spanish, they have a tendency to place adjectives before nouns (*la pequeña casa*), which is the rule for English but not for Spanish.

Speakers' ethnicity can also influence their general verbal style. For example, Jewish Americans may engage in a style of talking about problems that non-Jews perceive as complaining (Bowen, 2012); some Native American tribes use teasing as a form of public rebuke (Shutiva, 2012); and some Chinese Americans who live in the southern United States are particularly likely to let other speakers choose conversational topics (Gong, 2012). When two ethnic or racial groups speak the same language but use different syntax, lexical items, or verbal style, one or both of the groups may view the other's verbal style as incorrect, as a failed attempt at proper speech rather than as a dialect with its own rules (Ellis & Beattie, 1986).

These views can have important real-life implications—political and monetary. Take the controversy about **African American Vernacular English**—a version of English that has its roots in West African, Caribbean, and U.S. slave languages. There is no agreed-on definition of African American Vernacular English; some linguists emphasize the international nature of the language (as a linguistic consequence of the African slave trade); others stress that it is a variety of English (e.g., the equivalent of Black English) or as different from English and viewed as an independent language. Yet we should also keep in mind that "there is no single and correct way to be 'African American.' These identities are negotiated in context and situationally emergent" (Hecht, Jackson, & Ribeau, 2003, p. 2).

African American Vernacular English

a version of English that has its roots in West African, Caribbean, and U.S. slave languages

In his book, *"You are an African American, so why are you talking like a white person,"* Jeffrey Walker (2010) encourages African Americans to practice **code switching**— or change the way that they speak in different situations. Code switching is an important linguistic practice that helps speakers of different languages and dialects to change the way that they speak to communicate more effectively in mainstream culture, while also demonstrating cultural group membership in other situations. For example, some African Americans may use African American Vernacular English when speaking in social settings with other African Americans to demonstrate their community membership, but use a more standard English when speaking in a professor context.

Code switching

the practice of changing language or dialect to accommodate to the communication situation

Education and Occupation

We will discuss education and occupation together because they are often mutually influencing. For example, medical doctors speak a similar language because they share a profession, but also because they were educated similarly. Typically, the more educated people are, the more similarly they speak (Hudson, 1983). Thus, larger dialect differences occur between Easterners and Midwesterners if they have not been to college than if they have doctoral degrees. This does not mean that all lawyers talk the same or that all professors speak similarly; rather, it suggests that differences become less pronounced as people receive more education.

Education affects dialect in part because any given university or college attracts people from different parts of the country. Therefore, college students have contact with a variety of dialects. At the same time, as students attend college they develop similar vocabularies from their shared experiences and learn similar terms in their classes. For example, you may never have used the term *dyad* to refer to two people before you went to college, but this is a term you might encounter in a range of courses, including psychology, sociology, anthropology, and communication.

jargon

the specialized terms that develop in many professions

Physicians, like members of other professions, develop specialized terms called jargon.

Your occupation also influences the specialized terms you use to communicate. The specialized terms that develop in many professions are called **jargon**. Professors routinely speak of *tenure, refereed journals,* and *student credit hours.* Physicians speak of *contusions* (bruises), *sequelae* (results), and *hemorrhagic stroke* (a stroke where a blood vessel bursts). In fact, most occupations have their own jargon. In addition to influencing your lexical choices, your occupation may also influence your overall communication style—including tone of voice and some nonverbal behaviors. For example, nursery school teachers are often recognizable not only

by their vocabulary but also by the rhythm, volume, and expressivity of their communication style.

To sum up, then, various features of language—phonology, syntax, semantics, and pragmatics—contribute to the development of meaning in verbal communication. These features combine with individual influences in language use, such as gender, age, and level of education, to create one's specific communication style. However, we have not yet covered every aspect of verbal communication. We now turn to the influence of societal forces on verbal communication.

4 The Individual, Verbal Communication, and Society: Language, Perception, and Power

4 Describe the relationships between language, perception, and power.

How do societal forces influence verbal communication? Culture and power are two of the most important influences. Culture impacts verbal communication primarily through its influence on language and perception. Perception plays a key role in communication. Power is connected to verbal communication because within society, some language styles are viewed as more powerful, with consequences for both the powerful and the powerless.

Language and Perception

Scholars have long argued about the influence of language and culture on perception. The central issue they have debated is whether the words a culture has available to it influence how its members see and perceive the world around them. For example, the English language expresses action in the past, present, and future. Thus, English speakers may say "Alan went to the library" (past), "Alan is at the library" (present), or "Alan will be going to the library" (future). In contrast, Japanese makes no distinction between the present and future. Although the verb for "went" is *ikimashita*, the verb used for both "is" and "will be going" is the same, *ikimasu*. Because English and Japanese have two different verb structures, scholars have questioned whether English speakers and Japanese speakers think about present and future actions in different ways. Scholars who have debated this relationship between language and perception generally fall into two camps: the *nominalists* and the *relativists*.

Nominalists claim that any idea can be expressed in any language and that the structure and vocabulary of the language do not influence the speaker's perception of the world. According to nominalists, English and Japanese may express present and future in different ways, but English speakers and Japanese speakers still understand the distinction.

In contrast, the **relativists** argue that language serves not only as a way for us to voice our ideas but that, in addition, it "is itself the shaper of ideas, the guide for the individual's mental activity" (Hoijer, 1994, p. 194). This idea is the basis for the **Sapir-Whorf hypothesis**. The Sapir-Whorf hypothesis argues that the language people speak determines the way they see the world. Adherents to this hypothesis believe language is like a prison because it constrains the ways individuals can perceive the world (Deutscher, 2010). According to this hypothesis, the distinction between the present and the future is not as clear-cut for Japanese speakers as it

nominalists
those who argue that any idea can be expressed in any language and that the structure and vocabulary of the language do not influence the speaker's perception of the world

relativists
those who argue that language serves not only as a way for us to voice our ideas but "is itself the shaper of ideas, the guide for the individual's mental activity"

Sapir-Whorf hypothesis
idea that the language people speak determines the way they see the world (a relativist perspective)

is for English speakers. As another example, surfers have many more words for the types of waves in the ocean than do nonsurfers (Scheibel, 1995); the Sapir-Whorf hypothesis argues that, because of this, surfers perceive more types of waves than do others.

So how much does language influence perception? The Sapir-Whorf hypothesis position has been challenged by a number of scholars who investigate the connection between language and how we think. They represent a modified relativist position on the relationship between language and perception. For example, Steven Pinker (2007), a renowned cognitive scientist, cautions against assuming a simplistic connection between language and thought, and rejects the Sapir-Whorf assumption that the particular language we speak compels us to perceive the world in a particular way or prevents us from thinking in different ways. He uses the example of applesauce and pebbles to argue that we naturally categorize (and therefore label) these two substances differently (as "hunk" and "goo"). By looking at language from the perspective of our thoughts, Pinker shows that what may seem like arbitrary aspects of speech (the hunk–goo distinction) aren't arbitrary at all, but rather that they are by-products of our evolved mental machinery. In sum, all languages have the formal and expressive power to communicate the ideas, beliefs, and desires of their users. From this vast range of possibilities, human communities select what they want to say and how they want to say it. This view allows for more freedom than indicated by the Sapir-Whorf hypothesis.

Surfers have many more words for the types of waves in the ocean than do nonsurfers.

Which viewpoint makes more sense to you—nominalist or relativist? Why?

Language and Power

In many ways, language and power are inextricably connected. People in power get to define what languages and communication styles are appropriate. In addition, people who use language and communication according to the rules of the powerful may be able to increase their own power. This view of the relationship between language and power is explained by *cocultural theory*. **Cocultural theory** explores the role of power in daily interactions using the five following assumptions:

cocultural theory

explores the role of power in daily interactions

1. In each society, a hierarchy exists that privileges certain groups of people; in the United States, these groups include men, European Americans, heterosexuals, the able-bodied, and middle- and upper-class people.

2. Part of the privilege these groups enjoy, often subconsciously, is being able to set norms for what types of communication are acceptable or not acceptable (Orbe, 1998). Consequently, communication patterns of the dominant groups (in the United States, rich, male, White, educated, straight) tend to be more highly valued. For example, the preferred communication practice in many large corporations is that used by White males—direct, to the point, task oriented, and unemotional (Kikoski & Kikoski, 1999).

3. Language maintains and reinforces the power of these dominant groups, again, mostly subconsciously. Thus, people whose speech does not conform to what is valued in society may be excluded or negatively stereotyped. As we noted

previously, commentators sometimes characterize women's speech as sounding more tentative than male speech. Because society values male speech styles at work, women aspiring to corporate leadership positions may undertake a special effort to make their speech direct or tough enough, or to avoid being too cooperative or nurturing in their communication practices.

4. In the relationship realm, society tends to value a more female communication style, and men may be criticized for failing to communicate appropriately with their intimates. Remember that none of these language variations is inherently good or bad, powerful or powerless; it is the societal hierarchies that teach us how to view particular communication practices. Of course, not every White male is direct, to the point, and task oriented, nor does every woman speak tentatively at work. Nor is every woman supportive and self-disclosive and every man distant and terse in close relationships. These generalizations can help explain communication practices, but they should not solidify into stereotypes.

5. These dominant communication structures impede the progress of persons whose communication practices do not conform to the norms. For example, what are the consequences for women who do not conform to "male" communication norms in a corporation? Or for African Americans who do not conform to "White" communication norms of the organizations in which they work? Or for students who do not conform to the "middle-class" communication norms at a university? They may risk being labeled negatively ("not serious enough," "soft," "doesn't have what it takes") and marginalized.

Now, let's look at how these societal hierarchies affect attitudes toward words, accents, and dialects, and how they impact identity labels.

Power and Words

Attitudes about power can be built into language by certain roots or by the structure of the language. Consider words such as *chairman, fireman,* or the generic use of he and man to refer to people. In the past it was widely believed that it didn't matter whether we used masculine words to mean *human,* but in recent decades researchers discovered that people didn't think *human* when someone mentioned the word *man*—they thought about a man. Similarly, awareness of the inequality inherent in terms such as *Mr.* (not designating marital status) and *Mrs.* (which does) has resulted in the use of new, more equal terms such as *Ms.* and *he* or *she.*

Although some languages, such as Japanese or Korean, are strongly gendered (meaning that traditionally, men and women used almost a separate language), English is somewhat gendered, or androcentric. *Androcentrism* is the pairing of maleness with humanity and the consequent attribution of gender difference to females—often to women's disadvantage. Scholars recently reviewed fifty years of psychology articles for androcentric bias. Although they found few uses of he for *human,* information was still portrayed in a way that emphasized male as the norm. Male data was placed first in tables, and gender differences were often described as female—subconsciously assuming that male is the norm and female is different. Researchers point out that being different is not necessarily harmful but probably reflects some of the underlying stereotypes (and societal hierarchies) we have discussed previously (Hegarty & Buechel, 2006).

What are the implications for students? We argue that it's not about freedom of speech or being overly politically correct, but rather about audience and awareness. Gender-neutral language has gained support from most major textbook publishers, and from professional and academic groups, as well as major newspapers and law journals. As an English professor suggested, "You need to be able to express yourself according to their guidelines, and if you wish to write or speak convincingly to people who are influenced by the conventions of these contexts, you need to be conscious of their expectations."

Power and Accent

Where did people learn that an English accent sounds upper crust and educated? Or that English as spoken with an Asian Indian accent is hard to understand? Why do communicators often stereotype Black English as sounding uneducated? Although these associations come from many sources, they certainly are prevalent in the media. People have become so accustomed to seeing and hearing these associations that they probably don't even question them. In fact, William Labov, a noted sociolinguist, refers to the practice of associating a dialect with the cultural attitudes toward it as "a borrowed prestige model." For example, until the 1950s, most Americans thought that British English was the correct way to speak English (Labov, 1980); even today, people continue to think that an English accent sounds refined and educated. On the other hand, Southern drawls and Black English have become stigmatized so that today, people who speak them are often perceived negatively. For similar reasons, people often find the English accent of people from India (where English often is a first language) difficult to understand—as reported by our student in *It Happened to Me: Bart*.

Such language stereotypes can be "set off" in one's head before a person even speaks, when one *thinks*, generally because of the person's appearance, that she or he will not speak Standard English (Ruben, 2003). This is probably what happened to our student, Bart. Once he adjusted to the Indian English accent, he found he could understand his Indian professor just fine. (For examples of accents from many different language backgrounds, go to **classweb.gmu.edu/accent/**.)

How does language cause one group to become elevated and another denigrated? The answer lies partly in understanding the social forces of history and politics. The positive and negative associations about African American, White, and British English developed during the nineteenth and twentieth centuries when European Americans were establishing themselves as the powerful majority in the United States, while passing legislation that subjugated African Americans and other minority groups. Thus, it is not surprising that the languages of these groups were viewed so differently. Similarly, the English spoken by people from India was negatively stereotyped as the aberrant language of the colonized because England was the colonial power in India until the mid-twentieth century. Similar attitudes can be seen toward immigrant groups today; their accented English is often stigmatized, sometimes leading to language discrimination and lawsuits, as illustrated in *Did You Know? Language Discrimination*.

It Happened to Me

Bart

I recently had a course taught by an Asian Indian professor, and it took me some time to understand his accent and form of speaking. Sometimes I thought he was mumbling, and sometimes his speech sounded so fast that I couldn't understand it. After a couple of classes, my hearing disciplined itself to understand him better. In the end, I realized he was a fine teacher.

Power and Identity Labels

The language labels that refer to particular identities also communicate important messages about power relations. Members of more powerful groups frequently invoke labels for members of other groups without input from those group members. For example, straight people label gays but rarely refer to themselves as straight. White people use ethnic and racial labels to refer to others (*people of color, African American*, or *Black*) but rarely

Did You Know?

Language Discrimination

Should language discrimination be illegal? Are there jobs where speaking English with an accent would impair someone's ability to do the job? Does language discrimination happen outside of employment as well?

Language discrimination includes interlanguage discrimination and intralanguage discrimination. Interlanguage discrimination happens when people are treated differently because of the languages that they speak. In countries with an official language, discrimination can occur against those who do not speak the official language(s). Intralanguage discrimination happens when people are treated differently because they speak in a way that is not considered "proper" or the dominant language. In the United States, for example, someone who speaks Hawaiian pidgin or African American Vernacular English, may be treated differently than someone who speaks standard American English. Both kinds of discrimination can happen in job situations where someone is not hired or promoted because of an accent or is treated differently from other employees. Language discrimination can also happen in schools when students are forbidden to speak certain languages. In the United States, for example, some schools require students to speak English, not only in class but also outside of class. Language discrimination can also happen in social settings when someone is rebuffed because of the way they speak.

In contrast, some accents are preferred. For example, some U.S. Americans find a British or French accent to be attractive. Others like the Irish accent or accents from Australia or New Zealand. Some people like or dislike Southern accents, New England accents, and other varieties of English. Do you find yourself treating others with different accents in different ways?

Attempts to impose languages on others can be a legacy of colonialism. English, French, and Spanish are widely spoken around the world, largely as a result of a history of colonialism. Does requiring people to speak a particular language raise a human rights issue? Some languages that used to be more widely spoken are now marginalized, such as Irish; and some others have become extinct, such as Susquehannock (spoken by the Native Americans along the Susquehanna River). When we discriminate against people who speak in certain ways or speak certain languages, we are discriminating against the individuals, not just the accents or languages. The legacy of these histories in the contemporary global context means that we need to think about who should learn whose languages, as seen in the case of the New York Yankees in the Alternative View.

Think about labels and terms we have for males and females. Why do you think so many more negative terms exist for females than for males?

refer to themselves as *White*. This power to label seems "normal," so most people don't think twice about specifying that a physician is a "woman doctor," but never describing one as a "male doctor." Or they might identify someone as a gay teacher but not a white teacher (even if this teacher is both). People usually don't think about the assumptions that reflect societal power relations; in sum, individuals feel the need to mark minority differences, but they tend not to identify majority group membership.

Not only do the more powerful get to label the less powerful, but they may also use language labels to stigmatize them. However, the stigma comes from the power relations, not from the words themselves. For example, in the Polish language, the word *Polack* simply means "a man from Poland," but the stigma associated with the term comes from the severe discrimination practiced against Eastern Europeans in the early twentieth century, which led to jokes and stereotypes that exist to this day. The term *Oriental* originated when Western countries were attempting to colonize, and were at war with, Asian countries—and the connotative meaning was *exotic* and *foreign*. Today, many Asians and Asian Americans resent this label. Read about one of our student's opinions on the topic in *It Happened to Me: Hiroko*.

This resentment can make communication more difficult for Hiroko and those who use this term to refer to her. As this example reveals, understanding the dictionary meanings of words does not always reveal the impact of identity labels.

It Happened to Me

Hiroko

I get really tired of people referring to me as "Oriental." It makes me sound like a rug or a cuisine. I refer to myself as Asian American or Japanese American. I know people probably don't mean anything negative when they use it, but it makes me uncomfortable. If it's somebody I know well, I might ask them not to use that word, but usually I just don't say anything.

Alternative View

Who Should Learn Whose Languages?

The New York Yankees, a professional baseball team, hired four Japanese players, and although they are trying to learn English, some of the Yankee players are also trying to learn Japanese. Many other languages are spoken in professional baseball (and other sports). Which players should learn the languages of the other players? What does it mean to other players that a teammate has learned their languages?

There are many different reasons why people choose to learn other languages. Sometimes work environments like professional sports may lead people to try to learn another language. Sometimes people believe that they will have more economic opportunities if they learn another language. Sometimes people have more personal, familial reasons for studying another language. They may have family members who speak another language. Learning someone else's language is a tremendous commitment and so it can communicate much more care and love to others that you have learned their language.

Members of minority communities are the best informants on the communicative power of specific labels.

Not everyone in an identity group has the same denotative meaning for a particular label. For example, some young women do not like to be called "girl"; they find it demeaning. Others are comfortable with this term. Some people view these calls for sensitivity in language as nothing more than unnecessary political correctness.

Moreover, the power of labels can change over time. In an earlier age, many viewed the term *WASP* (White, Anglo-Saxon, Protestant) as a descriptor or even a positive label; now, however, it is seen as rather negative (Martin, Krizek, Nakayama, & Bradford, 1999). The shift probably reflects the changing attitudes of Whites, who are now more aware of their ethnicity and the fact that they are not always the majority. Similarly, the term *Paddy* as in "paddy wagon" (a term for a police wagon) originally was a derogatory term; some older Irish Americans may still find it offensive. It reflected a stereotype, widely held one hundred years ago, of Irish men as drunks who had to be carted off to jail. Now that discrimination (and stereotyping) against the Irish has all but disappeared, this term has lost much of its impact.

In summary, language, power, and societal forces are closely linked. The societal environment profoundly influences the way people perceive the world and the language choices available to them. Those in power set the language and communication norms, often determining what verbal communication style is deemed appropriate or inappropriate, elegant or uneducated. They frequently get to choose and use identity labels for those who are less powerful. Those whose language does not fit the standard, or who are the recipients of negative labels, may feel marginalized and resentful, leading to difficult communication interactions.

5   Ethics and Verbal Communication

5   **Identify and give examples of confirming communication, disconfirming communication, and hate speech.**

In this section, we examine one specific type of language whose use may harm individuals or relationships.

Hate speech is legal in the United States, but many argue that it is unethical.

hate speech

use of verbal communication to attack others based upon some social category

As ethical communicators, where should we draw the line between free speech and unethical verbal communication?

Hate Speech

In the United States, we place a high value on freedom of speech. We have codified this value into our legal system, beginning with the First Amendment to the Constitution. However, freedom of speech is always balanced by competing societal interests. As the familiar saying goes, freedom of speech does not include the right to shout "fire!" in a crowded theater. But what about the right to express negative opinions about others? In the 1980s and 1990s, as U.S. society became more aware of the ethics of minority rights, the term *hate speech* began to be used (ACLU, 1994). **Hate speech**, or the use of verbal communication to attack others based on some social category such as race, ethnicity, religion, or sexuality, is seen as threatening an entire group or inciting violence against members of these groups. In the United States, the first-amendment guarantee of free speech is generally used to protect against laws that would make hate speech illegal (Liptak, 2008). However, many argue that even if hate speech is legal, it is unethical.

Many countries view the use of verbal communication to attack, demean, and degrade other groups of people as not only unethical, but also illegal. Canada's criminal code, for example, forbids speech, writing, and Internet postings that advocate genocide or that publicly incite hatred (Media Awareness Network, n.d.). As another example, in some European countries it is illegal to deny that the Holocaust occurred. In 2013, a Hungarian was given an eighteen-month suspended sentence and "has been ordered to visit Hungary's holocaust memorial centre, Auschwitz death camp or the Yad Vashem memorial in Israel" ("Holocaust Denier," 2013).

Sometimes even speaking another language from others can invoke anger and, sometimes physical aggression. In October 2013, a man in Madison, Wisconsin, encountered two men speaking to each other and he demanded they stop speaking Spanish and speak English. Although the two men were speaking Hebrew, not Spanish, "He then punched each of the two men in the face, leaving one with a swollen eye, while the other victim fell to the ground with the impact of the assault" (Terrero, 2013). Although people are free to speak in any languages they wish, sometimes negative feelings and attitudes arise when people are not speaking the dominant language.

Whether illegal or unethical, the use of verbal communication to attack others based on their group membership is often seen as an attack on the whole group, not just the person who is the receiver of such messages. See *Did You Know? Cyberbullying* for another example of using verbal communication to attack others.

Confirming and Disconfirming Communication

Although hate speech may be obviously unethical, there are other, less obvious types of communication that can be unethical because of the harm they can cause. One of these is *disconfirming communication*. **Disconfirming communication** occurs when people make comments that reject or invalidate a self-image, positive or negative, of their conversational partners (Dance & Larson, 1976). Consider the following conversation:

disconfirming communication

comments that reject or invalidate a positive or negative self-image of our conversational partners

TRACEY: Guess what? I earned an A on my midterm.

LOU: Gee, it must have been an easy test.

Did You Know?

Cyberbullying

Does the rapid pace of new technology development make cyberbullying difficult, or even impossible, to stop?

Cyberbullying has emerged as a serious problem as communication technologies have developed. The consequences can be as severe as the victims of the cyberbullying committing suicide. Cyberbullying is defined by the U.S. Department of Health and Human Services as:

> bullying that takes place using electronic technology. Electronic technology includes devices and equipment such as cell phones, computers, and tablets as well as communication tools including social media sites, text messages, chat, and websites.

As technology continues to develop, new apps become available that some people use for cyberbullying. Although the underling intent behind creating new apps might not be to allow new venues for cyberbullying, people often use apps for their own goals. One app that has gained popularity in cyberbullying is Yik Yak. This app has become popular among young people because it is perceived as beyond the surveillance of parents and educators, unlike Facebook or other social media sites. As new apps are developed, parents and educators might not be able to keep up with these new apps. As the technological landscape changes, cyberbullys will find new routes to harass others.

Although particular apps can be identified, is it possible to stay on top of all of the new communication technology and apps that are being developed?

SOURCE: U.S. Department of Health and Human Services. (n.d.). What is cyberbullying? Retrieved March 7, 2014, from: http://www.stopbullying.gov/cyberbullying/what-is-it/

Lou's response is an example of disconfirming communication because it suggests that Tracey could not have earned her A because of competence or ability. Consequently, his message disconfirms Tracey's image of herself. You can disconfirm people either explicitly ("I've never really thought of you as being smart") or implicitly (as Lou did).

How can messages such as these cause harm? Imagine that you received numerous disconfirming messages from people who are important to you. How might it affect you? Such messages not only can negatively influence your self-image, but they also can impair your relationships with the people who disconfirm you. For instance, Harry Weger, Jr. (2005) and John Caughlin (2002) have found that when couples engage in disconfirming behavior, their marital dissatisfaction increases. Disconfirming messages can harm both individuals and relationships and may be considered unethical as well as ineffective because they focus on the person.

If you want to avoid sending disconfirming messages, what should you do instead? You can provide others with confirming messages. Confirming messages validate positive self-images of others, as in the following example of **confirming communication**.

confirming communication
comments that validate positive self-images of others

TRACEY: Guess what? I earned an A on my midterm.

LOU: That's great. I know it's a tough class; you deserve to be proud.

OR LOU MIGHT SAY: Congratulations! I know you were studying very hard and you deserve that grade.

Confirming messages are not only more ethical, they are usually more effective. Most people enjoy communicating with those who encourage them to feel good about themselves. Although engaging in confirming communication will not guarantee that you will be instantly popular, if you are sincere, it will increase the effectiveness of your communication and ensure that you are communicating ethically. If using confirming communication does not come naturally to you, you can practice until it does.

You might be wondering how you can provide negative feedback to people without being disconfirming. We discuss how to do this in the next section.

6 Improving Your Verbal Communication Skills

6   Discuss ways to improve your own verbal communication skills.

When considering the ethics of language use, you should think about the effectiveness of your verbal choices. What are some guidelines for engaging in more effective verbal communication? We describe two ways in which you might improve: You can work on using "I" statements and also become more aware of the power of language.

"I" Statements

One type of disconfirming message involves making negative generalizations about others. Although you recognize that people are complex and variable, have you nevertheless found yourself making negative generalizations such as those listed here?

> "You are so thoughtless."

> "You are never on time."

As you can see, negative generalizations (which also are called "you" statements) are typically disconfirming. But, in the real world everyone lives in, some people *are* thoughtless, and some *are* consistently late. So is there an ethical and effective way to make your dissatisfaction known? Yes. You can use a type of message called an "I" statement. "I" statements allow you to express your feelings (even negative ones) by focusing on your own experiences rather than making negative generalizations (or "you" statements) about others.

"I" statements are conveyed through a three-part message that describes

1. the other person's behavior,
2. your feelings about that behavior, and
3. the consequences the other's behavior has for you.

Taking the examples just given and rewriting them as "I" statements, you could come up with:

> "When you criticize my appearance (behavior), I feel unloved (feeling), and I respond by withdrawing from you (consequence)."

> "I think I must be unimportant to you (feeling) when you arrive late for dinner (behavior), so I don't feel like cooking for you (consequence)."

"You" statements often lead recipients to feel defensive or angry because of the negative evaluation contained in the message and because the listener resents the speaker's position of passing judgment. "I" statements can lead to more constructive resolution of conflicts because they arouse less defensiveness. They also are more effective than "you" statements because the receiver is more likely to listen and respond to them (Kubany, Bauer, Muraoka, Richard, & Read, 1995). In addition, to make "I" statements, speakers have to explore exactly what they are dissatisfied with, how it makes them feel, and what the consequences of the other person's behavior are. "I" statements prevent speakers from attacking others to vent their feelings.

Although many communication scholars believe in the value of "I" statements, a recent study found that people reacted similarly to *both* "I" and "you" statements involving negative emotions. However, the authors point out that their study involved written hypothetical conflict situations. They admit that their results might have been different if they had studied real-life conflict situations (Bippus & Young, 2005).

Although "I" statements can be effective in a variety of contexts, this does not mean they are *always* appropriate. Situations may arise where others' behavior so violates what you believe is decent or appropriate that you wish to state your opinions strongly. Thus, if your friend abuses alcohol or takes illicit drugs, you may need to say, "You should not drive a car tonight" or "You need to get help for your addiction." The effectiveness of one's verbal communication must always be evaluated in the context of the situation, the relationships one has with others, and one's goal.

Become Aware of the Power of Language

Language is a powerful force that has consequences and ethical implications. Wars have been started, relationships have been ruined, and much anger and unhappiness has resulted from intentional and unintentional verbal messages. The old adage "Sticks and stones can break my bones, but words will never hurt me" is not always true. Words *can* hurt.

When a speaker refers to others by negative or offensive identity terms, the speaker not only causes harm, he or she also denies those labeled individuals their identities—even if it isn't intentional. For example, one of our students, Cynthia, told us how bad she felt when she realized that some of her gay coworkers were offended by her use of the term homosexual (instead of gay). They explained that homosexual was used as a description of a psychiatric disease by the American Psychiatric Association's list of mental disorders until 1973 and has a connotation of this sexual orientation as a cold, clinical "condition." Using her embarrassment as a learning experience, she initiated an enlightening discussion with her coworkers. She learned that often the best way to discover what someone "wants to be called" is to ask. However, a conversation of this nature can only occur in the context of a mutually respectful relationship—one reason to have a diverse group of friends and acquaintances.

Summary

Verbal communication plays a significant role in people's lives, assisting in relationship development, creating identities, and accomplishing everyday tasks. Language is the foundation of verbal processes and it functions in at least seven ways: instrumental, regulatory, informative, heuristic, interactional, personal, and imaginative. The four components of language study are phonology, the study of sounds; syntax, the grammar and rules for arranging units of meaning; semantics, the meaning of words; and pragmatics, the rules for appropriate use of language.

Individual influences on language include speakers' memberships in various identity groups (gender, age, regionality, ethnicity and race, education and occupation). When identities influence several aspects of language (vocabulary, grammar, and pronunciation), these speakers have distinct dialects. In other instances identity groups' language variations may be minor, involving only some pronunciation or word choices.

Societal forces affect verbal processes because they shape our perceptions and the power relationships that surround us. The language used in a given society influences its members' perceptions of social reality, whereas power relationships affect how its members' verbal patterns are evaluated.

Communicating more ethically involves avoiding hate speech and using confirming rather than disconfirming language. To improve your verbal communication skills, learn to use "I" statements when expressing dissatisfaction, and recognize the power of language.

Key Terms

instrumental	semantics	code switching
regulatory	denotative meaning	jargon
informative	connotative meaning	nominalists
heuristic	pragmatics	relativists
interactional	speech act theory	Sapir-Whorf hypothesis
personal language	dialect	cocultural theory
imaginative	lexical choice	hate speech
grammar	cohort effect	disconfirming communication
phonology	African American Vernacular	confirming communication
syntax	English	

Apply What You Know

1. For each scenario, write a paragraph describing a typical communication exchange. For each, think about the various elements of verbal communication: sounds, grammar, meaning (word choice), conversational rules, and contextual rules.

   - an informal family outing
   - a meeting with your advisor
   - a bar, where you are trying to impress potential partners

   Hint: Working in a small group, see whether you and your classmates can come up with some shared contextual rules for communication in these various situations. Give some reasons why you can or cannot come up with shared rules.

2. Take three sheets of paper and write one of the following words on each sheet: *garbage, milk, mother*. Take the first piece of paper and crumple it up and then stomp on it. Do the same with the second and third pieces. How did you feel crumpling up and stomping on the first piece of paper? The second? The third? What does this say perhaps about the difference between denotative and connotative meanings?

3. For each of the examples that follow, create an "I" statement that expresses your feelings about the situation:

   - Once again your roommate has borrowed some of your clothes without asking and has returned them dirty or damaged.
   - For the third time this semester, your instructor has changed the date of an exam.
   - Your good friend has developed a habit of canceling plans at the last moment.
   - Your romantic partner embarrasses you by teasing you about personal habits in front of friends.

   Form a group with two or three of your classmates. Take turns reading your "I" statement for each situation. Discuss the strengths and weaknesses of each statement. As a group, develop an "I" statement for each situation that best expresses the group's feelings without encouraging defensiveness in the receiver.

4. Locate five people who either grew up in different parts of the United States or who grew up in different countries. Try to include both men and women and people of different ages in your sample. Ask each person to answer the following questions:

   - What do you call a carbonated beverage?
   - How do you pronounce "roof"?
   - What expressions do you use that some other people have had trouble understanding?
   - What does the term *feminist* mean?
   - Who do you think talks "different"?

Glossary

African American Vernacular English a version of English that has its roots in West African, Caribbean, and U.S. slave languages

cocultural theory explores the role of power in daily interactions

code switching the practice of changing language or dialect to accommodate to the communication situation

cohort effect the influence of shared characteristics of a group that was born and reared in the same general period; the process by which historical events influence the perceptions of people who grew up in a given generation and time period

confirming communication comments that validate positive self-images of others

connotative meaning the affective or interpretive meanings attached to a word

denotative meaning the dictionary, or literal, meaning of a word

dialect a variation of a language distinguished by its vocabulary, grammar, and pronunciation

disconfirming communication comments that reject or invalidate a positive or negative self-image of our conversational partners

grammar the structural rules that govern the generation of meaning in a language

hate speech use of verbal communication to attack others based upon some social category

heuristic use of language to acquire knowledge and understanding

imaginative use of language to express oneself artistically or creatively

informative use of language to communicate information or report facts

instrumental use of language to obtain what you need or desire

interactional use of language to establish and define social relationships

jargon the specialized terms that develop in many professions

lexical choice vocabulary

nominalists those who argue that any idea can be expressed in any language and that the structure and vocabulary of the language do not influence the speaker's perception of the world

personal language use of language to express individuality and personality

phonology the study of the sounds that compose individual languages and how those sounds communicate meaning

pragmatics field of study that emphasizes how language is used in specific situations to accomplish goals

regulatory use of language to control or regulate the behaviors of others

relativists those who argue that language serves not only as a way for us to voice our ideas but "is itself the shaper of ideas, the guide for the individual's mental activity"

Sapir-Whorf hypothesis idea that the language people speak determines the way they see the world (a relativist perspective)

semantics the study of meaning

speech act theory branch of pragmatics that suggests that when people communicate, they do not just say things, they also *do* things with their words

syntax the rules that govern word order

References

Académie française. Exemples de remarques normatives, 9th edition. Retrieved March 6, 2014, from: http://www.academie-francaise.fr/le-dictionnaire-la-9e-edition/exemples-de-remarques-normatives.

Académie française. (2014, March 6). Replay. Retrieved March 6, 2014, from: http://www.academie-francaise.fr/dire-ne-pas-dire.

American Civil Liberties Union. (1994). Free speech: Hate speech on campus. Retrieved March 16, 2014, from: http://www.aclu.org/free-speech/hate-speech-campus.

American Heritage Dictionary of the English Language, (5th ed.) (2011). Boston: Houghton-Mifflin. Retrieved March 16, 2014, from: http://ahdictionary.com/.

Anderson, J. F., Beard, F. K., & Walther, J. B. (2010). Turn-taking and the local management of conversation in a highly simultaneous computer-mediated communication system. Language@Internet, Retrieved March 7, 2014, from: http://www.languageatinternet.org/articles/2010/2804.

Arana, G. (2013 January 10). Creaky voice: Yet another example of young women's linguistic ingenuity. Atlantic.com. Retrieved March 16, 2014, from: http://www.theatlantic.com/sexes/archive/2013/01/creaky-voice-yet-another-example-of-young-womens-linguistic-ingenuity/267046/.

Aylor, B., & Dainton, M. (2004). Biological sex and psychological gender as predictors of routine and strategic relational maintenance. *Sex Roles: A Journal of Research, 50*, 689–697.

Bippus, A. M., & Young, S. L. (2005). Owning your emotions: Reactions to expressions of self versus other-attributed positive and negative emotions. *Journal of Applied Communication Research, 33*, 26–45.

Bowen, S. P. (2012). Jewish and/or woman: Identity and communicative styles. In A. González, M. Houston, & V. Chen. (Eds.), (5th ed., pp. 47–52). New York: Oxford University Press.

Boxer, D. (2002). Nagging: The familial conflict arena. *Journal of Pragmatics, 34*, 49–61.

Burrell, N. A., Donohue, W. A., & Allen, M. (1988). Gender-based perceptual biases in mediation. *Communication Research, 15*, 447–469.

Caughlin, J. P. (2002). The demand/withdraw pattern of communication as a predictor of marital satisfaction over time: Unresolved issues and future directions. *Human Communication Research, 28*, 49–85.

Chomsky, N. (1957). *Syntactic Structures*, The Hague/Paris: Mouton.

Cohen, R. (2014, March 12). In defense of *I can't even*. Slate.com Retrieved March 16, 2014, from: http://www.slate.com/blogs/lexicon_valley/2014/03/12/language_i_can_t_even_is_just_the_newest_example_of_an_old_greek_rhetorical.html.

Crystal, D. (2003). *The Cambridge encyclopedia of the English language*. New York: Cambridge University Press.

Dance, F. E. X., & Larson, C. E. (1976). *The functions of human communication*. New York: Holt, Rinehart, & Winston.

Deutscher, G. (2010). Through the language glass: Why the world looks different in other languages. New York: Metropolitan Books.

"Duflot: 'appelez-moi Madame la minister.'; (2012, September 26). Le Figaro. Retrieved March 7, 2014 from: http://www.lefigaro.fr/flash-actu/2012/09/26/97001-20120926FILWWW00677-duflot-appelez-moi-madame-la-ministre.php

Duke, M. P., Fivush, R., Lazarus, A., & Bohanek, J. (2003). Of ketchup and kin: Dinnertime conversations as a major source of family knowledge, family adjustment, and family resilience (Working Paper #26). Retrieved March 16, 2014, from: http://www.marial.emory.edu/research/.

Edwards, J. V. (2004). Foundations of bilingualism. In T. K. Bhatia & W. C. Ritchie (Eds.), *The handbook of bilingualism* (pp. 7–31). Malden, MA: Blackwell.

Ellis, A., & Beattie, G. (1986). Variations within a language. *The psychology of language and communication.* (pp. 109–114). East Sussex, UK: Psychology Press.

Fromkin, V., & Rodman, R. (1983). *An introduction to language.* New York: Holt, Rinehart, and Winston.

Gong, G. (2012). When Mississippi Chinese talk. In A. González, M. Houston, & V. Chen (Eds.), *Our voices: Essays in culture, ethnicity, and communication* (5th ed., pp. 104–111). New York: Oxford University Press.

Gray, J. (2012). *Men are from Mars, women are from Venus* (20th anniversary ed). New York: HarperCollins.

Hannah, A., & Murachver, T. (2007). Gender preferential responses to speech. *Journal of Language and Social Psychology, 26*(3), 274–290.

Hecht, M. L., Jackson, R. L. II, & Ribeau, S. A. (2003). *African American communication.* Mahwah, NJ: Lawrence Erlbaum Associates.

Hegarty, P., & Buechel, C. (2006). Androcentric reporting of gender differences in APA journals: 1965–2004. *Review of General Psychology, 10*(4), 377–389.

Heilman, M. E. (2001). Description and prescription: How gender stereotypes prevent women's ascent up the organizational ladder. In "Gender, hierarchy and leadership," Ed. L. Carli & A. Eagly. *Journal of Social Issues, 57*(4), 657–674.

Heilman, M. E., Caleo, S., & Halim, M. L. (2010), Just the thought of it! Effects of anticipating computer-mediated communication on gender stereotyping. *Journal of Experimental Social Psychology, 46*(4), 672–675.

Hoijer, H. (1994). The Sapir-Whorf hypothesis. In L. Samovar & R. E. Porter (Eds.), *Intercultural communication: A reader* (pp. 194–200). Belmont, CA: Wadsworth.

Holocaust denier ordered to visit memorial. (2013, February 1). Sky News. Retrieved March 6, 2014, from: http://news.sky.com/story/1046315/holocaust-denier-ordered-to-visit-memorial.

Hudson, R. A. (1983*). Sociolinguistics.* London: Cambridge University Press.

Hyde, J. S. (2006). Gender similarities still rule. *American Psychologist, 61*(6), 641–642.

Kikoski, J. F., & Kikoski, C. K. (1999). *Reflexive communication in the culturally diverse workplace.* Westport, CT: Praeger.

Kim, M. S. (2002). *Non-Western perspectives on human communication.* Thousand Oaks, CA: Sage.

Kohonen, S. (2004). Turn-taking in conversation: Overlaps and interruptions in intercultural talk. *Cahiers, 10.1,* 15–32.

Kubany, E. S., Bauer, G. B., Muraoka, M., Richard, D. C., & Read, P. (1995). Impact of labeled anger and blame in intimate relationships. *Journal of Social and Clinical Psychology, 14,* 53–60.

Labov, W. (1980). The social origins of sound change. In W. Labov (Ed.), *Locating language in time and space* (pp. 251–265). New York: Academic Press.

Labov, W. (Ed.). (2005). *Atlas of North American English.* New York: Walter De Gruyter.

Leaper, C., & Ayres, M. M. (2007). A meta-analytic review of gender variation in adults' language use: Talkativeness, affiliative speech, and assertive speech. *Personality and Social Psychology Review, 11*(4), 328–363.

Liptak, A. (2008). Hate speech or free speech? What much of West bans is protected in U.S. *New York Times.* Retrieved March 16, 2014, from: http://www.nytimes.com/2008/06/11/world/americas/11iht-hate.4.13645369.html.

Martin, J. N., Krizek, R. L., Nakayama, T. K., & Bradford, L. (1999). What do White people want to be called? A study of self-labels for White Americans. In T. K. Nakayama & J. N. Martin (Eds.), *Whiteness: The communication of social identity* (pp. 27–50). Thousand Oaks, CA: Sage.

Media Awareness Network (n.d.). Criminal code of Canada: Online hate and free speech. Retrieved March 16, 2014, from: http://mediasmarts.ca/online-hate/online-hate-and-free-speech.

Mehl, M. R., & Pennebaker, J. W. (2003). The sounds of social life: A psychometric analysis of students' daily social environments and natural conversations. *Journal of Personality and Social Psychology, 84,* 857–70.

Mey, J. L. (2001). *Pragmatics: An introduction* (2nd ed.). Oxford, UK: Blackwell Publishing.

Mulac, A., Bradac. J. J., & Gibbons, P. (2001). Empirical support for the gender-as-culture hypothesis: An intercultural analysis of male/female language differences. *Human Communication Research, 27,* 121–152.

Nofsinger, R. (1999). *Everyday conversation.* Prospect Heights, IL: Waveland.

Orbe, M. P. (1998). *Constructing co-cultural theory: An explication of culture, power, and communication.* Thousand Oaks, CA: Sage.

Paramasivam, S. (2007). Managing disagreement while managing not to disagree: Polite disagreement in negotiation discourse. *Journal of Intercultural Communication Research, 36*(2), 91–116.

Pennebaker, J. W., & Stone, L. D. (2003). Words of wisdom: Language use across the life span. *Journal of Personality and Social Psychology, 82,* 291–301.

Philips, S. U. (1990). Some sources of cultural variability in the regulation of talk. In D. Carbaugh (Ed.), *Cultural communication and intercultural contact* (pp. 329–344). Hillsdale, NJ: Erlbaum.

Piaget, J. (1952). *The origins of intelligence in children.* New York: International Universities Press.

Pinker, S. (2007). *The stuff of thought: Language as a window into human nature.* New York: Viking.

Pinto, D., & Raschio, R. (2007). A comparative study of requests in heritage speaker Spanish, L1 Spanish, and L1 English. *International Journal of Bilingualism, 11*(2), 135–155.

Preston, D. R. (2003). Where are the dialects of American English at anyhow? *American Speech, 78,* 235–254.

Ramírez-Esparza, N., Gosling, S. D., Benet-Martínez, V., Potter, J. D., & Pennebaker, J. W. (2006). Do bilinguals have two personalities? A special case of cultural frame switching. *Journal of Research in Personality, 40,* 99–120.

Reid, S. A., Keerie, N., & Palomares, N. A. (2003). Language, gender salience, and social influence. *Journal of Language and Social Psychology, 22,* 210–233.

Ruben, D. L. (2003). Help! My professor (or doctor or boss) doesn't talk English! In J. N. Martin, T. K. Nakayama, & L. A. Flores (Eds.). *Readings in intercultural communication* (2nd ed., pp. 127–138). Boston: McGraw-Hill.

Sacks, H., Schegloff, E., & Jefferson, G. (1978). A simplest systematics for the organization of turn-taking for conversation. In J. Schenkein (Ed.), *Studies in the organization of conversational interaction* (pp. 7–55). New York: Academic Press.

Sagrestano, L. M., Heavey, C. L., & Christensen, A. (1998). Theoretical approaches to understanding sex differences and similarities in conflict behavior. In D. J. Canary & K. Dindia (Eds.), *Sex differences and similarities in communication: Critical essays and empirical investigations on sex and gender in interaction* (pp. 287–302). Mahwah, NJ: Erlbaum.

Sauerbrey A. (2013, September 25). How do you say "blog" in German? *New York Times.com* Retrieved March 6, 2014, from: http://www.nytimes.com/2013/09/26/opinion/how-do-you-say-blog-in-german.html?_r=0

Sbisa, M. (2002). Speech act in context, *Language & Communication, 22*, 421–436.

Schegloff, E. A. (2000) Overlapping talk and the organization of turn-taking for conversation, *Language in Society, 29*, 1–63.

Scheibel, D. (1995). Making waves with Burke: Surf Nazi culture and the rhetoric of localism. *Western Journal of Communication, 59*(4), 253–269.

Sedivy, J. (2012, March 28). Votes and vowels: A changing accent show how language parallels politics. *Discover*. Retrieved March 7, 2014, from: http://blogs.discovermagazine.com/crux/2012/03/28/votes-and-vowels-a-changing-accent-shows-how-language-parallels-politics/#.UxoiICifNiF.

Sellers, J. G., Woolsey, M. D., & Swann, J. B. (2007). Is silence more golden for women than men? Observers derogate effusive women and their quiet partners. *Sex Roles, 57*(7–8), 477–482.

Shutiva, C. (2012). Native American culture and communication through humor. In A. González, M. Houston, & V. Chen (Eds.), *Our voices: Essays in culture, ethnicity, and communication* (5th ed., pp. 134–138). New York: Oxford University Press.

Terrero, N. (2013, October 28). Wisconsin man arrested for punching two males for speaking "Spanish." *NBC Latino*. Retrieved March 6, 2014, from: http://nbclatino.com/2013/10/28/wisconsin-man-arrested-for-punching-two-males-for-speaking-spanish/

Walker, J. L. (2010). *"You are an African American, so why are you talking like a white person?"* Omaha, NE: P.T.C.E, Inc.

Weger, H., Jr. (2005). Disconfiming communication and self-verification in marriage: Associations among the demand/withdraw interaction pattern, feeling understood, and marital satisfaction. *Journal of Social and Personal Relationships, 22*, 19–31.

Wood, J. T. (2002). *Gendered lives: Communication, gender and cultures.* Belmont, CA: Wadsworth.

Credits

Photo Credits

Credits are listed in order of appearance.

Photo 1: Monkey Business/Fotolia

Photo 2: Sandor Kacso/Fotolia

Photo 3: Chris Rout/Alamy

Photo 4: Nyul/Fotolia

Photo 5: Robin Nelson/ZUMA Press/Newscom

Photo 6: Vivian Zink/Bravo/Everett Collection

Photo 7: WavebreakMediaMicro/Fotolia

Photo 8: EpicStockMedia/Fotolia

Photo 9: Hitdelight/Shutterstock

Photo 10: Leungchopan/Fotolia

Photo 11: Jim West/Alamy

Text and Art Credits

Cristina

Chomshy, N. (1957). Syntactic Structures, The Hague/Paris: Mouton.

Based on Académie française. Exemples de remarques normatives, 9th edition. Retrieved March 6, 2014 from: http://www.academie-francaise.fr/le-dictionnaire-la-9e-edition/exemples-de-remarques-normatives Académie française. (2014, March 6). Replay. Retrieved March 6, 2014 from: http://www.academie-francaise.fr/dire-ne-pas-dire Sauerbrey A. (2013, September 25). How do you say "blog" in German? New York Times. Retrieved March 6, 2014 from: http://www.nytimes.com/2013/09/26/opinion/how-do-you-say-blog-in-german.html?_r=0 "Duflot: 'Appelez-moi Madame la ministre.'" (2012, September 26). Le Figaro. Retrieved March 7, 2014 from: http://www.lefigaro.fr/flash-actu/2012/09/26/97001-20120926FILWWW00677-duflot-appelez-moi-madame-la-ministre.php;

American Heritage Dictionary of the English Language, 5th ed. (2011). Boston: Houghton-Mifflin. Retrieved March 16, 2014, from: http://ahdictionary.com/.

Heilman, M. E. (2001). Description and prescription: How gender stereotypes prevent women's ascent up the organizational ladder. In "Gender, hierarchy and leadership," Ed. L. Carli & A. Eagly. Journal of Social Issues, 57(4), 657-674. p. 658

Based on material from www.internetslang.com

Sedivy, J. (2012, March 28). Votes and vowels: A changing accent show how language parallels politics. Discover. Retrieved March 7, 2014, from: http://blogs.discovermagazine.com/crux/2012/03/28/votes-and-vowels-a-changing-accent-shows-how-languageparallels- politics/#.UxoiICifNiF

Fig 05.01 , Map by Matthew T.Campbell Spatial Grahpics and Analysis lab Department of cartograhphy and Geography East central University (oklahomo) Map Template courtesy of www.mymaps.com.

Hecht, M. L., Jackson, R. L. II, & Ribeau, S. A. (2003). African American communication. Mahwah, NJ: Lawrence Erlbaum Associates.

Hoijer, H. (1994). The Sapir-Whorf hypothesis. In L. Samovar & R. E. Porter (Eds.), Intercultural communication: A reader (pp. 194-200). Belmont, CA: Wadsworth.

Bart

Hiroko

Holocaust denier ordered to visit memorial. (2013, February 1). Sky News. Retrieved March 6, 2014, from: http://news.sky.com/story/1046315/holocaust-denier-ordered-to-visit-memorial.

Terrero, N. (2013, October 28). Wisconsin man arrested for punching two males for speaking "Spanish." NBC Latino. Retrieved March 6, 2014, from: http://nbclatino.com/2013/10/28/wisconsinman-arrested-for-punching-two-males-for-speaking-spanish/

U.S. Department of Health and Human Services. (n.d.). What is cyberbullying? Retrieved March 7, 2014, from: http://www.stopbullying.gov/cyberbullying/what-is-it/

Nonverbal Communication

CHAPTER TOPICS		Chapter Objectives

The Importance of Nonverbal Communication

What Is Nonverbal Communication?

Nonverbal Communication and the Individual

The Individual, Nonverbal Communication, and Society

Ethics and Nonverbal Communication

Improving Your Nonverbal Communication Skills

1 Describe the important role of nonverbal communication in social interaction.

2 Identify four factors that influence the meaning of nonverbal communication.

3 Define five nonverbal codes and discuss the five functions of nonverbal messages.

4 Explain how nonverbal communication can both trigger and express prejudice and discrimination.

5 Discuss six guidelines for ethical nonverbal communication.

6 Name five ways to improve your ability to interpret nonverbal behavior.

From Chapter 6 of *Human Communication in Society*, Fourth Edition. Jess K. Alberts, Thomas K. Nakayama, Judith N. Martin.
Copyright © 2016 by Pearson Education, Inc. All rights reserved.

Charee took her four-year-old sister with her to a group project meeting at which some members argued about how to present their class paper. After observing the interaction for a few minutes, her sister Anna whispered, "When it's your turn to talk, you have to make your mad face."

Even though Anna is only four years old, she is sensitive to the nonverbal behavior of others. She readily reads others' facial expressions and assigns meaning to them. From an early age, all children learn the basics of nonverbal communication (Boone & Cunningham, 1998); in fact, infants from an early age imitate others' nonverbal behavior. For example, when newborns observe caregivers sticking out their tongues, they imitate them and do the same (Als, 1977; Meltzoff & Prinz, 2002).

We take a close look at the intricacies of nonverbal communication and the many factors that shape nonverbal messages and their interpretation. First, we describe the importance of nonverbal communication, provide a definition, and explore how it differs from nonverbal behavior. We then give you an overview of the various types of nonverbal codes, and we examine the functions that nonverbal messages serve. We next explore how societal forces intersect with individuals' nonverbal communication. We conclude by discussing ethical issues in nonverbal communication and providing you with suggestions for improving your nonverbal communication skills.

1 The Importance of Nonverbal Communication

1 **Describe the important role of nonverbal communication in social interaction.**

nonverbal communication

nonverbal behavior that has symbolic meaning

Nonverbal communication plays an important role in social interaction. It helps us express and interpret the verbal aspects of communication—such as when a person:

- smiles to *reinforce* an expression of thanks;
- uses the "OK" sign to *substitute* for saying "I am all right";
- laughs flirtatiously to *contradict* the words, "I hate you";
- puts his fingers close together to *illustrate* how thin his new computer is.

Even young children understand and use nonverbal communication.

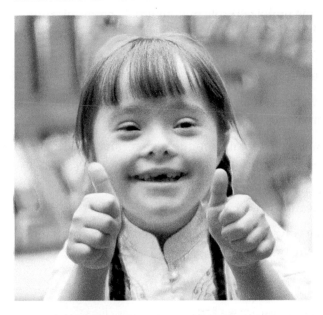

Nonverbal communication also influences how individuals interpret messages, especially those related to feelings, moods, and attitudes. Nonverbal cues are important to the expression of emotion because communicators are often more comfortable expressing their feelings nonverbally (such as by smiling or glaring) than they are stating them more explicitly through words (Mehrabian, 2007). For example, how often do you flatly tell a friend or colleague, "I am mad at you?" If you are like most people, this is a relatively rare event; instead, you probably rely on some type of nonverbal cue to indicate your dissatisfaction. The ability to decode others' nonverbal communication effectively helps you interpret the nuanced meanings in others' messages as well as how they feel—and how they feel about you. It also helps you respond better to those messages and feelings. This ability is particularly important in relationships. For instance, a study of nonverbal communication and marital satisfaction found that couples' ability to correctly decode their partner's nonverbal communication affect was connected to their relational satisfaction, especially for husbands (Koerner & Fitzpatrick, 2002).

If you would like to see how effectively you can identify others' facial expressions, visit this link:

http://www.questionwritertracker.com/quiz/61/Z4MK3TKB.html.

However, nonverbal communication can be complex and ambiguous—both for senders of messages to convey and for receivers of messages to interpret. Even though we begin learning nonverbal communication as children, we often have difficulty interpreting others' nonverbal communication. Why is this so? One reason is the fact that humans express a wide array of nonverbal behaviors, many of which can be quite subtle. Consequently, understanding nonverbal communication requires knowledge and skill.

However, beware of books, Web sites, and magazine articles that promise to teach you to "read a person like a book": there is no such thing as a key to decoding or interpreting every **nonverbal behavior** in every context. Why not? Because understanding nonverbal communication requires interpreting behavior and assigning meaning to it, and we don't always have the information we need to do that. If you are sitting in the library and notice a stranger staring at you, what does the stare mean? Does the person think he knows you? Is he interested in meeting you? Is he being aggressive? Or is the person simply lost in thought and only *appearing* to be gazing at you? As this example illustrates, nonverbal cues can be ambiguous. Because the meaning of nonverbal behavior is determined by a variety of factors, including context, culture, and even intentionality, it can be tricky to interpret a specific behavior.

nonverbal behavior
all the nonverbal actions people perform

In addition, nonverbal cues are continuous, meaning that people exhibit nonverbal behaviors virtually all the time they are conscious, and multiple behaviors act in concert to create a given message—or different messages, even unrelated ones. For example, imagine that Joan is talking to her husband about their need to spend time together to strengthen their marriage. Just as her husband asks, "What do you want to do about our marriage?" Joan happens to look over his shoulder at her computer screen and sees it displaying an error message. In frustration, she throws up her hands and sighs heavily. Joan was responding to her computer failure, but her husband thought she was responding to his question. He became upset, assuming she was expressing a wish to give up on their marriage.

Nonverbal communication also can be difficult to interpret because nonverbal cues are multichanneled; that is, they can be transmitted in a variety of ways simultaneously. Speakers can convey nonverbal messages through their facial expressions, voice qualities, eye gaze, posture, and gestures and by other channels we will discuss throughout this text. Moreover, because a variety of cues may occur at the same time, it can be difficult and confusing to keep up with everything (Schwartz, Foa, & Foa, 1983). If, for example, you are focusing on someone's face, you may miss important messages conveyed by the body.

"Pop psychology" treatments of nonverbal communication typically assume that each behavior has one meaning regardless of the context or who is performing it. Such explanations don't distinguish between nonverbal behavior and nonverbal communication; nor do they consider context, culture, individual variations in behavior, or the relationship that exists between the people being observed. All these factors, and more, can influence the meaning of a nonverbal behavior in a specific instance. So don't believe that just because someone has her arms crossed over her body, it means she is closed off to you. It may simply mean she needs a sweater.

Nonverbal messages are not only complex and ambiguous—they are also key components of communication. Understanding nonverbal communication can make you a better *verbal* communicator. In addition, nonverbal communication can help you navigate everyday life. For example, humans rely on nonverbal cues to determine

Public policy seeks to regulate nonverbal expression, such as what type of clothing people can wear.

whether other humans are a threat. In the television show *Going Tribal*, journalist Bruce Parry visited the remote Suri tribe in Ethiopia. As he approached the first tribal member, Parry carefully observed the tribesman thrust his bow and arrow at him and pace quickly back and forth while averting his eye gaze. Although many of the Suri's nonverbal behaviors communicated belligerence, the fact that he did not stare aggressively influenced Bruce to approach him slowly with a gift—which was accepted.

Similarly, on a daily basis people need to be able to read subtle nonverbal behaviors to assess how friendly or hostile others may be. This is especially true for individuals whose identities are less valued culturally or whose societal position makes them more vulnerable. Because of this vulnerability, such individuals tend to become quite adept at reading and interpreting nonverbal communication. For example, if Gary's boss walks into the office frowning and shaking her head, Gary may interpret this as meaning that she is in a bad mood; consequently, he may try to be especially helpful and avoid doing anything to provoke her. In a study that compared African Americans' and White Americans' ability to read the nonverbal behaviors of Whites, researchers found that African Americans were far better at detecting prejudicial attitudes as expressed in subtle nonverbal behavior than were Whites (Richeson & Shelton, 2005). Similarly, a study of heterosexual and gay men found that gay men were better able to identify the sexual orientation of unfamiliar men when watching videos of them (Shelp, 2002).

Nonverbal communication also is important because it can affect public policy decisions. For example, after several years of allowing students to wear just about anything they wished to school, many public schools now institute dress codes. Although some schools primarily regulate clothing that they see as "inappropriate" or too revealing, others require school uniforms. The supporters of this latter policy argue that school uniforms "help erase cultural and economic differences among students" (Isaacson, 1998) and improve student performance and attendance. Regulating school dress rests on the assumption that one form of nonverbal communication—attire—should be regulated because it can be distracting or even disruptive. Other examples of public policy attempts to regulate nonverbal expression include efforts to ban flag burning and to forbid the wearing of Muslim headscarves. Countries would not engage in efforts to control nonverbal expression if it were not so important.

2   What Is Nonverbal Communication?

2   Identify four factors that influence the meaning of nonverbal communication.

The nonverbal components of communication include all the messages that people transmit through means other than words. More specifically, communication scholar Valerie Manusov and psychologist Miles Patterson define nonverbal communication as "encompassing the sending and receiving of information through appearance, objects, the environment and behavior in social settings" (Manusov & Patterson, 2006, p. xi). Thus, they argue that we communicate nonverbally when we blow a kiss, scratch our arm, or wear clothing that signals our group membership. Even more frequently, nonverbal and verbal aspects of communication combine to convey messages, as when we indicate anger by turning our backs and saying "I don't want to talk with you right now."

However, not every scholar believes that all nonverbal behavior is communicative. These researchers argue that nonverbal communication occurs only when nonverbal behavior has symbolic meaning and is communicated intentionally (Burgoon, Buller, & Woodall, 1996). That is, they believe nonverbal communication stands for something, whereas nonverbal behavior may not. For example, from this perspective, scratching one's arm usually isn't intended by the scratcher, nor understood by the observer, to convey a particular message. Although it may provide information (that one's arm itches), it doesn't necessarily signal an *intentional* message. Rather, it would be considered an involuntary bodily "output." However, these scholars would argue that in baseball when a manager scratches his arm to signal that a runner on base should steal home, scratching the arm is symbolic and, therefore, an instance of nonverbal communication.

These sorority members signal their group membership nonverbally through their clothing and gestures.

Which of these two positions regarding nonverbal communication/nonverbal behavior seems more reasonable to you, and why? What evidence or reasoning influenced your decision? Finally, what difference does this distinction make?

Nonetheless, these scholars acknowledge that some nonverbal communication does lack the element of intentionality. For example, a smile may be understood as an expression of pleasure even if the smiler is unaware that he is smiling. Thus, if a behavior typically is used communicatively, then that behavior is understood to be part of our nonverbal "vocabulary" and will be interpreted as such, regardless of one's own conscious use of it (Burgoon, Buller, & Woodall, 1996).

However, scholars who prefer a broader definition of nonverbal communication argue that many actions one might consider just a "bodily output" can still convey messages nonverbally. For example, people usually cough because of a scratchy throat or yawn because they are tired, and when they engage in these behaviors others interpret their meaning. Of course, they also believe that when a person coughs as a signal to capture someone's attention or yawns to indicate he is bored, he is engaging in nonverbal communication.

As our discussion thus far suggests, most nonverbal behaviors have a variety of meanings—just as scratching one's arm can have multiple meanings. Therefore neither we, nor anyone else, can provide you with interpretations for specific nonverbal actions. Perhaps in part because of this difficulty, we cannot accurately estimate the amount of meaning that nonverbal communication contributes to the overall meaning in an interaction. This inability is revealed in *Did You Know? How Much Does Nonverbal Communication Contribute to Meaning?* where you can see why it can be difficult to estimate how much meaning nonverbal components convey in any message.

3 Nonverbal Communication and the Individual

3 Define five nonverbal codes and discuss the five functions of nonverbal messages.

If a smile is viewed as communicating pleasure even when the smiler doesn't intend to do so, then why don't all behaviors that are part of our nonverbal vocabulary always convey the same meaning? The answer is that assigning one simple meaning to a nonverbal behavior ignores the multiple meanings that may exist, depending on the context in which the behavior occurs. For example, you will read that when a person leans toward another (called a *forward body lean*), this is often a sign of interest or involvement. Does that mean that the forward body lean always indicates interest? Absolutely not! A person might lean forward for a variety of reasons: her stomach hurts, the back of her chair is hot, or her lower back needs to be stretched.

Did You Know?

How Much Does Nonverbal Communication Contribute to Meaning?

How much of the meaning of a message do you think is conveyed by its nonverbal components? Fifty percent? Seventy-five percent? One of the most common beliefs about communication is that more than 90 percent of the meaning of a message is transmitted by its nonverbal elements. However, in truth, we do not know! So where did this belief originate?

In 1967, psychologist Albert Mehrabian (along with Morton Wiener) wrote that 93 percent of the meaning of the utterances he examined was conveyed through the nonverbal aspects of communication. Specifically, he argued that 38 percent of meaning in his study was derived from paralinguistic cues (tone of voice, etc.) and 55 percent from facial expressions, leaving only 7 percent of meaning to be provided by the verbal message. After he published his findings, other people, researchers and non-researchers alike, began to generalize his claims about his one study to all communicative interactions.

However, a variety of scholars have contradicted this claim, either arguing for a different percentage (Birdwhistell, 1985) or suggesting that one cannot accurately determine how much words, context, nonverbal messages, and other factors actually contribute to the meaning of an utterance. Those who critique Mehrabian's analysis argue that his study exhibited several problems. First, it examined how people interpreted the meaning of single tape-recorded words, which is not how we naturally communicate. Second, he combined the results of two studies that most scholars believe should not be combined. Further, he did not consider the contributions to meaning made by gestures and posture. Also, he tried to estimate the contribution of particular nonverbal behaviors—for example, gesture versus facial expression. In practice, however, no one behavior is particularly useful in determining meaning. In other words, inferences made about the meaning of any given action are not all that reliable, nor are estimates of what percentage of the total message a single nonverbal cue communicates.

SOURCE: Birdwhistell, R. L. (1985). Kinesics and context: Essays in body motion communication. Philadelphia: University of Philadelphia Press.

Mehrabian, A. (1971, 2007). *Nonverbal communication.* Chicago, IL: Aldine de Gruyter.

Mehrabian, A., & Weiner, M. (1967). Decoding of inconsistent communication. *Journal of Personality and Social Psychology, 6,* 109–104.

To understand the meaning of a nonverbal behavior you have to consider the entire behavioral context, including what the person might be communicating verbally (Jones & LeBaron, 2002). Therefore, interpreting others' nonverbal behavior requires that you consider a variety of factors that can influence meaning. To interpret nonverbal communication, you also need to know the codes, or symbols and rules, that signal various messages. Finally, you will benefit from a familiarity with the variety of ways that nonverbal messages function. These are topics we take up next.

Influences on Nonverbal Communication

Culture is one of the more important factors that influence the meaning of nonverbal communication. This is not to say that many nonverbal cues and signals aren't shared; in fact, research shows that gaze is used to communicate aggression, dominance, and power as well as connection and nurturance across cultures and even species (Matsumoto, 2006); however, the specific manner in which gaze is used to communicate these messages can vary. For example, in many Arabic cultures, eye gaze during social interaction is more direct than is typical in the United States (Watson & Graves, 1966); thus, eye gaze that might be interpreted as friendly and involved in an Arabic culture could be perceived as somewhat aggressive by a U.S. American. Similarly, within the United States, gaze and visual behavior differ across sexes and ethnic groups, with women tending to gaze more than men (Briton & Hall, 1995) and African Americans often using more continuous eye gaze while talking and less while listening than do many Whites (Samovar & Porter, 2004).

Some nonverbal cues are used widely across cultures, such as nodding to mean yes—though this is not true in every culture. However, many nonverbal gestures have vastly different meanings in different cultures. In the United States, for instance, the "thumbs up" signals success and the "hitchhiker's thumb" asks for a ride, but these nonverbal signs carry potentially vulgar meanings in several other cultures.

In East Africa, instead of pointing with fingers, people often point with their lips—a gesture that is completely unfamiliar to most people in the United States. Differences in gestures also occur across ethnic groups in the United States. For example, historically Korean Americans tended to reserve smiling, shaking hands, and saying hello for friends and family; however, many immigrants changed this pattern of behavior once they recognized its meaning and importance in the United States (Young, 1999). Thus, the meaning of any nonverbal behavior is defined by the cultures of those interacting (Axtell, 1993; Segerstrale & Molnár, 1997).

In addition to culture, the relationship between the people interacting affects the meaning of nonverbal behaviors (Manusov, 1995). If a husband takes his wife's arm as they are crossing the street, the meaning likely is some mixture of care and affection; if a police officer were to do so, one probably would interpret it as an aggressive or controlling gesture. However, if a boss were to do the same with a subordinate, the meaning is more complex and potentially confusing or troubling. One might wonder whether she is being friendly, controlling, affectionate—or maybe too affectionate? How we interpret others' nonverbal behavior, then, is highly dependent on the type of relationship we have with them.

This gesture of support for the University of Texas Longhorns might be misinterpreted in Norway, where it is a sign of Satan.

nonverbal codes

distinct, organized means of expression that consists of symbols and rules for their use

Third, the meaning we attribute to someone's nonverbal behavior varies based on how well we know the communicator. For example, if a stranger smiles at you, you might interpret it as a gesture of friendliness because that is the meaning most often associated with this facial expression. However, if you know your best friend tends to smile when she is angry, then you will be more accurate at interpreting that her smile is a sign of her displeasure than would someone who did not know her well. Once we know people, then, we can usually read their nonverbal behavior and interpret its associated messages with more accuracy, as Abbad explains in *It Happened to Me: Abbad*. Finally, we tend to interpret individuals' nonverbal behavior based on their sex. For example, when women toss their hair, the behavior often is read as flirtatious—and therefore communicative. However, if a man does the same, we are more likely to believe he is just trying to get his hair out of his eyes—a nonverbal behavior that is not necessarily communicative. As we discuss throughout this text, sex differences in nonverbal and verbal communication are as a result of biological as well as social and cultural influences.

Nonverbal Codes

Nonverbal codes or signals are distinct, organized means of expression that consist of both symbols and rules for their use (Cicca, Step, & Turkstra, 2003). Although we describe a range of such codes in this section, we do not mean to imply that any one code occurs in isolation. Generally, a set of behaviors and codes together determines the meaning or significance of an action. For our purposes, we isolate a specific kind of behavior

It Happened to Me
Abbad

I am from the Middle East, and I arrived in the United States in 2000 with a couple of my friends. On a school break, we decided to travel to Washington, D.C. On the road, we stopped at a McDonald's to eat and to pray. As Muslims, we have to pray five times a day, and during the prayer we cannot talk at all. While in the middle of our prayer, a McDonald's employee approached and asked what we were doing. Since we could not talk, one of my friends used a hand gesture that in our culture means "wait for a minute." This hand gesture is expressed by holding all of one's fingers and thumb together sort of like a cup. For some reason, the employee understood the gesture as an invitation for a fight. I guess this is what it means in some parts of the United States. That's when the employee called 911. By the time the police officer arrived, we were done with our prayer. We explained we were new to this country and that the hand gesture we used means something else in our culture. We apologized to the employee for the misunderstanding and continued on our trip.

for analysis; in the real world, without knowing the context, interpretations about any behavior may be questionable or even wrong (Patterson, 1983). In this section, we'll look at the five types of nonverbal codes—*kinesics, paralinguistics, time and space, haptics,* and *appearance and artifacts*—to see how this system of nonverbal codes works.

KINESICS **Kinesics** is the term used to describe a system of studying nonverbal communication sent by the body, including gestures, posture, movement, facial expressions, and eye behavior. For clarity we group kinesic communication into two general categories, those behaviors involving the body and those involving the face.

THE BODY Our bodies convey many nonverbal messages. For example, we use **gestures** such as pointing, waving, and holding up our hands to direct people's attention, signal hello, and indicate that we want to be recognized. Communicators use four types of nonverbal gestures: *illustrators, emblems, adaptors,* and *regulators.* **Illustrators** are signals that accompany speech to clarify or emphasize the verbal messages. Thus, when people come back from a fishing trip they hold their hands far apart to indicate the size of the fish that got away. **Emblems** are gestures that stand for a specific verbal meaning; for example, raising one's hand in class indicates one wishes to speak and placing a finger parallel to one's lips signifies that others should be quiet. **Adaptors** are gestures we use to manage our emotions. Many adaptors are nervous gestures such as tapping a pencil, jiggling a leg, or twirling one's hair. Finally, people use **regulators** to control conversation; for example, if you want to prevent someone from interrupting you, you might hold up your hand to indicate that the other person should wait. In contrast, if you wish to interrupt and take the floor, you might raise a finger to signal your desire.

Gestures contribute a lot to our communication efforts; even their frequency can signal meaning. For instance, how much gesturing we do while speaking can indicate how involved we are in a conversation. Many people who are excited indicate their involvement by using many and varied gestures; those who have little involvement may indicate their lack of interest by their failure to gesture.

We also use our bodies to convey meaning through our posture and our movement. In general, posture is evaluated in two ways: by how *immediate* it is and by how relaxed it appears (Mehrabian, 1971; Richards, Rollerson, & Phillips, 1991). **Immediacy** refers to how close or involved people appear to be with each other. For example, when people like someone they tend to orient their bodies in the other person's direction, lean toward them, and look at them directly when they speak. How do people act when they wish to avoid someone? Typically, they engage in the opposite behavior. They turn their backs or refuse to look at them, and if they are forced to stand or sit near the person they dislike, they lean away from them. To understand this, imagine how you would behave if you were attempting to reject an unwanted amorous advance.

Relaxation refers to the degree of tension one's body displays. When you are at home watching TV, for instance, you probably display a relaxed posture: lounging in a chair with your legs stretched out in front of you and your arms resting loosely on the chair's arms. However, if you are waiting at the dentist's office, you may sit hunched forward, your legs pressed tightly together, and your hands firmly grasping the chair arms.

The way you walk or move also can communicate messages to others, particularly about your mood or emotional state. Sometimes you use movement deliberately to communicate a message—such as when you stomp around the apartment to indicate your anger. At other times, your movement is simply a nonverbal behavior—that is, you move naturally and unconsciously without any clear intentionality. Even when your movement is not intentional, observers can and do make judgments about you. One study found that observers could identify when pedestrians were sad, angry,

kinesics

nonverbal communication sent by the body, including gestures, posture, movement, facial expressions, and eye behavior

gestures

nonverbal communication made with part of the body, including actions such as pointing, waving, or holding up a hand to direct people's attention

illustrators

signals that accompany speech to clarify or emphasize the verbal message

emblems

gestures that stand for a specific verbal meaning

adaptors

gestures used to manage emotions

regulators

gestures used to control conversations

immediacy

how close or involved people appear to be with each other

relaxation

the degree of tension displayed by the body

happy, or proud, just from the way they walked (Montepare, Goldstein, & Clausen, 1987). However, some emotional states (anger) were easier to identify than others (pride), and some individuals were easier to classify than others. So although people consciously communicate a great deal with their body movements and gestures and observers interpret others' movements, some messages are more clearly transmitted than others. It should also be noted that many of the same factors discussed previously, such as culture, context, background knowledge, and gender, can affect the ability to interpret kinesic behavior.

THE FACE Facial expressions communicate more than perhaps any other nonverbal behavior. They are the primary channels for transmitting emotion, and the eyes, in particular, convey important messages regarding attraction and attention. Some research suggests that facial expressions of happiness, sadness, anger, surprise, fear, and disgust are the same across cultures and, in fact, are innate (Ekman & Friesen, 1969, 1986), although not all scholars agree. Through observations of deaf, blind, and brain-damaged children, researchers have concluded that commonality of facial expressions among humans is not the result of observation and learning but rather to genetic programming (Eibl-Eibesfeld, 1972; Ekman, 2003). To better understand the role of facial expressions in the communication of emotion, go to this Web site:

http://www.persuasive.net/blog/it-is-written-all-over-your-face-understanding-facial-expressions/

What nonverbal messages might be understood from this photo? Remember that a nonverbal behavior can have multiple meanings.

The ability to accurately recognize others' emotions gives individuals an edge in their interpersonal actions. For example, people with greater emotional recognition accuracy are effective in negotiations and are able to create more value for all parties and to achieve more favorable outcomes (Elfenbein, Maw, White, Tan, & Aik, 2007). If you are not adept at recognizing others' emotions, however, you can improve your ability to do so. A variety of studies show that individuals who are trained in emotion recognition and then receive feedback on their performance can improve their ability to recognize others' emotional expressions, especially if their targets are from different cultures than their own (Elfenbein, 2006).

Of course, people don't display every emotion they feel. Individuals learn through experience and observation to manage their facial expressions, and they learn which expressions are appropriate to reveal in what circumstances. In many cultures expectations of appropriateness differ for men and women. For example, in the United States, males are often discouraged from showing sadness, whereas females are frequently criticized for showing anger. In addition, women are routinely expected to smile, no matter how they feel, while relatively few men receive the same message. Whether or not they are conscious of such cultural expectations, many men believe they shouldn't feel strong emotions or don't want others to see them express strong emotions.

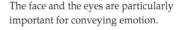

The face and the eyes are particularly important for conveying emotion.

Eye behavior is especially important in conveying messages for humans as well as animals. For example, both humans and dogs use prolonged eye gaze (a stare) to communicate aggression, and they avert their gaze when they want to avoid contact. Furthermore, eye behavior interacts with facial expressions to convey meaning. Thus, most people believe a smile is genuine only when the eyes "smile" as well as the lips. Actors such as Julia Roberts and Tom Cruise are particularly gifted at this; they can, at will, express what appears to be a genuine smile.

Like other types of nonverbal communication, context and culture shape the meanings people attach to

eye behavior. For example, cultures differ significantly in how long one is supposed to engage in eye contact and how frequently. Many Native Americans such as Cherokees, Navajos, and Hopis engage in minimal eye contact and many Arabic people maintain more intense and prolonged eye contact when they are listening compared to most White U.S. Americans (Chiang, 1993). Swedes tend to gaze infrequently but for longer periods of time, whereas southern Europeans gaze frequently and extensively (Knapp & Hall, 1992, 2001). Your relationship with others also affects how you interpret their eye behavior. Thus, you may find it appealing when a romantic partner gazes into your eyes but find the same behavior threatening when exhibited by a stranger. For an example of how differences in eye contact and facial expression can affect communication, see *Communication in Society: When You Smile on the Job.*

paraliguistics

all aspects of spoken language except for the words themselves; includes rate, volume, pitch, and stress

PARALINGUISTICS The vocal aspects of nonverbal communication are referred to as **paralinguistics**, which include rate, volume, pitch, and stress, among others. Paralinguistics are those aspects of language that are *oral* but not *verbal*. That is, paralinguistics describe all aspects of spoken language except the words themselves. For example, typically you recognize other speakers' voices in large part through their paralinguistics, or how they sound, rather than the specific words they say. For this reason, when you call a close friend or relative, you may expect them to recognize you just from hearing your voice on the telephone. If someone close to you fails to recognize your voice, you may feel hurt or offended, because their failing to do so suggests that perhaps they don't know you as well as you think they do. Paralinguistics are composed of two types of vocal behavior—*voice qualities* and *vocalizations*.

voice qualities

qualities such as pitch, rhythm, vocal range, and articulation that make up the "music" of the human voice

VOICE QUALITIES Voice qualities include speed, pitch, rhythm, vocal range, and articulation; these qualities make up the "music" of the human voice. We all know people whose voice qualities are widely recognized. For example, President Barack Obama's vocal qualities are frequently remarked on. One critic (Dié, 2008) described it as resembling that used by preachers, arguing that if you listen only to how the president speaks (rather than what he says), you would feel as if you were sitting in a small church in any Black neighborhood in the United States. He uses the same "ebb and flow," or rhythms and intonations, that are common to ministers' rhetorical style. To compare the vocal qualities of various presidents, go to **www.presidentsusa.net/ audiovideo.html** and listen to audio and video recordings of many presidents.

Communication in Society

When You Smile on the Job

Do you think it is reasonable for a retail store to require women cashiers to smile and make eye contact with all customers? Why or why not? Why do you think the female Safeway employees believed their smiles were the cause of the men's attention?

Have you noticed the smiles and greetings you receive when you shop at major grocery store chains such as Walmart and Safeway? Grocery stores weren't always such welcoming places. This friendly behavior, often called the "supermarket mandatory smile," began in the United States in the late 1990s. Although many stores encouraged this behavior, Safeway actually required its employees to greet customers with a smile and direct eye contact. However, some female employees

lodged complaints over this policy because they argued that male customers repeatedly propositioned them and asked them out on dates when they acted so friendly. Although Safeway denied that their policy was the cause of the men's behavior, they did eventually end it. If the organization had consulted nonverbal research on flirting, they might never have instituted the policy in the first place. One of the most common behaviors women use to signal their interest in men is a smile combined with eye contact and a slight tilt of the head (Trost & Alberts, 2009).

Trost, M. R., & Alberts, J. K. (2006). How men and women communicate attraction: An evolutionary view. In D. Canary & K. Dindia (Eds.) *Sex, gender and communication: Similarities and differences* (2nd ed.) 317–336. Mahwah, NJ: Lawrence Erlbaum

Speakers whose voices vary in pitch and rhythm seem more expressive than those whose voices do not. For example, actor Keanu Reeves is criticized by some as boring and inexpressive because they perceive his delivery as monotonous. (This worked to his advantage, however, during his role as Klaatu in *The Day the Earth Stood Still*.) Speakers also vary in how they articulate sounds, some pronouncing each word distinctly and others blurring their words and sounds. We tend not to notice this paralinguistic feature unless someone articulates very precisely or very imprecisely. If you have difficulty understanding a speaker, usually the fault lies not with how fast the person talks but with how clearly he or she articulates. When combined, the qualities of pitch and rhythm make your voice distinctive and recognizable to those who know you.

VOCALIZATIONS   **Vocalizations** are the sounds we utter that do not have the structure of language. Tarzan's yell is one famous example. Vocalizations include vocal cues such as laughing, crying, whining, and moaning, as well as the intensity or volume of one's speech. Also included are sounds that aren't actual words but that serve as fillers, such as "uh-huh," "uh," "ah," and "er."

The paralinguistic aspects of speech serve a variety of communicative purposes. They reveal mood and emotion; they also allow us to emphasize or stress a word or idea, create a distinctive identity, and (along with gestures) regulate conversation.

TIME AND SPACE   How people use time and space is so important to communication that researchers have studied their use and developed specialized terms to describe them. **Chronemics**, from the Greek word *chronos*, meaning "time," is the study of the way people use time as a message. It includes issues such as punctuality and the amount of time people spend with each other. **Proxemics** refers to the study of how people use spatial cues, including interpersonal distance, territoriality, and other space relationships. Let's see how these factors influence communication and relationships.

CHRONEMICS   People often interpret others' use of time as conveying a message, which removes it from the realm of behavior and places it in the realm of communication. For example, if your friend consistently arrives more than an hour late, how do you interpret her behavior? Culture strongly influences how most people answer this question (Hall & Hall, 1987). In the United States, time typically is valued highly; we even have an expression that "time is money." Because of this, most people own numerous clocks and watches. Events are scheduled at specific times and typically begin on time. Therefore, in the United States, lateness can communicate thoughtlessness, irresponsibility, or selfishness. A more positive or tolerant view might be that the perpetually late person is carefree.

Not all cultures value time in the same way, however. In some Latin American and Arab cultures, if one arrives 30 minutes or even an hour after an event is scheduled to begin, one is "on time." When people come together from cultures that value time differently, it can lead to conflict and a sense of displacement. This happened when one of our colleagues taught a class in Mexico. On the first class day, she showed up at the school shortly before the class was scheduled to begin. She found the building locked and no one around. And even though she knew that people in Mexico respond to time differently than she did, during her stay she never was comfortable arriving "late," and routinely had to wait outside the building until someone showed up to let her in.

The timing and sequencing of events convey a variety of messages. For example, being invited to lunch carries a different meaning than being invited to dinner, and being asked to dinner on a Monday conveys a different message than being asked to dinner on a Saturday. Events also tend to unfold in a particular order; so we expect informal interaction to precede intimate interaction and small talk to precede task talk. When these expectations are violated, we often attribute meaning to the violations, as shown in *Did You Know? Expectancy Violations*.

Think back to the last time you encountered someone you could tell was truly happy to see you. How could you tell? What nonverbal behaviors communicated the other person's happiness to you?

vocalizations

uttered sounds that do not have the structure of language

chronemics

the study of the way people use time as a message

proxemics

the study of how people use spatial cues, including interpersonal distance, territoriality, and other space relationships, to communicate

Did You Know?

Expectancy Violations

Think of a time when someone violated your expectations for nonverbal behavior. How did you interpret the behavior? Did you see it as a positive or negative violation? Why? How did you respond? How can a person use expectancy violation theory to increase liking?

Our expectations are one factor that influences our interpretations of others' nonverbal behavior. *Expectancy violation theory* states that when people violate our expectations, we tend to notice, become aroused, and attribute meaning to the violation, resulting in increased scrutiny and appraisal of the violator's behavior. For example, if you expect a stranger to shake your hand on being introduced, you likely will search for an explanation if she or he hugs you instead.

However, we don't necessarily interpret and respond to these violations negatively. Judee Burgoon and her colleagues repeatedly have shown that responses to another's violation of our expectations are influenced by how we perceive the violator. In other words, we judge a violation as positive or negative depending largely on whether we view the violator as someone with whom we'd like to interact. Thus, if the stranger who hugs you is attractive and you are single, you may evaluate this violation positively. This judgment shapes your response to the violation; in this case, if you interpret the hug positively, you may respond by hugging back (Burgoon & Hale, 1988; Burgoon & LePoire, 1993).

Burgoon, J. K., & Hale, J. L. (1988). Nonverbal expectancy violations: Model elaboration and application to immediacy behaviors. *Communication Monographs*, 55, 58–79.

Burgoon, J. K., & Le Poire, B. A. (1993). Effects of Communication expectancies, actual communication, and expectancy disconfirmation on evaluations of communicators and their communication behavior. *Human Communication Research*, 20(1), 67–96.

monochronically

engaging in one task or behavior at a time

polychronically

engaging in multiple activities simultaneously

In addition, some people use time **monochronically**, whereas others use it **polychronically**, and the differences can be perceived as transmitting a message (Hall, 1983; Wolburg, 2001). Individuals who use time monochronically engage in one task or behavior at a time—one reads *or* participates in a conversation *or* watches a movie. If you engage in multiple activities at the same time, you are using time polychronically. Historically in the United States, people have used time monochronically; however, now that technology is so pervasive, more people are using time polychronically as they send text messages, post pictures on Instagram, or read a few tweets as they interact with others. Unfortunately, people who use time monochronically may be insulted by those who use it polychronically, leading to comments such as "Put down that phone and pay attention to me when I talk to you!"

Whenever an individual's use of time differs from that of others, miscommunication is possible. If you tend to value punctuality more than others do, you may arrive at events earlier than expected and irritate your host, or you may be perceived as too eager. Similarly, if you don't value punctuality, you may discover that others won't schedule activities with you or are frequently annoyed with you for disrupting their plans. Relationships and communication benefit when the people involved understand how others value and use time.

PROXEMICS As we mentioned previously, proxemics is the study of how one uses space. People use variance in distance from others for two purposes: to create a sense of safety and comfort and to signal intimacy and closeness. First, individuals need to maintain sufficient space from others to feel safe in their surroundings. The more unfamiliar or uncomfortable one is with another person, the more space one requires. This is one reason we often feel uncomfortable riding on crowded buses or trains. In these cases, we are forced to maintain minimal space between ourselves and people we don't know. Interestingly, this psychological and physical need for safety results also occurs in virtual space. An individual's avatar responds to space violations the same way a person would in real life (Phillips, 1998).

Individuals' use of space also serves a communicative function. The distance people stand or sit from one another symbolizes physical or psychological closeness. For example, if you were sitting in an almost vacant theater and a stranger entered and proceeded to sit right next to you, how would you feel? If you are like many people in the United States, you might feel uncomfortable. On the other hand, if a longtime friend or your romantic partner walked into the theater and chose to sit rows away from you, how would you respond? You probably would be perplexed, perhaps even hurt or angry.

We respond to how close others sit or stand to us, because how much space we require to feel comfortable with others suggests how close or intimate we are them. That is, our physical closeness with others typically communicates our psychological closeness with them. Research by Edward T. Hall, a well-known anthropologist, has delineated four spheres or categories of space that reflect people's comfort and closeness with others (Hall, 1966). Let's take a look at each.

Intimate distance (zero to eighteen inches) tends to be reserved for those whom one knows very well. Typically, this distance is used for displaying physical and psychological intimacy, such as lovemaking, cuddling children, comforting someone, or telling secrets. **Personal distance** (eighteen to four feet) describes the space we use when interacting with friends and acquaintances. People in the United States often use the nearer distance for friends and the farther one for acquaintances, but cultures and personal preference strongly influence this choice. When others prefer closer distances than you do, you may find their closeness psychologically distressing; comedian Jerry Seinfeld has referred to these people as "close talkers." One of our students details her encounters with such a person in *It Happened to Me: Katarina*.

Social distance (four to twelve feet) is the distance most U.S. Americans use when they interact with unfamiliar others. Impersonal business with grocery clerks, sales clerks, and coworkers occurs at about four to seven feet, whereas the greatest distance is used in formal situations such as job interviews. **Public distance** (twelve to twenty-five feet) is most appropriate for public ceremonies such as lectures and performances, though an even greater distance may be maintained between public figures (such as politicians and celebrities) and their audiences.

One's culture, gender, relationship to others, and personality all influence whether one feels most comfortable at the near or far range of each of these spheres. In the United States, two unacquainted women typically sit or stand closer to each other than do two unacquainted men, whereas many men are more comfortable sitting or standing closer to unknown women than they are even to men they know (Burgoon & Guerrero, 1994). However, people in other cultures may prefer the closer ranges. Cultural disparities can result in a comedic cross-cultural "dance," where one person tries to get closer to the other and that person, made uncomfortable by the closeness, moves away.

What does the space between interactants in a given culture reveal? It can communicate intimacy or the lack of it; it also can communicate power and dominance. If person A feels free to enter person B's space without permission but refuses to allow B the same privilege, this lack of reciprocity communicates that A is dominant in the relationship. This situation is common between supervisors and subordinates and may exist in some parent–child relationships as well.

All humans, as well as animals, have strong feelings of territoriality. We exhibit territorial behavior when we attempt to claim control over a particular area. A primary way we attempt to claim and maintain control of a space is through personalization or marking, especially by use of artifacts. Thus, we alter spaces to make them distinctly our own through activities such as placing a fence around a residence or displaying family photos in an office. These markers are a form of nonverbal communication

intimate distance

(zero to eighteen inches) the space used when interacting with those with whom one is very close

personal distance

(eighteen inches to four feet) the space used when interacting with friends and acquaintances

social distance

(four to twelve feet) the distance most U.S. Americans use when they interact with unfamiliar others

public distance

(twelve to twenty-five feet) the distance used for public ceremonies such as lectures and performances

It Happened to Me

Katarina

I have a friend whom I like very much but who makes me really uncomfortable sometimes. She tends to lean in very close when she talks, especially if she has been drinking. One night, we were sitting together at a party. I sat in the corner of a couch while she leaned in to talk with me; I kept trying to pull my face away from hers while she talked until I was almost leaning over the back of the couch.

that specifies territorial ownership or legitimate occupancy (Becker, 1973). Markers function mainly to keep people away, thereby preventing confrontational social encounters. An unexpected manifestation of territoriality is described in *Did You Know? Space Invaders*.

Primary territories (areas under private control, such as houses and the bedrooms within them) serve as extensions of the owner's sense of identity, so markers there often include personally meaningful symbols reflecting the owner's style and taste (name plates, art objects, flower gardens). Public territories are less central to our self-concepts and, therefore, we tend to mark them with objects that are less personalized or that represent explicit claims to the space (for example, "reserved parking" signs). When someone violates a public territory, we tend to react with verbal retaliation, for example, asking the violator to leave. In contrast, we are likely to react strongly when someone violates our primary territory, for example, by seeking physical retaliation and legal sanctions (Abu-Ghazzeh, 2000).

haptics

the study of the communicative function of touch

It Happened to Me
Beth

I grew up in upper Michigan, where people rarely touch unless they know each other very well. Then I started working with a guy from the South. From the beginning, he touched me whenever we talked; he touched my arm, put his hand on my shoulder, or even put his arm on the back of my chair. This infuriated me! I thought he was being condescending and too familiar. Later, I realized that he does this with everybody. I understand he doesn't mean anything by it, but I still don't like it.

HAPTICS Although researchers in communication know that touch, or **haptics**, is important, it is among the least studied forms of nonverbal communication. Nonetheless, research does indicate that infants and

Did You Know?
Space Invaders

What do road rage, street harassment, and mob violence have in common? They all are responses to perceptions that one's space has been invaded.

Most articles on nonverbal communication and territory focus on how people "mark" their private and public spaces, such as when homeowners use fences to delineate their property lines or when students leave jackets on the seats they regularly occupy. Less often do we examine how invasions of space lead to anti-social behavior. However, like other animals, humans may respond aggressively when they believe their territory has been invaded.

A common type of space violation in the United Space occurs when one driver cuts off another driver. When an individual pulls into the lane ahead and causes them to slow down, some drivers become angry. They may engage in acts of road rage, such as chasing after the offender, driving them off of the road, or pulling a gun. Why would someone respond violently to a behavior that usually is only a minor inconvenience? People who do so typically have a strong sense of ownership over their cars and the spaces they occupy. They are likely to perceive that they have been disrespected and that the other person has willingly and arbitrarily invaded their territory. As a result, they feel the need to establish dominance over "their" space by responding aggressively.

Another regularly occurring response to perceived territory invasion is street harassment. Street harassment is a form of verbal or nonverbal harassment that has a sexual component. It is typified by debasing, objectifying, or threatening behavior designed to intimidate. Most women, and some gay men, have experienced it. How is this behavior a response to space invasions? Social control theory argues that street harassment is, at least in part, an effort on the part of some men to mark the public domain as their territory. In these cases, women without male partners are seen as violators of men's territory, and street harassment is viewed as a way to discourage them from intruding into this space alone (Lord, 2009). This behavior appears to be successful. A majority of women report that they have changed where they walk or live to avoid street harassment.

Yet another response to space intrusions is mob violence. You may have wondered why peaceful protests so often devolve into aggression. In part, they do so because as the group becomes more crowded, each person's zone of personal space become smaller, and as a result, people began to feel hostile. As the group continues to grow and personal space is rendered non-existent, individuals grow angrier and less civil, which can lead to violence. Even peaceful demonstrations can become disruptive, and angry ones can become lethal.

SOURCE: Lord, T. L. (2009). *The relationship of gender-based public harassment to body image, self-esteem, and avoidance behavior.* Unpublished dissertation. Ann Arbor, MI: ProQuest.

children need to be touched to be physically and psychologically healthy (Field, 2002). Also, although people vary considerably in how much or what type of touch they prefer, most enjoy being touched by those they care about. To understand how differences in preferences for touch affect relationships, see *It Happened to Me: Beth*.

Touch can be categorized into several general types (Givens, 2005), but people rarely notice the types unless a discrepancy occurs between their expectations and their experience. **Professional touch**, or **functional touch** is the least intimate; people who must touch others as part of their livelihood, such as medical and dental caregivers, hairstylists, and tailors, use this type of touch. Because touch often conveys intimacy, people who must use professional touch have to be careful of their interaction style; for example, they may adopt a formal or distant verbal communication style to counteract the intimacy of their touch. **Social-polite touch** is part of daily interaction. In the United States, this form of touch is more intimate than professional touch but is still impersonal. For example, many U.S. Americans shake hands when greeting acquaintances and casual friends, though in many European countries, such as France and Italy, hugging and kissing are appropriate forms of social touch. Even within the United States, people have different ideas about what types of touch are appropriate socially.

Friendship touch is more intimate than social touch and usually conveys warmth, closeness, and caring. Although considerable variation in touch may exist among friends, people typically use touch that is more intimate with close friends than with acquaintances or strangers. Examples include brief hugs, a hand on the shoulder, or putting one's arm loosely around another's waist or shoulders. **Love-intimate touch** most often is used with one's romantic partners and family. Examples are the long kisses and extended hugging and cuddling we tend to reserve for those with whom we are closest.

As is true of other forms of nonverbal communication, sex, culture, and power strongly influence patterns of touch. In the United States, heterosexual males are more likely to reserve hand-holding for their romantic partners and small children, whereas females touch other women more frequently and hold hands with older children, their close female relatives, and even female friends. In general, women tend to touch other women more frequently than men touch other men, and in cross-sex interactions, men are more likely to initiate touch than do women (Hall & Hall, 1990). However, in cross-sex interactions, the nature of the relationship influences touch behavior more than does the sex of the participants. Across all stages of heterosexual romantic relationships, partners reciprocate touch, so they do not differ in amount of touch (Guerrero & Andersen, 1991). However, men respond more positively to their partners' touch than do women (Hanzal, Segrin, & Dorros, 2008). In addition, men initiate touch more in casual romantic relationships, whereas women do so more often in married relationships (Guerrero & Andersen, 1994).

Each form of touch we have discussed thus far has a "positive" quality; but, of course, people also use touch to convey negative messages. For example, one study revealed that individuals (especially parents) use aggressive touch and withdrawal of affectionate touch with children to signal their displeasure (Guerrero & Ebesu, 1993). Aggressive touch can include grabbing, hitting, and pinching, whereas withdrawal of affection involves rejecting the touch attempts of others, as when one pushes another's arm away or refuses to hold hands. Both children and adults use aggressive touch with their peers as well, though in none of these instances is aggressive touch considered an appropriate or competent way to communicate.

Another type of touch that can be perceived negatively is **demand touching**, which is a type of touch used to establish dominance and power. Demand touching increases in hierarchical settings, such as at work. One significant characteristic of demand touching is that touchers typically have higher status and have more control over encounters than do receivers; this allows them more freedom of movement and

professional touch

type of touch used by certain workers, such as dentists, hairstylists, and hospice workers, as part of their livelihood; also known as *functional touch*

functional touch

the least intimate type of touch; used by certain workers such as dentists, hairstylists, and hospice workers, as part of their livelihood; also known as *professional touch*

social-polite touch

touch that is part of daily interaction in the United States; it is more intimate than professional touch but is still impersonal

friendship touch

touch that is more intimate than social touch and usually conveys warmth, closeness, and caring

love-intimate touch

the touch most often used with one's romantic partners and family

demand touching

a type of touch used to establish dominance and power

133

Demand touching is often used to establish dominance and power.

more visual contact. An everyday example of demand touch occurs when a supervisor stands behind a subordinate and leans over to provide directions, placing his or her hand on the subordinate's shoulder. The subordinate can't move easily or look directly at the supervisor, and the subordinate may feel both physically and psychologically constrained (Kemmer, 1992).

APPEARANCE AND ARTIFACTS In all cultures, individuals' appearance matters, as do their **artifacts**, or the clothing and other accessories they choose. Let's first consider appearance and how it operates as a nonverbal code.

In general, people's looks are believed to communicate something about them, and people develop expectations based on how others look. Hairstyle, skin color, height, weight, clothing, accessories such as jewelry, and other aspects of appearance all influence how we are perceived and how we perceive others. And in the United States, appearance is seen as especially important (Newport, 1999).

What is considered attractive, however, is influenced by one's culture and the time period in which one lives (Grammer, Fink, Joller, & Thornhill, 2003). Many people find it hard to believe that the Mona Lisa was considered a great beauty in her day, and even more people wonder who could ever have liked the clothes and hairstyles their own parents wore when they were young. Although the global village we live in now means the media transmit images that can be seen all over the world, cultures still vary in what they consider most attractive. The current ideal body type for women in the United States, as portrayed in the media, for example, is considered too thin and unfeminine by many African Americans (Duke, 2002). Although some American women get collagen injections to achieve full lips, our Japanese students tell us that such thick lips are not considered attractive in Japan. Some Europeans also dislike the defined musculature favored for males in magazines and television ads in the United States.

Ideals of what constitutes beauty differ according to time period, culture, class, and other factors.

In the United States, people invest considerable time, money, and energy adapting their appearance to cultural ideals of attractiveness. They diet, color and style their hair, frequent gyms and tanning booths, and even undergo extreme makeovers to be more attractive. People engage in all these efforts because the U.S. culture generally equates beauty with happiness, success, goodness, and desirability.

Although people face certain limits in reshaping their bodies and other physical attributes, they also have great flexibility in using clothing and other artifacts to convey important messages about themselves. In most business contexts, a suit is perceived to be authoritative and an indication of status. This is especially true of men; evaluations of their status often are based on their appearance and clothing (Mast & Hall, 2004). People also use artifacts to signal their occupations and identities. Nurses, flight attendants, and police officers wear uniforms to help others identify them and to send specific messages about their jobs (Gundersen, 1990). Thus, police officers wear paramilitary uniforms not only to allow us to easily identify them but also to reinforce their role in maintaining social order.

Individuals also choose their accessories and artifacts, such as purses, watches, jewelry, sunglasses, and even cars, to communicate specific messages about status, personality, success, or group membership. A student who carries a leather briefcase on campus creates a different image than one who carries a canvas backpack. On a typical college campus, it is fairly easy to differentiate the communication professors from the business professors and the engineering students from the theater majors based on their dress and artifacts. We might argue that in the United States, where it is not considered polite to announce one's status or success, people often use artifacts to make those announcements for them (Fussell, 1992).

As you can see from the preceding discussion, multiple categories of nonverbal behavior influence communication; these include kinesics, paralinguistics, chronemics and proxemics, haptics, and appearance and artifacts. These categories are, in turn, influenced by multiple individual and cultural factors. In the next section we explore how these categories work together to influence how we send and interpret messages.

What artifacts are important to you in terms of communicating your identity or status? If you had only one means of communicating high status, would you drive an expensive car, wear designer clothes, or live in an upscale neighborhood? What do you think your choice reflects about you?

The Functions of Nonverbal Messages

As mentioned previously, when people interpret nonverbal behaviors they don't isolate kinesics from haptics or proxemics from appearance; rather, they observe an integrated set of behaviors, consider the context and the individual, and then attribute meaning. If you see two people standing closely together in a public place, you wouldn't necessarily assume they were being intimate. Rather, you would examine how relaxed or tense their bodies appeared, evaluate their facial expressions and eye gaze, and consider the appropriateness of intimate displays in this public space (for example, a bar versus a church). Only then might you make an attribution about the meaning or function of the couple's behavior.

In general, scholars have determined that nonverbal behaviors serve five functions during interaction (Patterson, 1982, 2003). Those five functions are: communicating information, regulating interaction, expressing and managing intimacy, establishing social control, and signaling service-task functions. The most basic function is to communicate information, and this is the one we examine first.

COMMUNICATING INFORMATION   Most fundamentally, nonverbal messages are used to **communicate information**. From the receiver's point of view, much of a sender's behavior is potentially informative. For example, when you meet someone for the first time you evaluate the pattern of the sender's behavior to assess a variety of factors. First, you might evaluate the sender's general disposition to determine if it is warm and friendly or cool and distant. You likely will also assess her more fleeting nonverbal reactions to help you decide if she seems pleased to meet you or is just being polite. Finally, of course, you evaluate the person's verbal message. For example, does the speaker say, "I've really been looking forward to meeting you," or does she say, "I'd love to chat, but I've got to run"? You then combine all these pieces of information to ascribe meaning to the encounter.

communicating information
using nonverbal behaviors to help clarify verbal messages and reveal attitudes and motivation

Nonverbal communication helps individuals convey and interpret verbal messages. They can do this in five ways:

1. By repeating a message (winking while saying "I'm just kidding");
2. By highlighting or emphasizing a message (pointing at the door while saying "Get out!");
3. By complementing or reinforcing a message (whispering while telling a secret);
4. By contradicting a message (saying "I love your haircut" while speaking in a hostile tone and rolling one's eyes);
5. By substituting for a message (shaking one's head to indicate disagreement).

As these examples illustrate, using nonverbal communication effectively can make you a better *verbal* communicator.

REGULATING INTERACTION   Nonverbal communication also is used to **regulate interaction**. That is, people use nonverbal behaviors to manage turn-taking during conversation. Thus, if you want to start talking, you might lean forward, look at the current speaker, and even raise one finger. To reveal that you are finished with your

regulating interaction
using nonverbal behaviors to help manage conversational interaction

Various nonverbal behaviors regulate the interaction that occurs in a conversation.

expressing and managing intimacy

using nonverbal behaviors to help convey attraction and closeness

establishing social control

using nonverbal communication to exercise influence over other people

service-task functions

using nonverbal behavior to signal close involvement between people in impersonal relationships and contexts

Exercise trainers often use the service-task function of nonverbal communication.

turn, you may drop your volume and pitch, lean back, and look away from and then back toward the person you are "giving" your turn to. The regulating function tends to be the most automatic of the five, and most of us rarely think about it. The behaviors you use in this way include the more stable ones such as interpersonal distance, body orientation, and posture, as well as more fluid behaviors like gaze, facial expression, volume, and pitch, which are important in the smooth sequencing of conversational turns (Capella, 1985).

EXPRESSING AND MANAGING INTIMACY A third function of nonverbal communication, and the most studied, involves **expressing and managing intimacy**. The degree of your nonverbal involvement with another usually reflects the level of intimacy you desire with that person. If you meet someone new and notice your partner is leaning toward you, gazing into your eyes, nodding his head, and providing many paralinguistic cues such as "uh huh" as you talk, he is revealing a high degree of nonverbal involvement, which often signals attraction and interest. Of course, people can manipulate these behaviors to suggest attraction and involvement even if they are not experiencing these feelings. For example, in the workplace when subordinates talk with their supervisors, they often display fairly high levels of nonverbal involvement, regardless of their true feelings for their bosses.

ESTABLISHING SOCIAL CONTROL People also use nonverbal communication to exert or **establish social control**, or to exercise influence over other people. Individuals engage in the social control function when they smile at someone they want to do them a favor or when they glare at noisy patrons in a theater to encourage them to be quiet. You can use either positive or negative behaviors (or both) in your efforts to control others. People who are "charming" or very persuasive typically are extremely gifted at using nonverbal behavior to influence others.

When expressing and managing intimacy people tend to respond in similar, or reciprocal, ways to one another's nonverbal behavior. On the other hand, when engaging in social control, people tend to respond in complementary ways to one another's nonverbal behavior. To better understand the role of these responses in nonverbal interactions, see *Alternative View: Nonverbal Reciprocity or Nonverbal Complementarity?*

SIGNALING SERVICE-TASK FUNCTIONS Finally, nonverbal communication has a **service-task function**. Behaviors of this kind typically signal close involvement between people in impersonal relationships and contexts. For example, golf pros often stand with their arms around a novice golfer to help her with her golf swing, and massage therapists engage in intimate touch as part of their profession. In each of these cases, the behavior is appropriate, necessary, and a means to a (professional) end.

Accurately interpreting nonverbal messages is a complex endeavor, requiring awareness of a number of elements—factors that influence individuals' communication patterns, nonverbal communication codes and signals, and the communicative functions that nonverbal messages fulfill. However, in some senses, we have only shown you one piece of the picture, as we have thus far focused primarily on nonverbal communication as performed by individuals. In the next section, we expand the frame to explore how societal forces influence both the performance and interpretation of nonverbal messages and behavior.

Alternative View

Nonverbal Reciprocity or Nonverbal Complementarity?

Which of the following explanations seems more accurate to you? In what situations do you believe people are more likely to engage in nonverbal reciprocity? In nonverbal complementarity?

Nonverbal Reciprocity

Numerous studies provide evidence that many people unconsciously mimic their partner's postures, gestures, and other movements in social settings. Furthermore, this mimicry, or reciprocity, seems to increase liking and rapport between speakers. In turn, increased liking and rapport lead to more frequent mimicry. However, status or dominance affects who is likely to mimic whom. Lower status individuals are more likely to reciprocate the behaviors of higher status people, which may be unconsciously designed to increase liking and rapport (Chartrand & Bargh, 1999; Dijksterhuis & Smith, 2005).

Nonverbal Complementarity

A set of studies found that people respond to another's nonverbal power moves with complementary responses; that is, they respond to dominant behaviors with submissive ones and submissive behaviors with dominant ones (Tiedens & Fragale, 2003). Thus, if one person stares aggressively at another (a dominant behavior), the recipient of the stare is likely to look away (a submissive behavior). Furthermore, participants reported feeling comfortable with complementarity.

These studies specifically examined how people negotiate status in relationships with no prior hierarchy. Thus in groups and relationships in which everyone is on equal footing, the first dominant or submissive display by an individual may result from a random movement or a tactical strategy. Whatever the cause of the display, a hierarchical relationship can then result if an observer responds in a complementary fashion. Moreover, because people prefer to complement dominance with submissiveness, and vice versa, they are likely to promote that differentiation. Thus, nonverbal complementarity and the comfort associated with it may encourage hierarchical relationships and help maintain them. This phenomenon, then, may be one reason why hierarchies are so common and widespread.

Chartrand T. L., & Bargh J. A. (1999). The chameleon effect: The perception-behavior link and social interaction. *Journal of Personality and Social Psychology, 76,* 893–910.

Dijksterhuis, A., & Smith, P. K. (2005). What do we do unconsciously? And how? *Journal of Consumer Psychology 15*(3), 225–229.

Tiedens, L. Z., & Fragale, A. R. (2003). Power moves: Complementarity in dominant and submissive nonverbal behavior. *Journal of Personality and Social Psychology, 84,* 558–568.

4   The Individual, Nonverbal Communication, and Society

4   **Explain how nonverbal communication can both trigger and express prejudice and discrimination.**

Nonverbal communication, like all communication, is heavily influenced by societal forces and occurs within a hierarchical system of meanings. One's status and position within the societal hierarchy, as well as one's identity, are all expressed nonverbally. However, the more powerful elements in society often regulate these expressions. In addition, nonverbal communication can trigger and express prejudice and discrimination. Let's see how this operates.

Nonverbal Communication and Power

Nonverbal communication and power are intricately related—especially via the nonverbal codes of appearance and artifacts. In the United States, power is primarily based on an individual's access to economic resources and the freedom to make decisions that affect others. Economic resources are typically revealed or expressed through nonverbal codes. In spring 2014, style blogs commented on the $3,800 Chanel "graffiti" purse that Gwyneth Paltrow sported. Stylists found the beat up, deconstructed bag to be "hideous." So why would Patrow carry an expensive bag that most people agree is ugly? She likely did so because people display wealth through the clothing and accessories they wear (as well as the quality of their haircuts, and the value of their homes and cars). What better way is there to signal wealth than by showing that one has so many purses that one can afford to carry an expensive, unattractive bag on occasion? Whether one can afford to buy the latest designer fashions, or only to shop in discount stores, communicates clearly one's social class and power. English professor Paul Fussell (1992) provides an extensive description of how nonverbal messages communicated in our everyday lives reveal class standing. Consider, for example, the messages communicated by one's home. Fussell notes that the longer the driveway, the less obvious the garage, and the more manicured the grounds, the higher is one's socioeconomic class.

People use nonverbal cues to communicate their own status and identities, and to evaluate and interpret others' status and identities. Based on these interpretations, people—consciously and unconsciously—include and exclude others, and approve or disapprove of others. For example, in wealthy communities, people who don't look affluent may be stopped and questioned about their presence. (This practice was taken to its furthest extent when George Zimmerman confronted Trayvon Martin about his presence in his future stepmother's community.) More overtly, gated communities offer clear nonverbal messages about who belongs and who does not belong to a community. Of course, it isn't just the wealthy who use artifacts to convey their identity and belonging. Gang members, NASCAR fans, football fans, and many others also use attire as well as gestures to signal their individual and group identities.

The use of nonverbal cues to communicate social class extends beyond the use of appearance and artifacts. For example, psychology professors Michael Kraus and Dach Keltner (2009) examined individuals' use of nonverbal communication while interacting with a stranger. In these interactions they found that people with high socioeconomic status were more likely to display nonverbal signs of disengagement, such as doodling, and fewer signs of engagement, such as smiling and nodding, than people with lower socioeconomic status. In addition, people who observed these interactions could correctly guess the participants' social class from their nonverbal behavior. Thus, nonverbal communication reproduces—or recreates—the society and social classes in which we live.

The NBA issued rules governing NBA players' off-court dress to help shape the images they present to the public.

Although all groups use nonverbal communication to convey identity, more powerful segments of society typically define what is allowed. For example, many corporations have dress codes designed to communicate a particular professional image to the public. For the same reason, they may also have rules that regulate nonverbal expression of men's facial hair. The military and many police organizations have policies on tattoos as well (Zezima, 2005). Because these organizations are hierarchical, the decisions made by those in power in the organization must be followed by those who wish employment there.

In 2005, the National Basketball Association issued rules governing the off-court dress of NBA players: They are to dress in "business casual" whenever engaged in team or league business, and they are specifically excluded from wearing sleeveless shirts, shorts, T-shirts, headgear of any kind, chains, pendants, and sunglasses while indoors. See http://worklaw.jotwell.com/does-the-nbas-dress.code-violate-title-vii/ for more information on this topic. Through these dictums, the organization is attempting to regulate not only the players' clothing, but also their expression of their identities. Of course, not all players support these regulations (Wise, 2005). Some NBA players feel that the ban on chains and other jewelry was racially motivated. In short, this new policy "called attention to a generational chasm between modern professional athletes, many of whom are Black, and their mostly White paying customers" (Wise, 2005, p. A-1).

The number and range of dress codes and regulations on appearance underscore the powerful impact that nonverbal cues can have. The more powerful segments of society also define what is most desirable and attractive in our culture. For example, cosmetic corporations spend $231 billion annually on the development of beauty products and advertising to persuade consumers to buy them. The largest cosmetic companies have expanded to China where the nation's 451 million women are of great interest to the cosmetics market—which doubled to $8 billion between 2001 and 2006 (Carvajal, 2006). The media broadly communicate to us the definitions of beauty. This is why many U.S. Americans believe that blonde hair is better than brown, thin is better than fat, large breasts are better than small, and young is better than old—beliefs that are not shared universally. Messages promoting a specific type of youth and beauty might seem rather harmless, until one considers the consequences for those who are not thin and blonde, especially those who have no possibility of meeting the dominant standards of beauty. How does this hierarchy of attractiveness affect their communication with others? Do people respond to them negatively because of their appearance? Might they feel marginalized and resentful—even before they interact with others who more clearly meet the dominant standards?

Nonverbal expressions also are an important part of cultural rituals involving societal expectations. For example, in U.S. culture it is traditionally considered unacceptable to wear white to a wedding unless one is the bride, whereas black or other dark colors are considered appropriate to wear to funerals. Aspects of dress are important in the United States at other cultural events, particularly for women. The outfits worn to the Academy Awards and other "show business" honor ceremonies are reviewed and evaluated and are a topic of great interest for many people. Similarly, what the president's wife wears on Inauguration Day and at subsequent parties is a subject of conversation; in fact, the First Lady's wardrobe is discussed and critiqued every day on TV, in blogs, and in magazines. The interest (and evaluation) of these nonverbal expressions, such as clothing, is driven by societal forces. In all of these cases, women know that their nonverbal messages will be carefully scrutinized and evaluated.

Nonverbal Communication, Prejudice, and Discrimination

At the intersection of societal forces and nonverbal communication are prejudice and discrimination. Both can be triggered by nonverbal behavior and are also expressed through nonverbal behavior. Let's look at how this works. First, one's race and ethnicity, body shape, age, or style of dress—all of which are communicated nonverbally—can prompt prejudgment or negative stereotypes. How often do people make a snap judgment or generalization based on appearance? Second, prejudice and discrimination are expressed nonverbally. In some extreme cases, nonverbal signals have even triggered and perpetrated hate crimes. For example, one night in Phoenix, Arizona, Avtar (Singh) Chiera, a small-business owner and a Sikh, waited outside his business for his son to pick him up. Two White men pulled up in a small red pickup truck, yelled at him, and then opened fire on him. Because of anger over the events of 9/11, the two men likely targeted him as an

This antigroping sign from Japan illustrates a common problem in many parts of the world. What are the ethical issues in this nonverbal behavior?

Arab because of his turban and beard, even though Sikhs are neither Arab nor Muslim (Parasuram, 2003). In this encounter, nonverbal messages were the most important; the words spoken (if any) were of minimal impact.

Although the example of the shooting of Chiera is extreme, there are many other more subtle ways that prejudice can be communicated nonverbally—for instance, averting one's gaze or failing to reciprocate a smile. It can be as subtle as shifting your gaze, leaning your body away, or editing your speech. Sociologist A. G. Johnson (2001, pp. 58–59) gives a list of specific nonverbal behaviors that can be interpreted as prejudicial. These are mostly noticed only by the person experiencing them and often happen unconsciously and unintentionally:

- Not looking at people when we talk with them;
- Not smiling at people when they walk into the room, or staring as if to say, "What are you doing here?" or stopping the conversation with a hush they have to wade through to be included in the smallest way;
- Not acknowledging people's presence or making them wait as if they weren't there;
- Not touching their skin when we give them something;
- Watching them closely to see what they're up to;
- Avoiding someone walking down the street, giving them wide berth, or even crossing to the other side.

Given the potential consequences of nonverbal communication, you may find it helpful to consider how your nonverbal communication reflects your own ethical stance. To guide you in making appropriate and ethical choices, in the next section we explore the ethics of nonverbal communication.

5   Ethics and Nonverbal Communication

5   Delineate six guidelines for ethical nonverbal communication.

The ethics of nonverbal communication are actually quite similar to the ethics of communication in general. When people engage in behavior such as deceiving or threatening others or name-calling, their nonverbal behavior typically plays a central role in their messages. For instance, liars use nonverbal behavior to avoid "leaking" the deception, and they may also use it to convey the deceptive message. Moreover, deceivers may feel that lying nonverbally—for example, by remaining silent—is less "wrong" than lying with words. In the Old Testament, Joseph's brothers were jealous of their father's affection for him, so they sold Joseph into slavery. When they returned without him, however, they didn't "tell" their father what happened; instead they gave him Joseph's bloody coat and let their father draw the conclusion that wild animals had killed Joseph. In this way, they deceived their father without actually speaking a lie. What do you think? Is it better, or less unethical, to lie nonverbally than it is to do so verbally?

When communicators use nonverbal cues that ridicule, derogate, or otherwise demean others, they run the risk of their behavior being viewed by others as unethical. For example, if someone speaks in a patronizing vocal tone, screams at the less powerful, or touches others inappropriately, would you view this behavior as unethical? What if people respond to others' communication in a way that misrepresents how they actually feel? For instance, if they laugh at a racist or sexist joke even though they dislike it, would you see that behavior as unethical?

Because these are the types of decisions you have to make routinely throughout your life, here are some guidelines for ethical nonverbal communication to help you make those decisions. Consider whether:

- your nonverbal behaviors reflect your real attitudes, beliefs, and feelings;
- your nonverbal behaviors contradict the verbal message you are sending;
- your nonverbal behaviors insult, ridicule, or demean others;
- you are using your nonverbal behavior to intimidate, coerce, or silence someone;
- you would want anyone to observe your nonverbal behavior;
- you would want this nonverbal behavior directed to you or a loved one.

Although there is no litmus test for evaluating the ethics of every nonverbal message in every situation, if you keep these guidelines in mind, they will help you make better, more informed decisions.

6 Improving Your Nonverbal Communication Skills

6 Name five ways to improve your ability to interpret nonverbal behaviour.

By now you may be wondering how to decide what a set of behaviors means. How do you decide, for example, if your sports coach's touch is appropriately intimate (service-task) or just intimate? In the workplace, how can you determine whether your subordinate genuinely likes you and your ideas (nonverbal involvement) or is merely trying to flatter you (social control)?

One way you can assess your own and others' nonverbal communication is to examine how it interacts with verbal messages (Jones & LeBaron, 2002). That is, how congruent (similar) are the two sets of messages? When the two types of messages are **congruent**, they are often genuine (or we assume them to be so). For example, a positive verbal message ("I like you") combined with a positive nonverbal message (smile, forward body lean, relaxed posture) usually conveys a convincing positive message. However, it is also possible that people who are good at deception are able to offer congruent messages while lying, and those who are less adept at communicating may unintentionally offer contradictory messages when telling the truth. Given all of this, what other factors could you rely on to help you decide whether a congruent message is truthful?

Of course, verbal and nonverbal messages can also purposely **contradict** one another. When using sarcasm, people intentionally combine a positive verbal message ("what a nice pair of shoes") with a contradictory or negative nonverbal message (a hostile tone). However, at other times people offer contradictory messages unintentionally or carelessly. Caretakers often confuse children (and encourage misbehavior) by telling a child to stop a particular behavior while smiling or laughing. How does a child interpret this message? Most children will accept the nonverbal aspect of the message and ignore the verbal (Eskritt & Lee, 2003.)

In addition to assessing the congruence of the verbal and nonverbal components of a message, you improve your comprehension of nonverbal messages by analyzing the context, your knowledge of the other person, and your own experiences. For example, if you are playing basketball and a teammate slaps you on the rear and says "good going," the message may be clear. Given the context, you may read it as a compliment and perhaps a sign of affection or intimacy. But what if the slap on the rear occurs at work after an effective presentation? Given that such behavior is generally

congruent
verbal and nonverbal messages that express the same meaning

contradicting
verbal and nonverbal messages that send conflicting messages

The meaning of this nonverbal behavior is strongly affected by the context.

inappropriate in a business context, you probably will (and should) more closely assess its meaning. You might ask yourself whether this person simply lacks social skills and frequently engages in inappropriate behavior. If so, the message may be inappropriate but still be meant in a positive fashion. In contrast, if the person knows better and has touched you inappropriately at other times, the behavior may be intentionally designed to express inappropriate intimacy or social control.

Here are a few more suggestions to keep in mind:

- Recognize that others' nonverbal messages don't always mean the same as yours.
- Be aware of individual, contextual, and cultural factors that influence meaning.
- Ask for additional information if you don't understand a nonverbal message or if you perceive a contradiction between the verbal and nonverbal messages.
- Remember that not every nonverbal behavior is intended to be communicative.
- Don't place too much emphasis on fleeting nonverbal behaviors such as facial expression or vocal tone; rather, examine the entire set of nonverbal behaviors.

Summary

Nonverbal messages are an important component of communication. They help you interpret and understand verbal messages and, in doing so, help you more effectively navigate your everyday life. Studying nonverbal communication is particularly important because it is complex and ambiguous.

Nonverbal communication is defined as all the messages that people transmit through means other than words. To understand the meaning of a nonverbal messages, you have to consider the entire behavioral context, including culture, relationship type, background knowledge, and gender. Nonverbal communication occurs through five codes or types of signals: kinesics, paralinguistics (vocal qualities), chronemics and proxemics (time and space), haptics (touch), and appearance and artifacts. These codes can combine to serve one of five functions, such as communicating information, regulating interaction, expressing and managing intimacy, exerting social control, and performing service-task functions.

Power relationships as well as societal norms and rules influence the range of nonverbal behaviors we are allowed to perform and how those behaviors are interpreted. In addition, everyone needs to be aware that nonverbal communication can trigger and express prejudice and discrimination. Thus, nonverbal communication has ethical aspects one must consider when composing one's messages.

You can become more effective in interpreting others' nonverbal communication by assessing the congruence of the verbal and nonverbal components of a message; analyzing the context, your knowledge of the other person, and your own experiences; recognizing that others' nonverbal messages don't always mean the same as yours do; asking for additional information if you don't understand a nonverbal message; and remembering that not every nonverbal behavior is intended to be communicative.

Key Terms

nonverbal communication
nonverbal behavior
nonverbal codes
kinesics
gestures
illustrators
emblems
adaptors
regulators
immediacy
relaxation
paralinguistics
voice qualities

vocalizations
chronemics
proxemics
monochronically
polychronically
intimate distance
personal distance
social distance
public distance
haptics
professional touch
functional touch
social-polite touch

friendship touch
love-intimate touch
demand touching
artifacts
communicating information
regulating interaction
expressing and managing
  intimacy
establishing social control
service-task functions
congruent
contradicting

Apply What You Know

1. **Waiting Times** How long is the "appropriate" amount of time you should wait in each of the following situations? Specifically, after how long a period would you begin to feel angry or put out? Estimate waiting times for:

   a. your dentist
   b. a checkout line in a department store
   c. a movie line
   d. a friend at lunch
   e. a friend at dinner
   f. being on hold on the telephone
   g. your professor to arrive at class
   h. a stop light
   i. your romantic partner at a bar
   j. your professor during office hours.

   Do you see any patterns in your expectations for waiting times? What influences your expectations most—your relationship with the other party? The comfort of the waiting area? Your ability to control events? Compare your waiting times with others' to see how similar or different they are.

2. **Violating Norms for Proximity** For this exercise we would like you to violate some of the norms for spacing in your culture. Try standing slightly closer to a friend or family member than you normally would, then note how they react. If you have a romantic partner or very close friend, sit much farther from them than you normally would. For example, in a theater, sit one seat away from him or her, or sit at the opposite end of the couch if you would typically sit closer. Pay attention to the reactions you elicit. Finally, when talking with an acquaintance, increase the distance between you each time the other person tries to decrease it and see how the other person responds. What do these responses to your space violations reveal to you regarding the importance of spacing norms in the United States?

   NOTE: Be careful in your selection of people with whom you violate norms of space, and be prepared to explain why you are behaving so oddly.

Explore

1. Go to a Web site such as Michigan State University's Presidential Audio Recordings or Archer Audio Archives and compare the vocal qualities of four presidents—two presidents who served before the widespread use of television and two who have served since. What role do you think vocal versus visual cues played in the popularity of each president? Are there presidents whose appearance you find more appealing than their vocal qualities? Are there presidents whose vocal qualities you find more appealing than their appearance?

2. The study of facial expressions of emotion is complex and ongoing. Recently, researchers have begun studying the effect of Botox (which paralyzes facial muscles) on facial expressions and emotional response. Go to a Web site such as PsychCentral's *Facial Expressions Control Emotions* or WebMD's *Botox May Affect Ability to Feel Emotions* and read the articles. Based on what you read, write a brief paper in which you hypothesize how the use of Botox could affect interpersonal interaction.

Glossary

adaptors gestures used to manage emotions

artifacts clothing and other accessories

chronemics the study of the way people use time as a message

communicating information using nonverbal behaviors to help clarify verbal messages and reveal attitudes and moods

congruent verbal and nonverbal messages that express the same meaning

contradicting verbal and nonverbal messages that send conflicting messages

demand touching a type of touch used to establish dominance and power

emblems gestures that stand for a specific verbal meaning

establishing social control using nonverbal behavior to exercise influence over other people

expressing and managing intimacy using nonverbal behaviors to help convey attraction and closeness

friendship touch touch that is more intimate than social touch and usually conveys warmth, closeness, and caring

functional touch the least intimate type of touch; used by certain workers, such as dentists, hairstylists, and

143

hospice workers, as part of their livelihood; also known as *professional touch*

gestures nonverbal communication made with part of the body, including actions such as pointing, waving, or holding up a hand to direct people's attention

haptics the study of the communicative function of touch

illustrators signals that accompany speech to clarify or emphasize the verbal messages

immediacy how close or involved people appear to be with each other

intimate distance (zero to 18 inches) the space used when interacting with those with whom one is very close

kinesics nonverbal communication sent by the body, including gestures, posture, movement, facial expressions, and eye behavior

love-intimate touch the touch most often used with one's romantic partners and family

monochronically engaging in one task or behavior at a time

nonverbal behavior all the nonverbal actions people perform

nonverbal codes distinct, organized means of expression that consists of symbols and rules for their use

nonverbal communication nonverbal behavior that has symbolic meaning

paralinguistics all aspects of spoken language except the words themselves; includes rate, volume, pitch, stress

personal distance (eighteen inches to four feet) the space used when interacting with friends and acquaintances

polychronically engaging in multiple activities simultaneously

professional touch type of touch used by certain workers, such as dentists, hairstylists, and hospice workers, as part of their livelihood; also known as *functional touch*

proxemics the study of how people use spatial cues, including interpersonal distance, territoriality, and other space relationships, to communicate

public distance (12 to 25 feet) the distance used for public ceremonies such as lectures and performances

regulating interaction using nonverbal behaviors to help manage turn-taking during conversation

regulators gestures used to control conversation

relaxation the degree of tension displayed by one's body

service-task functions using nonverbal behavior to signal close involvement between people in impersonal relationships and contexts

social distance (4 to 12 feet) the distance most Americans use when they interact with unfamiliar others

social-polite touch touch that is part of daily interaction in the United States; it is more intimate than professional touch but is still impersonal

vocalizations uttered sounds that do not have the structure of language

voice qualities qualities such as speed, pitch, rhythm, vocal range, and articulation that make up the "music" of the human voice

---

References

Abu-Ghazzeh, T. M. (2000). Environmental messages in multiple family housing: Territory and personalization. *Landscape Research, 25*, 97–114.

Als, H. (1977). The newborn communicates. *Journal of Communication, 2*, 66–73.

Axtell, R. (1993). *Do's and taboos around the world.* New York: Wiley.

Becker, F. D. (1973). Study of special markers. *Journal of Personality and Social Psychology, 26*, 429–445.

Birdwhistell, R. L. (1985). *Kinesics and context: Essays in body motion communication.* Philadelphia: University of Philadelphia Press.

Boone, R. T., & Cunningham, J. G. (1998). Children's decoding of emotion in expressive body movement: The development of cue attunement. *Developmental Psychology, 34*, 1007–1016.

Briton, N. J., & Hall, J. A. (1995). Beliefs about female and male nonverbal communication. *Sex Roles, 32*, 79–90.

Burgoon, J. K., & Guerrero, L. K. (1994). Nonverbal communication. In M. Burgoon, F. G. Hunsaker, & E. J. Dawson (Eds.), *Human communication* (pp. 122–171). Thousand Oaks, CA: Sage.

Burgoon, J. K., & Hale, J. L. (1988). Nonverbal expectancy violations: Model elaboration and application to immediacy behaviors. *Communication Monographs, 55*, 58-79.

Burgoon, J. K., & Le Poire, B. A. (1993). Effects of Communication expectancies, actual communication, and expectancy disconfirmation on evaluations of communicators and their communication behavior. *Human Communication Research, 20*(1), 67-96.

Burgoon, J. K., Buller, D. B., & Woodall, W. G. (1996). *Nonverbal communication: The unspoken dialogue.* New York: Harper & Row.

Capella, J. (1985). The management of conversations. In M. L. Knapp & G. R. Miller (Eds.), *Handbook of* interpersonal communication (pp. 393–435). Beverly Hills, CA: Sage.

Carvajal, D. (2006, February 7). Primping for the cameras in the name of research. *New York Times.* Retrieved February 23, 2006, from: http://www.nytimes.com/2006/02/07/business/07hair.html?ex=1139979600&en=f5f94cb9d81a9fa8&ei=5070&emc=eta1.

Chartrand T. L., & Bargh J. A. (1999). The chameleon effect: The perception-behavior link and social interaction. *Journal of Personality and Social Psychology, 76,* 893–910.

Chiang, L. H. (1993, October). Beyond the language: Native Americans' nonverbal communication. Paper presented at the Annual Meeting of the Midwest Association of Teachers of Educational Psychology, Anderson, IN: October 1–2.

Cicca, A. H., Step, M., & Turkstra, L. (2003, December 16). Show me what you mean: Nonverbal communication theory and application. *ASHA Leader, 34,* 4–5.

Dié, L. (2008, November, 9). Obama: Speech patterns analyzed. *News Flavor: U. S. Politics.* Retrieved May 31, 2011, from: http://newsflavor.com/category/politics/us-politics/.

Dijksterhuis, A., & Smith, P. K. (2005). What do we do unconsciously? And how? *Journal of Consumer Psychology 15*(3), 225–229.

Duke, L. (2002). Get real! Cultural relevance and resistance to the mediated feminine ideal. *Psychology and Marketing, 19,* 211–234.

Eibl-Eibesfeld, I. (1972). Similarities and differences between cultures in expressive movement. In R. A. Hinde (Ed.), *Nonverbal communication* (pp. 297–314). Cambridge: Cambridge University Press.

Ekman, P. (2003). *Emotions revealed: Recognizing faces and feelings to improve communication and emotional life.* New York: Times Books.

Ekman, P., & Friesen, W. V. (1969). The repertoire of nonverbal behavior: Categories, origins, usage and coding. *Semiotica, 1,* 49–98.

Ekman, P., & Friesen, W. V. (1986). A new pan-cultural expression of emotion. *Motivation and Emotion, 10*(2), 159–168.

Elfenbein, H. A. (2006). Learning in emotion judgments: Teaching and the cross-cultural understanding of facial expressions. *Journal of Nonverbal Communication, 30,* 21–36.

Elfenbein, H. A., Maw, D. F., White, J., Tan, H. H., & Aik, V. C. (2007). Reading your counter-part: The benefit of emotion recognition accuracy for effectiveness in negotiation. *Journal of Nonverbal Behavior, 31,* 205–223.

Eskritt, M., & Lee, K. (2003) Do actions speak louder than words? Preschool children's use of the verbal-nonverbal consistency principle during inconsistent communication. *Journal of Nonverbal Behavior, 27,* 25–41.

Field, T. (2002). Infants' need for touch. *Human Development, 45,* 100–104.

Fussell, P. (1992). *Class: A guide through the American status system.* New York: Touchstone Books.

Givens, D. B. (2005). *The nonverbal dictionary of gestures, signs, and body language cues.* Spokane, WA: Center for Nonverbal Studies Press.

Grammer, K., Fink, B., Joller, A., & Thornhill, R. (2003). Darwinian aesthetics: Sexual selection and the biology of beauty. *Biological Reviews, 78,* 385–408.

Guerrero, L. K., & Andersen, P. A. (1991). The waxing and waning of relational intimacy: Touch as a function of relational stage, gender, and touch avoidance. *Journal of Social and Personal Relationships, 8,* 147–165.

Guerrero, L. K., & Andersen, P. A. (1994). Patterns of matching and initiation: Touch behavior and touch avoidance across romantic relationship stages. *Journal of Nonverbal Behavior, 18,* 137–153.

Guerrero, L. K., & Ebesu, A. S. (1993, May). While at play: An observational analysis of children's touch during interpersonal interaction. Paper presented at the annual conference of the International Communication Association, Washington, D.C.

Gundersen, D. F. (1990). Uniforms: Conspicuous invisibility. In J. A. Devito & M. L. Hecht (Eds.), *The nonverbal communication reader* (pp. 172–178). Prospect Heights, IL: Waveland.

Hall, E. T. (1966). *The hidden dimension.* New York: Doubleday.

Hall, E. T. (1983). *The dance of life.* Garden City, NY: Doubleday.

Hall, E. T., & Hall, M. R. (1987). *Hidden differences: Doing business with the Japanese.* Garden City, NY: Anchor.

Hall, E. T., & Hall, M. R. (1990). *Understanding cultural differences: Germans, French and Americans.* Yarmouth, ME: Intercultural Press.

Hanzal, A., Segrin, C., & Dorros, S. M. (2008). The role of marital status and age on men's and women's reactions to touch from a relational partner. *Journal of Nonverbal Behavior, 32,* 21–35.

Isaacson, L. A. (1998). Student dress codes. *ERIC Digest, 117.* Retrieved June 15, 2006, from: http://eric.uoregon.edu/publications/digests/digest117.html.

Johnson, A. G. (2001). *Privilege, power, and difference.* Boston: McGraw-Hill.

Jones, S. E., & LeBaron, C. D. (2002). Research on the relationship between verbal and nonverbal communication: Emerging integration. *Journal of Communication, 52,* 499–521.

Kemmer, S. (1992). Are we losing our touch? *Total Health, 14,* 46–49.

Knapp, M. L., & Hall, J. A. (1992). *Nonverbal communication in human interaction* (3rd ed.). New York: Holt, Rinehart and Winston.

Knapp, M. L., & Hall, J. A. (2001). *Nonverbal communication in human interaction.* Belmont, CA: Wadsworth.

Koerner, A., & Fitzpatrick, M.A. (2002). Nonverbal communication and marital adjustment and satisfaction: The role of decoding relationship relevant and relationship irrelevant affect. *Communication Monographs, 68*(1), 33–51.

Kraus, M., & Keltner, D. (2009). Signs of socio-economic status: A thin-slicing approach. *Psychological Science, 20,* 99–106.

Lord, T. L. (2009). *The relationship of gender-based public harassment to body image, self-esteem, and avoidance behavior.* Unpublished dissertation. Ann Arbor, MI: ProQuest.

Manusov, V. (1995). Reacting to changes in nonverbal behaviors: Relational satisfaction and adaptation patterns in romantic dyads. *Human Communication Research, 21,* 456–477.

Manusov, V., & Patterson, M. (2006). *Handbook of nonverbal communication.* Thousand Oaks, CA: Sage

Mast, M. S., & Hall, J. A. (2004). Who is the boss and who is not? Accuracy of judging status. *Journal of Nonverbal Behavior, 28,* 145–165.

Matsumoto, D. (2006). Culture and nonverbal behavior. In V. Manusov & M. Patters (Eds.). *Handbook of nonverbal communication* (pp. 219–235), Thousand Oaks, CA: Sage.

Mehrabian, A. (1971). *Nonverbal communication.* Chicago: Aldine-Atherton.

Mehrabian, A. (2007). *Nonverbal communication.* Chicago, IL: Aldine de Gruyter.

Mehrabian, A., & Weiner, M. (1967). Decoding of inconsistent communication. *Journal of Personality and Social Psychology, 6,* 109–-104.

Meltzoff, A. N., & Prinz, W. (2002). *The imitative mind: Development, evolution, and brain bases.* Cambridge, England: Cambridge University Press.

Montepare, J. M., Goldstein, S. B., & Clausen, A. (1987). The identification of emotions from gait information. *Ethology and Sociobiology, 6,* 237–247.

Newport, F. (1999). Americans agree that being attractive is a plus in American society. Gallup Poll Monthly, 408, 45–49.

Parasuram, T. V. (2003, October 23). Sikh shot and injured in Arizona hate crime. *Sikh Times.* Retrieved February 24, 2006, from: http://www.sikhtimes.com/news_052103a.html.

Patterson, M. L. (1982). A sequential functional model of nonverbal exchange. *Psychological Bulletin, 89,* 231–249.

Patterson, M. L. (1983). *Nonverbal behavior.* New York: Springer.

Patterson, M. L. (2003). Commentary. Evolution and nonverbal behavior: Functions and mediating processes. *Journal of Nonverbal Behavior, 27,* 201–207.

Phillips, J. (1998). Personal space in a virtual community. In Carat, C. M., & Lund, A. (Eds.)., *Summary of the Conference in Human Factors in Computing Systems,* (347–348). New York: ACM.

Richards, V., Rollerson, B., & Phillips, J. (1991). Perceptions of submissiveness: Implications for victimization. *Journal of Psychology, 125*(4), 407–411.

Richeson, J. A., & Shelton, J. N. (2005). Brief report: Thin slices of racial bias. *Journal of Nonverbal Behavior, 29,* 75–86.

Samovar, L. & Porter, R. (2004). *Communication between cultures.* Thomson, Wadsworth.

Schwartz, L. M., Foa, U. G., & Foa, E. B. (1983) Multichannel nonverbal communication: Evidence for combinatory rules. *Journal of Personality and Social Psychology, 45,* 274–281.

Segerstrale, U., & Molnár, P. (1997). (Eds.), *Nonverbal communication: Where nature meets culture* (pp. 27–46). Mahwah, NJ: Erlbaum.

Shelp, S. (2002). Gaydar: Visual detection of sexual orientation among gay and straight men. *Journal of Homosexuality, 44,* 1–14.

Tiedens, L., & Fragale, A. (2003). "Power moves: Complementarity in dominant and submissive nonverbal behavior." *Journal of Personality and Social Psychology, 84,* 558–568.

Trost, M. R., & Alberts, J. K. (2009). How men and women communicate attraction: An evolutionary view In D. Canary & K. Dindia (Eds.), *Sex, gender and communication: Similarities and differences* (2nd ed, pp, 317–336). Mahwah, NJ: Lawrence Erlbaum

Watson, O., & Graves, T. (1966). Quantitative research in proxemic behavior. *American Anthropologist, 68,* 971–985.

Wise, T. (2005, October 23). Opinions on NBA dress code are far from uniform. *Washington Post,* p. A01. Retrieved February 24, 2006, from: http://www.washingtonpost.com/wp-dyn/content/article/2005/10/22/AR2005102201386.html.

Wolburg, J. M. (2001). Preserving the moment, commodifying time, and improving upon the past: Insights into the depiction of time in American advertising. *Journal of Communication, 51,* 696–720.

Young, R. L. (1999). *Understanding misunderstandings.* Austin: University of Texas Press.

Zezima, K. (2005, December 3). Military, police now more strict on tattoos. *The San Diego Union-Tribune.* Retrieved February 22, 2006, from: http://www.signonsandiego.com/uniontrib/20051203/news_1n3tattoo.html.

Credits

Photo Credits

Credits are listed in order of appearance.

Photo 1: Denys kuvaiev/Fotolia

Photo 2: Claudia Wiens/Alamy

Photo 3: Steve Skjold/Alamy

Photo 4: Alen-D/Fotolia

Photo 5: J.P. Wilson/Icon SMI 320/J.P. Wilson/Icon SMI/ Newscom

Photo 6: Magann/Fotolia

Photo 7: Burlingham/Fotolia

Photo 8: Sylvie Bouchard/Fotolia

Photo 9: Robert Kneschke/Shutterstock

Photo 10: Mark Cuthbert/ABACAUSA.COM/Newscom

Photo 11: Photos.com/Jupiterimages/Getty Images

Photo 12: AISPIX by Image Source/Shutterstock

Photo 13: RIA Novosti/Alamy

Photo 14: Andrew D. Bernstein/NBAE/Getty Images

Photo 15: TWPhoto/Corbis

Photo 16: DAVE KAUP/AFP/Newscom

Text and Art Credits

Isaacson, L. A. (1998). Student dress codes. ERIC Digest, 117. Retrieved June 15, 2006, from http://eric.uoregon. edu/publications/digests/digest117.html

Manusov, V., & Patterson, M. (2006). Handbook of nonverbal communication. Thousand Oaks, CA: Sage.

Based on, Birdwhistell, R. L. (1985). Kinesics and context: Essays in body motion communication. Philadelphia: University of Philadelphia Press. Mehrabian, A. (1971, 2007). Nonverbal communication. Chicago, IL: Aldine de Gruyter. Mehrabian, A., & Weiner, M. (1967). Decoding of inconsistent communication. Journal of Personality and Social Psychology, 6, 109–104.

Abbad

Trost, M. R., & Alberts, J. K. (2006). How men and women communicate attraction: An evolutionary view In
D. Canary & K. Dindia (Eds.) Sex, gender and communication: Similarities and differences 2nd ed, (pp, 317–336). Mahwah, NJ: Lawrence Erlbaum.

Burgoon, J. K., & Hale, J. L. (1988). Nonverbal expectancy violations: Model elaboration and application to immediacy behaviors. Communication Monographs, 55, 58–79. Burgoon, J. K., & Le Poire, B. A. (1993). Effects of Communication expectancies, actual communication, and expectancy disconfirmation on evaluations of communicators and their communication behavior. Human Communication Research, 20(1), 67–96.

Katarina

Beth

Lord, T. L. (2009). The relationship of gender-based public harassment to body image, self-esteem, and avoidance behavior. Unpublished dissertation. Ann Arbor, MI: ProQuest.

Based on, Chartrand T. L., & Bargh J. A. (1999). The chameleon effect: The perception-behavior link and social interaction. Journal of Personality and Social Psychology, 76, 893–910. Dijksterhuis, A., & Smith, P. K. (2005). What do we do unconsciously? And how? Journal of Consumer Psychology 15(3), 225–229. Tiedens, L. Z., & Fragale, A. R. (2003). Power moves: Complementarity in dominant and submissive nonverbal behavior. Journal of Personality and Social Psychology, 84, 558–568.

Wise, T. (2005, October 23). Opinions on NBA dress code are far from uniform. Washington Post, p. A01. Retrieved February 24, 2006, from http://www.washingtonpost.com/wp-dyn/content/article/2005/10/AR2005102201386.html

Johnson, A. G. (2001). Privilege, power, and difference. Boston: McGraw-Hill.

Listening and Responding

From Chapter 7 of *Human Communication in Society*, Fourth Edition. Jess K. Alberts, Thomas K. Nakayama, Judith N. Martin.
Copyright © 2016 by Pearson Education, Inc. All rights reserved.

Listening and Responding

CHAPTER TOPICS		Chapter Objectives
The Importance of Listening	1	Identify six reasons why listening is important.
What is Listening? Four Stages	2	Describe the four stages of listening.
Listening and the Individual: Influences and Barriers	3	Describe the influences on listening and barriers to effective listening.
The Individual, Listening, and Society: Hierarchy, Contexts, and Community	4	Understand the role of societal forces (hierarchy, contexts, and community) in listening.
Ethics and Listening	5	Describe ethical challenges in listening.
Improving Your Listening Skills	6	Discuss two ways to improve your own listening behavior.

"Listening retains its position as the most widely used daily communication activity."

Charee wonders if her listening skills are deteriorating. After taking a class in communication and learning about both bad listening habits and effective strategies for listening, she realized that she often doesn't listen to what others are saying because she's busy thinking of the next thing she's going to say. She also started thinking about the impact of what her professor calls "chronic earbud attachment syndrome"—the "addiction" that she and many of her fellow students have to their earbuds. Although this doesn't impact their *ability* to listen, she thinks it probably affects their *opportunities* to listen, perhaps meaning she misses out on little things that humans hear throughout the day that help make sense of the world and maybe also sends a negative message to others. She thinks about the fact that in the past if she entered an elevator with her professor, she would have to converse or stand in silence. Now she can avoid the interaction. She says it was hard, and it took conscious effort, but she's been trying to take more listening opportunities and also to listen to what others say and acknowledge their thoughts before she responds. She thinks it's helped because now she even finds the discussions in classes more productive and interesting.

Listening may be the single most important skill in the communication process because communication doesn't exist without a listener! (Lacey, 2013, p. 168) But most of us, like Charee, don't really think about it very much. Why is this? Perhaps because listening seems like a passive skill, unlike speaking or writing. Or perhaps we think that listening can't be taught or learned. After all, few college courses teach listening theory and practice. However, as we'll discover, a great deal of academic research focuses on the listening process, which includes not only hearing what others say but also critically evaluating messages and responding. Communication experts have shown that by being aware of the dynamics of listening and working on being better listeners, we can become better communicators overall.

We will first identify six important reasons for improving listening and responding skills. We will then describe the process of listening as well as some of the influences and barriers to effective listening. Finally, we'll discuss the role of societal forces in listening, ethical issues related to listening, and suggestions for becoming a more effective listener.

1   The Importance of Listening

1   Identify six reasons why listening is important.

You might not understand why it is important to learn about listening. After all, it seems rather automatic, something we don't think about often. As this section shows, however, improving our listening skills can lead to many personal and professional benefits.

The first important reason for learning more about listening is that we spend so much time doing it! Listening is the primary communication activity for college students (Janusik & Wolvin, 2009), and experts estimate that they spend 55 percent of their total average communication day listening. About half that time is spent in interpersonal listening (class, face-to-face conversations, phone, listening to voice messages) and the other half in media listening (Emanuel et al., 2008). In fact, media listening, in the broadest sense, encompasses a variety of online activities, including social media such as Facebook and Twitter—which provide a steady stream of messages (Crawford, 2009). In addition to the pervasiveness of listening in our daily communication, there are five other important reasons for learning about listening: Better listening skills can lead to improved cognition, improved academic performance, enhanced personal relationships, enhanced professional performance, and even better health. Let's look at each of these in turn.

Second, having better listening skills can improve your memory, give you a broader knowledge base, and increase your attention span (Diamond, 2007). The brain is like any other muscle; you have to use it to improve it. The more you exercise it, the better you'll be able to process and remember information. The first step in exercising the brain is to pay better attention when others are speaking. You can't remember something if you never learned it, and you can't learn something—that is, encode it into your brain—if you don't pay enough attention to it.

A third, related reason to learn more about listening is that good listening skills can enhance academic performance. Not surprisingly, a number of research studies have shown that college students who have good listening skills are better students than those who are less effective listeners (Cooper & Buchanan, 2010). The most recent research shows that one of the most important outcomes of classes on listening is that students become more aware of what constitutes good listening (Beall, Gill-Rosier, Tate, & Matten, 2008). Although this indicates that a college course can help you identify the skills needed to be a good listener, you may need a lot of practice and attention to skill building on your own to become an effective listener. This is what Charee, in the opening vignette, realized.

Better listening is also linked to enhanced personal relationships—a fourth reason to learn more about listening. Effective communication skills can lead to enhanced personal relationships. This is also true for listening skills. It's easy to understand how better listening can lead to fewer misunderstandings, which in turn can lead to greater satisfaction, happiness, and a sense of well-being for us and those we care about (Floyd, 2014).

A fifth reason to improve listening skills is because leaders in many professions have long emphasized that effective listening is a highly desirable workplace skill; in fact, the ability to listen effectively is still one of the top three skills sought in job applicants (Janusik, 2010, p. 193). Poor listening skills can be costly: the consequences include wasted meeting time; inaccurate orders/shipments; lost sales; inadequately informed, misinformed, confused, or angry staff and customers; unmet deadlines; unsolved problems; wrong decisions; lawsuits; and poor employee morale (Battell, 2006). Listening skills are particularly important in medical contexts (Meldrum, 2011; Shepherd & King, 2014). Physicians with good listening skills have more satisfied patients, and better listening skills can even have monetary value because doctors with better listening skills have fewer malpractice lawsuits (Davis, Foley, Crigger, & Brannigan, 2008).

What makes listening so important in professional contexts? Part of the answer may lie in that fact that (as with personal relationships) better listening at work means fewer misunderstandings, less time lost on the job, and greater productivity (Diamond, 2007). People who are perceived to be good listeners in work settings are likely to be perceived as having leadership qualities (Kluger & Zaidel, 2013), and listening seems to play an interesting role in career advancement as well. One study showed that as workers move into management positions, listening skills become more important (Welch & Mickelson, 2013), particularly critical and comprehensive listening—listening that involves close attention to the verbal and nonverbal aspects to the message. As shown in the *Communication in Society* box, managers with effective listening skills probably develop good relationships with their employees, which can actually lead to more productivity.

Learning to be a better listener can boost academic performance.

Students spend about half of their listening time in media listening.

Listening skills are particularly important in medical contexts.

Communication in Society

Effective Listening Skills of Managers

The article summarized here describes the results of recent research emphasizing the importance of managers' communication skills. Do you think these findings can be generalized to other work contexts—for example, supervisors in fast-food restaurants or line managers in factories? Why or why not?

Communication scholars at the Institute for Behavioral Research in the Netherlands wanted to learn more about the impact of managers' communication with their employees. They surveyed about 500 employees in a large telecommunications company, asking them to rate their supervisors' communication skills and then answer questions about their own satisfaction with their supervisors, commitment to the organization, how well they thought the organization was functioning, and so on. It turns out that supervisors' communication skills, especially their listening skills, have far-reaching effects in the organization. The results of

the survey showed that the most important factor in employees' satisfaction with their supervisor was their supervisor's listening behaviors—which then had a domino effect. That is, employees who were most satisfied with their supervisors had a stronger commitment to the organization, and a clearer notion of the values and potential of the organization—all of which likely leads to lower turnover and enhanced productivity. The researchers emphasized the importance of good, trusting relationships between managers and workers—fostered by listening skills where managers take time to listen and respond to employees and are open to employee feedback, even negative feedback. "While quick wins and positive stories are easier to communicate....bad news has to be told and listened to" (p. 125).

SOURCE: van Vuuren, M., de Jong. M. D. T., & Seydel, E. R. (2007). Direct and indirect effects of supervisor communication on organizational commitment. *Corporate Communications, 12*(2), 116–128.

Finally, you may not know that good listening can actually lead to improved health—our sixth and final reason for learning how to be a better listener. Some studies show that when we listen attentively, heart rate and oxygen consumption are reduced, which leads to increased blood and oxygen to the brain—a healthy cardiovascular condition (Diamond, 2007). Health psychologist James J. Lynch (1985) conducted pioneering research showing that human interaction (or the lack of it) can dramatically affect cardiovascular systems. He found that when the patients talked about their own problems, their blood pressure increased to high levels. However, when the patients listened to a nonthreatening personal story or the reading of a passage from a book, the patients' blood pressure dropped to much lower levels because they momentarily focused on something outside themselves (cited by Shafir, 2003, p. 241). These results suggest that listening—an important aspect of personal connectedness—can improve human health.

Now that we've discussed the importance of learning about listening, the next section describes the process of listening, which shows that listening is much more than just hearing what others are saying.

2 What Is Listening? Four Stages

2   Describe the four stages of listening.

The first step in striving to improve listening skills is to understand exactly what we mean when we talk about listening. Thus, we first provide a definition and then describe the process of listening.

Although there are various definitions for **listening**, the one we'll use is provided by the International Listening Association. Listening is "the process of receiving, constructing meaning from, and responding to spoken and/or nonverbal messages" (ILA, 1995, p. 4; Wolvin, 2013, p. 104). As you can see, this definition includes the concept of the decoding phase of the communication process. It involves four stages: *hearing, understanding, evaluating,* and *responding* (Rosenfeld & Berko, 1990).

listening

the process of receiving, constructing meaning from, and responding to spoken and/or nonverbal messages

hearing

the stage when listeners pick up the sound waves directed toward them

Let's see how this might work. **Hearing** occurs when listeners pick up the sound waves directed toward them. Suppose you're sitting in your apartment deep into Facebook and you hear sounds in the kitchen; it's your roommate, Josie, returning from her job as a server in a restaurant near campus. She yells out, "Guess what happened at work today?" For communication to occur, you must first become aware that information is being directed at you. In other words, you have to hear the sounds. But of course, hearing something is not the same as understanding or evaluating the information—the next steps. This means that hearing is not the same as listening. Hearing is really only the first step.

understanding

interpreting the messages associated with sounds or what the sounds mean

Once you sense that sounds are occurring, you have to interpret the messages associated with the sounds—that is, you have to **understand** what the sounds mean. The meaning you assign affects how you will respond—both physiologically and communicatively. In the example of your roommate, Josie, you understand her words—she's asking you to guess what happened at her work that day.

evaluating

assessing your reaction to a message

After you understand (or at least believe you understand) the message you have received, you **evaluate** the information. When you evaluate a message, you assess your reaction to it. For example, what do you think Josie is really asking you? Did something incredibly important happen to her at work? Or does she ask you this every time she returns from work, so that you know it doesn't matter what you answer because she is going to tell you some long, drawn-out story about people she works with whom you don't know? Or is she trying to engage you in conversation because you have both been busy and haven't seen each other much lately? As you can see, critical thinking skills are important in evaluating what you have heard—what are the possible interpretations of the message sent? What are the logical interpretations?

responding

showing others how you regard their message

Finally, you **respond** to messages. Maybe you decide that you really want to hear what Josie's going to tell you or at least want to have a conversation with her and you tell her so—"no, I can't imagine what happened at work today, tell me!" Your response provides the most significant evidence to others that you are listening. Responding means that you show others how you regard their messages. For example, you could have responded to Josie in a sarcastic tone, letting her know that you'll listen but you're not really interested; or you could have just said "hmmm," telling her you don't even want to engage in a conversation. Even failing to respond is a type of response! Not answering a text message or not replying to a Tweet or FB message is a response of sort. You can respond in numerous ways; however, your response will be influenced by *how* you listen.

In addition to these phases of listening, we need to recognize that the total process of listening as a communication process is complex, involving motivations (we have to want to listen), cognitions, emotions, and behaviors (Bodie, Worthington, Imhof, & Cooper, 2008). In addition, some communication experts expand the definition of listening to include lurking—following Tweets, blog and Facebook posts—without responding (*see Alternative View: Lurkers as Listeners*).

Think of a recent conflict you had, and describe how listening behaviors might have influenced the outcome. How might it have been different if those involved had spent more time listening instead of talking?

Now that you understand the process of listening, the next section shows how an individual's personal characteristics influence listening and responding. We also describe how different situations require different types of listening skills.

3   Listening and the Individual: Influences and Barriers

3   **Describe the influences on listening and barriers to effective listening.**

Do you have any friends who are especially good listeners? Any who are not so good? Do you find it easier to listen in some situations than in others?

Alternative view

Lurkers as Listeners

The work summarized here suggests a new way of defining listening—suggesting that just by attentiveness to the new many messages we attend to each day, we are listening, even if we don't respond. What do you think? Does listening only occur in face-to-face settings? Do we have to respond explicitly to be a listener?

Some communication scholars have suggested that we broaden our definition of listening—given all the new communication technologies. For example, they suggest that participation in various online activities—reading blogs, streaming videos, lurking on social media sites, attending to messages in Facebook, following tweets or RSS feeds—all constitute listening. They argue that even though the lurkers or "listeners" may not respond by posting messages, they directly contribute to

the community by acting as a "gathered audience" who are engaged as listeners and are necessary to provoke the senders to keep speaking.

Further, they note that listening to several (or several hundred) Twitter users or Facebook friends requires a real skill: "One needs to inhabit a stream of multilayered information, often leaping from news updates to a message from a friend experiencing a stressful situation, to information about what a stranger had for lunch, all in the space of seconds. Some will require attention; many can be glimpsed and tuned out" (Crawford, 2009, p. 529).

SOURCES: Crawford, K. (2009). Following you: Discipline of listening in social media. *Continuum: Journal of Media & Cultural Studies, 23*(4), 525–535.

Lacey, K. (2013). *Listening Publics: The Politics and Experience of Listening in the Media Age.* Cambridge: Polity.

Although some studies have identified general listening skills (see *Communication in Society: The "Big Five" of Listening Competency*), there are many factors that influence whether listening in any particular situation is easier or more difficult. In this section, we describe some of these factors, including individual listening styles and individual characteristics such as gender, age, and nationality. Finally, we discuss physical and psychological barriers to listening.

Influences on Listening

Not everyone listens in the same way; our personal listening habits may be influenced by gender, age, ethnicity, or even certain idiosyncratic patterns. These influences can then affect how we respond to others. Let's look first at the various listening styles and then turn to other characteristics that may influence how we listen and respond.

LISTENING STYLES According to experts, a **listening style** is a set of "attitudes, beliefs, and predispositions about the how, where, when, who, and what of the

listening style
a set of attitudes, beliefs, and predispositions about the how, where, when, who, and what of the information receiving and encoding process

---

Communication in Society

The "Big Five" of Listening Competency

A recent online questionnaire asked 1,319 students to describe, what it means to be an effective listener. The results revealed the following top or "Big Five" dimensions of effective listening.

Notice how each of these dimensions is associated with the phases of listening (hearing, sensing, and so on). Are there other skills that you would add?

1. Openness or willingness to listen
2. Ability to read nonverbal cues
3. Ability to understand verbal cues

4. Ability to respond appropriately
5. Ability to remember relevant details

Although these skills are important and confirm findings from previous studies, the authors of the study note that other factors, such as age, maturity, and personal experiences, influence an individual's listening competence. In addition, they note that the study design did not address the influence of context or interpersonal relationship.

SOURCE: Cooper, L. O., & Buchanan, T. (2010). Listening competency on campus: A psychometric analysis of student listening. *International Journal of Listening, 24*(3), 141–163.

information reception and encoding process" (Watson, Barker, & Weaver, 1995, p. 2). To put it more simply, it is "the way people prefer to receive oral information" (Watson et al., 1995, p. 9). Researchers have identified four listening styles used in various situations (Bodie & Worthington, 2010; Watson et al., 1995) and find that a given individual will tend to prefer to use just one or two of these styles (Barker & Watson, 2000).

Each listening style emphasizes a particular set of skills that are useful for responding to others in particular situations. The point of this is not that you should strive to develop a particular style or that having a particular style ensures you will be a good listener, but that your listening style should vary somewhat by context or situation. And, indeed, studies have shown that most people do vary their listening style from situation to situation (Imhof, 2004).

action-oriented listening style

listening style that reflects a preference for error-free and well-organized speaking

ACTION-ORIENTED LISTENING STYLE The **action-oriented listening style** reflects a preference for error-free and well-organized speaking, with an emphasis on active responding. People using this style focus more on the content of the message than on the person delivering it, and they want to not only hear the message, but also to do something with it. They may get impatient if a speaker is not direct or concise enough.

informational listening

listening skills that are useful in situations requiring attention to content

The action-oriented style requires **informational listening** skills, useful in situations requiring attention to content. For example, at work you probably listen primarily for content, to make sure you understand the instructions of your boss, supervisor, or coworkers. Informational listening skills are also useful at school, during course lectures, or when professors give detailed instructions about assignments. How can you improve your informational listening skills? Here are some suggestions:

1. Attend to what the speaker is saying: Maintain eye contact; face the person, and lean toward him or her. Show the speaker that you *want* to understand what he or she is saying.

2. Don't judge the speaker prematurely: Making mental judgments can prevent you from understanding the content of the speaker's message.

3. Paraphrase: Reflect the speaker's words back to make sure you understand and let the speaker know you are listening—for example, if your professor is describing instructions for an assignment, you might say, "You're saying that the five-page paper needs to cite at least ten different research sources."

4. Clarify: Ask questions to clear up any confusion or seek more information. For example, if you don't completely understand your professor's instructions, you might ask, "How should we submit the paper? Can we email it to you or do you want us to hand it to you in class?"

5. Review and summarize: Periodically review and summarize to make sure you understand the information. Summarizing captures the overall meaning of what has been said and puts it into a logical and coherent order, but summaries should not add any new information. After your summary, you might also ask, "Is that correct?" so that the speaker still has control. For example, you might say, "So we hand in a five-page research paper to you in class Thursday on the topics we discussed today? Is this correct?"

content-oriented listening style

a listening style that reflects an interest in detailed and complex information, simply for the content itself

CONTENT-ORIENTED LISTENING STYLE The **content-oriented listening style** reflects an interest in detailed and complex information, simply for the content itself. People using this style prefer debate or argument content over simpler speech; they attend to details and are interested in the quality of the speech. Critical thinking skills are particularly important in this style.

critical listening

listening skills that are useful in a wide variety of situations—particularly those involving persuasive speaking

This style involves the informational listening skills detailed previously and an additional set of **critical listening** skills (Mooney, 1996), which go hand in hand with critical thinking skills. These skills are useful in a wide variety of situations, particularly those involving persuasive speaking—for example, when you are listening to a political speech or a sales pitch—or even in more informal settings, such as when friends or acquaintances try to persuade you to see their point of view about an issue or activity. Here are some suggestions for developing critical listening skills:

1. Consider the speaker's credibility. Is this speaker qualified to make these arguments? Is this speaker trustworthy?

2. Listen between the lines. Are the words and the body language consistent? Are the content and the emotion in harmony?

3. Evaluate the messages being sent and their implications. Ask yourself, "What conclusions can be drawn from what is being said? Where is this leading?"

4. Weigh the evidence. Does what is being said make sense? Are the speaker's opinions logical? Are they supported by fact?

5. Periodically review and summarize. As with informational listening, you need to periodically check to make sure you understand the message. Ask yourself, "Do I have it straight? Do I understand the speakers' arguments and main points?"

PEOPLE-ORIENTED LISTENING STYLE People using this style are interested in hearing about others' experiences, thoughts, and feelings and finding areas of common interest. The **people-oriented listening style** is often associated with friendly, open communication and an interest in establishing ties with others rather than in controlling them (Villaume & Bodie, 2007). The people-oriented style is particularly useful in informal personal situations, as when we are listening to friends, family, and relational partners.

People-oriented listening involves **supportive listening** skills, focused not only on understanding information but also "listening" to others' feelings—which they may communicate nonverbally (Bodie & Jones, 2012; Bodie, Vickery, & Gearhart, 2013). Consider the following suggestions for effective supportive listening (Fowler, 2005). Notice also how many of them involve nonverbal behaviors on the listener's part, and also the overlap with informational listening skills:

1. Put the other person at ease. Give space and time and "permission to speak." Do this by showing that you *want* to hear the speaker. Look at him or her. Nod when you can agree. Encourage the speaker to talk.

2. Remove distractions. Be willing to take out your earbuds, close a door and stop texting, checking Facebook, or surfing on your iPad. Let the speaker know he or she has your full attention.

3. Empathize with the other person, especially if he or she is telling you something personal or painful; take a moment to stand in the other person's shoes, to look at the situation from his or her point of view. Empathy can be expressed by (a) being a sounding board, which means allowing the person to talk while maintaining a nonjudgmental, noncritical manner; (b) resisting the impulse to discount the person's feelings with stock phrases like "it's not really that bad" or "you'll feel better tomorrow"; and (c) paraphrasing what you think the person really means or feels. This can help the person clarify his or her thoughts and feelings—for example, "It sounds like you're saying you feel overwhelmed by the new project"—and communicates that you understand the emotions and feelings involved.

4. Be patient. Some people take longer to find the right word, make a point, or clarify an issue.

5. Be aware of your own emotions. Being supportive can sometimes be challenging and may cause stress on the part of the listeners (Jones, 2011). As we'll discuss, emotions can be a barrier to effective listening.

people-oriented listening style
a listening style that is associated with friendly, open communication and an interest in establishing ties with others

supportive listening
listening skills focused not only on understanding information but also "listening" to others' feelings

People-oriented listening involves listening not only to words but also to others' feelings.

Time-oriented listening can be effective in emergencies when information must be communicated quickly and concisely.

time-oriented listening style

a listening style that prefers brief, concise speech

Consider the various listening styles and think about which style(s) you tend to use. Which are you less likely to use? Which sets of skills might you need to work on to become a more effective listener?

TIME-ORIENTED LISTENING STYLE   The **time-oriented listening style** prefers brief, concise speech. Time-oriented listeners don't want to waste time on complex details; they just want the aural equivalent of bullet points. They may check their email or send a text when they think someone is taking too long to get to the point. They may also state how much time they have for an interaction to keep the interaction concise and to the point. No specific set of skills accompanies this style; in fact, this style seems to involve rather ineffective listening behavior, except in cases where time is of the essence and concise information is imperative (e.g., emergency situations). If you find yourself using this style in many situations, you may want to consider which of the other three styles may be more effective.

In conclusion, to become a more effective listener in a variety of personal and professional contexts, identify your preferred style(s) and then work on developing the skill sets that accompany the other styles. For example, if you tend to be a people-oriented listener, you might improve your informational and critical listening skills. On the other hand, if you tend to prefer the content-oriented style, you might work to develop your supportive listening skills.

INDIVIDUAL IDENTITY CHARACTERISTICS   Now let's turn to other individual influences on listening behaviors. How do individual identity characteristics such as gender, age, and ethnicity affect listening behaviors? Do males and females tend to listen differently? Do older people listen in a different way than do younger people? And a related set of questions: Should we adapt our listening behaviors depending on who we are listening to? For example, should we listen to children differently from adults? Let's look at how the experts weigh in on answers to these questions.

Gender   Some scholars think that in general men and women not only differ in their listening styles, but that women tend to be better listeners than men. Other researchers have found no gender differences in listening behavior (Pearce, Johnson, & Barker, 2003; Imhof, 2004). Before looking at the research on this topic, let's discuss the issue of gender stereotypes—that is, the common perceptions people have concerning gender and listening.

Two communication scholars have identified common gender-based listening stereotypes: Men, they say, are supposedly logical, judgmental, interrupting, inattentive, self-centered, and impatient, whereas women are stereotyped as emotional, noninterrupting, attentive, empathetic, other-centered, responsive, and patient (Barker & Watson, 2000). And there is some evidence suggesting that individuals with strong feminine orientation prefer a person-centered listening style, and more masculine individuals prefer a more task-oriented style (Johnson, Weaver, Watson, & Barker, 2000).

For example, a recent study, asking five hundred staff workers and managers in a variety of industries to rate themselves on a Listening Competency Scale, found some gender differences: Both female staff and managers rated themselves as more competent at therapeutic (supportive) listening, and overall, female managers scored higher than the male managers (Welch & Mickelson, 2013). Most behavioral scientists believe that although some innate gender differences may exist, most behavioral differences between men and women are influenced more by cultural norms than biology. To sum it up, there do seem to be a few gender differences in listening behaviors, but both men and women can demonstrate feminine and masculine listening behaviors (Bodie & Fitch-Hauser, 2010). Remember, too, that gender differences are not fixed and given; people of both genders can learn to be effective listeners.

Age Do you listen differently to your parents than to your younger siblings? The fact is that people have different communication capacities and skill levels during various life stages, which means that we often adapt our listening behaviors depending on the age of the speaker (Brownell, 2012). We can and should adapt our listening behaviors for children (Clark, 2005). For example, because young children are in the process of developing their communication skills, they struggle sometimes to interpret the meanings of others and to follow adult conversational norms—that is, to listen when others are speaking, not interrupt, and respond to instructions. Be patient when they "break" conversational rules or are struggling to say something; children have more

to say than they can express. You can demonstrate patience and involvement by giving them your undivided attention, maintaining eye contact when they're speaking and asking questions; in other words, be a good listening role model (Brownell, 2012). And be aware of the impact your feedback and responses have. Children tend to think literally, so if you tell them that a big bad witch is going to come and take them away if they misbehave, they may fear that this will actually happen.

Listening to children involves adjusting one's listening style and being tolerant of children's "breaking" conversational rules.

Teenagers may also require some special listening behaviors. In many cultures, including the United States, teenagers are in a crucial stage of learning to be independent. Part of this process may involve closing off channels of communication or being critical of parents and other adults. As with children, listening effectively to teenagers involves patience and restraint—not asking too many questions or giving too much criticism, being available to listen when the teen wants to talk, and acknowledging when the teenager acts responsibly (Barker & Watson, 2000; Nichols, 2009).

As we get older, listening may become more difficult if hearing ability is an issue. We'll discuss hearing disability in the next section, under barriers to listening. However, not everyone who is old is deaf or has diminished mental abilities. Assuming that they are—that is, yelling or treating listeners like children—can be hurtful and insulting (Froemming & Penington, 2011).

Nationality Do people in all cultures consider listening equally important? The answer is no. Generally speaking, people in Western countries (U. S. and Europe) tend to place more emphasis on speaking skills, whereas many Asians consider listening to be the most important communication skills and are taught early that they *must* be good listeners (Beall, 2010, p. 233). In addition, there are cultural differences in what people consider appropriate nonverbal expressions of listening and responding (Imhof & Janusik, 2006). In most western cultures, good listening is demonstrated by eye contact, head nods, and some back-channeling vocalizations such as "hmmm" and "oh." However, in some countries, such as Vietnam and Thailand, good listening behavior (listening respectfully) involves avoiding eye contact. In other countries, such as Japan, good listening may involve responding with lots of head nods, back-channeling, and even saying "yes, yes," which actually means, "I hear you," not "I agree with you" (Fujii, 2008).

Here, however, to summarize, factors that can influence an individual's listening behavior include gender, age, ethnicity, and nationality, as well as one's own listening style preferences and the particular situation. Still, one cannot assume that an individual will listen in a particular way just because she or he belongs to a certain gender, age, or nationality group. Listening is a complex behavior, and numerous factors beyond these kinds of identity characteristics can serve as barriers, the topic we turn to next.

Fatigue is a common barrier to listening.

Barriers to Listening

Like Charee in the opening vignette, people have many reasons for not listening to others. Some typical ones include physical and physiological barriers, psychological barriers, conflicting objectives, and poor listening habits (Robertson, 2005). Let's explore in more detail how these factors can interfere with effective listening.

PHYSICAL AND PHYSIOLOGICAL BARRIERS Physical barriers to listening include a noisy environment or physical discomforts that make it difficult to concentrate. We have all had the experience of trying to listen to someone in a noisy bar or in a room with a loud television, or while standing outside with traffic whizzing by on a busy highway. Physical barriers are the most elemental; if we can't hear because of the noise around us, it doesn't matter how refined our listening skills are.

Another physical barrier is fatigue. Whether a listener is tired from lack of sleep or from high stress, it can be a barrier to good listening. For example, it's difficult for students to listen effectively in class when they are exhausted; and it's difficult for parents to listen to children when they are stressed out from working hard and managing their many responsibilities. As we hope you understand by now, listening well takes effort and requires alertness and focus—both of which may be absent when one is tired.

Another type of listening barrier is physiological—for example, a hearing disability. Good listening is a skill, but it is also strongly affected by a person's physical ability to hear. The Hearing Loss Association of America estimates that more than 35 million people in the United States have a hearing loss that could be treated and, in fact, an increasing number of younger people have hearing problems associated with Personal Media Players (PMP) (Johnson-Curiskis, 2012). (See *Did You Know? Statistically Speaking, How Many People Are Deaf or Hard of Hearing?*) Unfortunately, many people with hearing loss do not treat it—whether because of vanity (not wanting to wear a hearing aid), lack of funds, or lack of knowledge about the disability. Getting over this barrier may mean recognizing and treating the disability or, in the case of mild impairment, asking people to enunciate more clearly and use adequate speech volume.

PSYCHOLOGICAL BARRIERS Common psychological barriers that prevent us from listening effectively are boredom and preoccupation. The human mind can process information at a rate of about six hundred words per minute, about three times faster than the typical speaker can talk. This phenomenon is sometimes labeled the "thought-speech differential" (Brownell, 2012, p. 81). Consequently, as Charee discovered, your mind has plenty of time to wander, and you can easily become distracted or bored, which will certainly undermine the amount that you listen to and retain.

Preoccupation, or distracted listening, is a related psychological barrier. During an interaction, people often think of other things and, thus, do not listen to what is being said. Preoccupation can be caused by having an extensive to-do list and feeling stress about getting it all done. Two other common sources of preoccupation include having a personal agenda in a conversation (Shafir, 2003) and being emotional.

How can having a personal agenda in a conversation lead to preoccupation and inattentive listening? As one example, let's say you've just met someone in a social setting who is the head of a corporation where you would like to work. During your conversation, you do your best to impress her as she talks about her professional activities and ideas; you smile, nod enthusiastically, and try to act in a professional manner. However, when you finally get to speak, you repeat ideas that she has just expressed or ask questions that she has already answered. Why? Because you weren't listening; you were too preoccupied with your own agenda to hear what

Did You Know?

Statistically, How Many People Are Deaf or Hard of Hearing?

How often do you assume that the person listening to you has good hearing? How might this assumption influence how you respond and, ultimately, the outcomes of your communication encounters? How might you modify your way of speaking if you knew you were speaking to someone with a hearing loss?

Statistically, how many people are deaf or hard of hearing? It is actually difficult to estimate because some people may not wish to identify themselves as having a hearing loss, or the questions may not ask directly if a person has a hearing loss. People who are hard of hearing refers to people with hearing loss ranging from mild to severe. They usually communicate through spoken language and can benefit from hearing aids, captioning and assistive listening devices. People who are deaf mostly have profound hearing loss, which implies very little or no hearing. They often use sign language for communication.

Here are some interesting facts about hearing loss:

- About 2 to 3 out of every 1,000 children in the United States are born with a detectable level of hearing loss in one or both ears. More than 90 percent of deaf children are born to hearing parents.
- One in eight people in the United States (13 percent, or 30 million) aged 12 years or older has hearing loss in both ears.
- Hearing loss increases with age. About 2 percent of adults aged 45 to 54 have disabling hearing loss. The rate increases to 8.5 percent for adults aged 55 to 64 and nearly 25 percent of those aged 65 to 74 and 50 percent of those who are 75 and older have disabling hearing loss.
- Men are more likely than women to report having hearing loss
- Approximately 15 percent of Americans (26 million people) between the ages of 20 and 69 have high frequency hearing loss due to exposure to noise at work or during leisure activities

Hearing loss can have important academic, social, and emotional impacts. Hearing loss can delay spoken language development and academic performance. Hearing loss affects individuals ability to communicate and can lead to of loneliness, isolation, and frustration, particularly among older people with hearing loss.

SOURCES: (2014, February) *World Health Organization Media Center Fact Sheet* Retrieved October 5, 2014, from http://www.who.int/mediacentre/factsheets/fs300/en/. *National Institute on Deafness and Other Communication Disorders (NIDCD) Quick Statistics.* Retrieved October 5, 2014, from http://www.nidcd.nih.gov/health/statistics/pages/quick.aspx.

she was saying. In this case, you probably failed to do the one thing you wanted to do—impress her. These kinds of listening failures can lead to frustration and maybe even feelings of low self-worth. What is the lesson, then? Listeners do better to put their own goals aside during a conversation and focus on the priorities and concerns of their conversational partner.

A second source of preoccupation comes from strong emotions. For example, some older Americans identify emotional triggers that cause them to tune out and they give several excellent tips for younger people communicating with them. The use of the pause-filler "like" is especially annoying, as well as "false familiarity", for example, someone calling them by their first names or using the term "you guys" (Froemming & Penington, 2011). Likewise, if you are frustrated or irritable for whatever reason, you are more likely to interpret casual comments as criticism. On the other hand, even joy, for example, can make a person too preoccupied to listen and can also influence how he or she understands and reacts to messages, so if something wonderful has just happened to you, you may be concentrating on your good news and how you are going to celebrate, rather than focusing on the speaker. Thus, a wide variety of emotions can distract you and influence how you listen and respond in communicative interactions (Nichols, 2009).

Emotions can also make people defensive and thus impair their listening abilities. Defensive listening occurs when

Strong emotions can interfere with listening by making people defensive, overly sensitive, or hostile.

someone perceives, anticipates, or experiences a threat (Nichols, 2009). In such cases, the listener often puts up a "wall" for protection. These walls can distort incoming messages, leading to misinterpretation. For example, one of our colleagues described how her emotional reactions to her father hindered her ability to listen to him: "We had such a rotten relationship that every time he even opened his mouth to speak, I was so defensive, so sure he was going to criticize me or yell at me that I never even heard a word he said." Some people are more defensive than others; their personalities and experiences have influenced them to respond defensively to many messages. However, certain types of messages are more likely to elicit defensive listening. Messages that are evaluative, controlling, superior, or dogmatic tend to prompt a defensive reaction.

Preconceived ideas about issues or participants can also trigger strong emotions. For example, sometimes we allow negative past experience with a person to interfere; that is, if you expect your sibling (or father) to be angry at you, you will likely interpret any comment as hostile—as was the case with our colleague and her father. For another example, if you are usually sarcastic, then others are likely to hear even your compliments as insults. Unfortunately, people often find it difficult to acknowledge their own preconceptions, let alone recognize those of others. Good advice here is to use your past experience to help you learn about the world, but do not rely on it as your only source for evaluating a present situation.

The psychological barriers discussed here can act as "filters that allow only selected words and ideas into our consciousness ... [they can also] screen out the less comfortable and uncomfortable messages, [so that] only pieces of message are received—the comfortable pieces" (Shafir, 2003, p. 46). The end result is that these barriers can stifle the potential for developing meaningful relationships and new ideas.

CONFLICTING OBJECTIVES   A third barrier to listening involves conflicting objectives. How people understand and react to others' communicative attempts depends in part on their objective(s) for the conversation. For example, how do you listen to a lecture when your instructor announces, "This will be on the midterm"? How do you listen when told the material will *not* be on a test? Your different objectives for these situations are likely to influence how well you listen.

Sometimes participants to a conversation differ in their objectives for an interaction. For example, during a business meeting Ignacio's objective was to explain a new procedure for evaluating employees, whereas Roberta's objective was to get a raise. Consequently, the two focused on different aspects of their conversation, assigned different meanings to what occurred, and remembered different aspects of their meeting. Of course, people may have multiple objectives for an interaction, each of which will influence how they listen and respond.

POOR LISTENING HABITS   As it turns out, people can more easily define poor listening than effective listening. Similarly, people can more easily identify the listening habits and flaws of others than they can their own. In our opening story, Charee saw other students' poor listening behaviors—although she also recognized her own.

Here are five common ineffective listening behaviors, which result in not really getting the speaker's message.

1. **Wandering:** Probably the most common. The listener's mind wanders from time to time, not really focused on what the speaker is saying. The words go in one ear and out the other.
2. **Rejecting:** The listener "tunes out" the speaker at the beginning of the message, often because of a lack of respect or dislike for the speaker.
3. **Judging:** The listener focuses on what the speaker says, but makes a hasty evaluation of the speaker's message, ignoring the remainder of the message.

4. **Predicting:** So common—the listener gets ahead of the speaker and finishes her thoughts; again, missing at least some of the speaker's message.

5. **Rehearsing:** The listener is thinking about what she is going to say next.

Are there other annoying habits you would like to add to this list? Are you guilty of any of these? Most of us are. Perhaps the most important way to avoid these bad habits is to first become more aware of our own listening behavior and to really focus on the speaker rather than on our own thoughts, feelings, and what we're going to say next. As we've mentioned, however, societal factors can have an important impact on one's ability to listen effectively, and this is the subject we turn to next.

It is easier to identify poor listening habits in others than in ourselves.

4   The Individual, Listening, and Society: Hierarchy, Contexts, and Community

4   **Understand the role of societal forces (hierarchy, contexts, and community) in listening.**

As emphasized throughout this text, communication behaviors do not exist solely on the individual level but are a complex interaction of individual and societal factors, reflected in our Synergetic Model of communication. Let's examine listening as it's affected by three levels of societal forces: social hierarchy, context, and community.

Social Hierarchy

Societal norms and social hierarchy influence much of our communication behaviors, and listening is no exception. Let's look more closely at how this works. Every society transmits messages about who is most powerful and important, and these are the people who set the communication norms. How do these messages affect our listening and responding?

Each time we meet someone for the first time, we immediately evaluate whether that person is worth listening to. We mentally go through our personal (influenced by society's) criteria. If the person doesn't meet the criteria, the person's words "become fainter and fainter until only our thoughts fill our attention" (Shafir, 2003, p. 57). Some of the most crucial information to be gained as listeners—like people's names—gets lost while we process acceptability checklists. Three important "filters" are social status, physical appearance, and vocal cues.

Review the listening barriers described in the text. Which do you think are the most common in your own life? Which do you think are the most difficult to overcome? What is the evidence for your answers to these questions?

SOCIAL STATUS   One criterion on many people's acceptability checklist is social status. We ask ourselves: Is this person worthy of my time and attention? Most of us are more attentive and listen more closely to those we consider equal to us or higher in society's hierarchy. For example, we listen closely to the words of physicians, teachers, successful business people, and celebrities. Rebecca Z. Shafir (2003), a renowned speech pathologist and listening expert, recounts the story of a manager of a large department who, as part of his power trip, ordered his staff to follow him down the hall as they asked questions or presented ideas (like the scheming boss, Wilhelmina, in the TV sitcom *Ugly Betty*):

> He rarely made eye contact with his subordinates and walked past them as they spoke. Yet, when conversing with his peers or those higher on the administrative ladder, a dramatic change in his voice and body language

took place. He looked them in the eye and smiled, nodding his head at any comment or suggestion. He laughed uproariously at their jokes and thanked them profusely for their unique insights. (p. 53)

Shafir goes on to say that this manager's attention to status overrode his ability to gain the voluntary cooperation of his staff and resulted in ineffective management, low staff morale, and high turnover. Regardless of the positions we hold, most of us are similarly influenced by systems of hierarchy, and these systems are sometimes tinged with prejudice. For example, do we listen with as much attention to people who have less education? Perhaps not, as Danny found out in *It Happened to Me*.

It Happened to Me

Danny

Being in college, I'm a part of a culture that's very different from the culture where I grew up. In college, people value talking about ideas, learning new information, and working toward becoming more "educated." When I go home, however, I have to remember that not everyone in my family, and not all of my friends, went to college. They don't understand a lot of the jargon I use, and they don't know about the things I've studied. I try to be mindful of this when I visit; I don't want to sound condescending. I also try to remember that their opinions are equally valid and that I need to listen as attentively to them as I do to my college friends.

PHYSICAL APPEARANCE One of the most common obstacles to listening relates to physical appearance. Societal forces set the norms for physical attractiveness, which include being physically able-bodied, having symmetrical features, and embodying certain weight and height norms. This means that many people hold stereotypes about people with disabilities or physical challenges (e.g., people who are extremely overweight or small), and they often find it difficult to listen to them, avoiding eye contact or ignoring the person entirely. One of our colleagues, Tanya, had a stroke as a young adult and uses a walker or wheelchair. She describes a common situation she encounters:

> It really irritates me sometimes when I'm in public and people avoid looking at me, look at my husband instead and ask him what I want. Why can't they listen to what *I'm saying* and respond to *me*?

In sum, social hierarchies can act as a filter that, in turn, influences people's listening behaviors.

VOCAL CUES In addition to social status and appearance, vocal cues (the *way* a person talks) can also be a filter that influences how people listen to others. Sometimes these judgments are factually accurate. For example, people can often tell by hearing someone's voice whether the speaker is male or female, young or old. However, a recent study showed that people make other judgments about a person, in addition to gender and age, based on the pitch and sound of their voice

Physical appearance has a strong effect on listening. How well do you listen when the speaker has a disability or other characteristic that makes you feel uncomfortable?

(Imhof, 2010). In this study, the researchers found that people with higher pitched voices were judged by others to be more outgoing and open, but less conscientious and less emotionally stable. The judgments stem from societal cues and assumptions that link people's vocal cues to personality. Another study found that job applicants with a U.S. Midwestern accent were evaluated more positively than those with a foreign accent (Deprez-Sims & Morris, 2010).

The important question is, how do we listen to people we consider "less conscientious" or "less emotionally stable" or foreign? Something to keep in mind is whether we are making unwarranted judgments that then influence how we listen.

The point here is that these "filters," based on social hierarchy, can prevent us from listening to others with openness and in a nonjudgmental manner that is usually thought of as part of effective listening. However, several experts have pointed out that it is probably not really possible to "set aside prejudices" and "consider all people as equal," so that setting these goals as a necessary and sufficient condition for effective listening means almost certain failure. Rather, they suggest that we see them as ideals—goals to strive *toward*. In so doing, certainly becoming aware of our "filters" is a first step (Bodie, 2010; Floyd, 2010).

Listening in Context

As discussed previously, different contexts may call for different listening styles and behaviors. For example, in professional contexts we generally focus on content or action listening, whereas in social contexts we generally focus more on people and relationship affirmation. With friends, we are often called on to listen sympathetically and with little judgment, establishing empathy and communicating a recognizable "*feeling* of being heard" (Shotter, 2009, p. 21).

In professional contexts, too, whether one is working on an assembly line or as a manager, listening with empathy is important because it enables people to understand each other and get the job done (Battell, 2006; Imhof, 2001). At the same time, employees must be cautious about letting their work relationships get too personal. For example, when Donna's new boss, Lena, asked Donna to be Facebook friends, Donna was flattered. However, when Lena posted nasty messages about her divorce and aired problems she was having with her children, and continued these conversations at work, Donna soon found that Lena's personal issues were taking lots of time and keeping her from getting work done. In addition, she discovered that her coworkers were critical of her for being unable to keep things on a professional level. The lesson, then, is that colleagues need to balance task and relational listening skills (Nichols, 2009).

Societal forces may affect listening behavior in any context. For example, some individuals are the victims of prejudice, discrimination, or even bullying in social or workplace contexts because of gender, age, race, ethnicity, or sexual orientation. When this happens, they may not be able to easily adapt their listening behavior. Others' bullying or discriminatory reactions to them may completely undermine their attempts to demonstrate good communication skills. Deborah Tannen's (1994) influential work showed how women's contributions in office meetings were often not listened to, and similarly, a disabled person might display good listening skills in a conversation by making eye contact, leaning forward, and paying close attention, but these good communication skills can be undermined if the speaker expresses prejudice toward the listening disabled person by *avoiding* eye contact in return, or by ignoring the disabled person's contribution by not listening when that person becomes the speaker.

Listening and Community

Communication scholar David Beard (2009) reminds us that in addition to all the voices in various hierarchies and contexts we listen to every day, we also listen to **soundscapes**—the everyday sounds in our environments. Together these sounds establish a community identity. For example, in many small towns, church bells—or in some countries, the imam calling Muslims to prayer five times daily—help define the boundaries of regional or religious communities and shape a community identity.

soundscape
the everyday sounds in our environments

Community-specific soundscapes can also vary with generational differences. Contrast the technological soundscapes of your parents' and grandparents' generation—the hiss of the needle on a record player, the sound of rotary phone dialing (and perhaps even a live operator's voice), the chimes of the NBC logo, the screech of dial-up Internet access—with your own soundscapes. What were the soundscapes of the neighborhood where you grew up? What sounds do you hear every day that may represent your generational identity and communities? Perhaps more importantly, how do these affect you? Are they comforting? Irritating? Are there some that you tune out? Perhaps they are so much a part of the sound "background" that we don't consider their effect on us.

Although, as you've seen, the quality of one's listening is subject to powerful social forces as well as individual factors such as listening style, gender, and age, we do have some latitude for making choices about our own behavior. In other words, we do make ethical decisions about listening—the topic we turn to next.

5   Ethics and Listening

5   Describe ethical challenges in listening.

People have several ethical decisions to make about listening. These decisions include choosing what you will listen to and when, as well as how you will respond when listening to other people or to the soundscapes that surround you.

To begin, choosing to listen or not is an ethical decision, in both face-to-face and mediated communication contexts (Beard, 2009; Lacey, 2013; Stoltz, 2010). Just because someone wants to tell you something doesn't mean you have to listen. And sometimes the act of listening—or refusing to—means taking a moral stand. For example, let's say a friend of yours tweets a vicious rumor about another person or tells a racist joke. You have an ethical decision to make. How are you going to respond? Are you going to retweet it? Ignore it?

You can tell your friend you don't want to hear any more or even gently explain why you don't want to. Or you can do nothing, sacrificing honesty to avoid making yourself (and others) feel uncomfortable. What are the consequences of each of these decisions? If you listen to something offensive and pass it on, you are in effect agreeing with the tweet. It may be awkward to tell your friend (either at the moment or later) that you don't want to listen to such remarks, but the friend may think twice before sending similar tweets in the future. Obviously, there are no easy answers; you need to consider the consequences and possible outcomes in each situation as you make these ethical decisions.

Let's say you overhear some information or see a text message not intended for you. What are some guidelines for dealing with this information? you might first consider the expectations of the individual who sent the message. Perhaps this person has made it clear that he or she wants this information kept private. Or you might consider that if you were in this person's position, you would want the information to be kept private. Or perhaps you know that the sender does not mind if the information is shared more widely—but what about the person to whom the message is addressed? You need to consider his or her wishes, too. Depending on the privacy expectation, the ethical decision might be to listen to or read the message—or not. Would the sender or addressee feel harmed? Would any benefit result from your listening to the message? The answer to these questions probably depends a great deal on your relationships with the sender and addressee. A close friend may not mind your listening in on messages; someone you don't know very well may object strenuously.

Mediated communication contexts also can pose ethical issues with regard to listening. The fact is that we receive more messages and hear many more voices than ever possible in our parents' or grandparents'

Ethical listening involves knowing how to handle confidentiality if you receive a message not intended for you.

time. Communication expert Kate Lacey says we need a new set of listening skills to help us cope with this barrage of messages and to be selective in our listening choices; we train in "public speaking," but not "public listening" (p. 190). She notes that on the one hand, we have an ethical responsibility to "grant right of audience" to those who would otherwise not be heard because they present opportunities to expand our horizons, and of course we need to balance openness with critical thinking. On the other hand, much of our new media listening is increasingly narrowed—device settings/apps that program what we hear (music, talk, TV, Web sites) to our idiosyncratic preferences (Lacey, 2013). Here are some choices we make, as listeners, to become more or less ethical beings, in our mediated world:

1. The choice to cut ourselves off from listening to our immediate environments: As Charee discussed in the chapter opening, we can choose to listen alone (putting on the headset/earbuds), which sometimes might be a positive, self-constructive act. At other times, however (e.g., in a work situation or at home when our relational partner wants to talk), doing so can be isolating and damaging to relationships.

2. The choice to listen selectively: For example, we can choose to listen to media "candy" or to media that enhance and inspire us as people. We can choose to listen to a friend's choice of media, so we can discuss it together, or we can listen only to our own choices.

3. The choice not to listen: For example, in the public arena, we can decide to listen (or not listen) to a political speaker who espouses ideas we oppose. Our choice has a potential impact on us and our thinking because listening implies the possibility of change in attitudes and behavior. Listening to a political speaker (or even a friend) promoting ideas and beliefs that we disagree with may open us up to ideas previously unexplored or may reinforce our own beliefs. Choosing never to listen to opposing views ensures that we won't alter our beliefs or learn to defend them in a logical and constructive way.

4. The choice to listen together: For example, when we attend a music concert or a political rally, we open ourselves to being part of a community of music fans or political sympathizers (Beard, 2009). The consequences of the decision to listen with a particular community may open up opportunities for new experiences that may alter our future thinking or behavior.

The point is that all these choices are just that—choices. Although we don't usually consider these types of choices when we think of listening, the decisions we make regarding them do influence our communication life—influencing our communication identity and relationships with those important to us.

6   Improving Your Listening Skills

6   Discuss two ways to improve your own listening behavior.

As we have shown, listening (including responding appropriately) is an important communication skill. As is the case with all communication skills, however, there are no surefire, easy recipes for becoming a more effective listener. Still, two guidelines might help you improve.

Identify Poor Habits

As noted, most people have some poor listening habits, particularly in our close and intimate relationships, where partners often develop irritating practices such as finishing the other person's sentences, interrupting, and "tuning out" the other person. These irritating behaviors crop up especially if you are an action- or time-oriented listener.

Interrupting or completing other people's sentences are barriers to listening that we can all learn to overcome if we try.

Ask yourself, then: What keeps you from really listening? Which filters block your ability to hear and understand what others are saying? Overcoming listening barriers—especially those that are reinforced by social hierarchies—can be challenging.

Perhaps one way to overcome those societal messages is through awareness that our listening behaviors play an important role in the outcome of communication encounters. A number of research studies have shown that when people listen attentively to one another, the speaker is more likely to speak coherently. On the other hand, when listeners do not pay careful attention, speakers tend to be less coherent. Put another way, regardless of who they are or their social location, when speakers feel they are listened to with respect and attentiveness, they become better communicators and vice versa.

Strive for Mindful Listening

Applying the concept of mindful listening, described by renowned listening expert Rebecca Z. Shafir (2003), can help. Mindful listening, which is a specific kind of mindfulness, is based on Eastern philosophy and Zen Buddhism; it is defined by focus, concentration, and compassion, and it can bring health, peace, and productivity to our everyday lives. This holistic approach requires that we listen with the heart, body, and mind, and for most of us, that means a major change in attitude. Mindful listening focuses on the *process* of listening versus the *payoff*.

Shafir suggests that to be a better listener to each of our friends, family, and acquaintances, we need to understand their "movie." What does that mean? Shafir compares listening to movies with listening to people. Most of us don't have trouble focusing on and paying attention while watching a movie; we get caught up in the plot, the emotion, and the characters. Why, she asks, should listening to people be any different? To continue the comparison, if we approach a listening opportunity with the same self-abandonment as we do a movie, think how much more we might gain from those encounters (Shafir, 2003).

Being a mindful listener requires three elements:

1. the desire to get the whole message,
2. the ability to eliminate the noisy barriers discussed previously, and
3. the willingness to place your agenda lower on the priority list than the speaker's.

Mindful listening is based on empathy—the ability to identify with and understand someone else's feelings. As listening expert Michael Nichols states it, listening is not just taking in information; it is also "bearing witness" to, validating, and affirming another's expression. The core of listening, he says, is "to pay attention, take an interest in, care about, validate, acknowledge, be moved … appreciate" (2009, p. 14).

Summary

Listening is considered to be one of the most important communication skills, partly because we spend so much time doing it! In addition, better listening skills can lead to improved cognition, improved academic performance, enhanced personal relationships, enhanced professional performance, and even better health.

Listening is defined as "the process of receiving, constructing meaning from, and responding to spoken and/or nonverbal messages" and occurs in four stages: hearing, understanding, evaluating, and responding. Not everyone listens in the same way; our personal listening habits may be influenced by our gender, age, ethnicity, or even our own predominant listening style, which can be people-, action-, content-, or time-oriented. Action-oriented style involves informational listening skills; content-oriented style involves informational and critical listening skills; people-oriented style involves supportive listening skills. People have many reasons for not listening to others, but some typical ones include physical or physiological barriers, psychological barriers, conflicting objectives, and poor listening habits.

Finally, listening habits and preferences are influenced by societal forces: contexts and hierarchies. Ethical considerations also come into play with respect to listening behavior. Ethical decisions include choosing what to listen to and when, how to respond when listening to other people or to the soundscapes around us, including media. Although we can offer no surefire, easy recipes for becoming a more effective listener, two guidelines might help: Identify your poor listening habits or barriers, and practice mindful listening.

Key Terms

listening
hearing
understanding
evaluating
responding

listening style
action-oriented listening style
informational listening
content-oriented listening style
critical listening

people-oriented listening style
supportive listening
time-oriented listening style
soundscape

Apply What You Know

1. When you are in class or in a large group, notice how people listen to each other and respond. Reflect on what you think is more or less effective about others' listening skills. Then apply what you observed to your own listening skills.

2. Ask someone to observe your listening skills over a period of time. This person can be a parent, friend, teacher, or romantic partner. Ask the observer to give you constructive feedback on how you can improve your listening skills. Try to implement those suggestions.

Glossary

action-oriented listening style   a style that reflects a preference for error-free and well-organized speaking

content-oriented listening style   a style that reflects an interest in detailed and complex information, simply for the content itself

critical listening   listening skills that are useful in a wide variety of situations—particularly those involving persuasive speaking

evaluating   assessing your reaction to a message

hearing   the stage when listeners pick up the sound waves directed toward them

informational listening   listening skills that are useful in situations requiring attention to content

listening   the process of receiving, constructing meaning from, and responding to spoken and/or nonverbal messages

listening style   a set of attitudes, beliefs, and predispositions about the how, where, when, who, and what of the information receiving and encoding process

people-oriented listening style   a style that is associated with friendly, open communication and an interest in establishing ties with others

responding   showing others how you regard their message

soundscape   the everyday sounds in our environments

supportive listening   listening skills focused not only on understanding information but also "listening" to others' feelings

time-oriented listening style   a style that prefers brief, concise speech

understanding   interpreting the messages associated with sounds or what the sounds mean

---

References

Barker, L., & Watson, K. (2000). *Listen up: How to improve relationships, reduce stress, and be more productive by using the power of listening*. New York: St. Martin's Press.

Battell, C. (2006). *Effective listening*. ASTD Press.

Beall, M. L. (2010). Perspectives on intercultural listening In A. D. Wolvin (Ed.), *Listening and human communication in the 21st century* (pp. 232–238). Malden, MA: Wiley-Blackwell.

Beall, M. L., Gill-Rosier, J., Tate, J., & Matten, A. (2008). State of the context: Listening in education. *The International Journal of Listening, 22*, 123–132.

Beard, D. (2009). A broader understanding of the ethics of listening: Philosophy, cultural studies, media studies and the ethical listening subject. *The International Journal of Listening, 23*(1), 7–20.

Berke, J. (2010, September 6). Hearing Loss—Demographics—Deafness Statistics. Retrieved March 28, 2014, from: http://deafness.about.com/cs/earbasics/a/demographics.htm.

Bodie, G. D. (2010). Treating listening ethically. *International Journal of Listening, 24*(3), 185–188.

Bodie, G. D., & Fitch-Hauser, M. (2010). Quantitative research in listening: Explication and overview. In A. D. Wolvin (Ed.), *Listening and human communication in the 21st century* (pp. 46–93). Malden, MA: Wiley-Blackwell.

Bodie, G. D., & Jones, S. M. (2012). The nature of supportive listening II: The role of verbal person centeredness and nonverbal immediacy. *Western Journal of Communication, 76*(3), 250–269.

Bodie, G. D., & Worthington, D. L. (2010). Revisiting the Listening Styles Profile (LSP-16): A confirmatory factor analytic approach to scale validation and reliability estimation. *International Journal of Listening, 24*(2), 69–88.

Bodie, G. D., Vickery, A. J., & Gearhart, C. C. (2013). The nature of supportive listening, I: Exploring a relation between supportive listeners and supportive people. *The International Journal of Listening, 27*(1), 39–49.

Bodie, G. D., Worthington, D., Imhof, M., & Cooper, L. (2008). What would a unified field of listening look like? A proposal linking past perspectives and future endeavors. *The International Journal of Listening, 22*, 103–122.

Brownell, J. (2012*). Listening: Attitudes, principles and skills* (5th ed). Boston: Pearson.

Clark. A. (2005). Listening to and involving young children: A review of research and practice. *Early Child Development and Care, 175*(6), 489–505.

Cooper, L. O., & Buchanan, T. (2010). Listening competency on campus: A psychometric analysis of student listening. *International Journal of Listening, 24*(3), 141–163.

Crawford, K. (2009). Following you: Discipline of listening in social media. *Continuum: Journal of Media & Cultural Studies, 23*(4), 525–535.

Davis, J., Foley, A., Crigger, N., & Brannigan, M. C. (2008). Healthcare and listening: A relationship for caring. *The International Journal of Listening, 22*, 168–175.

Deprez-Sims, A-S., & Morris, S. B. (2010). Accents in the workplace: Their effects during a job interview. *International Journal of Psychology, 45*(6), 417–426.

Diamond, L. E. (2007). *Rule #1: Stop talking! A guide to listening*. Cupertino, CA: Listeners Press.

Emanuel, R., Adams, J., Baker, K., Daufin, E. K., Ellington, C., Fitts, E., Himsel, J., Holladay, L., & Okeowo, D. (2008). How college students spend their time communicating. *The International Journal of Listening, 22*(1), 13–28.

Floyd, J. (2010). Provocation: Dialogic listening as reachable goal. *International Journal of Listening, 24*(3), 170–173.

Floyd, K. (2014). Empathic listening as an expression of interpersonal affection. *International Journal of Listening, 28*, 1-14.

Fowler, K. (2005). Mind tools on active listening. Retrieved December 7, 2009, from: http://www.mindtools.com/CommSkll/Mind20Tools20Listening.pdf.

Froemming, K. J., & Penington, B. A. (2011). Emotional triggers: Listening barriers to effective interactions in senior populations. *The International Journal of Listening, 25*, 113–131.

Fujii, Y. (2008). You must have a wealth of stories: Cross-linguistic differences between addressee support behaviour in Australian and Japanese. *Multilingua, 27*(4), 325–370.

Imhof, M. (2001). How to listen more efficiently: Self-monitoring strategies in listening. *The International Journal of Listening, 5*, 2–19.

Imhof, M. (2004). Who are we as we listen? Individual listening profiles in varying contexts. *The International Journal of Listening, 18*, 39–44.

Imhof, M. (2010). Listening to voices and judging people. *International Journal of Listening, 24*(1), 19–33.

Imhof, M., & Janusik, L. A. (2006). Development and validation of the Imhof-Janusik listening concepts inventory to measure listening conceptualization differences between cultures. *Journal of Intercultural Communication Research, 35,* 79–98.

International Listening Association (1995, April). An ILA Definition of Listening. *ILA Listening Post, 53,* 1–4.

Janusik, L. A. (2010). Listening pedagogy: Where do we go from here? In A. D. Wolvin (Ed.), *Listening and human communication in the 21st century* (pp. 193-224). Malden, MA: Wiley-Blackwell.

Janusik, L. A., & Wolvin, A. D. (2009). 24 hours in a day: A listening update to the time studies. *International Journal of Listening, 23*(2), 104–120.

Johnson-Curiskis, N. (2012). Hearing screening. *International Journal of Listening, 26*(2), 71–74.

Jones, S. M. (2011). Supportive listening. *International Journal of Listening, 25,* 85–103.

Kluger, A. N., & Zaidel, K. (2013). Are listeners perceived as leaders? *International Journal of Listening, 27*(2), 73–84.

Lacey, K. (2013). *Listening Publics: The Politics and Experience of Listening in the Media Age.* Cambridge: Polity.

Lynch, J. J. (1985). *Language of the heart: The body's response to human dialogue.* New York: Basic Books.

Meldrum, H. (2011). The listening practices of exemplary physicians. *International Journal of Listening, 25*(3), 145–160.

Mooney, D. (1996) Improving your listening skills. Retrieved December 7, 2009, from: http://suicideandmentalhealthassociationinternational.org/improvlisten.html.

National Institute on Deafness and Other Communication Disorders (NIDCD) Quick Statistics. Retrieved October 5, 2014, from, http://www.nidcd.nih.gov/health/statistics/pages/quick.aspx

Nichols, M. P. (2009). *The lost art of listening* (2nd ed.). New York: The Guilford Press.

Pearce, C. G., Johnson, I. W., & Barker, R. T. (2003). Assessment of the Listening Styles Inventory: Progress in establishing reliability and validity. *Journal of Business and Technical Communication, 17*(1), 84–113.

Robertson K. (2005). Active listening: More than just paying attention. *Australian Family Physician, 34*(12), 1053–1055

Rosenfeld, L. B., & Berko, R. (1990). *Communicating with competency.* Glenview, IL: Scott, Foresman/Little.

Shafir, R. Z. (2003). *The Zen of listening* (2nd ed). Wheaton, IL: Quest Books.

Shepherd, T. A., & King, G. (2014). Clinical scenario discussions of listening in interprofessional health care teams. *International Journal of Listening, 28*(1), 47–63.

Shotter, J. (2009). Listening in a way that recognizes/realizes the world of "the other." *The International Journal of Listening, 23*(1), 21–43.

Stoltz, M. (2010). Response: Choice and ethics in listening situations. *International Journal of Listening, 24*(3), 177–178.

Tannen, D. (1994). *Talking from 9 to 5.* New York: William Morrow.

van Vuuren, M., de Jong. M. D. T., & Seydel, E. R. (2007). Direct and indirect effects of supervisor communication on organizational commitment. *Corporate Communications, 12*(2), 116–128.

Villaume, W. A., & Bodie, G. D. (2007). Discovering the listener within us: The impact of trait-like personality variables and communicator styles on preferences for listening style. *International Journal of Listening, 21*(2), 102–123.

Watson, K. W., Barker, L. L., & Weaver, J. B. (1995). The Listening Styles Profile (LSP-16): Development and validation of an instrument to assess four listening styles. *Journal of the International Listening Association, 9,* 1–13.

Welch, S. A., & Mickelson, W. T. (2013). A listening competence comparison of working professionals. *International Journal of Listening, 27*(2), 85–99.

Wolvin, A. (2013). Understanding the listening process: Rethinking the 'one size fits all' model. *International Journal of Listening, 27*(2), 104–106.

(2014, February) *World Health Organization Media Center Fact Sheet.* Retrieved October 5, 2014, from: http://www.who.int/mediacentre/factsheets/fs300/en/

Credits

Photo Credits

Credits are listed in order of appearance.

Photo 1: StockLite/Shutterstock

Photo 2: Jupiterimages/Getty Images

Photo 3: Kathy deWitt/Alamy

Photo 4: Riccardo Piccinini/Shutterstock

Photo 5: Bruce Chambers,/ZUMA Press/Newscom

Photo 6: AISPIX by Image Source/Shutterstock

Photo 7: Chuck Savage/Alamy

Photo 8: Renay Johnson/ZUMAPRESS/Newscom

Photo 9: Matthias Tunger/Digital Vision/Getty Images

Photo 10: Spencer Grant/PhotoEdit

Photo 11: Fotosearch/Getty Images

Photo 12: Denise Hager/Catchlight Visual Services/Alamy

Text and Art Credits

International Listening Association (1995, April). An ILA Definition of Listening. ILA Listening Post, 53, 1-4. p. 4.

van Vuuren, M., de Jong. M. D. T., & Seydel, E. R. (2007). Direct and indirect effects of supervisor communication on organizational commitment. Corporate Communications, 12(2), 116–128.

Based on Crawford, K. (2009). Following you: Discipline of listening in social media. Continuum: Journal of Media & Cultural Studies, 23(4), 525-535. Lacey, K. (2013). Listening Publics: The Politics and Experience of Listening in the Media Age. Cambridge: Polity.

Crawford, K. (2009). Following you: Discipline of listening in social media. Continuum: Journal of Media & Cultural Studies, 23(4), 525-535. p. 529.

Based on Cooper, L. O., & Buchanan, T. (2010). Listening competency on campus: A psychometric analysis of student listening. International Journal of Listening, 24(3), 141–163.

Watson, K. W., Barker, L. L., & Weaver, J. B.(1995). The Listening Styles Profiles (LSP-16): Devlopment and validation of an instrument to assess four listening styles. Journal of the International Listening Association, 9, 1-13.

Watson, K. W., Barker, L. L., & Weaver, J. B.(1995). The Listening Styles Profiles (LSP-16): Development and validation of an instrument to assess four listening styles. Journal of the International Listening Association, 9, 1-13.

Based on (2014, February) World Health Organization Media Center Fact Sheet. Retrieved October 5, 2014, from http://www.who.int/mediacentre/factsheets/fs300/en/, National Institute on Deafness and Other Communication Disorders (NIDCD) Quick Statistics. Retrieved October 5, 2014, from http://www.nidcd.nih.gov/health/statistics/pages/quick.aspx demographics.htm

Shafir, R. Z. (2003). The Zen of listening (2nd ed). Wheaton, IL: Quest Books.

Shafir, R. Z. (2003). The Zen of listening (2nd ed). Wheaton, IL: Quest Books; pp. 157–158, Shafir, R. Z. (2003). The Zen of listening (2nd ed). Wheaton, IL: Quest Books.

Danny

Shotter, J.(2009) Listening in the way that recognizes/realizes the world of "the other". The International Journal of Listening. 23(1), 21-43.

Nichols, M. P. (2009). The lost art of listening (2nd ed.). New York: The Guilford Press.

Communication Across Cultures

From Chapter 8 of *Human Communication in Society*, Fourth Edition. Jess K. Alberts, Thomas K. Nakayama, Judith N. Martin.
Copyright © 2016 by Pearson Education, Inc. All rights reserved.

Communication Across Cultures

CHAPTER TOPICS	Chapter Objectives

The Importance of Intercultural Communication

What Is Intercultural Communication?

Intercultural Communication and the Individual: Borders Dwellers

Intercultural Communication and the Individual: Cultural Values

Intercultural Communication and the Individual: Dialectics

The Individual, Intercultural Communication, and Society: Politics, History, and Power

Ethics and Intercultural Communication

Improving Your Intercultural Communication Skills

1 Identify four reasons for learning about intercultural communication.

2 Define *intercultural communication*.

3 Identify three groups of border dwellers.

4 Identify six cultural values that influence communication.

5 Describe the dialectical approach to intercultural communication.

6 Explain the roles that politics, history, and power play in communication between people from different cultural backgrounds.

7 Give three guidelines for communicating more ethically with people whose cultural backgrounds differ from your own.

8 Discuss three ways to improve your own intercultural communication skills.

"Many, if not most, of your daily interactions are intercultural in nature."

Charee has become good friends with Kaori, a Japanese exchange student. Kaori's English is really good, but sometimes they misunderstand each other when they text. For example, Charee recently learned that when she uses terms like byb or ttyl or makes sarcastic remarks such as "what a great idea, Einstein!" in text messages, Kaori doesn't understand. Kaori didn't tell Charee that she didn't understand, but just didn't respond to the messages. She only explained later when Charee became concerned about the lack of response and pressed Kaori to tell her if something was wrong.

Kaori's story illustrates several points about intercultural communication. First, intercultural contact is a fact of life in today's world; and second, although intercultural contact can be enriching, it can also bring challenges and misunderstanding, especially in mediated communication such as text messaging. In Kaori's case, communicating in English in text messages is especially challenging because of the lack of nonverbal cues. She explained to Charee that she doesn't always feel comfortable telling people when she doesn't understand. She said that in Japan, people generally avoid direct communication and prefer to be more indirect, as we will discuss later. Kaori is an example of someone living "on the border"—between two cultures—having to negotiate sometimes conflicting sets of languages and cultural values.

In today's world, we typically have many opportunities to meet people from different cultures. You may sit in class with students who are culturally different from you in many ways—in nationality, ethnicity, race, gender, age, religion, sexual orientation, and physical ability. In addition, today's widespread access to communication technologies and foreign travel provides many opportunities for intercultural encounters beyond the classroom. But the many political, religious, and ethnic conflicts around the globe may inspire doubt about the ability of people from different cultures to coexist peacefully. Interethnic violence in Sudan and other African nations, in the former Soviet Union, and in the Middle East; clashes between Buddhists and Hindus in India; and tension in the United States between African Americans and Whites may lead people to believe that cultural differences necessarily lead to insurmountable problems. However, we believe that increased awareness of intercultural communication can help prevent or reduce the severity of problems that arise due to cultural differences.

In this chapter, we'll first explore the importance of *intercultural communication* and define what we mean when we use this term. Next, we will describe the increasingly common experience of individuals who must negotiate different cultural realities in their everyday lives. Then we'll examine how culture influences our communication and present a dialectical perspective on intercultural communication. Finally, we'll discuss how society affects communication outcomes in intercultural interactions and provide suggestions for how one can become a more ethical and effective intercultural communicator.

1 The Importance of Intercultural Communication

1 **Identify four reasons for learning about intercultural communication.**

How many reasons for studying intercultural communication can you think of? If you are like many students, entering college has given you more opportunities than ever before for intercultural contact, both domestically and internationally. You will communicate better in these situations if you have a good understanding of intercultural communication. In addition, increased knowledge and skill in intercultural communication can improve your career effectiveness, intergroup relations, and self-awareness. Let's look at each of these reasons more closely.

Increased Opportunities for Intercultural Contact

Experts estimate that more than a billion people travel each year. People leave their countries for many reasons, including national revolutions and civil wars (Syria and Sudan) and natural disasters (floods in Europe and Indonesia, earthquake in Japan). Experts estimate there are currently 36 million displaced persons and persecution forced an average of twenty-three thousand people per day to leave their homes and seek protection elsewhere (United Nations High Commissioner for Refugees [UNHCR], 2013). Sometimes, in a process called **diaspora**, whole groups of people are displaced to new countries as they flee genocide or other untenable conditions or are taken forcefully against their will. Diasporic groups often attempt to settle together in communities in the new location while maintaining a strong ethnic identity and a desire to return home. Historically, diasporic groups include slaves taken from Africa in the 1700s and 1800s, Jews persecuted throughout centuries and relocating around the world, Chinese fleeing famine and wars in the nineteenth and twentieth centuries, and Armenians escaping Turkish genocide in early 1900s (Pendery, 2008; Waterston, 2005). More recent diasporas in the 1990s include Eritreans from Ethiopia, Albanians from Kosovo, and Chechnyans from Russia (Bernal, 2005; Koinova, 2010). Some experts refer to the current Latino diaspora, the increasing numbers of Latin Americans who settle outside their homelands, or the Katrina diaspora, the thousands of Hurricane Katrina survivors who are still unable to return home (Anderson, 2010). Some migrants travel to new lands voluntarily for economic opportunities (to make a better life for themselves or their families) or personal reasons (to join family or friends abroad). Read interesting facts about worldwide migration patterns below (Facts about Global Migration, 2013).

Interesting Facts about Global Migration 2013:

- International migration is at an all time high (232 million migrants in 2013).
- Europe and Asia are hosts to the largest number of international migrants, 72 and 71 million respectively. North America hosts the third largest number (53 million).
- The top 10 migrant corridors are Mexico to the United States (12 million), Ukraine to Russian Federation (3.6 million), Russian Federation to Ukraine (3.5 million), Bangladesh to India (3.1 million), Turkey to Germany (2.8 million), Kazakhstan to Russian Federation (2.6 million), Afghanistan to Pakistan (2.4 million), China to the United States (1.9 million), Philippines to the United States (1.8 million), and India to the United States (1.5 million).
- Refugees represent a small percentage of immigrants worldwide (7% of all international migrants).
- The majority of refugees worldwide are hosted by the following rather small countries: Jordan (2.6 million), Palestine (2.2 million), Pakistan (1.7 million), Syria (1.2 million), Iran (0.9 million), and Germany (0.5 million).

SOURCES: (2013) *World Migration Report 2013: Migrant well-being and development*. Geneva, Switzerland: International Organization for Migration. (2013, September). *Population facts* No. 2013/2. United Nations Department of Economic and Social Affairs, Population Division. www.unpopulation.org.

diaspora
the movement, migration, or scattering of a people away from an established or ancestral homeland

Did You Know?

Meeting Other Travelers Adds Depth to Argentina Visit

Have you had experiences with people from other cultures that changed how you saw the world or the United States? If so, what was it about those interactions that changed your views? If you could change other countries' views of the United States, what would you want to tell them?

Allison, from the United States, is an exchange student in Argentina. Here's an excerpt from her travel blog:

We went to the North West last week; four of us stayed in a youth hostel there. I felt like I had discovered a secret that had been hidden from me all my life. I IMMEDIATELY felt at home. It was just a bunch of kids all traveling from all parts of the world just hanging out and meeting people and sharing all their stories. Our first friends we met were two Canadian kids who had been backpacking through South America the past two months. We spent a lot of time with them drinking mate (the traditional Argentine tea) and chatting about all their experiences in South America. There was a Venezuelan girl and a Japanese girl. It was a pleasure sharing a room with them. In talking to everyone I became even more aware of how misinformed about international news we are in America and how uncommon it is for us to actually be interested enough to really be concerned about what's going on in the rest of the world.

I had a really intriguing conversation with an Israeli soldier who had been traveling through South America during his time off. Hearing his stories was absolutely heartbreaking … all that he was forced to see and to do was absolutely awful! No one of any age should have to endure those things, and he's been doing it since he was 18. I guess that's how it is for people that live in countries where that's just their reality. They become accustomed to falling asleep with gun shots outside their window and getting up to go to work not having any idea what their day will hold and whether or not they'll die. It's awful and such a foreign concept to us; maybe we should make it more of a reality….

SOURCE: Allison Nafziger Travel Blog. Reprinted by permission of Allison Nafziger.

Increasing numbers of people travel for pleasure, some 1,035 million in 2013 ("Tourism Highlights," 2013). Many people, like the student Kaori in the opening story, also travel for study. According to the Institute of International Education, approximately 800,000 international students study in the United States each year and approximately 280,000 U.S. students study overseas (*Open Doors 2013*). Many students study abroad because of the exciting opportunities that exist for intercultural encounters, as exchange student Allison describes in *Did You Know? Meeting Other Travelers Adds Depth to Argentina Visit*.

Another source of increased opportunity for intercultural contact exists because of the increasing cultural diversity in the United States. According to 2010 U. S. census figures, there are continuing dramatic increases in ethnic and racial diversity, and in the next several decades the United States will become a "plurality nation" in which the non-Hispanic white population remains the largest single group, but no group is in the majority (Cooper, 2012).

As shown in Figure 1, the Hispanic population will more than double in size and constitute approximately 30 percent of the population by 2060; in the same time period, the Asian American population will also double in size and will constitute about 8 percent of the total population. African Americans will remain approximately the same in numbers and compose almost 14 percent of the population; Whites will continue to be a smaller majority as minority populations increase in number. The group that will increase the most is the "two or more races" category, which is projected to more than triple. The nation's elderly population will more than double in size from 2012 through 2060, as the baby-boom generation enters the traditional retirement years. The number of working-age Americans and children will grow more slowly than the elderly population and will shrink as a share of the total population (U.S. Census Bureau projections, 2012).

Of course, communication technologies also provide increased opportunity for intercultural encounters. You can play video games with students in

Figure 1 Population by Race and Ethnicity, Actual and Projected: 1960, 2005, and 2050 (percentage of total)

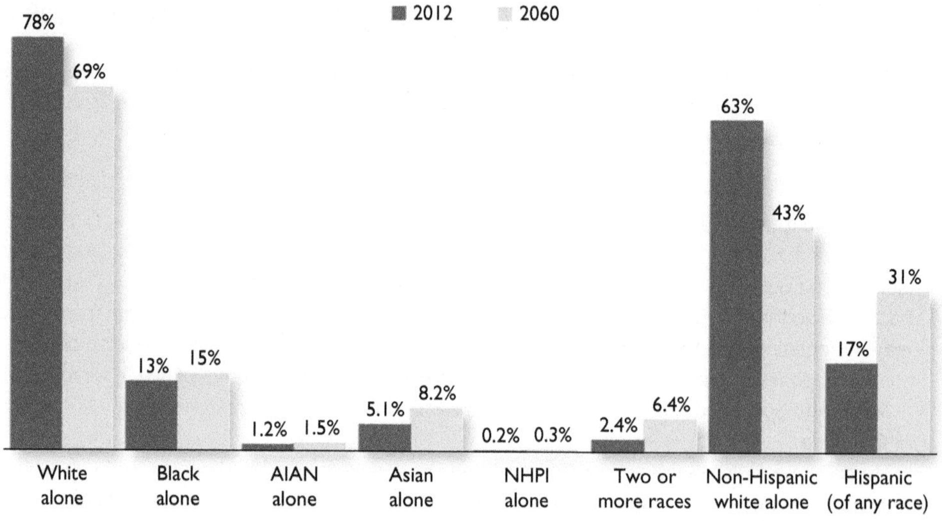

AIAN = American Indian and Alaska Native; NHPI = Native Hawaiian and other Pacific Islander
SOURCE: U.S. Census Bureau projections, 2012

How multicultural is your circle of friends? How many of your friends differ from you in nationality, religion, class, gender, age, sexual orientation, or physical ability?

China, get acquainted with a former exchange student's friends and family on Facebook, debate rock climbing techniques with climbers from Norway to New Zealand on a sports blog, or collaborate with students from around the country for a virtual team project in one of your classes. In the next sections, we will discuss the opportunities that these types of contacts offer—and the benefits to be had from learning more about the intricacies of intercultural communication.

Enhanced Business Effectiveness

Studying intercultural communication can lead to greater success in both domestic and international business contexts. In the domestic context, the U.S. workforce is becoming increasingly diverse as the general population does the same. Furthermore, businesses are becoming more multinational as virtual communication makes it faster and cheaper to collaborate with vendors and customers around the globe. Many industries are also outsourcing services overseas to countries where wages are lower (e.g., Latin and South America, China, Vietnam) and sometimes to former colonies where the colonizer's language is already firmly established. For example, British and U.S. businesses have outsourced services to Ireland and India, and French businesses have sent jobs to Tunisia and Morocco (Bertrand, 2011).

Even though the trend toward globalization is no longer a new phenomenon, a primary cause for international business failures is still lack of attention to cultural factors. For example, Walmart lost hundreds of millions of dollars and finally gave up trying to establish stores in Germany. They failed in part because Walmart executives mistakenly assumed they could transfer their U.S. cultural practices lock, stock, and barrel to the German context. German workers rebelled at the Walmart practice of a Walmart chant every morning; they also rebelled at being told they had to smile (a practice that some male shoppers interpreted as flirting). Although it's faced some recent challenges in China and Mexico, Walmart seemed to learn from their German experience and has been mostly successful in its international expansion (Landler & Barbaro, 2006; Loeb, 2013).

Improved Intergroup Relations

Although we cannot blame all the world's political problems on ineffective intercultural communication, the need for better communication and understanding between countries and ethnic groups is clear. A case that is particularly important to U.S. citizens is improving relationships with people in the Middle East. Many experts think that to facilitate better relationships in this region, the United States should establish meaningful contact with average citizens in the Muslim world, which is something that cannot be accomplished through military force or traditional diplomacy. One way to do this is to acquire intercultural knowledge and skills through learning the language, culture, and history of a country or region and being able to listen (Finn, 2003). U.S.-sponsored programs such as the Peace Corps and the Fulbright scholarship were designed with this kind of intercultural exchange and understanding in mind.

Intercultural communication expertise also can facilitate interethnic relations, which have frequently involved conflict. Consider the ethnic struggles in Bosnia and the former Soviet Union; the war between Hutus and Tutsis in Rwanda (Africa); the continued unrest in the Middle East; and the racial and ethnic struggles and tensions in neighborhoods of many U.S. cities. These conflicts often call for sophisticated skills of intercultural communication and **peacebuilding**, or working toward equilibrium and stability in a society so that disputes do not escalate into violence and war. For example, communication scholar Benjamin Broome (2003, 2004) has successfully facilitated interethnic relations on the island of Cyprus, which is one of the most heavily fortified regions in the world. Through his efforts over many years, small groups of Greek and Turkish Cypriots have worked together to identify communication barriers and propose suggestions for improved relations between their two groups (Broome & Jakobsson, 2006). It should be acknowledged, however, that even with sophisticated intervention, miscommunication and intercultural conflicts can persist: witness the long-standing conflicts in the Middle East, where peacebuilding efforts have long been part of the attempts at resolution. In some cases, people are not motivated to resolve these "intractable conflicts," which are "exceptionally complex, usually involving issues of identity, meaning, justice, and power, often resisting even the most determined attempts at resolution" (Broome & Collier, 2012, p. 1). Although we must admit that there is no easy cure-all for intercultural tensions and misunderstandings, intercultural communication skills are certainly valuable in this area.

peacebuilding
working toward stability in a region to prevent conflicts from escalating into war

Enhanced Self-Awareness

The final reason for studying intercultural communication is to increase self-awareness. This may seem like a contradiction, but it is not. Intercultural exploration begins as a journey into the cultures of others but often results in increased self-knowledge and understanding (Braskamp, Braskamp, & Merrill, 2009). People often learn more about themselves and their own cultural background and identities by coming into contact with people whose cultural backgrounds differ from their own, as our student discovered during her stay in South Africa (see It Happened to Me: Susan).

What you learn about intercultural communication may depend on your social and economic position. For example, individuals from minority racial and ethnic groups in the United States may learn to be a bit wary of intercultural interactions and expect some slights, such as a Chinese American colleague who is sometimes approached

Intercultural contact is a fact in today's world. Many, if not most, of our daily interactions are intercultural in nature.

at professional meetings by White communication professors who assume she is a waitress and ask her to take their drink order!

On the other hand, White and middle-class individuals may find that intercultural learning includes an enhanced awareness of privilege, such as a White colleague who tells of feeling uncomfortable staying at a Caribbean resort, where he was served by Blacks whose ancestors were brought there as slaves by Europeans colonizers. Although he realized that it was his relative privilege that allows him to travel and experience new cultures and places, he also wondered whether this type of travel simply reproduces those same historical postcolonial economic patterns.

With these reasons for studying intercultural communication in mind, we need to define precisely what we mean by intercultural communication and culture, which is the subject we turn to next.

It Happened to Me
Susan

I rarely ever thought about being White or an American until my family and I spent a year in South Africa. Then, I thought about both every day, especially about my being White. The official language of South Africa is English, but even though we technically spoke the same language as the South Africans, my family and I had problems. It started when we were to be picked up from the airport in a *combie*, but I didn't know what that was. It turned out to be a van! Small pick-up trucks were *bakkies*, traffic signals were *robots*, and friends wanted to collect my *contact details*, which meant that they simply wanted the number of my *mobile*, better known as a cell phone, and our address. I felt that every time I opened my mouth, everyone *knew* I was American. The Black/White thing was even more pronounced. When we went down to the flea market or to the Zulu mass at the church we attended, we stood out like "five white golf balls on a black fairway" as my husband liked to say. I wondered if the self-consciousness I felt being White was the same as an African American has walking down the street in America.

2   What Is Intercultural Communication?

2   *Define* intercultural communication.

intercultural communication

communication that occurs in interactions between people who are culturally different

Generally speaking, **intercultural communication** refers to communication that occurs in interactions between people who are culturally different. This contrasts with most communication studies, which focus on communicators in the same culture. Still, in practice, intercultural communication occurs on a continuum, with communication between people who are relatively similar in cultural backgrounds on one end and people who are extremely different culturally on the other. For example, your conversations with your parents would represent a low degree of "interculturalness" because you and your parents belong to two different cultural (age) groups and you probably have much in common—nationality, religion, and language. On the other hand, an interaction with a foreign teaching assistant who has a different nationality, language, religion, age, socioeconomic status, and gender would represent a high degree of interculturalness. Although these two examples represent different ends on the continuum, they are both intercultural interactions. So you can see that many, if not most, of your daily interactions are intercultural in nature.

culture

learned patterns of perceptions, values, and behaviors shared by a group of people

heterogeneous

diverse

The two essential components of intercultural communication are, of course, culture and communication. Having read this far in your text, you should have a good understanding of communication. However, we think it is worthwhile to review our definition of **culture**. Culture is defined as *learned patterns of perceptions, values, and behaviors shared by a group of people*. It is dynamic (it changes), **heterogeneous** (diverse), and operates within societal power structures (Martin & Nakayama, 2014, p. 32). Next we explore how these features of culture impact individuals' intercultural interactions.

3 Intercultural Communication and the Individual: Border Dwellers

3 **Identify three groups of border dwellers.**

However, not all cultural differences have equal impact on one's interactions. For example, although your parents may sometimes seem to come from a different culture, age differences generally have a less dramatic effect on people's interactions than do ethnic and national differences. Here we will examine some of the cultural differences that affect individuals' interactions with one another. We begin by exploring three types of intercultural interactions that can occur when individuals from different cultures coexist. We then explore specific cultural values that shape individuals' communication experiences, and we conclude this section by examining the ways that individuals within a culture can be both similar to and different from one another.

Intercultural Communication on the Borders

Because of increased opportunities for cultural contact, more people find themselves living a multicultural life. Travelers, racial and ethnic groups that live in proximity, immigrants, and people whose intimate partners come from other cultural backgrounds are only some of the groups that live between cultures, or as **border dwellers**. Here we refer to people who live on cultural borders as border dwellers because they often experience contradictory cultural patterns; thus, they may have to move between ethnicities, races, religions, languages, socioeconomic classes, or sexual orientations. One can become a border dweller in one of three ways: through travel, through socialization (co-cultural groups), and through participation in an intercultural relationship. Let's look at each in turn.

BORDER DWELLERS THROUGH TRAVEL Individuals travel between cultures both voluntarily and involuntarily, and for both long and short periods. **Voluntary short-term travelers** include study-abroad students, corporate personnel, missionaries, and military people. **Voluntary long-term travelers** include immigrants who settle in other locations, usually seeking what they perceive is a better life, as is the case for many immigrants who come to the United States. **Involuntary short-term travelers** include refugees forced into cultural migration because of war, famine, or unbearable economic hardship. For example, many people fled Iraq and Afghanistan during the wars there and only return when they feel it is safe to do so (UNHCR, 2013). **Involuntary long-term travelers** are those who are forced to permanently migrate to a new location, including the many diasporic groups referred to previously.

When people think of traveling or living in a new culture, they tend to think that learning the language is key to effective intercultural interaction; however, intercultural communication involves much more than language issues. Most sojourners find there are two types of challenges: (1) dealing with the psychological stress of being in an unfamiliar environment (feeling somewhat uncertain and anxious) and (2) learning how to behave appropriately in the new culture, both verbally (e.g., learning a new language) and nonverbally, for example, bowing instead of shaking hands in Japan (Kim, 2005).

The first of these two challenges is often called *culture shock*. **Culture shock** is a feeling of disorientation and discomfort resulting from the unfamiliarity of surroundings and the lack of familiar cues in the environment. Sometimes people even experience culture shock when they move from one region of the United States to another (e.g., relocating from Boston to Birmingham or from Honolulu to Minneapolis). When

border dwellers

people who live between cultures and often experience contradictory cultural patterns

voluntary short-term travelers

people who are border dwellers by choice and for a limited time, such as study-abroad students or corporate personnel

voluntary long-term travelers

people who are border dwellers by choice and for an extended time, such as immigrants

involuntary short-term travelers

people who are border dwellers not by choice and only for a limited time, such as refugees forced to move

involuntary long-term travelers

people who are border dwellers permanently but not by choice, such as those who relocate to escape war

culture shock

a feeling of disorientation and discomfort as a result of the lack of familiar environmental cues

reverse culture shock/reentry shock

culture shock experienced by travelers on returning to their home country

travelers return home, they may experience similar feelings, known as **reverse culture shock or reentry shock**, which is a sort of culture shock in one's own home location. After being gone for a significant amount of time, aspects of one's own culture may seem somewhat foreign, as the student Maham discovered on his return home to Pakistan after living in the United States for four years (see *It Happened to Me: Maham*).

There are many reasons why an individual may be more, or less, successful at adapting to a new culture. Younger people who have had some previous traveling experience seem to be more successful than older people and first-time travelers. On the other hand, if the environment is hostile or the move is involuntary, adaptation may be especially difficult and the culture shock especially intense. For example, many evacuees from Hurricane Katrina were forced to relocate. In some instances, they were greeted with great sympathy and hospitality in the new locations; in other instances they were subjected to considerable racism ("Rabbi: My radio," 2005). Asian, African, and Latino students in the United States tend to have a more difficult adaptation because of experiences of discrimination and hostility based on their race/ethnicity (Jung, Hecht, & Wadsworth, 2007; Lee & Rice, 2007). Although we may think that anti-immigrant attitudes are a recent phenomenon in the United States because of the number of immigrants or where they come from, historians remind us that today's immigrants have much in common with previous immigrants—including anti-immigrant attitudes. It also turns out that specific locations within the United States tend to be more receptive to international visitors. A recent study found that international students have more positive experiences in the South than in the Northeast United States and fare better in smaller towns than big metropolitan centers (Gareis, 2012).

It Happened to Me

Maham

I would say that I experienced culture (reentry) shock when I visited Pakistan after moving away from there four years ago. In those four years, I had basically forgotten the language and became very unfamiliar with the culture back home. Even though I enjoyed my visit to Pakistan a lot, I had problems adjusting to some of the ways of life. I was not familiar with the bargaining system ... where people can go to the store and bargain for prices. I felt very out of place.... As I spent more time there, I got adjusted and used to how people did things there.

For diasporic groups, whether relocated within their own country or in a foreign country, the culture shock and disorientation can be complicated and even extended

Alternative View

Immigrants

How important is it to reject your own home culture in adapting to a new culture? How can immigrants use their own cultural traditions to help make a smooth transition to the new culture? What could we in the host country do to help immigrants transition successfully to the United States?

Some people seem to think that the key to successfully adapting to a new culture is to completely reject one's home culture. However, some experts suggest that maintaining a strong connection to one's original language and culture actually facilitates a smooth transition to the new culture. Scholar Lucas Torres asked immigrants themselves, in focused interviews as well as quantitative survey questionnaires, what they thought were the knowledge and skills that lead to successful

cultural adaption of Latinos to the United States. Although some of his findings are expected—ambition, perseverance, hard work, good communication/relational skills—they also answered that it was important to maintain the traditional Latino culture (cultural practices such as celebrating holidays, keeping up language skills, strong connections with family and cultural values of respect). They explained that these practices actually serve as strong motivators to successfully adapt—as one said "Competent Latinos embrace their cultures, and because they do.... I think they derive some sort of, I guess, motivation for them to pull forward" (p. 587).

SOURCE: Torres, L. (2009). Latino definitions of success: A cultural model of intercultural competence. *Hispanic Journal of Behavioral Sciences, 31*, 576–593.

because of their strong desire to return home and a feeling of rootlessness. As one Iraqi refugee said, after fleeing war and terrible violence, only to encounter unemployment and poverty in the United States, "We came to this country for the future of our children. We have no future" (Yako & Biswas, 2014, p. 143).

One thing that can ease culture shock and make cultural adaptation easier is taking time to observe and listen. Communication scholar Gerry Philipsen (2010) suggests hanging out where people meet to talk, peer over shoulders, sit for a while and listen, visit social Web sites, "situate oneself wherever there is communicative conduct and watch it and listen to it, with eyes and ears alert and open" to the new communication practices going on around you (p. 166). Something else that helps is having a social support network. This can come from organizations such as an international student office or a tourist bureau that can assist with housing, transportation, and so forth. Close relationships with other travelers or host-country acquaintances, as in the case of Charee and Kaori, can also provide support in the form of a sympathetic ear; through these relationships sojourners can relieve stress, discuss, problem solve, acquire new knowledge, or just have fun (Geeraert, Demoulin, & Demes, 2014; Sobré-Denton, 2011).

The role of social support is even more crucial for long-term travelers, such as immigrants. Diasporic individuals often maintain strong relationships with other members of their group, providing for each this much needed social support, sometimes through cyber communities or in face-to-face interaction (Bernal, 2005; Pendery, 2008). If there is little social support or the receiving environment is hostile, immigrants may choose to separate from the majority or host culture, or they may be forced into separation (Berry, 2005).

Another option for immigrants is to adapt in *some* ways to the new culture, which means accepting some aspects, such as dress and outward behavior, while retaining aspects of the old culture. For many recent immigrants to the United States, this has been a preferred option and seems to lead to less stress. For example, Asian Indians constitute one of the largest immigrant groups in the United States. Many have successfully adapted to U.S. life both professionally and socially. Still many retain viable aspects of their Indian culture in their personal and family lives—continuing to celebrate ethnic or religious holidays and adhering to traditional values and beliefs (Hegde, 2012). Some experts suggest that this integration of two cultures is a model for successful cultural adaptation (see *Alternative View: Immigrants*).

However, this integration of two cultures is not always easy, as we'll see in the next section. Families can be divided on the issues of how much to adapt, with children often wanting to be more "American" and parents wanting to hold on to their native language and cultural practices (Ward, 2008).

BORDER DWELLERS THROUGH SOCIALIZATION The second group of border dwellers is composed of people who grow up living on the borders between cultural groups. Examples include ethnic groups, such as Latinos, Asian Americans, and African Americans, who live in the predominantly White United States, as well as people who grow up negotiating multiple sexual orientations or religions. In addition to those who must negotiate the two cultures they live within, the United States has increasing numbers of multiracial people who often grow up negotiating *multiple* cultural realities (Yen, 2011).

There are many famous multiracial U.S. Americans, including singers Rihanna (Afro-Bajan, Irish and Afro-Guyanese) and Nicki Minaj (East Indian and Afro-Trinidadian), and actors Dwayne Johnson (also known as The Rock), who is Black and Samoan, and Wentworth Miller (father is African American, Caucasian, and Native American and mother is Middle Eastern and Caucasian). Genetic experts point out that many of these multiracial individuals are a recent phenomenon. Their complex web of ancestors, originating from distant world regions, could have encountered each other in the United States only within the past one hundred years (Wells, 2002).

Members of minority groups sometimes find themselves in a kind of cultural limbo—not "gay" enough for gay friends, not "straight" enough for the majority; not Black enough or White enough.

Sometimes multiracial U.S. Americans have to respond, at some point, to criticism that they do not sufficiently align themselves with one or another of their racial groups. Vin Diesel has been criticized for refusing to discuss his Black racial heritage, whereas Dwayne Johnson originally was condemned for not recognizing his Black heritage but later was praised for attending the Black Entertainment Television awards. Many recognize their unique positions, in limbo between but also potential bridges between two cultures. For example, children raised in biracial homes find they are often able to, as adults, relate easily with individuals of both races. They fit in easily with both whites and blacks and often have diverse friendship networks.

Border dwellers through socialization include many multiracial individuals and families. How might the concept of border dwellers change as these many children grow up?

BORDER DWELLERS THROUGH RELATIONSHIPS   Finally, many people live on cultural borders because they have intimate partners whose cultural background differs from their own. Within the United States, increasing numbers of people cross borders of nationality, race, and ethnicity in this way, creating a "quiet revolution" (Root, 2001). In fact, by 2010, 15 percent of all new marriages in the United States were between spouses of a different race or ethnicity—more than double the number in 1980 (Wang, 2012). Overall, partners in interethnic and interracial romantic relationships have faced greater challenges than those establishing relationships across religions, nationalities, and class groups.

Did you know that until June 12, 1967, it was illegal in Virginia (and 13 other states) for Whites and Blacks to marry? This ban against miscegenation (interracial sexual relationships) was challenged in Virginia by Mildred and Richard Loving, who had been married in 1958 in Washington, D.C. (where interracial marriages were permitted). In 1967, the Supreme Court declared Virginia's anti-miscegenation ban unconstitutional, thereby ending all race-based legal restrictions on marriage in the United States. Attitudes toward intercultural relationships have changed significantly in the ensuing decades, particularly attitudes toward interracial relations. For example, in recent surveys, two-thirds of Americans say it "would be fine" with them if a member of their own family were to marry outside their own racial or ethnic group, which is more than double the number in 1986, and the young are the most accepting (Wang, 2012).

However, such relationships are not without their challenges. The most common challenges involve negotiating how to live on the border between two religions, ethnicities, races, languages, and, sometimes, value systems. A recent study of intercultural marriages, some based on religious and some on racial and ethnic differences, found that communication played an important role in the success of these relationships. That is, open communication about the differences helped promote relationship growth. If partners were able to understand, appreciate, and integrate each other's similarities and differences, they would be able to use these in an enriching manner (Reiter & Gee, 2009).

The balancing act between cultures can be especially challenging when friends, family, and society disapprove (Fiebert, Nugent, Hershberger, & Kasdan, 2004). A Jewish professor who married a Muslim woman reflects on how people would react if he decided to convert to Islam:

> What a scandalous action! My family would be outraged and my friends startled. What would they say? How would I be treated? What would colleagues at the university do if I brought a prayer rug to the office and, say, during a committee meeting, or at a reception for a visiting scholar, insisted on taking a break to do my ritual prayers? (Rosenstone, 2005, p. 235).

These challenges can be even more pronounced for women because parents often play an important role in whom they date and marry. It turns out that women are much more likely than men to mention pressure from family members as a reason that interethnic dating would be difficult (Clark-Ibanez & Felmlee, 2004).

NEGOTIATING CULTURAL TENSIONS ON THE BORDERS   How do people negotiate the tensions between often-contradictory systems of values, language, and nonverbal behavior of two or more cultures? The answer depends on many factors, such as one's reason for being on the border, length of stay or involvement, receptivity of the dominant culture, and personality characteristics of the individuals (Kim, 2005).

In most cases, people in such situations can feel caught between two systems; this experience has been described as feeling as if one were swinging on a trapeze, a metaphor that captures the immigrant's experience of vacillating between the cultural patterns of the homeland and the new country, or between two ethnic or religious groups (Hegde, 1998). Typically, cultural minorities are socialized to the norms and values of both the dominant culture and their own; nonetheless, they often prefer to enact those of their own. They may be pressured to assimilate to the dominant culture and embrace it, yet those in the dominant culture may still be reluctant to accept them as they try to do so. Communication scholar Karla D. Scott (2013) conducted focus groups with Black women who lived and work in predominantly white environments to understand better how they navigate between the two cultures, and they all talked about how they simultaneously work to dispel negative stereotypes and to convey an identity of competence and success: "Immediately when I step into a setting where I'm the only Black, I'm feeling like all eyes are upon me, for my entire race, especially Black women. My tone changes, the way I speak, following the rules of language—not that I don't do it anyway, but I'm more alert, making sure that I don't stumble over certain words" (p. 319).

Americans have become much more accepting of interracial and gay marriages and dating relationships in the recent past.

Managing these tensions while living on the border and being multicultural can be both rewarding and challenging. Based on data from interviews she conducted, Janet Bennett (1998) described two types of border dwellers or, as she labeled them, "marginal individuals": *encapsulated marginal people* and *constructive marginal people*.

Encapsulated marginal people feel disintegrated by having to shift cultures. They have difficulty making decisions and feel extreme pressure from both groups. They try to assimilate but never feel comfortable or at home.

In contrast, **constructive marginal people** thrive in their "border" life and, at the same time, recognize its tremendous challenges. They see themselves as choice makers. They recognize the significance and potential of being "in between." For example, communication scholar Lisa Flores (1996) shows how Chicana feminist writers and artists acknowledge negative stereotypes of Mexican and Mexican American women—illiterate Spanglish-speaking laborers, passive sex objects, servants of men and children—and transform them into images of strength. In their descriptions and images, Chicana artists are strong, clever bilinguals, reveling in their dual Anglo-Mexican heritage. In so doing, they create a kind of positive identity "home" where they are the center. In addition, they gain strength by reaching out to other women (women of color and immigrant women), and together strive to achieve more justice and recognition for women who live "in the middle" between cultural worlds.

To summarize, people can find themselves living on cultural borders for many reasons: travel, socialization, or involvement in an intercultural relationship. Although border dwelling can be challenging and frustrating, it also can lead to cultural insights and agility in navigating intercultural encounters.

encapsulated marginal people

people who feel disintegrated by having to shift cultures

constructive marginal people

people who thrive in a border-dweller life, while recognizing its tremendous challenges

4   Intercultural Communication and the Individual: Cultural Values

4   Identify six cultural values that influence communication.

The Influence of Cultural Values on Communication

Culture influences verbal and nonverbal communication. You might think that these differences would be important to understanding intercultural communication, however, just as important is understanding **cultural values**, which are the beliefs that are so central to a cultural group that they are never questioned. Cultural values prescribe what *should* be. Understanding cultural values is essential because they so powerfully influence people's behavior, including their communication. Intercultural interaction often involves confronting and responding to an entirely different set of cultural values. Let's see how this works.

Social psychologist Geert Hofstede (1998, 2010) and his colleagues conducted a massive study, collecting 116,000 surveys about people's value preferences in approximately eighty countries around the world. Psychologist Michael Bond and his colleagues conducted a similar, though smaller, study in Asia ("Chinese Culture Connection," 1987). Although these studies identify value preferences of national cultural groups, they can also apply to religious and ethnic or racial groups, socioeconomic class groups, and gender groups. For example, anthropologists Florence Kluckhohn and Fred Strodtbeck (1961) conducted a study that identified the contrasting values of three cultural groups in the United States: Latinos, Anglos, and American Indians. Recently, communication scholars have identified cultural values of other racial groups: African Americans and Asian Americans. Together, all these studies identified a number of cultural values.

As you read about these cultural value orientations, please keep three points in mind. These guidelines reflect a common dilemma for intercultural communication scholars—the desire to describe and understand communication and behavior patterns within a cultural group and the fear of making rigid categories that can lead to stereotyping:

1. The following discussion describes the *predominant* values preferred by various cultural groups, not the values held by *every person* in the cultural group. Think of cultural values as occurring on a bell curve: Most people may be in the middle, holding a particular value orientation, but many people can be found on each end of the curve; these are the people who *do not go along* with the majority.

2. The following discussion refers to values on the cultural level, not on the individual level. Thus, if you read that most Chinese tend to prefer an indirect way of speaking, you cannot assume that every Chinese person you meet will speak in an indirect way in every situation.

3. The only way to understand what a particular individual believes is to get to know the person. You can't predict how any one person will communicate. The real challenge is to understand the full range of cultural values and then learn to communicate effectively with others who hold differing value orientations, regardless of their cultural background.

Now that you understand the basic ground rules, let's look at six key aspects of cultural values.

INDIVIDUALISM AND COLLECTIVISM   One of the most central value orientations identified in this research addresses

cultural values

beliefs that are so central to a cultural group that they are never questioned

In individualistic cultures, the nuclear family household is most common [just parent(s) and children]: children are raised to be autonomous and to live on their own by late adolescence, whereas parents are expected to not "be a burden" on their children when they age.

whether a culture emphasizes the rights and needs of the individual or that of the group. For example, many North American and northern European cultural groups, particularly U.S. Whites, value individualism and independence, believing that one's primary responsibility is to one's self (Bellah, Madsen, Sullivan, Swidler, & Tipton, 2007; Hofstede et al., 2010). In relationships, those with this **individualistic orientation** respect autonomy and independence, and they do not meddle in another's problems unless invited. For example, in cultures where individualism prevails, many children are raised to be autonomous and to live on their own by late adolescence (although they may return home for short periods after this). Their parents are expected to take care of themselves and not "be a burden" on their children when they age (Triandis, 1995).

In contrast, many cultures in South America and Asia hold a more **collectivistic orientation** that stresses the needs of the group, as do some Hispanic and Asian Americans in the United States (Ho, Rasheed & Rasheed, 2004). Some argue that working-class people tend to be more collectivistic than those in the middle or upper class (Dunbar, 1997). For collectivists, the primary responsibility is to relationships with others; interdependence in family, work, and personal relationships is viewed positively. Collectivists value working toward relationship and group harmony over remaining independent and self-sufficient. For example, giving money to a needy cousin, uncle, or aunt might be preferable to spending it on oneself. Or sharing belongings, such as cars, computers, mobile phones may be expected in collectivist communities. In many collectivist cultures, too, children often defer to parents when making important decisions, like accepting a new job or choosing a spouse (McGoldrick, Giordano, & Garcia-Preto, 2005).

As noted previously, however, not all Japanese or all Indians are collectivistic, nor are all U.S. Americans individualistic. A recent book by journalist Colin Woodard (2012) maintains that there are significant regional differences here in the degree of commitment to individual freedom or conversely, sacrifice for the good of the community. In addition, generational differences may exist within countries where collectivism is strong. For example, some Japanese college students show a strong preference for individualism whereas their parents hold a more collectivistic orientation—which sometimes leads to intercultural conflict (Matsumoto, 2007). Young people in many Asian countries (e.g., Korea, Vietnam) are increasingly influenced by Western capitalism and individualism and are now making their own decisions regarding marriage and career, rather than following their family's wishes—a practice unheard of 50 years ago (Shim, Kim, & Martin, 2008). In addition, not all cultures are as individualistic as U.S. culture or as collectivistic as Japanese culture. Rather, cultures can be arranged along an individualism–collectivism continuum (Ting-Toomey, 2010) based on their specific orientations to the needs of the individual and the group.

PREFERRED PERSONALITY In addition to differing on the individualism–collectivism spectrum, cultural groups may differ over the idea of the **preferred personality**, or whether it is more important to "do" or to "be" (Kluckhohn & Strodtbeck, 1961). In the United States, researchers have found that *doing* is the preferred value for many people, including European Americans, Asian Americans, and African Americans (Ting-Toomey, 1999). In general, the "doing mode" means working hard to achieve material gain, even if it means sacrificing time with family and friends. Other cultural groups, for example, many Latinos, prefer the *being* mode—which emphasizes the importance of experiencing life and the people around them fully and "working to live" rather than "living to work" (Hecht, Sedano, & Ribeau, 1993).

individualistic orientation

a value orientation that respects the autonomy and independence of individuals

collectivistic orientation

a value orientation that stresses the needs of the group

As you were growing up, in what ways were you reared to be individualistic? Collectivistic? Which orientation was the predominant cultural value of your family?

preferred personality

a value orientation that expresses whether it is more important for a person to "do" or to "be"

In many collectivist cultures, adult children often defer to parents when making important decisions.

*What kinds of communication prob-
lems might occur when members of a
diverse work team hold different value
orientations toward being and doing?
How might someone who usually uses
a being mode view someone with a doing mode, and vice versa?*

Some scholars suggest that many African Americans express both a doing mode, fighting actively against racism through social activity for the good of the community, and a being mode, valuing a sense of vitality and open expression of feeling (Hecht, Jackson, & Ribeau, 2002). Cultural differences in this value orientation can lead to communication challenges. For example, many Latinos believe that Anglos place too much emphasis on accomplishing tasks and earning money and not enough emphasis on spending time with friends and family or enjoying the moment (Kikoski & Kikoski, 1999).

view of human nature

a value orientation that expresses whether humans are fundamentally good, evil, or a mixture

HUMAN NATURE A third value difference concerns the **view of human nature**—in particular, whether humans are considered fundamentally good, evil, or a mixture. The United States, for example, was founded by the Puritans who believed that human nature was fundamentally evil (Hulse, 1996). In the years since the founding of the country, a shift occurred in this view, as evidenced in the U.S. legal and justice systems. It emphasizes rehabilitation, which suggests a view of humans as potentially good. In addition, the fact that the U.S. justice system assumes people are innocent until proven guilty indicates that people are viewed as basically good.

In contrast, cultural groups that view humans as essentially evil, such as some fundamentalist religions, emphasize punishment over rehabilitation. Some evidence indicates that U.S. Americans in general are moving again toward this view of human nature. For example, state laws such as the "three-strikes rule" emphasize punishment over rehabilitation by automatically and significantly increasing the prison sentences of persons convicted of a felony who have been previously convicted of two or more violent crimes or serious felonies. Also, incarceration rates in the United States have increased by more than 500 percent since the early 1970s, and among developed countries, the United States now has the highest percentage of incarcerated individuals—more than China, Cuba, and Russia (Mahapatra, 2013). As you might imagine, people who differ on the question of human nature can have serious disagreements on public policies concerning crime and justice.

human–nature value orientation

the perceived relationship between humans and nature

HUMAN–NATURE RELATIONSHIP A fourth value that varies from culture to culture is the perceived relationship between humans and nature, or the **human–nature value orientation**. At one end of this value continuum is the view that humans are intended to rule nature. At the other extreme, nature is seen as ruling humans. In a third option, the two exist in harmony. Unsurprisingly, the predominant value in the United States has been one of humans ruling over nature, as evidenced in the proliferation of controlled environments. Phoenix, Arizona, for example, which is in a desert, has more than two hundred golf courses—reflecting the fact that Arizonans have changed the natural environment to suit their living and leisure interests. In other parts of the United States, people make snow for skiing, seed clouds when rain is needed, dam and reroute rivers, and use fertilizer to enhance agricultural production. Such interventions generally reflect a belief in human control over nature (Trompenaars & Hampden-Turner, 2012).

In contrast, many in the Middle East view nature as having predominance over humans. This belief that one's fate is held by nature is reflected in the common Arabic saying *"Enchallah"* ("Allah willing"), suggesting that nature will (and should) determine, for example, how crops will grow. A comparable Christian saying is "God willing," reflecting perhaps a similar fatalistic tendency in Christianity. Interestingly, many Spanish-speaking Christians express the same sentiment with the word *"Ojalá,"* which is rooted in *"Enchallah"* and originates from the centuries when southern Spain was a Muslim province.

Many American Indians and Asians value harmony with nature. People who hold this cultural orientation believe that humans and nature are one and that nature enriches human life. For many traditional American Indians, certain animals such as buffalo and eagles are important presences in human activity (Porter, 2002). For example, the use of feathers can be an important part of the sundance, a religious ceremony practiced by many different American Indian groups. In this ceremony, the eagle is viewed as the link between humans and creator. When people see an eagle in the sky during a ceremony, they are especially thankful because the eagle flies highest of all birds and the moment it disappears into the skies, people's prayers are heard. These traditions show high regard and utmost respect for these animals and reflect a belief in the close and important relationship between humans and nature ("Eagle aviary allows American Indians to continue heritage", 2005).

In the United States, differences arise between real estate developers, who believe that humans take precedence over nature, and environmentalists and many Native American groups, who believe that nature is as important as humans. This conflict has surfaced in many disagreements; for example, in controversies over water rights in Oregon between Indian tribes who want to maintain water levels for endangered fish they traditionally harvest, denying water to farmers downstream (Barboza, 2013) and between loggers and environmentalist over the endangered spotted owl, which are now also threatened by the more aggressive barred owl in the southwestern United States (Sahagun, 2014).

Reverence for nature plays an important role in many American Indian ceremonies.

POWER DISTANCE Power distance, the fifth value orientation, refers to the extent to which less powerful members of institutions and organizations within a culture expect and accept an unequal distribution of power (Hofstede et al., 2010). In Denmark, Israel, the United States, and New Zealand many people value small power distances. Thus, most people in those countries believe that inequality, although inevitable, should be minimized, and that the best leaders emphasize equality and informality in interactions with subordinates. In many situations, subordinates are expected to speak up and contribute.

Societies that value large power distance—for example, Mexico, the Philippines, and India—are structured more around a hierarchy in which each person has a rightful place, and interactions between supervisors and subordinates are more formal (Hofstede et al., 2010). Seniority, age, rank, and titles are emphasized more in these societies than in small power distance societies. In addition, a preference for informal communication tends to go along with small power distance orientation.

People who are used to large power distances may be uncomfortable in settings where hierarchy is unclear or ambiguous and communication tends to be informal. For example, international students who come from countries where a large power distance value predominates may initially be uncomfortable in U.S. college classrooms, where relations between students and teachers are informal and characterized by equality, especially in online classes, a situation described in *It Happened to Me: Nagesh*.

In contrast, U.S. Americans abroad often offend locals when they treat subordinates at work or home too informally—calling them by their first names, treating them as if they were friends. For example, when former President George W. Bush visited Europe, he referred to the Belgian Prime Minister by his first name, Guy. This surprised and amused many Belgians, who are accustomed to more formality.

Note that value orientations often represent a cultural ideal rather than a reality. Although many Americans say they desire

power distance

a value orientation that refers to the extent to which less powerful members of institutions and organizations within a culture expect and accept an unequal distribution of power

It Happened to Me
Nagesh

I was amazed when I took my first online class at an American university. The students seemed very disrespectful toward the teacher and toward each other. In discussions, they addressed the teacher very informally, just like "hey, I have a question!" They didn't address the professor by title, and they would openly disagree with each other. In my country (India), students would never behave this way toward a teacher. I found it difficult to speak up in this kind of online classroom situation.

small power distance, the truth is that rigid social and economic hierarchies exist in the United States. Most Americans are born into and live within the same socioeconomic class for their whole lives (Moving on up, 2013).

LONG-TERM VERSUS SHORT-TERM ORIENTATION The research identifying the five values we've described has been criticized for its predominately western European bias. In response to this criticism, a group of Chinese researchers developed and administered a similar, but more Asian-oriented, questionnaire to people in 22 countries around the world ("Chinese Culture Connection," 1987). They then compared their findings to previous research on value orientations and found considerable overlap, especially on the dimensions of individualism versus collectivism and power distance. These researchers did identify one additional value dimension that previous researchers hadn't seen—**long-term versus short-term orientation.**

This dimension reflects a society's attitude toward virtue or truth. A **short-term orientation** characterizes cultures in which people are concerned with possessing one fundamental truth, as reflected in the **monotheistic** (belief in one god) religions of Judaism, Christianity, and Islam. Other qualities identified in the research and associated with a short-term orientation include an emphasis on quick results, individualism, and personal security and safety (Hofstede et al., 2010).

In contrast, a **long-term orientation** tends to respect the demands of virtue, reflected in Eastern religions such as Confucianism, Hinduism, Buddhism, and Shintoism, which are all **polytheistic** religions (belief in more than one god). Other qualities associated with a long-term orientation include thrift, perseverance, and tenacity in whatever one attempts, and a willingness to subordinate oneself for a purpose (Bond, 1991, 2010).

Although knowing about these value differences can help you identify and understand problems that arise in intercultural interactions, you might be concerned that this approach to the study of intercultural communication leads to generalizing and stereotyping. The next section presents an approach that helps counteract this tendency to think in simplistic terms about intercultural communication.

5   Intercultural Communication and the Individual: Dialectics

5   **Describe the dialectical approach to intercultural communication.**

A Dialectical Approach

Dialectics has long existed as a concept in philosophical thought and logic. In this text we introduce it as a way to emphasize simultaneous contradictory truths. Thus, a **dialectical approach** helps people respond to the complexities of intercultural communication and to override any tendencies to stereotype people based on cultural patterns. This concept may be difficult to understand because it is contrary to most formal education in the United States, which often emphasizes **dichotomous thinking,** in which things are "either/or"—good or bad, big or small, right or wrong. However, a dialectical approach recognizes that things may be "both/and." For example, a palm tree may be weak *and* strong. Its branches look fragile and weak, and yet in a hurricane it remains strong because the "weak" fronds can bend without breaking. Similar dialectics exist in intercultural communication; for example, Didier may be a Frenchman who shares many cultural characteristics of other French people, but he also is an individual who possesses characteristics that make him unique. So, he is both similar to and different from other French people. A dialectical approach emphasizes the fluid, complex, and contradictory nature of intercultural interactions.

---

long-term versus short-term orientation

the dimension of a society's value orientation that reflects its attitude toward virtue or truth

short-term orientation

a value orientation that stresses the importance of possessing one fundamental truth

monotheistic

belief in one god

long-term orientation

a value orientation in which people stress the importance of virtue

polytheistic

belief in more than one god

dialectical approach

recognizes that things need not be perceived as "either/or," but may be seen as "both/and"

dichotomous thinking

thinking in which things are perceived as "either/or"—for example, "good or bad," "big or small," "right or wrong"

Dialectics exist in other communication contexts such as relationships. Six dialectics that can assist you in communicating more effectively in intercultural interactions are discussed next.

CULTURAL–INDIVIDUAL This dialectic emphasizes that some behaviors, such as ways of relating to others, are determined by our culture, whereas others are simply idiosyncratic, or particular to us as individuals. For example, Robin twists her hair while she talks. This idiosyncratic personal preference should not be mistaken for a cultural norm. She doesn't do it because she is female, or young, or Protestant, or African American. Although it isn't always easy to tell whether a behavior is culturally or individually based, taking a dialectical approach means that one does not immediately assume that someone's behavior is culturally based.

PERSONAL–CONTEXTUAL This dialectic focuses on the importance of context or situation in intercultural communication. In any intercultural encounter, both the individual and the situation are simultaneously important. Let's take the example of a French student and a U.S. student striking up a conversation in a bar. The immediate situation has an important impact on their communication, so their conversation would probably differ dramatically if it occurred at a synagogue, mosque, or church. The larger situation, including political and historical forces, also plays a role. In the build-up to the Iraq War of 2003, for example, some French students encountered anti-French sentiment in the United States. At the same time, the characteristics of the specific individuals also affect the exchange. Some U.S. students would ignore the immediate or larger situation and reject the anti-French sentiment—especially if they were opposed to the war themselves. Others would attach great importance to the larger context and view the French students negatively. The point is that reducing an interaction to a mere meeting of two individuals means viewing intercultural communication too simplistically.

DIFFERENCES–SIMILARITIES Real, important differences exist between cultural groups; we've identified some of these. However, important commonalities exist as well. One of our students summed up this point nicely in *It Happened to Me: Angelina*.

STATIC–DYNAMIC Although some cultural patterns remain relatively stable and static for years, they also can undergo dynamic change. For example, many people form impressions about American Indians from popular films such as *Smoke Signals*—or even children's movies like *Pocahontas* or *The Indian in the Cupboard*, which portray Indians living the rural life they lived centuries ago—even though the majority of Indians in the United States today live in urban areas (American Indians, 2010). A static–dynamic dialectic requires that you recognize both traditional and contemporary realities of a culture.

HISTORY/PAST–PRESENT/FUTURE An additional dialectic in intercultural communication focuses on the present and the past. For example, one cannot fully understand contemporary relations between Arabs and Jews, Muslims and Christians, or Catholics and Protestants without knowing something of their history. At the same time, people cannot ignore current events. For example, the conflict over where Yasser Arafat was to be buried in the autumn of 2004 flowed from a complex of historical and contemporary relations. His family had resided for

It Happened to Me
Angelina

In my first year of college, I had the most memorable friendship with a person from the Middle East. Through this friendship I learned a lot about the way people from the Middle East communicate with friends, family, and authority. My new friend and I differed in many ways—in religion, culture, nationality, race, and language. However, we were both female college students, the same age, and we shared many interests. She dressed like I did and styled her hair similarly, and we shared many ideas about the future and concerns about the world.

Although being white involves cultural advantages, being poor involves disadvantages.

generations in Jerusalem and wanted him laid to rest there. Israel, having current control of Jerusalem and viewing Arafat as a terrorist leader of attacks against Israel, refused.

PRIVILEGE–DISADVANTAGE In intercultural interactions, people can be simultaneously privileged and disadvantaged (Johnson, 2006). This can become quite clear when one travels to developing countries. Although U.S. Americans may be privileged in having more money and the luxury of travel, they can also feel vulnerable in foreign countries if they are ignorant of the local languages and customs. Poor Whites in the United States can be simultaneously privileged because they are White and disadvantaged because of their economic plight (Engen, 2012). As a student, you may feel privileged (compared to others) in that you are acquiring a high level of education, but you may also feel economically disadvantaged because of the high cost of education.

This dialectical approach helps us resist making quick, stereotypical judgments about others and their communication behavior. A single person can have individualistic and collectivistic tendencies, can be both culturally similar and different from us, and can be culturally privileged in some situations and culturally disadvantaged in others (Ting-Toomey, 2010). All these elements affect communication in both business and personal relationships.

6 The Individual, Intercultural Communication, and Society: Politics, History, and Power

6   **Explain the roles that politics, history, and power play in communication between people from different cultural backgrounds.**

As you have probably gathered by now, intercultural communication never occurs in a vacuum but must be understood in the context of larger societal forces. In this section, we first focus on social, political, and historical forces; second, we turn our attention to the role of power in intercultural communication.

Political and Historical Forces

That societal forces can affect intercultural encounters is exemplified by the varying reactions toward some immigrant groups after the attacks of September 11, 2001. Scholar Sunil Bhatia (2008) found, through interviews with Asian-Indian Americans, that these immigrants experienced reactions from others that caused them to question their "American" identity. Before 9/11, they considered themselves well-adapted to U.S. culture. However, after 9/11, people treated them differently. Their neighbors, who knew them well, were much friendlier and sympathetic. However, some strangers were more hostile to them (sometimes mistaking non-Muslims for Muslims). Thus, they were reminded that they were different; they were not completely accepted as Americans by the U.S. majority.

Historical forces also can influence contemporary intercultural interaction, as we noted in our discussion of dialectics. For example, although slavery is long gone in the United States, one could not understand contemporary Black–White relations in this country without acknowledging its effect. Author James Loewen (2010) describes the twin legacies of slavery that are still with us: (1) social and economic inferiority for Blacks brought on by specific economic and political policies from 1885 to 1965 that led to inferior educational institutions and exclusion from labor unions, voting rights, and the advantage of government mortgages; (2) cultural racism instilled in Whites. The election of Barack Obama as the first African American U.S. president demonstrates significant progress in interracial relations and has presented new opportunities for cross-racial dialogue (Dyson, 2009). However, the intense political and social conversations that have occurred since the election, often centering on race (e.g., the shooting of Michael Brown, an unarmed black teenager, by a white police officer in Ferguson, Missouri), might also demonstrate that the historical legacies of racism impact interracial encounters even today (Martin, Trego, & Nakayama, 2010). In fact, a recent Reuters poll found that 40 percent of white Americans and 25 percent of non-white Americans report that they have no friends of another race and that Americans remain fairly racially segregated (Dunsmuir, 2013).

As a society, which institutions or contexts now promote the best opportunities for interracial contact? Neighborhoods? Educational institutions? Churches, synagogues, and other places of worship? The workplace? Neighborhoods and workplaces do not seem to provide opportunities for the *type* of contact (intimate, friendly, equal-status interaction) that facilitates intercultural relationships (Johnson & Jacobson, 2005). On the other hand, it appears that *integrated* religious institutions and educational institutions provide the best opportunities for intercultural friendships and the best environment to improve interracial attitudes (Johnson & Jacobson, 2005). For example, a study of six California State University campuses found that the students on these campuses interacted equally, in interracial and intraracial encounters (Cowan, 2005). These campuses are diverse; no single ethnic or racial group is a majority. However, a more recent study cautions that sometimes students in multicultural campus assume that they have intercultural relationships just by virtue of being surrounded by cultural diversity and may not make the effort to actually pursue intercultural friendships (Halualani, 2008).

Intercultural Communication and Power

The more powerful groups in society establish the rules for communication, and others usually follow these rules or violate them at their peril (Orbe, 1998). A number of factors influence who is considered powerful in a culture. For example, being White in the United States has more privilege attached to it than being Latino. Although most Whites do not notice this privilege and dominance, most minority group members do (Bahk & Jandt, 2004). Being male also has historically been more valued than being female, and being wealthy is more valued than being poor. Further, being able-bodied is traditionally more valued than being physically disabled (Allen, 2010; Johnson, 2006). Every society, regardless of power distance values, has these kinds of traditional hierarchies of power. Although the hierarchy is never entirely fixed, it does constrain and influence communication among cultural groups.

How do power differences affect intercultural interaction? They do so primarily by determining whose cultural values will be respected and followed. For example, even though the United States is increasingly diverse culturally, faculty, staff, and students in most U.S. universities adhere to the values and communication norms set by the White, male-dominant groups. These values and communication norms emphasize individualism. Thus, although group work is common in many courses, professors usually try to figure out how to give individual grades for it, and most students are encouraged to be responsible for their own work. Moreover, the university is run on monochronic time, with great emphasis placed on keeping schedules and meeting deadlines—and these deadlines sometimes take precedence over family and other personal responsibilities. The communication style most valued in this culture also is individual-oriented, direct and to the point, and extremely task-oriented, as is the case in many organizations in the United States (Kikoski & Kikoski, 1999).

What is the impact for those who come from other cultural backgrounds and do not fit into this mold—say, for those who have collectivistic backgrounds and value personal relationships over tasks and homework assignments? Or for those, like Kaori, whose preferred communication style is more indirect? They may experience culture shock; they also may be sanctioned or marginalized—for example, with bad grades for not participating more in class, for not completing tasks on time, or for getting too much help from others on assignments.

cocultural group

a significant minority group within a dominant majority that does not share dominant group values or communication patterns

To more fully consider these problems we need to introduce the concept of the **cocultural group**, meaning significant minority groups within a dominant majority that do not share dominant group values or communication patterns. Examples include some Native American, Mexican American, and Asian American individuals who choose not to assimilate to the dominant, White U.S. culture. Researcher Mark Orbe (1998) suggests that cocultural group members have several choices as to how they can relate to the dominant culture: They can assimilate, they can accommodate, or they can remain separate. He cautions that each strategy has benefits and limitations. For example, when women try to assimilate and "act like men" in a male-oriented organization, they may score points for being professional, but they also may be criticized for being too masculine. When African Americans try to accommodate in a largely White management, they may satisfy White colleagues and bosses, but earn the label "oreo" from other African Americans. In contrast, resisting assimilation or remaining apart may result in isolation, marginalization, and exclusion from the discussions where important decisions are made.

Communication in Society

African American TV Families: Diverse Enough?

This author writes about the debate over the role of reality television shows reflecting or shaping our views on racial and economic diversity. How important do you think it is that television shows, especially reality TV, reflect or critique social reality?

Does diversity matter in reality TV? Tamar Braxton of *Braxton Family Values*, on WEtv, explained why her family chose to do a reality show: she noted that it was important "especially for our black community" to show audiences people to whom they could relate. And it makes sense for the network's bottom line—attracting a large diverse audience

[However,] it should also be noted that the families on some reality television can't be used to generalize about families of any race; they're really rich: e.g. *Braxton Family Values*, where one sister is singer Toni Braxton, and *The Real Housewives of Atlanta*, part of a franchise where affluence is the common experience.

So although there may be racial diversity, is the lack of socioeconomic diversity of African-American TV families, scripted and unscripted, a problem? As Cynthia Bailey, of *The*

Real Housewives of Atlanta, says, she couldn't identify with the *Cosby Show* when she was growing up. "That wasn't what my family was like," she says. "In my mind, that was almost a rich black family."

Some experts think this is a problem. Communication professor Catherine Squires, author of *African Americans and the Media*, says that because television shows, especially reality television, are supposed to reflect reality, "[l]ooking at rich, black people acting out after you've looked at rich, white people acting out, does that give people who aren't rich and black any sense of what the black people closer to their lives are like?" And even a show like *Real Housewives*, which is relatively diverse across the franchise, represents each racial group as largely cut off from the others. Squires says that, while the monoracial nature of television does reflect ongoing segregation everywhere from schools to Hollywood, such mirroring means it's all the more important to notice.

SOURCE: Rothman, L. (2012, July 8). Essence Fest 2012: Is reality TV still not diverse enough? *Time.com*. Retrieved March 22, 2014, from: http://entertainment.time.com/2012/07/08/essence-reality-tv-family-panel/.

7 Ethics and Intercultural Communication

7 **Give three guidelines for communicating more ethically with people whose cultural backgrounds differ from your own.**

It is difficult to engage in meaningful communication if people are unwilling to suspend or reexamine their assumptions about the world.

How can you communicate more ethically across cultures? Unfortunately, no easy answers exist, but a few guidelines may be helpful.

First, remember that everyone, including you, is enmeshed in a culture and thus communicating through a cultural lens. Recognizing your own cultural attitudes, values, and beliefs will make you more sensitive to others' cultures and less likely to impose your own cultural attitudes on their communication patterns. Although you may feel most comfortable living in your own culture and following its communication patterns, you should not conclude that your culture and communication style are best or should be the standard for all other cultures. Such a position is called *ethnocentrism*. Of course, appreciating and respecting other cultures does not mean you don't still appreciate and respect your own.

Second, as you learn about other cultural groups, be aware of their humanity and avoid the temptation to view them as an exotic "other." Communication scholar Bradford Hall (1997) has cautioned about this tendency, which is called the "zoo approach."

When using such an approach, we view the study of culture as if we were walking through a zoo admiring, gasping, and chuckling at the various exotic animals we observe. One may discover amazing, interesting, and valuable information by using such a perspective and even develop a real fondness of these exotic people, but miss the point that we are as culturally "caged" as others and that they are culturally as "free" as we are (Hall, 1997, p. 14). From an ethical perspective, the zoo approach denies the humanity of other cultural groups. For example, the view of African cultures as primitive and incapable led Whites to justify colonizing Africa and exploiting its rich resources in the nineteenth century.

Third, you will be more ethical in your intercultural interactions if you are open to other ways of viewing the world. The ways that you were taught about the world and history may not be the same as what others were taught. People cannot engage in meaningful communication if they are unwilling to suspend or reexamine their assumptions about the world. For example, some Europeans believe that the United States becomes involved in other countries' affairs so that it can control its oil interests, whereas many U.S. Americans believe that concern over human rights is the motivation. If neither group will consider the opinion of the other, they will be unlikely to sustain a mutually satisfying conversation.

8 Improving Your Intercultural Communication Skills

8 **Discuss three ways to improve your own intercultural communication skills.**

How can you communicate more effectively across cultures? As with ethics, no magic formula exists, but here are several suggestions.

Increase Motivation

Perhaps the most important component is *motivation*. Without the motivation to be an effective communicator, no other skills will be relevant. Part of the problem in longstanding interethnic or interreligious conflicts—for example, between the Israelis and the Palestinians—is the lack of interest, on both sides, in communicating more effectively. Some parties on both sides may even have an interest in prolonging conflict. Therefore, a strong desire to improve one's skills is necessary.

Increase Your Knowledge of Self and Others

In addition to being motivated, you become a more effective intercultural communicator if you educate yourself about intercultural communication. Having some knowledge about the history, background, and values of people from other cultures can help you communicate better, both face to face and online. When you demonstrate this type of knowledge to people from other cultures, you communicate that you're interested in them and you affirm their sense of identity. Obviously, no one can know everything about all cultures; nonetheless, some general information can be helpful, as can an awareness of the importance of context and a dialectical perspective.

Self-knowledge also is important. If you were socialized to be individualistic and direct in your communication style, you may initially have a hard time understanding collectivistic tendencies or indirect communication. Once you become aware of these differences, however, you can more easily communicate with someone who holds a different perspective. Growing up in a middle-class family may also influence your perceptions. Many middle-class people assume that anyone can become middle class through hard work. But this view overlooks the discrimination faced by people of color, members of religious minorities, and gays and lesbians. How can you increase your cultural self-awareness? Perhaps the best way is to cultivate intercultural encounters and relationships.

Developing facility in intercultural communication occurs through a cyclical process. The more one interacts across cultures, the more one learns about oneself, and then the more prepared one is to interact interculturally, and so on. However, increased exposure and understanding do not happen automatically. Being aware of the influence of culture on oneself and others is essential to increasing one's intercultural experience and competence (Ting-Toomey, 2010).

Where should you start? You can begin by examining your current friendships and reach out from there. Research shows that individuals generally become friends with people with whom they live, work, and worship. So your opportunities for intercultural interaction and self-awareness are largely determined by the type of people and contexts you encounter in your daily routine.

Wahoo, the Cleveland Indians mascot, is a controversial figure. To some, Wahoo represents an offensive stereotype; to others, an expression of pride in the team. How might we respond to a similar caricature of African Americans or White Americans?

Avoid Stereotypes

Cultural differences may lead to stereotyping and prejudices. Normal cognitive patterns of generalizing make our world more manageable. However, when these generalizations become rigid, they lead to stereotyping and prejudices. Furthermore, stereotyping can become self-fulfilling (Snyder, 2001). That is, if you stereotype people and treat them in a prejudiced or negative manner, they may react in ways that reinforce your stereotype.

On the other hand, we must note, overreacting by being "sweet" can be equally off-putting. African Americans sometimes complain about being "niced" to death by Whites (Yamato, 2001). The guideline here is to be mindful that you might be stereotyping. For example, if you are White, do you only notice bad behavior when exhibited by a person of color? Communicating effectively across cultural boundaries is a challenge—but one we hope you will take up.

Summary

Four reasons for learning about intercultural communication are increased opportunity, increased business effectiveness, improved intergroup relations, and enhanced self-awareness. Intercultural communication is defined as communication between people from different cultural backgrounds, and culture is defined as learned patterns of perceptions, values, and behaviors shared by a group of people. Culture is dynamic and heterogeneous, and it operates within power structures. Increasing numbers of individuals today live on cultural borders—through travel, socialization, or relationships. Being a "border dweller" involves both benefits and challenges.

Six core cultural values differentiate various cultural groups, and these value differences have implications for intercultural communication. A dialectical approach to intercultural communication can help individuals avoid quick generalizations and stereotyping. There are at least six intercultural communication dialectics: cultural–individual, personal–contextual, differences–similarities, static–dynamic, history/past–present/future, and privilege–disadvantage.

Society plays an important role in intercultural communication because intercultural encounters never occur in a vacuum. Societal forces, including political and historical structures, always influence communication. Power is often an important element in that those who hold more powerful positions in society set the rules and norms for communication. Those individuals who do not conform to the rules because of differing cultural backgrounds and preferences may be marginalized. To ensure that you are communicating ethically during intercultural interactions, attend to the following: avoid ethnocentric thinking, recognize the humanity of others, and remain open to other ways of understanding the world. Finally, you can become a more effective intercultural communicator in at least three ways: by increasing your motivation, acquiring knowledge about self and others, and avoiding stereotyping.

Key Terms

diaspora
peacebuilding
intercultural communication
culture
heterogeneous
border dwellers
voluntary short-term travelers
voluntary long-term travelers
involuntary short-term travelers
involuntary long-term travelers
culture shock

reverse culture shock/reentry
  shock
encapsulated marginal people
constructive marginal people
cultural values
individualistic orientation
collectivistic orientation
preferred personality
view of human nature
human–nature value
  orientation

power distance
long-term versus short-term
  orientation
short-term orientation
monotheistic
long-term orientation
polytheistic
dialectical approach
dichotomous thinking
cocultural group

Apply What You Know

1. **Cultural Profile** List all the cultural groups you belong to. Which groups are most important to you when you're at college? When you're at home? Which groups would be easiest to leave? Why?
2. **Intercultural Conflict Analysis** Identify a current intercultural conflict in the media. It can be conflict between nations, ethnic groups, or gender. Read at least three sources that give background and

information about the conflict. Conduct an analysis of this conflict, answering the following questions:

- What do you think are the sources of the conflict?
- Are there value differences?
- Power differences?
- What role do you think various contexts (historical, social, and political) play in the conflict?

Glossary

border dwellers people who live between cultures and often experience contradictory cultural patterns

cocultural group a significant minority group within a dominant majority that does not share dominant group values or communication patterns

collectivistic orientation a value orientation that stresses the needs of the group

constructive marginal people people who thrive in a border-dweller life, while recognizing its tremendous challenges

cultural values beliefs that are so central to a cultural group that they are never questioned

culture learned patterns of perceptions, values, and behaviors shared by a group of people

culture shock a feeling of disorientation and discomfort due to the lack of familiar environmental cues

diaspora group of immigrants, sojourners, slaves, or strangers living in new lands while retaining strong attachments to their homelands

dialectical approach recognizes that things need not be perceived as "either/or," but may be seen as "both/and"

dichotomous thinking thinking in which things are perceived as "either/or"—for example, "good or bad," "big or small," "right or wrong"

encapsulated marginal people people who feel disintegrated by having to shift cultures

heterogeneous diverse

heuristic use of language to acquire knowledge and understanding

human–nature value orientation the perceived relationship between humans and nature

individualistic orientation a value orientation that respects the autonomy and independence of individuals

intercultural communication communication that occurs in interactions between people who are culturally different

involuntary long-term travelers people who are border dwellers permanently but not by choice, such as those who relocate to escape war

involuntary short-term travelers people who are border dwellers not by choice and only for a limited time, such as refugees forced to move

long-term versus short-term orientation the dimension of a society's value orientation that reflects its attitude toward virtue or truth

long-term orientation a value orientation in which people stress the importance of virtue

monotheistic belief in one god

peacebuilding working toward stability in a region to prevent conflicts from escalating into war

polytheistic belief in more than one god

power distance a value orientation that refers to the extent to which less powerful members of institutions and organizations within a culture expect and accept an unequal distribution of power

preferred personality a value orientation that expresses whether it is more important for a person to "do" or to "be"

reverse culture shock/reentry shock culture shock experienced by travelers upon returning to their home country

short-term orientation a value orientation that stresses the importance of possessing one fundamental truth

view of human nature a value orientation that expresses whether humans are fundamentally good, evil, or a mixture

voluntary long-term travelers people who are border dwellers by choice and for an extended time, such as immigrants

voluntary short-term travelers people who are border dwellers by choice and for a limited time, such as study-abroad students or corporate personnel

References

Allen, B. (2010). *Difference matters: Communicating social identity* (2nd ed). Waveland Press.

Allison Nafziger Travel Blog. Reprinted by permission of Allison Nafziger.

American Indians by the Numbers (From the U. S. Census Bureau 2010). Retrieved March 17, 2014, from: http://www.infoplease.com/spot/aihmcensus1.html.

Anderson, E. (2010, August 26). One town's post-Katrina diaspora. *msnbc.msn.com*. Retrieved September 7, 2011, from: http://www.msnbc.msn.com/id/38851079/ns/us_news-katrina_five_years_later/t/one-towns-post katrina-diaspora/.

Bahk, M., & Jandt, F. E. (2004). Being white in America: Development of a scale. *Howard Journal of Communications, 15*, 57–68.

Barboza, T. (2013, May 7). Water war between Klamath River farmers, tribes poised to erupt. *LA Times*. Retrieved March 17, 2014, from: http://articles.latimes.com/2013/may/07/local/la-me-klamath-20130507.

Bellah, R. N., Madsen, R., Sullivan, W. M., Swidler, A., & Tipton, S. M. (2007). *Habits of the heart: Individualism and commitment in American life, with a new preface*. Los Angeles: University of California Press.

Bennett, J. M. (1998). Transition shock: Putting culture shock in perspective. In M. J. Bennett (Ed.), *Basic concepts in intercultural communication: Selected readings* (pp. 215–224). Yarmouth, ME: Intercultural Press. First published in 1977, in N. C. Jain (Ed.), *International and Intercultural Communication Annual, 4*, 45–52.

Bernal, V. (2005). Eritrea on-line: Diaspora, cyberspace, and the public sphere. *American Ethnologist, 32,* 660–675.

Berry, J. W. (2005) Acculturation: Living successfully in two cultures. *International Journal of Intercultural Relations, 29,* 697–712.

Bertrand, O. (2011). What goes around, comes around: Effects of offshore outsourcing on the export performance of firms. *International Business Studies, 42*(2), 334–344.

Bhatia, S. (2008). 9/11 and the Indian diaspora: Narratives of race, place and immigrant identity. *Journal of Intercultural Studies, 29*(1), 21–39.

Bond, M. (1991). *Beyond the Chinese face.* Hong Kong: Oxford University Press.

Bond, M. (Ed.) (2010). *The Oxford handbook of Chinese psychology.* New York: Oxford University Press.

Braskamp, L. A., Braskamp, D. C., Merrill, K. C. (2009). Assessing progress in global learning and development of students with education abroad experiences. *Frontiers: The Interdisciplinary Journal of Study Abroad, 13,* 101–118.

Broome, B. J. (2003). Responding to the challenges of third-party facilitation: Reflections of a scholar-practitioner in the Cyprus conflict. *Journal of Intergroup Relations, 26*(4), 24–43.

Broome, B. J. (2004). Building a shared future across the divide: Identity and conflict in Cyprus. In M. Fong and R. Chuang (Eds.), *Communicating ethnic and cultural identity* (pp. 275–294). Lanham, MD: Rowman and Littlefield, Publishers.

Broome, B. J., & Collier, M. J. (2012). Culture, communication, and peacebuilding: A reflexive multi-dimensional contextual framework. *Journal of International and Intercultural Communication, 5*(4), 245–269.

Broome, B. J., & Jakobsson H. A. (2006). Building peace in divided societies: The role of intergroup dialogue, in J. Oetzel and S. Ting-Toomey (Eds.), *Handbook of Conflict Communication* (pp. 627–662). Thousand Oaks, CA: Sage Publications.

Chinese Culture Connection (1987). Chinese values and the search for culture-free dimensions of culture. *Journal of Cross-Cultural Psychology, 18,* 143–164.

Clark-Ibanez, M. K., & Felmlee, D. (2004). Interethnic relationships: The role of social network diversity. *Journal of Marriage and Family, 66,* 229–245.

Cooper, M. (2012, 13 December). Census officials, citing increasing diversity, say U. \S. will be a 'Plurality Nation'. *New York Times,* p. A20.

Cowan, G. (2005). Interracial interactions of racially diverse university campuses. *Journal of Social Psychology, 14,* 49–63.

Dunbar, R. A. (1997). Bloody footprints: Reflections on growing up poor white. In M. Wray & A. Newitz (Eds.), *White trash: Race and class in America* (pp. 73–86). New York: Routledge.

Dunsmuir, L. (2013, August 8). Many Americans have no friends of another race: poll. Retrieved March 22, 2014, from: http://www.reuters.com/article/2013/08/08/us-usa-poll-race-idUSBRE97704320130808.

Dyson, M. E. (2009). An American man, an American moment. *Ebony, 64*(3), 90–94.

Eagle aviary allows American Indians to continue heritage. (2005, March 3). newswise.com. Retrieved March 22, 2014, from: http://www.newswise.com/articles/eagle-aviary-allows-american-indians-to-continue-heritage.

Engen, D. (2012). Invisible identities: Notes on class and race. In A. González, M. Houston, V. Chen (Eds.), *Our voices: Essays in culture, ethnicity and communication* (5th ed., pp. 223–239). New York: Oxford University Press.

Fiebert, M. S., Nugent, D., Hershberger, S. L., & Kasdan, M. (2004). Dating and commitment choices as a function of ethnicity among American college students in California. *Psychological Reports, 94,* 1293–1300.

Finn, H. K. (2003). The case for cultural diplomacy. *Foreign Affairs, 82,* 15.

Flores, L. A. (1996). Creating discursive space through a rhetoric of difference: Chicana feminists craft a homeland. *Quarterly Journal of Speech, 82,* 142–156.

Gareis, E. (2012). Intercultural friendship: Effects of home and host region. *Journal of International and Intercultural Communication, 5*(4), 309–328.

Geeraert, N., Demoulin, S., & Demes, K. A. (2014). Choose your (international) contact wisely: A multilevel analysis on the impact of intergroup contact while abroad. *International Journal of Intercultural Relations, 38*(2014), 86–96

Hall, B. J. (1997). Culture, ethics and communication. In F. L. Casmir (Ed.), *Ethics in intercultural and international communication* (pp. 11–41). Mahwah, NJ: Erlbaum.

Halualani, R. T. (2008). How do multicultural university students define and make sense of intercultural contact? A qualitative study. *International Journal of Intercultural Relations, 32,* 1–16.

Hecht, M., Sedano, M., & Ribeau, S. (1993). Understanding culture, communication, and research: Application to Chicanos and Mexican Americans. *International Journal of Intercultural Relations, 17,* 157–165.

Hecht, M. L., Jackson R. L., II, & Ribeau, S. (2002). *African American Communication: Exploring identity and culture* (2nd ed.). Hillsdale, NJ: Erlbaum.

Hegde, R. S. (1998). Swinging the trapeze: The negotiation of identity among Asian Indian immigrant women in the United States. In D. V. Tanno & A. González (Eds.), *Communication of identity across cultures* (pp. 34–55). Thousand Oaks, CA: Sage.

Hegde, R. S. (2012). Hybrid revivals: Ethnicity and South Asian celebration. In A. González, M. Houston, V. Chen (Eds.), *Our voices: Essays in culture, ethnicity and communication* (5th ed., pp. 158–163). New York: Oxford University Press.

Ho, M. K., Rasheed, J. M., & Rasheed, M. N. (2004). *Family therapy with ethnic minorities* (2nd ed). Thousand Oaks, CA: Sage.

Hofstede, G. (1998). *Masculinity and femininity.* Thousand Oaks, CA: Sage.

Hofstede, G., Hofstede, G. J., & Minkov, M. (2010). *Cultures and organizations: Software of the mind* (3rd ed.). Boston: McGraw-Hill.

Hulse, E. (1996). Example of the English Puritans. *Reformation Today, 153.* Retrieved June 13, 2006, from: http://www.puritansermons.com/banner/hulse1.htm.

Johnson, A. G. (2006). *Privilege, power and difference.* Thousand Oaks, CA: Sage.

Johnson, B. R., & Jacobson, C. K. (2005). Context in contact: An examination of social settings on Whites' attitudes toward interracial marriage. *Journal of Social Psychology, 68,* 387–399.

Jung, E., Hecht, M. L., & Wadsworth, B. C. (2007). The role of identity in international students' psychological well-being in the United States: A model of depression level, identity gaps, discrimination, and acculturation. *International Journal of Intercultural Relations, 31,* 605–624.

Kikoski, J. F., & Kikoski, C. K. (1999). *Reflexive communication in the culturally diverse workplace.* Westport, CT: Praeger.

Kim, Y. Y. (2005). Adapting to a new culture: An integrative communication theory. In W. B. Gudykunst (Ed.), *Theorizing about intercultural communication* (pp. 375–400). Thousand Oaks, CA: Sage.

Kluckhohn, F., & Strodtbeck, F. (1961). *Variations in value orientations.* Chicago: Row, Peterson & Co.

Koinova, M. (2010). Diasporas and secessionist conflicts: The mobilization of the Armenian, Albanian, and Chechen diasporas. *Ethnic and Racial Studies, 34,* 333–356.

Landler, M., & Barbaro, M. (2 August 2006). Walmart finds its formula doesn't fit every culture. *New York Times.* Retrieved March 6, 2014, from: http://www.nytimes.com/2006/08/02/business/worldbusiness/02walmart.html?pagewanted=al.

Lee, J. J., & Rice, C. (2007). Welcome to America? International student perceptions of discrimination. *Higher Education, 53,* 381–409.

Loeb, W. (2013, March 7). Successful global growers: What we can learn from Walmart, Carrefour, Tesco, Metro. *forbes.com.* Retrieved March 17, 2014, from: http://www.forbes.com/sites/walterloeb/2013/03/07/walmart-carrefour-tesco-metro-successful-global-growers-what-can-we-learn-from-them/.

Loewen, J. W. (2010). *Teaching what* really *happened.* New York: Teachers College, Columbia University.

Mahapatra, L. (2013, August 14). Prisoners per 100,000: U.S. has highest incarceration rate in the world. *International Business Times.* Retrieved March 17, 2014, from: http://www.ibtimes.com/prisoners-100000-us-has-highest-incarceration-rate-world-chart-1384305.

Martin, J. N., & Nakayama, T. K. (2014). *Experiencing intercultural communication: An introduction* (4th ed.). Boston: McGraw-Hill.

Martin, J. N., Trego, A., & Nakayama, T. K., (2010). The relationship between college students' racial attitudes and friendship diversity. *Howard Journal of Communications, 21*(2), 97–118.

Matsumoto, D. (2007). *The new Japan: Debunking seven cultural stereotypes.* London, ME: Nicholas Brealey.

McGoldrick, M., Giordano, J., & Garcia-Preto. (Eds.). (2005). *Ethnicity and family therapy* (3rd ed.). New York: Guilford Press.

Moving on up: Why do some Americans leave the bottom of the economic ladder, but not others? (2013, November). A brief from the PEW Charitable Trusts. Retrieved March 22, 2014, from: http://www.pewstates.org/uploaded-Files/PCS/Content-Level_Pages/Reports/2013/Moving_On_Up.pdf.

Open Doors 2013: Institute of International Education, Retrieved March 5, 2014 from http://www.iie.org/Research-and-Publications/Open-Doors/Data/International-Students; and http://www.iie.org/Research-and-Publications/Open-Doors/Data/US-Study-Abroad.

Orbe, M. P. (1998). *Constructing co-cultural theory: An explication of culture, power, and communication.* Thousand Oaks, CA: Sage.

Pendery, D. (2008). Identity development and cultural production in the Chinese diaspora to the United States, 1850–2004: New perspectives, *Asian Ethnicity, 9*(3), 201–218.

Philipsen, G. (2010). Some thoughts on how to approach finding one's feet in unfamiliar cultural terrain. *Communication Monographs, 77*(2), 160–168.

(2013, September). *Population facts* No. 2013/2. United Nations Department of Economic and Social Affairs, Population Division. www.unpopulation.org

Porter, T. (2002). The words that come before all else. *Native Americas, 19,* 7–10.

Rabbi: My radio show pulled because of racism (2005, September 27). *The Associated Press.* Retrieved October 10, 2005, from: http://www.newsmax.com/archives/ic/2005/9/22/173035.shtml.

Reiter, M. J., & Gee, C. B. (2009). Open communication and partner support in intercultural and interfaith romantic relationship: A relational maintenance approach. *Journal of Social and Personal Relationships, 25*(4), 539–599.

Root, M. P. P. (2001). *Love's revolution: Interracial marriage.* Philadelphia: Temple University Press.

Rosenstone, R. A. (2005). My wife, the Muslim. *Antioch Review, 63,* 234–246.

Rothman, L. (2012, July 8). Essence Fest 2012: Is reality TV still not diverse enough? Time.com. Retrieved March 22, 2014, from: http://entertainment.time.com/2012/07/08/essence-reality-tv-family-panel/.

Sahagun, L. (2014, February 24). Northern spotted owls are being ousted by barred owl invaders. *LA Times,*

Retrieved March 17, 2014, from: http://www.latimes.com/science/sciencenow/la-sci-sn-barred-owl-invasion-20140224,0,4292055.story.

Scott, K. D. (2013). Communication strategies across cultural borders: Dispelling stereotypes, performing competence, and redefining Black womanhood. *Women's Studies in Communication, 36*, 312–329.

Shim, Y-J., Kim, M-S., & Martin, J. N. (2008). *Changing Korea: Understanding culture and communication.* New York: Peter Lang.

Snyder, M. (2001). Self-fulfilling stereotypes. In P. S. Rothenberg (Ed.), *Race, class & gender in the U.S.* (5th ed., pp. 511–517). New York: Worth.

Sobré-Denton, M. (2011). The emergence of cosmopolitan group cultures and its implications for cultural transition: A case study of an international student support group. *International Journal of Intercultural Relations, 35*, 79–91.

Ting-Toomey, S. (1999). *Communicating across cultures.* New York: Guilford.

Ting-Toomey, S. (2010). Applying dimensional values in understanding intercultural communication. *Communication Monographs, 77*(2), 169–180.

Torres, L. (2009). Latino definitions of success: A cultural model of intercultural competence. *Hispanic Journal of Behavioral Sciences, 31*, 576-593.

Tourism Highlights. (2013). Retrieved March 5, 2014, from: file:///F:/Red%20USB%20DISK/HCIS%20Revisions%202013/Intercultural%20Chapter/unwto_highlights%202013.pdf.

Triandis, H. C. (1995). *Individualism & collectivism.* Westview Press.

Trompenaars, F., & Hampden-Turner, C. (2012). *Riding the waves of culture: Understanding diversity in global business* (3rd ed.). Boston: McGraw-Hill.

United Nations High Commissioner for Refugees. (2013). *UNHCR Mid year trends 2013* Retrieved March 6, 2014, from: http://www.unhcr.org/52af08d26.html.

U.S. Census Bureau projections show a slower growing, older, more diverse nation a half century from now. (2012, December 12). U.S. Census Newsroom. Retrieved March 6, 2014, from: http://www.census.gov/ewsroom/releases/archives/population/cb12-243.html.

Wang, W. (2012). *The rise of intermarriage: Rates characteristics vary by race and gender.* Pew Research. Retrieved March 17, 2014, from: http://www.pewsocialtrends.org/2012/02/16/the-rise-of-intermarriage/.

Ward, C. (2008). Thinking outside the Berry boxes: New perspectives on identity, acculturation and intercultural relations. *International Journal of Intercultural Relations, 32*, 105–114.

Waterston, A. (2005). Bringing the past into the present: Family narratives of Holocaust, exile, and diaspora: The story of my story: An anthropology of violence, dispossession, and diaspora. *Anthropological Quarterly, 78*, 43-61.

Wells, S. (2002). *The journey of man: A genetic odyssey.* Princeton, NJ: Princeton University Press.

Woodard, C. (2012). *American nations: A history of the eleven rival regional cultures of North America.* New York: Penguin Books.

(2013) *World Migration Report 2013: Migrant well-being and development.* Geneva, Switzerland: International Organization for Migration.

Yako, R. M., & Biswas, B. (2014). "We came to this country for the future of our children. We have no future": Acculturative stress among Iraqi refugees in the United States. *International Journal of Intercultural Relations, 38*, 133–141

Yamato, G. (2001). Something about the subject makes it hard to name. In M. L. Andersen & P. H. Collins (Eds.), *Race, class, and gender: An anthology* (4th ed., pp. 90–94). Belmont, CA: Wadsworth.

Yen, H. (2011, February 3). Census estimates show big gains for US minorities. Yahoo! News. Retrieved February 6, 2011, from http://news.yahoo.com/s/ap/20110203/ap_on_re_us/us_census2010_population

Credits

Photo Credits

Credits are listed in order of appearance.

Photo 1: Minneapolis Star Tribune/ZUMA Press/Newscom

Photo 2: Lisa F. Young/Fotolia

Photo 3: Marcin Sadlowski/Fotolia

Photo 4: Ashwin/Fotolia

Photo 5: DNF-Style/Fotolia

Photo 6: Lisa F. Young/Fotolia

Photo 7: Mast3r/Fotolia

Photo 8: All India Images/Panorama Productions/Inc./Alamy

Photo 9: Ashwin/Shutterstock

Photo 10: Anders Ryman/Alamy

Photo 11: Monart Design/Fotolia

Photo 12: Tony Freeman/PhotoEdit

Photo 13: MANDEL NGAN/AFP/Getty Images/Newscom

Photo 14: Tony Dejak/AP Images

Text and Art Credits

Based on (2013) World Migration Report 2013: Migrant well-being and development. Geneva, Switzerland: International Organization for Migration; (2013, September). Population facts No. 2013/2. United Nations Department of Economic and Social Affairs, Population Division. www.unpopulation.org

Allison Nafziger Travel Blog. Reprinted by permission of Allison Nafziger.

Fig 02, U.S. Department of Commerce Economics and Statistics Administration U.S Census Bureau.

Broome, B. J., & Collier, M. J. (2012). Culture, communication, and peacebuilding: A reflexive multi-dimensional contextual framework. Journal of International and Intercultural Communication, 5(4), 245–269.

Susan

Maham

Based on Torres, L. (2009). Latino definitions of success: A cultural model of intercultural competence. Hispanic Journal of Behavioral Sciences, 31, 576-593.

Torres, L. (2009). Latino definitions of success: A cultural model of intercultural competence. Hispanic Journal of Behavioral Sciences, 31, 576-593.(p. 587).

Philipsen, G. (2010). Some thoughts on how to approach finding one's feet in unfamiliar cultural terrain. Communication Monographs, 77(2), 160–168.

Pearson Education, Inc.

Root, M. P. P. (2001). Loves's revolution: Interracial marriage. Philadelphia, PA: Temple University Press.

Rosenstone, R. A. (2005). My wife, the Muslim. Antioch Review, 63, 234–246.; pp. 20-21, FROM: Larabell, J. (2014, January 15). Sobering advice for anyone contemplating a cross-cultural marriage. Retrieved March 17, 2014, from http://www.larabell.org/cross.html.

Scott, K. D. (2013). Communication strategies across cultural borders: Dispelling stereotypes, performing competence, and redefining Black womanhood. Women's Studies in Communication, 36, 312–329.

Bennett, J. M. (1998). Transition shock: Putting culture shock in perspective. In M. J. Bennett (Ed.), Basic concepts in intercultural communication: Selected readings (pp. 215–224). Yarmouth, ME: Intercultural Press. First published in 1977, in N. C. Jain (Ed.), International and Intercultural Communication Annual, 4, 45–52.

Nagesh

Angelina

Based on Rothman, L. (2012, July 8). Essence Fest 2012: Is reality TV still not diverse enough? Time.com. Retrieved March 22, 2014 from http://entertainment.time.com/2012/07/08/essence-reality-tv-family-panel/

Communicating Through Social and Other Interactive Media

From Chapter 14 of *Human Communication in Society*, Fourth Edition. Jess K. Alberts, Thomas K. Nakayama, Judith N. Martin.
Copyright © 2016 by Pearson Education, Inc. All rights reserved.

Communicating Through Social and Other Interactive Media

CHAPTER TOPICS	Chapter Objectives
The Importance of Interactive and Social Media	**1** Identify two reasons for learning about interactive media.
What Are Interactive Media?	**2** Identify and describe interactive media.
How Does Interactive Media Use Affect Our Communication Choices?	**3** Describe the dimensions of interactive media and how these dimensions combine into a framework for understanding the use of interactive media.
Interactive Media and the Individual	**4** Describe issues that can arise in identity and relationship development when using interactive media.
The Individual, Communication Technology, and Society	**5** Understand the role of power and privilege in interactive media use.
Ethics and Interactive Media	**6** Identify and describe three ethical challenges involving interactive media use.
Improving Your Mediated Communication Skills	**7** Discuss ways to improve your own mediated communication skills.

> *"Experts predict the Internet will become 'like electricity'—less visible, yet more deeply embedded in people's lives for good and ill"*
> —Digital Life in 2025, *Pew Report, 2014* —J. G. Ballard

Charee just heard that a friend's mother has been diagnosed with a serious illness. Charee would like to contact her friend, but she's not sure how best to get in touch. Should she call her? Send a message through Facebook, the way she usually gets in touch with her? Contact her with a text message? She started to think about all the communication choices she has every day and the impacts of those choices. For example, her mother got offended when she just sent a text message on Mother's day instead of phoning her. Her grandmother refuses to text, so Charee has to talk with her on the phone, which she really doesn't like. Some of her friends will only communicate through Facebook.

Charee's thinking about her communication choices illustrates a number of issues we will address. For example, given the many choices we have to connect with people in our daily lives, how do we decide which is the most appropriate? How do people use technology to communicate in different contexts and with different people? How has the pervasiveness of technology impacted the way we communicate with others? And how does the constant "connectivity" to others affect our identities and our interpersonal relationships?

The focus of mass media is one-way mediated communication produced by large industries intended for a large audience, such as television, radio, and films. Here we focus on **interactive media**, or mediated communication, which relies on technologies such as the Internet and mobile phones and other devices (for example, tablets). First, we describe how interactive media play an important role in our lives and define what we mean by interactive media. As you'll see, social media is the largest group of interactive media—which is why it's included in the title. However, as we will explain later, interactive media also include text messaging and email, which are not technically social media. Then we examine individuals' use of interactive media, including identity issues and impacts on personal and work relationships. We then shift the focus to societal forces—examining how gender, race/ethnicity, and socioeconomic class impact interactive media use and who does (and does not) have access to these and other communication technologies. Finally, we discuss ethical issues related to interactive media use and conclude with suggestions for improving your own skills in using communication technologies.

interactive media
a collection of mediated communication technologies that are digital and converging and tend to be mobile

1   The Importance of Interactive and Social Media

1   **Identify two reasons for learning about interactive media.**

Interactive media are a constant reality in our lives and affect our daily activities in multiple ways. This pervasiveness provides the first and primary reason for learning more about this topic. A second reason is that understanding interactive media and having good media skills will help you be more successful personally and professionally.

First, we say that interactive media are pervasive because most of us interact with these communication technologies almost constantly, especially on mobile devices. In fact, experts have described young people as a "tethered generation," meaning they are connected to media 24/7 (Mihailidis, 2014; Turkle, 2011). As one college student said, "I constantly check my phone for messages even though it does not ring or vibrate....I cannot help it. I do it all the time, every day." Another said that "when I am without it, it is like I lost my arm" (Milhailidis, 2014, p. 64). And these students are not alone. Ninety percent of U.S. Americans have mobile phones, and even 77 percent of older Americans (65 years old and older) now have mobile phones (Mobile technology fact sheet, 2014; Smith, 2014b). A recent study reported that 44 percent of mobile phone owners have slept with their phone next to their bed because they wanted to make sure they didn't miss any calls, text messages, or other updates during the night (Mobile technology fact sheet, 2014).

We should note that mobile communication technology is one of the fastest-growing communication technologies in history, in a little more than thirty years the mobile communications user base has grown to more than six billion subscribers worldwide (Wei, 2013). Although this has been a huge boon for many people around the globe, it presents challenges to communication researchers (and textbook authors) in trying to understand and study the implications of these interactive mobile media for our daily lives. Communication technologies come and go at a rapid rate. By the time researchers design a study, the particular technology may have lost prominence (remember MySpace, pagers, car phones, Xanga?), and the study results can then seem irrelevant. In addition, it's difficult to predict which technologies will be important in the future (Boase, 2013).

That said, we have to start somewhere to describe the role of interactive media in our everyday lives, and most experts agree that we currently use communication technologies primarily for (1) connecting with others and (2) consuming content (verbal and visual). In our "culture of connectivity" (van Dijck, 2013), perhaps the most important interactive media activity, particularly for young people, worldwide, is the opportunity to develop and maintain relationships. A recent study of almost eight hundred students in eight universities on three continents found that the most common use of mobile phone was to send text messages and secondly to check social network sites (Facebook, Twitter, Instagram, etc.). In fact, about 30 percent said they checked their social networking site (SNS) app(s) more than thirteen times in a twenty-four-hour period (Mihailidis, 2014). Seventy three percent of online adults interact with SNSs and 42 percent use multiple SNSs (Facebook and Instagram most common, but many others are frequently accessed). These interactive media offer many ways to stay connected, and as Charee discovered, present many communication choices. Our friends can know immediately what books we're reading, what brand of sunscreen we've purchased, the restaurant where we're eating, films we're watching, and lots of other information about our daily activities. Location service apps on mobile phones allow us to connect with others in the same physical location, ranging from meeting friends (Meetup, Foursquare) to potential sexual or romantic relationships (e.g., Grindr for gay men; Tinder and Blendr for straight people). Of course, different social media platforms have different audiences that require different approaches. What you would post on LinkedIn, for example, is different than what you post on Facebook or Pinterest or Twitter. We are constantly making choices about which information we want to share with which friends/acquaintances/colleagues and in which medium. Throughout this text, we will examine how this pervasive connectivity can affect our communication choices as well as our sense of identity, personal privacy, and romantic, work, and acquaintance relationships.

Another important interactive media activity is searching for information/consuming content (visual and verbal). Some activities may be less interactive (e.g., getting directions, movie/restaurant reviews, stock quotes, weather reports, news headlines, watching funny cat videos), but others are quite interactive—reading and commenting on political/news/opinion blogs, posting your own opinion on restaurant reviews, or sending that funny cat video to a friend with a message about your own cat experiences. The study cited previously also reported that college students got most of their news and political opinions from SNSs (Mihailidis, 2014), which shows how these two activities (connecting and consuming content) can overlap. In addition to major news blogs (e.g., *Huffington Post*), there are personal blogs in which people document their everyday activities and express their opinions, thoughts, feelings, and religious beliefs (Cheong, 2010; Cheong, Halavais, & Kwon, 2008; Cheong & Poon, 2009).

Twitter is especially popular because it allows us to "follow" people we don't know, but is also transformative in that it allows millions to quickly disseminate *and discuss* marketing, political, sports news, and personal information as part of the larger web of social media (Bruns & Stieglitz, 2013; Osborne & Dredze, 2014). For example, some experts note that Twitter has "disrupted" the traditional mass media coverage of sporting events, where spectators are passive audience to televised sporting events. Twitter allows consumers to interact with teams, organizations, and athletes in a *public* way not possible in mass media contexts or even through text messaging or SNSs like Facebook (Pegoraro, 2014).

Interacting with others around information also offers opportunities for civic engagement and political activism. Social media played an important role in the political turmoil of the "Arab Spring" in Egypt and other Mideast countries in 2011— when citizens revolted against and eventually toppled oppressive governments. Communicating through these media helped citizens make decisions about participating in protests, implementing logistics, and determining the likelihood of success. Further, these media provided sources of information the government could not control (Tufekci & Wilson, 2012).

Some experts worry about our overreliance on interactive media for information; they say that we only "skim" and don't make an effort to remember the information we find because it's always at our fingertips. As a result, they speculate, we are becoming less able to concentrate and recall information (Bennhold, 2011; Carr, 2008). In addition, as with mass media selective exposure, we often tailor the material we access on interactive media to conform to our particular tastes and opinions, perhaps cutting ourselves off from a range of views and opinions.

Now that we've discussed the pervasiveness of interactive media in our lives, let's examine the second reason for studying about interactive media: the fact that an understanding of these media and good technological skills can help ensure personal and professional success. As we'll see later, understanding the sometimes complex role that interactive media play in interpersonal relationships and employee–employer relationships is essential. Interpersonally, knowing about the specific characteristics of various media and their effects on relationships is crucial. Understanding organi-

Text messages and instant messages are increasingly popular ways to communicate in the United States, particularly for adolescents and college students.

zational rules and practices involving interactive media, including surveillance, privacy concerns, and "netiquette," will serve you well. There are frequent news stories about employees who lost their jobs or were penalized as a result of not understanding the informal or formal rules about media behavior in the workplace (Wiley, 2013).

It's easy to see that many everyday activities and transactions that used to be conducted face to face are now being carried out using communication technologies. Before looking at how these media forms affect our everyday communication, our identity, and our relationships, let's discuss what we mean by the term interactive media.

2   What are Interactive Media?

2   **Identify and describe interactive media.**

We define interactive media as a collection of mediated communication technologies that are digital and converging and tend to be mobile, all accessed on a variety of devices, from desktop and laptop computers, smartphones, tablets, and other mobile devices. Let's unpack this definition a little further and distinguish interactive media from mass media. In contrast to face-to-face (FtF) communication, both mass media and interactive media are mediated forms of communication, meaning that the messages are carried through an *intervening* system of **digital** electronic storage before being transmitted between two or more people.

In contrast to mass media in which messages are generally one-to-many, interactive media messages converge, meaning that they can be sent one to one, one to many, or many to many. Also in contrast to mass media, they are interactive, meaning that communication goes both ways and permits individuals to connect and interact with others. So what are examples of interactive media? There are many, but the easiest description is: Interactive media is **social media** *plus text messages and email*. Social media is "a group of Internet-based, Web (World Wide Web, or WWW) applications that allow the creation and exchange of user-generated content" (Kaplan & Haenlein, 2010, p. 61).

Business scholars Andreas Kaplan and Michael Haenlein (2010) identify six categories of social media: (1) blogs, (2) **Social Networking Sites (SNSs)** such as Facebook, (3) Virtual social worlds such as Second Life, (4) Collaborative projects such as wikis, (5) Content communities like YouTube, and Pinterest, and (6) **Massively Multiplayer Online Games (MMOGs)** such as World of Warcraft. These categories are not set in stone. Twitter, for example, is an SNS but is also categorized as a microblog. Remember, that in addition to social media, interactive media also include text messaging and email.

One of the characteristics of interactive media is new versions are always emerging. It is a dynamic form of communication, and increasingly mobile. Distinctions between mass and new media are becoming more and more blurred. For example, some mass media forms like television reality shows can be viewed on mobile devices that allow for audience reaction and participation. And some media, like podcasts, although relatively new, may not allow interaction in a way that is similar to traditional mass media. For our purposes, we focus on the *interactive* elements of new media, where the "real give and take of social life" in cyberspace occurs (Walther & Parks, 2002, p. 3).

How does this mobility and constant connection with others through interactive media affect our communication choices? Before addressing this question, we need to understand how various communication technologies differ from each other and from FtF communication—the topic we turn to next.

3   How Does Interactive Media Use Affect Our Communication Choices?

3   **Describe the dimensions of interactive media and how these dimensions combine into a framework for understanding the use of interactive media.**

Because interactive media are rapidly changing forms of communication, it is difficult to arrive at definitive conclusions about their exact role in everyday life. Researching these forms of communication can be like trying to hit a moving target. Still, with a basic understanding of what interactive media are, and some of the ways they can differ, we can get some sense of their increasingly important role.

digital

information that is transmitted in a numerical format based on only two values (0 and 1)

social media

group of Internet-based applications that allow the creation and exchange of user-generated content

Social Networking Sites (SNSs)

web-based service where people construct their profiles, identify others with whom they share a connection, and interact with others within the system

Massively Multiplayer Online Games (MMOGs)

text-based "virtual reality" games in which participants interact with enrichments, objects, and other participants

To begin, consider this question that Charee faced: How should she decide whether to communicate a message by text, Facebook post, phone, or in person? Like Charee, perhaps you have had an issue to discuss with a friend or acquaintance and were unsure what the most effective mode of communication would be. If so, you had good reason to feel unsure. Interactive media differ in important ways, and these differences can affect the outcome of your conversation.

One way to understand these differences is to show how interactive media vary along two dimensions, employing two sets of theories and ideas about communication theories: (1) Media characteristics: media richness and social presence and (2) social processes: self presentation and self disclosure.

MEDIA CHARACTERISTICS There are two characteristics that differentiate various interactive media. First, some forms of new communication technologies lack the capability of carrying nonverbal cues. Second, some are also asynchronous in nature—which means a delay may occur between the time the message is sent and when it is responded to. Nonverbal cues play an important role in understanding the totality of a person's message. When we speak face to face, we see the other person's gestures, facial expressions, and attire, we hear their sighs, accent, or dialect; these are just a few of the many cues we use to fully understand what a person means. Some interactive media, however—like text messages and tweets—eliminate all of those cues that help us to determine what is being communicated.

Another variation in interactive media forms is the degree to which the exchange of messages is synchronous or asynchronous. FtF communication and media like the telephone and Skype chats are **synchronous**; that is, messages are sent and received at the same time. However, email, blog posts, and video recordings are **asynchronous**; that is, messages may be received at a later time. The distinction between synchronous and asynchronous messages can be blurred (Rettie, 2009). Text messaging may be synchronous or not, depending on how quickly the other person acknowledges or responds to the message. In some instances, one can choose to make a media interaction asynchronous (e. g., putting phone on silent, used only for voicemail).

When you send a mediated message through an asynchronous medium, it is almost impossible to know if the other person has received your message because you don't receive any "in the moment" response. A challenge in text messaging is when to respond. What do silences mean in interactive media? In FtF interaction, silences can be meaningful and are usually interpreted by nonverbal cues to mean hesitation, reflection, or perhaps anger. But silence after posting a new Facebook status or sending a text message might mean anything, ranging from lack of interest to a technology glitch. Yet, the implications for relationships can be important (Pettigrew, 2010).

Two theories can help us understand the impact of lack of and presence of nonverbal cues and degree of synchronicity in various interactive media: media richness theory and social presence theory. **Media richness theory** describes the potential information-carrying capacity of a communication medium (Daft & Lengel, 1984, 1986). According to this theory, FtF communication is the richest medium for communicating because you can see facial expressions and body gestures as well as hear the tone, speed, and quality of a person's voice. All these factors relay a tremendous amount of information and allow you to interpret and respond to messages more accurately. You not only hear the words, or the content of the message, but you also receive the relational messages that are being sent nonverbally and that reveal how that person feels about you. If the other person is smiling, leaning toward you, and maintaining eye contact, you probably infer that the person is happy or glad to talk with you. If the person is scowling and avoiding eye contact, you might infer that she or he is angry or unhappy with you.

According to media richness theory, some types of mediated communication do allow for a certain amount of richness. Consider video/audio communication, or

synchronous
communication in which messages are sent and received at the same time

asynchronous
communication in which messages are sent and received at different times

media richness theory
theory that describes the potential information-carrying capacity of a communication medium

Skype. When you communicate using a webcam, you might miss some immediate context cues, such as body posture or gestures, but you have the benefit of seeing some of the nonverbal behaviors of the person you're communicating with. The telephone is a less rich medium, revealing some paralinguistic cues (for example, tone of voice), but no facial expression, eye gaze, or gestures.

The least-rich media, according to media richness theory, are text-based messages—email, text messaging, and tweets. But nonverbal cues aren't completely absent here, either. Some relational/nonverbal information *can* be communicated in these text-based media, with emoticons, such as ☺, and abbreviations like LOL. Messages can also be made "richer" in some technologies by altering the font color, using animation or icons (Sheer, 2011).

Of course, writing (including writing emails and text messages) is a form of communication that includes some techniques for expressing mood and feelings. For example, moods can be expressed by punctuation, by the length of sentences, and by numbers of adjectives or adverbs. Writers can also communicate intonation by emphasizing particular words in a sentence or by repetition.

Social presence refers to the feelings of psychological closeness or immediacy that people experience when they interact with each other (Short, Williams, & Christie, 1976). This closeness is communicated through nonverbal cues, such as smiling, leaning forward, and relaxed body posture, and through synchronous communication. **Social presence theory** suggests that FtF communication is generally high in this kind of social presence, and that media vary in the amount of social presence they convey. For example, talking on the telephone conveys less social presence than FtF interaction, but more than email communication—where all nonverbal cues are eliminated. The implication is that media low in social presence (such as texting, emailing, and tweets) may seem more impersonal, less "relationship-focused."

SOCIAL PROCESSES   A second way that interactive media can vary is in the type of self-presentation and self-disclosure allowed. These are not specific theories, but are important notions in the field of communication. We are motivated to control the impressions others have of us (self-presentation)—to influence them to think of us in the ways we want and also to create an image that is consistent with our self-concept and our personal identity. So when you create your Facebook profile, change your FB status or post photos of your travels to Nepal on Instagram, you are engaging in and controlling your self-presentation—what others think of you. If, in a given social media platform, you want others to see you as a serious professional, you will post information that is consistent with this self-concept. If you want to present yourself as a fun-loving party animal, you will probably post other information.

One of the important aspects of self-presentation is self-disclosure. And mutual self disclosure is a crucial step in the development of relationships. The more we disclose to others, the more others tend to self-disclose to us, which in turn strengthens a relationships. One way that we can understand the variation in social media is the degree of self-disclosure it requires and the type of self-presentation it allows. So when you create your Facebook or LinkedIn profile, you are required to disclose some information about yourself (you also have the opportunity to disclose a lot more); when playing Warcraft or other online games you disclose much less.

Combining these two dimensions—media richness characteristics (richness/social presence) and social processes (self-disclosure/self-presentation)—results in the framework presented in Table 1—and helps us understand how these interactive media vary and the options they present in making communication choices. Concerning media richness/social presence, blogs are the lowest as they are text-based

social presence

degree of psychological closeness or immediacy engendered by various media

social presence theory

theory that suggests face-to-face communication is generally high in social presence, and that media vary in the amount of social presence they convey

Think of a recent conflict you had and describe how it might have been different if the communication media had been different. How might it have gone over the telephone? Face to face? Text messaging?

Table 1 Interactive Media Characteristics

		Social presence/Media richness		
		Low	Medium	High
Self-Presentation/ Self-disclosure	**High**	Blogs, email, and text messaging	Social networking sites (e.g., Facebook)	Virtual Social worlds (e.g., Second Life)
	Low	Collaborative projects (e.g., Wikipedia)	Content communities (e.g., YouTube)	Virtual game worlds (e.g., World of Warcraft)

SOURCE: Adapted from Kaplan & Haenlein, 2010, p. 62

and do not allow for synchronous interaction; the same is true for email and text messaging—depending on how quickly the receiver responds. SNSs are higher in that they allow for photos and some "richer" communication, and virtual social worlds are the highest as encounters there are synchronous. On the self-presentation/self-disclosure dimensions, collaborative projects are low because they are mostly text based (few photos or videos can be posted) and allow for simple exchanges and relatively little self-disclosure; content communities and SNSs enable more self-disclosure than content communities. Finally, the highest level of self-presentation/self-disclosure is a virtual social world.

This framework can be useful in at least two ways: First, it shows the tremendous number and variation of communication opportunities we have in our everyday lives. Second, this framework can be used to think through and guide our communication choices—in terms of how much to disclose, how to present ourselves to others, and how much social presence or media richness we desire. Individuals make many different choices every day. In the opening vignette, Charee was trying to decide how to communicate with her friend about her mother's illness. In this case, she might decide that social presence/media richness was necessary for that interaction, and so would phone her. On the other hand, when she wanted to ask her professor about a course requirement, she assumed that social presence or synchronicity was not required, so emailing would be a fine choice. A person may choose to switch media in the same conversation (Madianou & Miller, 2013), depending on the topic. Our student Rosemary started getting into an argument with a friend on Facebook through posts and comments and then switched to private messaging to continue the discussion.

How do you decide? One of the complicating issues of some interactive media is that your communication can potentially be seen and received by many different audiences. In FtF encounters, you know who you are addressing your message to. When Charee is talking to her mother or grandmother face to face, she tailors her messages specifically to them (and may use different communication styles and word choices than she would use with her close friends). However, when she posts on Facebook or sends a Tweet, these message can potentially be seen by many, and she can't easily adapt her message to all these potential audiences. Scholar danah boyd (2014) describes this phenomenon as **"collapsing contexts"**—meaning we don't always know exactly who we are speaking to (what the communication context is) when we send a message on social media, and this leads to another characteristic of social media— **"spreadability,"** which is the ease with which content can be spread. That is, our messages can be forwarded, retweeted, and quickly seen by hundreds of people, complicating our communication choices even more! This leads some individuals to create different Facebook pages, one with their real name which is more public and another with a name that only close friends can see, or using multiple SNSs for various audiences. Our communication choices today are clearly challenging. We'll discuss further the topic of these communication choices in the next section on identity.

collapsing contexts

in social media, not knowing exactly who is reading one's posts

spreadability

the ease with which content can be spread on social media

People use multiple media in addition to FtF interactions to fit their social needs.

Although experts mostly agree on these characteristics of various media, they do not always agree on the specific impacts these characteristics have on our communication choices and relationships. Some experts point to the positive and some point to the negative aspects of interactive media. Some experts suggest that the digital future is only bright—bringing more connectivity, maximizing human potential, more civic engagement, democracy and equality. Others point to the downside: heavy social media use can lead to physical isolation from others and dissatisfaction with one's own life—resulting from constant comparisons with others' lives and experiences (Kross et al., 2013), more abuses and abusers in cyber relationships (bullying, stalking, pornography, identity theft), and more surveillance and intrusion into private lives (Anderson & Rainie, 2014).

However, seeing social media and technology in general as all good or all evil for human interaction is too simplistic. What is clear is that they play an increasingly important role in our lives and that people use multiple media in addition to FtF interactions to fit their social needs and lifestyles. It seems more useful to view interactive media through a dialectical lens. A dialectical perspective emphasizes simultaneous contradictory truths, recognizing that things may be "both/and"—both good and bad, strong and weak—and that we each have to navigate this media landscape, making the best choices we can. And this complexity of choice should not be a surprise, considering the pace of technology development and how much we still have to learn about interactive media capacities. With these thoughts in mind, let's look at a related topic—how personal identity is performed and managed in interactive media use.

Alternative View

Alone Together

Do you agree with Turkle's premise that pervasive connectivity actually makes us less connected to other people? Why or why not?

In a 2011 book, media expert Sherry Turkle challenges us to reexamine our assumptions about technology being the answer to intimacy and connections. She thinks that, although we are constantly in contact with each other—*tethered* to our technology—we sometimes choose technologies that merely substitute for human intimacy and that the technology is taking us "places we don't want to go." She offers as proof that adults would rather email, coworkers would rather leave voicemail messages, and teenagers would rather text. These technologies give us control over our relationships and actually distance us from others; as she puts it, "Technology makes it easy to communicate when we wish and to disengage at will" (2011, p. 13). A thirteen-year-old tells her that she hates the phone and never listens to voicemail but finds texting just right. Texting puts us in touch, but not too close.

Turkle describes the story of Ellen, working in Paris, who used Skype to connect with her grandmother in Philadelphia.

Twice a week they would talk for an hour. But, unbeknownst to her grandmother, Ellen was multitasking during the conversation—typing away on her keyboard answering emails. So it wasn't a *real* connection because Ellen wasn't really present. And Ellen reportedly felt guilty about her actions.

Later, in a 2012 TED (Technology Entertainment Design) talk, Turkle gives another example. She describes the creation of furry stuffed animal-like social robots designed to be with and comfort lonely older people. Dr. Turkle thinks this is proof that we're abdicating our human responsibility and what makes us human: the ability to care for others in intimate ways. We substitute technology for intimacy.

Turkle concludes that we should continually examine the benefits and challenges of our "connectivity culture," always asking "how we got to this place and whether we are content to be here" (2011, p. 2).

SOURCES: Turkle, S. (2011). *Alone together: Why we expect more from technology and less from each other*. New York: Basic Books.

Turkle, S. (2012, February). TED talk: Connected, but alone? Retrieved May 25, 2014, from: http://www.ted.com/talks/sherry_turkle_alone_together#t-755215.

4✶ Interactive Media and the Individual

4 **Describe issues that can arise in identity and relationship development when using interactive media.**

Clearly, interactive media use presents us with a range of choices, and those choices can have a powerful impact on communication between individuals in terms of identity, and in turn, personal relationships. Let's examine the way this works.

Managing Identity

The range of communication choices in interactive media has profound implications for how we manage our identity online. Social media provides many opportunities to be seen and admired and to self-disclose. At the same time, some media (Twitter, Internet forums) allow us to control the amount of information we disclose about ourselves. All these options provide a fluidity to our identities that we don't have in FtF communication. One's identity or self-concept is developed and expressed through communication with others. From the framework presented in the previous section, we can see that identity/self-presentation/self-disclosure would be most relevant to communication on blogs, SNSs, and virtual social worlds. How do you present yourself and manage impressions that others have of you on these sites, given the characteristics and range of possibilities discussed in the previous section?

SELF-PRESENTATION ONLINE In using interactive media, you often make decisions about what kind of information to reveal about yourself. There seem to be three (overlapping) types of information that can be disclosed:

1. Standard information (for example, name, gender, profile picture);
2. Sensitive personal information—details that could be used to locate/identify or to threaten or harm (for example, email address, birthday, birth year, employer, job position, profile picture, photo albums);
3. Potentially stigmatizing information—information that could result in stigmatization within society (for example, religious views, political views, birth year, sexual orientation, photos).

An important question in deciding how much and what type of information to disclose: Who are your intended/"imagined" audiences? Some students see their Facebook profile/page as a professional platform, almost like a resume, where potential employers can read about their academic achievements and intern experiences. Others see it as a place to hang out with good friends and discuss the latest partying activities. For young people working out issues around their sexual identity or sexual practices, participation in interactive media can be tricky. On the one hand it can provide communities of support but also exposes them to potential discrimination or reactions from people they may not want to see this aspect of their identity development.

Perhaps one of the biggest challenges in how to present yourself and manage your online identity is that you don't know exactly who might be listening or reading. You may discover that your intended audience is not who is responding. For example, one student described his frustration when he posts messages about playing his latest favorite retro video game (Legend of Zelda) and his cousins make fun of his "lame" interest and mock him. Even worse, his sister also annoys him by responding to his posts intended for his friends ("fell asleep in boring Mr. K.'s class") when she plays the older sister role in her posts ("hey bro, you shouldn't do that, should be paying attention"). Not only that, she keeps responding to his friends' posts, which he thinks violates a social code. He has stopped posting as much and reset his privacy settings, but says it makes him sad because he would like to share things with his family but wants to have control over his self-presentation online (Boyd, 2014). Sometimes young people have their intended self-presentation sabotaged by others—when friends tag them in photos or post photos of them engaging in activities they'd rather not have others see. Or they have also been embarrassed (often intentionally) by their parents on their SNSs—who post inappropriate photos and/or comments (Winter, 2014). Another consequential audience is the **lurkers**, people who see and read material posted on SNSs but don't comment. Most lurkers are harmless, but underage users should remember that accepting "followers" they don't know could result in their photos and videos ending up on pedophile Web sites, especially given that Facebook has made it easier to search for public content (Levin, 2013).

Some decisions about what to reveal on SNSs may be related to a person's age, with younger people disclosing more. One long time Facebook user bemoaned her earlier days of FB postings, her four year long "lapse of judgment" following high school. She describes photos of herself where she was:

> sticking out my tongue, flopping on couches, stuffing my face with food, wearing too-short tops ... attempting to show I was having an amaaaaazing time (whoooo!!!!), all in all, trying much, much too hard. There was an album titled, I'm cringing even now, "Bro'ing and Ho'ing out—Spring Break 07" (Bosker, 2014).

She goes on to say that her (millennial) generation seems less inclined now to make their lives an open book, are more selective in what they post on Facebook and opt for less public sharing—preferring erasable Snapchats, private Picasa albums, and the one-on-one WhatsApp. When Facebook users were asked what they disliked about Facebook, the number-one response was people sharing too much information about themselves (Smith 2014b). Oversharing can also have negative professional impacts; potential employers can access profile information, and according to one study, 34 percent of employers surveyed admit to dismissing a candidate from consideration because of what they found on social networking sites.

Interestingly, one recent study found a "privacy paradox," that although online users said they were concerned about privacy, their behaviors didn't seem to mirror those concerns because they reported revealing quite a bit of personal and sensitive information, especially if their friends and acquaintances also shared (Taddicken, 2014). Revealing information on SNSs is also related to other factors. For example, perhaps not surprisingly, people with low self-esteem tend to accept friend requests from people they don't know well, reveal more information about themselves, and present exaggerated information. For example, someone might say he plays in a band, when in reality his older brother plays in a band and he gets to play occasionally with them when they practice. In contrast, popular users tend to disclose information strategically to further enhance their popularity—for example, changing their profile picture often to show them having fun at parties, public events, and traveling and changing their Facebook profiles often to note new activities or interests (Tazghini & Siedlecki, 2012; Zywica & Danowski, 2008). Additionally, single people tend to reveal more demographic and personal information, probably because they feel that information is needed to attract partners (Nosko, Wood, & Molema, 2010).

Another aspect of self-presentation is listing friendship links, and on SNSs, "friends" can be used to provide context—to remind users of the imagined audiences they hope to interact with. But adding too many friends can have the opposite effect—raising doubts about one's popularity and desirability (Tong, Van Der Heide, Langwell, & Walther, 2008). Fascination with fame and celebrity is associated with more frequent Facebook and Twitter use, for example, following celebrities and trying to integrate them into their own social networks (Greenwood, 2013).

lurkers

people who read, observe, but do not actively participate in online communities/sites

ANONYMITY AND PSUEDOANONYMITY   When you communicate via Twitter or in an online forum, or post a comment on YouTube, others may not know your age, gender, race, nationality, or many of the other cues that affect perceptions of individuals. The degree to which people should be able to remain anonymous online has been vigorously debated. Facebook founders have strongly advocated for the "real-name web," saying that real names allow people to better connect to their offline friends, thereby strengthening social connections. Others, like activist Christopher Pool, strongly disagree, believing that tying real names to content is an unnecessary burden. Pool, known for years only as "moot," was founder of 4chan.org, which spawned LOLcats (humorous photos of cats with superimposed text written in a form of broken English known as lolspeak), and the Internet hacking group "anonymous" that has targeted corporations, governments, and child predators. 4chan.org allows and encourages anonymous postings (Hogan, 2012). It does seem that there is increasingly less opportunity for anonymity online as more and more of our lives and information about our "real" selves is posted, persistent, and available for searching. The old adage of "There are no erasers on the Internet" is still very true. Getting rid of information once it's out on the Internet can be difficult, if not impossible. For example, if you deactivate your Facebook account, the information remains stored on the Web site. To entirely delete your Facebook account, you have to fill out a form and tell Facebook exactly why you want to leave (Larson, 2014).

There are at least three issues in the complex relationship between anonymity and identity in online communication (Wood & Smith, 2005). The first has to do with the informative aspect of the identity. On the one hand, knowing something about the person sending information gives a context for judging his or her messages. If you know, for example, that the person answering your medical question online is a doctor, that person seems more credible than a person who does not have a medical degree. On the other hand, because information on age, gender, and race can form the basis for stereotyping and prejudice, some anonymity presents the possibility of interactions somewhat free of prejudice.

A second issue regarding anonymity is its capacity to liberate speech. For example, without knowing who has issued a statement, the legal restrictions on speech are difficult to enforce. So if someone is misrepresenting oneself online and makes racist or libelous statements, it is almost impossible to implement legal sanctions. On the other hand, anonymity can give people courage to express unpopular opinions or question conventional wisdom, which they might be afraid to do in FtF interaction. Some young people find anonymity gives a sense of freedom that they don't have on SNSs where parents or other authority figures are always watching, or even on sites or online games where they construct a pseudo identity (boyd 2014).

The third issue related to anonymity is that in some ways, the freedom that people feel as a result of their anonymity may lead them to be less responsible communicators (Anderson, 2014a). For example, anonymity can lead to irresponsible and destructive online behavior, like **trolling**. For example, a recent report outlined how male online players denigrate, harass, and drive off female would-be gamers, and how anti-Chinese racism is expressed in hostile in-game interactions and in YouTube rants (Yee, 2014). In addition, anonymity facilitates email rumors and hoaxes (e.g., the suggestion that swallowing active dry yeast before drinking alcohol prevents you from getting drunk or messages that companies like Microsoft will give away free money to people who forward the email message to five additional people). For information about evaluating these types of messages, check out Snopes.com.

Also annoying are the millions of **spam** messages (unwanted commercial messages and advertisements sent through email), which might be greatly reduced if addresses or spammers' identities were easier to trace. **Phishing**—the practice of trying fraudulently to get consumer banking/credit card or other personal information, such as usernames, passwords, social security numbers—is another problem for

trolling
posting Internet messages meant to intentionally anger or frustrate in order to provoke reactions from others

spam
unwanted commercial messages and advertisements sent through email

phishing
the practice of trying fraudulently to get consumer banking and credit card information

215

interactive media users. Increasing numbers of fake emails are "warning" users that their account information needs to be updated and then pointing to Web sites that ask the user to enter personal or financial information. Although technology companies and banks aggressively pursue those who send spam and phishing messages, apprehending and prosecuting them is difficult (Kleinman, 2014). This leads to a good reason to be careful about how much personal information to disclose on SNSs; spammers have used freely accessible profile data from SNSs to craft phishing schemes that appear to originate from a friend on the network. Targets are much more likely to give away information to this "friend" than to a perceived "stranger."

cyberbullying

the deliberate and repeated misuse of communication technology by an individual or group to threaten or harm others

Another form of bad behavior online is **cyberbullying**—"the deliberate and repeated misuse of communication technology by an individual or group to threaten or harm others" (Roberto & Eden, 2010, p. 198). Cyberbullying differs from traditional bullying partly because it is anonymous, it can occur anywhere (through voice, text, picture, or video messages on cell phones and through social networking sites, chat rooms, and so on), and an infinite number of viewers can observe or participate. Research shows that cyberbullying can have many negative consequences for victims, ranging from psychological problems like depression, anxiety, and low self-esteem to disastrous consequences, as in the tragic case of Tyler Clementi, who committed suicide after being harassed by his roommate, who used a webcam to spy on his trysts with another man and then sent tweets with info about how others could watch the hookups (Boyle, 2012). Some experts report that approximately 25 percent of minors are victims of cyberbullying and about 15 percent admit that they cyberbullied others, leading many schools to implement cyberbullying prevention programs. Communities are also beginning to seriously enforce anti-cyberbullying laws (Ferman, 2014; Patchin, 2014). Students, who are gay, lesbian, bisexual, transgender, or queer (GLBTQ), are often the targets of bullies, and some experts suggest that bullying is not always just aggressive behavior but often reflects the socially accepted norm of marginalizing those outside the norm (e.g., GLBTQ). They propose rethinking intervention programs to include challenges to the culturally accepted and perpetuated inequities regarding gender, racial, ethnic, and sexual identities (Payne & Smith, 2013).

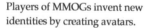

Players of MMOGs invent new identities by creating avatars.

The final form of online behavior related to anonymity is deception. If you have represented yourself as something you are not on a Facebook or other social media profile, you are not alone. Many people say they put false information on their social networking sites and they give many reasons for doing so. In some cases, it's a strategy for projecting a more positive image (e.g., lying about one's salary, weight, achievements), or for some, it's about achieving privacy because they become more and more aware of the consequences of having their posted information taken out of context. Fabricating data on these sites may protect from unwanted advances from strangers, but for young people, it can also shield them from the watchful eyes of their parents (boyd, 2014), or be a strategy for finding out what "friends" think of them by starting an online conversation about oneself, using a false identity.

However, some children are lying about their age to create accounts on SNSs—most of which have an age limit of thirteen—leaving them open to fraud and predators (Byrne, Katz, Linz, & Mcilrath, et al., 2014), although some experts think the media focus on online risks to children is misplaced. They say that children and teens who engage in risky behavior online are often struggling offline (with unsafe home environments, addicted parents, etc.) and that in fact technology can often help keep children safe (boyd, 2014). A Web site called http://www.findyourmissingchild.org/ provides instructions for how parents can use social media to find missing children.

Beyond anonymity is the phenomenon of **pseudoanonymity**, or projecting a false identity. For example, people can invent identities through acceptable means in MMOGs such as "World of Warcraft," "EverQuest II," "Karaoke Revolution," and in virtual worlds such as Second Life and Entropia Universe. Some young people take their participation in these games seriously, they enjoy playing with people outside of their offline world of school and work, and create an online identity, often different from their offline identity. There are rarely negative consequences because this "deception" is expected.

Similarly, virtual worlds like Second Life, also provide opportunities to create an alternative identity for socializing or pedagogical purposes or commercial ventures. In these virtual worlds, as many as ten thousand people—or their **avatars**, digital alter egos or versions of themselves—can be present at the same time, engaged in activities from hanging out, to holding charity fundraisers, or to operating sex clubs. Some players purposely construct their avatars in ways that reflect their actual physical characteristics; others construct them based on skills or attractiveness (boyd, 2014). These virtual social worlds can also be used for education and training. Some universities have developed sites on Second Life where professors and students can interact; CAVA is a simulation that teaches students about dealing with date violence (http://www.totemlearning.com/cava/) and major corporations use virtual simulation educational games for teaching about leadership, diversity, and other important issues (Routledge & de Freitas, 2013).

Although there seems to be increasing acceptance of the real-name Web, some experts maintain that there should be a place for pseudonyms and some anonymity online. They point out that these allow people "to express their competitive urges in gaming environments, their health concerns on specialist sites, their political appetites on blogs, without these getting in the way of each other or personal and professional obligations" (Hogan, 2012, p. 14). In addition, it can provide some measure of safety in interactive media sites for those potential victims of cyberbullying (for example, GLBTQ teens and domestic abuse victims).

To summarize, interactive media technologies afford many possibilities for performing and managing identities, but these possibilities should be balanced with consideration of safety and ethical concerns, as well as impression management concerns. Let's now turn our attention to how relationships develop and are maintained through interactive media.

② Relationship Development

You probably have some relationships that exist only online, such as with acquaintances you met in an online course or on an SNS, although it appears that people are using SNSs less to make new friends and more to strengthen relationships with their existing friends. Let's consider the impact of mediated communication on three types of relationships: friendships, romantic relationships, and relationships in the workplace.

FRIENDSHIPS Although online and offline relationships have much in common, interactive media can affect our relational development in at least a couple significant ways. First, you can come into contact with many more people online than you ever would in person, so online relationships may offer many more potential partners than offline life.

Second, relationships that are initiated or maintained through interactive media also overcome limits of time and space. You do not have to (ever) be in close proximity to these people and you do not (ever) have to exchange messages at the same time, and you can stay in close contact almost 24/7. What are the implications of these characteristics for these relationships?

There has been much debate about whether social media in particular yield overall positive or negative effects on relationships in general. A recent longitudinal

pseudoanonymity
projecting a false identity

avatars
digital alter egos or versions of oneself, used in MMOGs

How many personal details do you think people should disclose on their SNS pages? Is there any information that you think should be routinely disclosed? Never disclosed? How much do you disclose? Why?

study found that overall, SNS users reportedly had more FtF interaction with close friends and a greater number of acquaintances than those who did not use SNSs. This suggests that SNS communication does not replace intimacy or FtF communication. However, users also reported more loneliness than nonusers, especially males; so maybe heavy SNS use also increases feelings of isolation and loneliness (Brandtzaeg, 2012).

It is clear that we cannot assume that interactive media has all positive (or negative) effects on communication or relationships. For this reason, we prefer a dialectical view of interactive media's affect on relationships and assume that *interactive media BOTH strengthens AND weakens relationships.*

The lack of nonverbal cues on some media can weaken relationships. Not being able to see the expression on your friend's face while she texts you about a problem she's having might result in your not realizing how unhappy she is. However, media scholars also point out that the reduced nonverbal cues can have a positive effect on communication because these cues (such as appearance or accent) can sometimes trigger stereotypes. For example, viewing email or text messages, we may not be able to determine someone's race, gender, age, ability–disability and so are less likely to show prejudice or discrimination in online communication (Merryfield, 2003).

Similarly, asynchronicity may weaken personal relationships because the notion of friendship includes shared experiences, feelings, and activities. So, when you receive terrific news that you want to share with your best friend, telling him or her through a delayed text message (if your friend does not immediately respond to your message) does not have the same impact that a FtF conversation or phone call would.

However, media scholars also point out that the asynchronicity of mediated messages can have positive effects on relationships. For example, it can give people time to formulate a message, which can be helpful for shy people and others as well (Baker & Oswald, 2010). In fact, in one study, young people explained that although there were often misunderstandings, they preferred mobile text messaging over other forms of communication partly because it gave them more time to ponder and think about what they were trying to express (Coyne, Stockdale, Busby, Iverson, & Grant, 2011). Asynchronicity, allowing the time to formulate thoughts into words, can also be useful when communicating in a foreign language (Thompson & Ku, 2005).

Online relationships may be both more durable and fragile. An example of the greater durability of online relationships is that if you have a relationship that is strictly online and you relocate to a faraway place, the relationship may not be affected. As people are increasingly mobile, new communication technologies afford more continuity than was possible before. On the other hand, online relationships can be somewhat more fragile, partly because they require some skepticism. As we discussed previously, deception frequently occurs in the initial stages of online relationships. There are also people who drop out because they find the pressures of SNS "performance" too stressful (agonizing over how to present themselves, which photos to post, whether their photos and music picks are "cool" enough, and so on). And some decide to stop participating in "the throwaway friendships of online life" (Turkle, 2011, p. 275).

How can you effectively navigate social networking sites, for example, where online relationships are developed? Because the information you post on SNSs is potentially accessed by hundreds or thousands of people, you should consider carefully how much and what type of information you post. It's useful to ask yourself: Do you know who has access to the information? Do you know how it will be used? How much information do you want to share with others?

However, when moving an online relationship offline, the timing may be important; some experts suggest that it is better to move a relationship offline fairly soon after an initial meeting, before people develop an idealized notion of their online partner and have unrealistic expectations (Ramirez & Zhang, 2007).

ROMANTIC RELATIONSHIPS Who becomes involved in online romantic relationships, and how does online romance differ from in-person romance? According to one survey, 50 percent of respondents said they knew someone who had met a romantic partner online (Friedman, 2011). Many online romance Web sites feature a scientific approach, which often includes compatibility and personality testing and seems to cover all ages and income levels (Match, OkCupid, Tinder, eHarmony). Some specialize in niche marketing focusing on religion (Jewish, Catholic, Christian), race/ethnicity (interracial, Black, Latino), or age (OurTime for singles older than 50). Others use matching activities, such as social gaming (Tagged), photography (Jazzed), or as mentioned previously, physical location (Tinder, Sonar, Are you Interested?, Skout, Plenty of Fish) (13 Best dating apps, 2012).

"If you really want to know why I'm dumping you, you may want to check out my website where there's a long, detailed explanation posted."

There are several qualities of online communication that are particularly relevant to romantic relationships: the ease of finding similar others and of achieving intimate exchanges (McKenna, Green, & Gleason, 2002). To begin, it's easy to see how one can meet people with similar interests via online forums or communities where people gather precisely because they share an interest. According to one student, "when you like a girl it's much easier to send a friend request than to ask for her phone number. Then you can check out her photos, her profile information and her posts.... if you're still interested, chances are she's worth pursuing" (Bennhold, 2011). Second, online communication may give rise to easier, quicker self-disclosure and intimacy (as we have noted). For example, on Internet dating sites, profiles are set up to reveal extensive information about potential partners—describing their personality, interests (what they read, music they listen to, and so forth), ideal date, and political persuasion. It is easy to see how mediated communication in this context may lead to relationships in which people develop intimacy more quickly.

However, developing online relationships poses dangers and can provide opportunities for deception (as described in *It Happened to Me: Jacqueline*). In one study of online dating practices, researchers found that 50 percent of the participants admitted to lying about their looks, relationship status, age, weight, socioeconomic status, or interests (Whitty, 2007). Another found that older daters were more likely to misrepresent age, and men were more likely to misrepresent personal assets and interests, attributes, and relationship goals. Women were more likely to misrepresent weight (Hall, Park, Song, & Cody, 2010). However, online daters also report that they usually assume some deception and learn to "correct" for it: "One woman mentioned that if a profile said a man was 5'11" she would assume he was probably 5'9"; a

It Happened to Me
Jacqueline

My first year in college I met a guy in one of my online courses—we were on the same team for our group project. We seemed to have a lot in common. We had the same major, film studies, and we talked a lot about our favorite (obscure) movies and traded recommendations for movie watching. He said he wasn't on Facebook, which seemed a little odd to me, but we mostly communicated through text messages and some phone conversations. We lived about 50 miles apart and finally did get together a few times. Finally, I found out (through another student in the class) that he did have a Facebook page—using his middle name—and a wife and two kids! I felt betrayed and was much more cautious after that about forming friendships in online courses.

man said that if a woman said she was 'average' body type, he would assume she was slightly heavy" (Heino, Ellison, & Gibbs, 2010).

catfishing

creating an intentionally deceptive social media profile

And as noted previously, more serious deception can occur with the practice of **catfishing**—creating an intentionally deceptive social media profile, sometimes even including fake photos, bios, friends, and so on, often with the goal of making a romantic connection. Of course the person who is catfishing needs to avoid any offline contact with the intended target and the motivation may be a search for a close relationship, or the satisfaction of manipulating another (D'Costa, 2014). More sinister, even criminal motives are increasingly prevalent; many people have been swindled out of money by someone who poses as a potential suitor and asks for money after gaining the trust and interest of a dating partner. One woman met a man on a popular dating site. They emailed, texted, and talked on the phone; he sent flowers and so on. Later in the relationship he asked for money for his daughter's tuition and later, for money to help fund his oil rig business—which even had a fake business Web site. She sent him a total of $300,000 before one of her friends contacted the authorities (Flacy, 2014). Despite the potential risks, people can and do form close, lasting relationships online. Many of the same things that make offline romantic relationships work are important in online relationships, like intimacy, trust, and communication satisfaction. In fact, it appears that interactive media and constant connectivity *can* strengthen romantic relationships. Although not replacing FtF expressions of affection, a quick text message to say "I luv u:)" or a phone call while doing routine errands enables couples to continue expressing affection throughout the day. Interestingly, in one study married heterosexual couples used a larger variety of media (phone, social networking, blogs, and webcams) than dating couples (Coyne, 2011).

However, there are also downsides to the constant connectivity of new media in maintaining romantic relationships (Dainton & Noller, 2013). Experts have found that the use of Facebook is associated with increased jealousy in romantic relationships and relational dissatisfaction (Elphinston, 2011). For example, one young man describes how he monitors his girlfriend's Facebook page to see what other guys write (Bennhold, 2011). Similarly, the connectedness of text messaging can be seen as stifling or even as harassing if one partner insists on constant communication (Duran, Kelly, & Rotaru, 2011; Pettigrew, 2010), and some (more than 40 percent of respondents in one study!) complain that their partners are too distracted by cell phones. Others argue about the amount of time their partners spend on particular online activities (Lenhart & Duggan, 2014).

Terminating romantic relationships, given all the communication choices, can be particularly challenging. In one study, researcher Illana Gershon (2010) interviewed college students about their media choices in breaking up with a romantic partner. Although almost all said that face to face was the most appropriate way to end a relationship, they often chose interactive media for various stages of breakup. The particular communication form chosen varied a great deal, and they believed the particular choice affected the message that was sent but didn't always agree on the particular affect (e.g., some saw texting as intimate because the phone is always with you, whereas others saw it as distancing because of message length limit), which often complicated the relationship negotiation. Some used a variety of media, initiating the break up by text, then talking on the phone and finishing by face to face. A few ended relationships by changing their Facebook status, because they didn't want to deal with the partner's reaction over the phone or face to face.

cloud storage

storage of data online on multiple servers, accessible from multiple locations

WORK RELATIONSHIPS Most workers report that communication technologies have improved their ability to do their job, share ideas with coworkers, and work in a flexible way. For example, one software company has seventeen employees at three locations: Phoenix, Arizona; Cape Cod, Massachusetts; and Philadelphia, Pennsylvania. All their documents are in **cloud storage**; they communicate regularly through Yammer, an internal SNS designed especially for businesses. They have monthly video conference meetings and meet face to face from time to time. These interactive technologies mean that none of the employees had to relocate when they were hired, and through media technologies, they stay connected and productive. Although interactive technologies generally have positive effects on work relationships, some concerns exist. According to a recent study, many workers think that these technologies result in longer hours and increased stress levels because many continue their work after they get home and are expected to read email and be available for cell phone calls after work (Turkle, 2011). The impact varies, however, depending on the type of relationship—whether it is a superior–subordinate relationship or a peer relationship.

Superior–Subordinate Communication At least three areas of concern center on interactive media in the workplace: status and boundary issues, surveillance issues, and confidentiality issues. A major impact of online communication in the workplace is its status-leveling effect. With email, anyone can have instant access to superiors. On the other hand, this status leveling can also raise boundary issues: How much online interaction is appropriate between boss and employees? Should you ask to friend your boss on Facebook? Should a supervisor request to friend a subordinate? The answer is probably not because it blurs the work–personal relationships in unproductive ways (Calderon, 2013). Communication technologies also give superiors a way of checking up on subordinates. Messages sent through email may be stored forever on company servers, so management can monitor employees' correspondence. Also, if you are Facebook friends with an employee, you can check his or her account and see if it is used during the day when they are at work!

Many companies monitor employee email and Internet usage, and Web-based security cameras are increasingly common. Also, technologies such as GPS and employee badges with radio frequency identification (RFID) tags provide an even higher level of employee monitoring. These tracking systems can record, display, and archive the exact location of any employee—both inside and outside the office—at any time. Use of the GPS tracking software, fairly common now, placed on the company-owned smartphones of a pest control company's employees led to two employees being dismissed: one for meeting a woman during work hours and the other for just not working. Other software allows employers to see every photo, text message, or email sent over company phones. A theft-monitoring software used in 392 restaurants resulted in a 22-percent reduction in server theft (Ante & Weber, 2013). Some employees view this surveillance as a violation of privacy, and one study showed that workers who were electronically monitored reported higher levels of job boredom, psychological stress, depression, anger, and fatigue (Brustein, 2013).

Although most companies see the benefit of social networking sites as a way to advertise products and even bolster employee relationships (some large corporations have their own in-house versions of Facebook, such as Yammer), they are skeptical of giving employees access to social media during work hours, partly because of fear of decreased productivity, also known as "social notworking." One study estimated that the personal use of SNSs was costing the British economy $2.3 billion annually, and another concluded that if companies banned employees from using Facebook, they could increase productivity by 1.5 percent ("Yammering away at the office," 2010). Another new media concern for employers is losing

It Happened to Me
Cruzita

I sent my manager an email requesting some time off, but she didn't receive it. When I found out that I did not get the weekend off, I was mad at her, but she had no idea I had sent her an email. If my manager and I had communicated face to face, we would not have had a mix up of this kind.

control of their image, as in the case of a DTE Energy employee who lost her job after posting negative comments on Facebook referring to their customers (Wiley, 2013). Employers also worry about employees leaking confidential information through social media messages—loss of corporate, confidential, or customer information or making inappropriate public statements about the company.

Another issue concerns decisions about what should be handled in person or online. Just as in romantic relationships, bad news (termination, negative job performance reviews) should probably be communicated in person. On the other hand, communicating electronically gives workers the opportunity to think carefully about their communication before sending it, but it can result in misunderstandings. For an example of the type of workplace misunderstandings that can occur using email, read *It Happened to Me: Cruzita.*

Peer Communication Although interactive media may make the communication between workers more efficient and effective, access to certain kinds of information often decreases when one relies on online communication. For example, in FtF work contexts, you can observe colleagues in the next office during meetings and talk with them in the halls or mailroom, but if you communicate online with a coworker at a different location, you have little information about them. This lack of information increases uncertainty as well as the potential for disagreements and misunderstanding, as one of our students describes in *It Happened to Me: Mei-Lin*. To minimize these misunderstandings and build trust among personnel, some employers try to arrange periodic FtF meetings or even promote social networking communication among coworkers.

It Happened to Me
Mei-Lin

I sent an urgent email to a colleague requesting information for a report I was writing. He didn't respond, and I became very irritated at his lack of response. A few days later, I found out that his child had been in a serious accident, and he missed work for several days. If we had been located in the same office, I would have known immediately what was wrong, would have responded more appropriately to his absence, and could have gotten the information I needed in some other way.

To summarize, interactive media provides opportunities and challenges for relationship development and maintenance, and each type of relationship, whether a friendship, a romance, or a work relationship, has unique challenges. When we expand the frame of reference beyond individuals, as we do in the next section, we encounter a new set of new media-related issues and challenges—those posed by societal forces.

5 The Individual, Communication Technology, and Society

5 **Understand the role of power and privilege in interactive media use.**

All media activities—whether for fun, socializing, or information seeking—are enacted by humans within a social context and the larger society. These activities both reflect and influence larger societal norms. For example, some of the same social hierarchies that exist in the larger society also exist in the realm of interactive media. When we sort people out by various identities (for example, gender, ethnicity, or race), we find differences not only in how many of them use communication technologies (see Table 2) but also in how they are perceived to use these media. In this section, we'll first look at how various identities influence technology use and then examine some of the inequalities in communication technologies use.

Table 2 The demographics of smartphone ownership (2014)*

Percent of U.S. adults within each group who own a smartphone	
All adults	58
Gender	
Men	61
Women	57
Age	
18–29	83
30–49	74
50–64	49
65 and older	19
Race/Ethnicity	
White, non-Hispanic	53
Black, non-Hispanic	59
Hispanic	61
Household Income	
Less than $30,000	47
$30,000–$49,999	53
$50,000–$74,999	61
$75,000 and higher	81
Education Level	
High school grad or less	44
Some college	67
College (plus post-college education)	71
Geographic Location	
Urban	64
Suburban	60
Rural	43

*N = 1,0006, except for race/ethnicity where n = 2,008

SOURCE: Mobile Technology Fact Sheet. (2014) *Pew Internet & American Life Project*. Retrieved May 20, 4014, from http://www.pewinternet.org/fact-sheets/mobile-technology-fact-sheet/.

Gender, Age, Ethnicity, and Technology Use

Let's consider gender first. In 2007, when college students were asked to identify various computer activities as either "masculine," "feminine," or "neutral," they identified arcade-style computer games as the most masculine activity, as well as high-tech peripherals (for example, digital cameras), banking, and downloading music. In contrast, they identified emailing, studying online, and shopping as feminine activities (Selwyn, 2007). These perceptions seem to represent traditional gender roles—men being more action oriented and females more interpersonally oriented. How accurate are these stereotypes today?

As it turns out, some of the perceptions are accurate and others are not. Males are more likely than females to play online games and to play a larger variety of games, although female players are increasing in numbers (Galarneau, 2014). Hacking also seems to be a predominantly male activity and most computer code is written by males (Humphreys & Vered, 2014). Men participate more in online political activities than women (Wei, 2012). Not surprisingly, more men than women tend to major in and pursue careers in computer science or other technology-related fields (Marder, 2012).

Women tend to email more and more likely to use and access social networking sites in general (Wei, 2012). This is particularly true of Pinterest; women are four

The fastest-growing group of Internet users is people age 70 and older.

times as likely as men to access Pinterest (Duggan & Smith, 2013). Nevertheless, some of the stereotypes about gender are unfounded. For example, some evidence shows males and females having equal levels of computer skills (Cheong, 2008), and it seems likely that both genders are equally likely to shop online and take online courses. Taken together, then, this evidence suggests that the use of communication technologies only partially reinforces gender stereotypes.

How do other identities—such as age—interact with interactive media use? As one might expect, young people are still more comfortable with new technologies than older folks, and they tend to use communication technologies in more and different ways (Smith 2014c; Wei, 2012). The younger you are, the more likely you are to own a smartphone, tablet, and e-book reader and use social media than are older people (Smith, 2014c; Wei, 2012). However, the stereotype of older people avoiding technology is somewhat inaccurate. Although older folks do tend to use interactive media less, the fastest-growing group of Internet users is older people (age 70 and older), and the number of older people (age 50 and older) who visit SNSs has increased significantly in the last few years (Duggan & Smith, 2013c).

Social media use also varies somewhat with race. It turns out that the Black American presence on Twitter is significant, and several communication experts have studied the "Black Twitter" phenomenon. Forty percent of eighteen to twenty-nine-year-old African Americans who use the Internet say that they use Twitter, compared to 28 percent of young whites (Smith, 2014a). Further, many Blacks (not all!) seem to use Twitter differently than other racial/ethnic groups. They form tighter clusters on the network; that is, they follow one another more readily, retweet each other more often, and more of their posts are @-replies (directed at other users). Their tweets are most visible in "trending topics"—a real-time list of the most tweeted-about subjects (Brock, 2012). Media expert Farhad Manjoo gives the example of the hashtag #wordsthatleadtotrouble that started one day, and people worldwide responded in a viral "call and response" Twitter conversation, competing to outdo each other in "ever more hilarious, bizarre, or profane posts" ("we need to talk," "the condom broke," "I didn't know she was your sister" [Manjoo, 2010]). It was a top-trending topic the next day, and it turns out that most of the tweets were from Black people. Manjoo and other experts suggest that Twitter is particularly conducive to the strong participative oral traditions within many Black communities—the "call and response" between minister and congregation or the "playin' the dozens," which are playful back and forth insults (Brock, 2012; Florini, 2014).

Stereotypes of ethnic, racial, and gender groups persist online. Studies show that characters in video games are overwhelmingly White and male. Outside of sports video games, only a few Black characters exist, and often they are portrayed as gangsters or street people. Latinos and Native Americans are extremely underrepresented as video game characters; female characters are more likely to be represented by partially nude avatars of an unrealistic body type. Although there are many White male game players, the population of gamers worldwide includes female gamers, people of different racial and cultural backgrounds, and gamers of varying ages. The typical gamer is not necessarily a White male adolescent, which seems to be the assumption of video game creators (Cheong & Gray, 2011; Williams, Martins, Consalvo, & Ivory, 2009).

As you can see, people use social media in different ways and not everyone is equally represented in the communication technology revolution, nor does everyone have equal access to digital life and cyberspace, which is perhaps the most important way that societal forces affect interactive media use.

Power, Access, and Digital Inequalities

According to a recent Pew Internet and American Life Project report, about 15 percent of Americans are not online at all (Zickuhr, 2014), and in many countries, only a tiny fraction of the population has access to computers and the Internet. This inequality of access between the technology "haves" and the "have nots"—once referred to as the **digital divide**—is probably more accurately viewed now as a continuum of digital inequalities rather than a divide (Wei, 2012). These inequalities exist within the United States and also on a global scale. Although there is high Internet access in Western Europe, North America, and East Asia, usage in developing countries—especially in Africa—is sparse. In Africa, Internet penetration is 18 percent, compared with 48 percent in East Asia, 12 percent in South Asia, 25 percent in Southeast Asia, and 29 percent in Central Asia; 37 percent in the Middle East, 34 percent in Latin America, 47 percent in South America, 78 percent in Western Europe, 63 percent in Oceania (Australia, New Zealand), and 81 percent in North America (Anderson, 2014b). Many developing countries lack landline services, but their mobile phone usage is growing exponentially; it's estimated that 95 percent of the world's population now owns a cell phone (Anderson, 2014b, Global Digital Statistics, 2014), allowing people to connect in ways never possible before (Alzouma, 2012; Chuma, 2014).

digital divide

inequity of access between the technology "haves" and "have nots"

Why do differences in digital access and use matter? In a global information society, information is an important commodity that everyone needs to function. In addition, to function effectively in society, people need **cultural capital** (Bourdieu, 1986), or certain bodies of cultural knowledge and cultural competencies. Those with the most power in a society decide what constitutes cultural capital, and it is passed down from parents to children, just as economic capital is.

cultural capital

cultural knowledge and cultural competencies that people need to function effectively in society

In the United States and much of the world, cultural capital includes the ability to use communication technologies in appropriate ways, and digital exclusion is one of the most damaging forms of exclusion in our increasingly digitized world. What hinders people from acquiring **technocapital**, that is, access to technological skills and resources? Without these skills and knowledge, one can feel disconnected from the center of society (Wei, 2012). For example, a researcher told of a man who had little experience with computers. When the man went for a haircut, he was told to check in online, either with his phone or on the computer at the counter. He was too embarrassed to admit not knowing how to do this, so he left the shop without getting a haircut. Why is this man on the far side of the digital inequalities continuum? What factors keep him, and others, from having digital technocapital?

technocapital

access to technological skills and resources

Cultural capital includes the knowledge enabling people to make use of interactive media.

WHO HAS ACCESS TO INTERACTIVE MEDIA? Inequalities in digital access and usage is decreasing in some ways. For example, gender differences in digital access—once a feature underlying the digital divide in the United States—have all but disappeared, and cell phone ownership is almost universal. Racial and ethnic disparities are also shrinking for some media use, especially the more recent technologies (Smith, 2014a). However, some experts say that disparities based on income, education, and urban-rural groups persist. Let's look more closely at what they mean by this statement.

As shown in Table 2, Hispanics and African Americans have higher smartphone ownership rates than Whites (61 percent; 59 percent versus 53 percent). Although all smartphone users can access the Internet by phone, Blacks and especially Latinos are more likely than Whites to rely *only* on mobile phones because they are less likely to have access to a computer or broadband Internet at home, especially older and less educated Blacks (Smith, 2014a). What are the implications? It is difficult or impossible to accomplish some important activities with a smartphone, such as updating a résumé and conducting a job search

online. Thus, these ethnic groups are at a disadvantage, which illustrates the new configuration of digital inequalities; it has to do with how one *uses* interactive media. Communication scholar Lu Wei suggests that to understand digital inequalities, we should measure the number of online activities one engages in (**multimodality**), not just whether one has access to the Internet or a particular media device (like a smartphone). That is, the more digital activities one pursues (e.g., check email, log on to Facebook, write on Twitter, share a video on YouTube, post a picture on Flickr, move money from one account to another on a banking site, and update and post a resume on LinkedIn), the more digitally empowered one is. We'll explore the relationship between multimodality and digital inequalities further a little later.

In addition, socioeconomic status and education level make a big difference in Internet access, smartphone ownership, and some social media use for all ethnic or racial groups. People who make more than $75,000 a year are much more likely to be online and own a smartphone, and use SNSs such as LinkedIn and Pinterest than those making less than $30,000. Similarly, those with some college education are much more likely to be online, own a smartphone, and use SNSs such as LinkedIn and Pinterest than those without a high school diploma (Anderson & Rainie, 2014; Duggan & Smith, 2013, Fox & Rainie, 2014).

The rural, urban, and suburban divide also persists for some technologies (Mobile technology fact sheet, 2014). As you can see from Table 2, people in rural areas are much less likely to own a smartphone as those in urban or suburban areas (43 percent versus 64 percent; 60 percent) and less likely to use the Internet (83 percent versus 88 percent; 87 percent) (Fox & Rainie, 2014).

As we've mentioned, age is also a digital divide factor: 90 percent of young people ages eighteen to twenty-nine have access to computers and are online, compared with 56 percent of people ages sixty-five and older ("Demographics of Internet users," 2014). Older people are also less likely to be mobile phone and smartphone users and less likely to visit almost all SNSs except for Facebook (Duggan & Smith, 2013; Fox & Rainie, 2014;). And disability is also associated with lower new media access and use; even with analysis control for all demographic factors (age, income, education, and so on), people with disabilities are less likely to have Internet access and less likely than other Internet users to have high-speed access or wireless access (Fox, 2011). Although many people with disabilities visit SNSs such as Facebook and use them in the same ways as non-disabled, many sites do not provide full access to persons with disabilities, especially people with visual disabilities. In addition, some individuals with disabilities regard Facebook as an unsafe environment, where they may be discriminated against because of their disabilities, especially if they use it for professional networking (Shpigelman & Gill, 2014).

Overall, then, in the United States, the people most likely to have access to and use interactive media:

- Are young or middle-aged.
- Have a college degree or are currently students.
- Have a comfortable income.
- Live in an urban or suburban area.
- Are physically abled.

Globalization and Digital Inequalities

Compared with those in the United States, even larger digital inequalities exist on a global scale. The issues of who does and does not have technocapital and whose culture dominates it are relevant in our current global economy. Why? Some activists and policymakers hope that a world

multimodality

the range or breadth of Internet activities

Socioeconomic status and education are strong factors in the digital divide.

facilitated by new communication technologies, economic globalization—meaning increased mobility of goods, services, labor, and capital—can lead to a more democratic and equitable world. And some evidence supports this hope. For example, outsourcing American jobs to overseas locations has provided income opportunities for many in English-speaking countries such as India. And, despite some governments' attempts to limit their citizens' access to new media, the Internet provides information, world news, and possibilities for interpersonal communication that were not available previously.

In addition, interactive media have been used successfully by advocates of social change. Social media such as Facebook and Twitter enable organizers to reach many people quickly and can be used to recruit people, organize collective action, raise awareness and shape attitudes, raise money, and increase communication with decision makers. For example, in one survey, 56 percent of respondents said they have seen an online group come together to help a person or community solve a problem (Fox & Rainie, 2014). Social media played an especially prominent role in the millions of dollars raised for amyotrophic lateral sclerosis (ALS) research during the "Ice Bucket Challenge" in Summer 2014. Participants who were nominated (usually via social media like Facebook, Twitter, Instagram) were filmed (and posted on social media) having a bucket of ice water poured on their heads and then nominating others to do the same. When nominated, participants usually had 24 hours to comply or forfeit by way of a charitable financial donation. However, other evidence suggests that new media technologies primarily benefit wealthy Western nations, promoting their cultural values and technology and enriching their countries. Evidence here includes the fact that Western countries control and profit from the majority of new media hardware and software.

REDUCING DIGITAL INEQUALITIES: WHAT KEEPS PEOPLE OFFLINE? To understand how to reduce these digital inequalities we need to better understand why some people lack technocapital. Fourteen percent of Americans have never been online and are categorized as the "truly disconnected"; this number has recently decreased. They are more likely to be older (65 and older), no high school degree, and have an annual income of less than $30,000. The primary reason given is that they are just not interested or doesn't seem relevant; the second most common reason is that it's too frustrating or difficult; and third, it that it is too expensive (Zickuhr, 2014).

As we've seen, there are other groups that are digitally connected but less so than other groups. Experts have conducted a number of studies and advanced several theories to explain these inequalities. One theory that explains why some people accept new technologies and others don't is the diffusion of innovations, which was developed by Everett Rogers (2003). The theory suggests that for people to accept a new technology such as a computer or a smartphone, they have to see it as useful and compatible with their values and lifestyle. Moreover, if people important to the individual (e.g., an adolescent's peers) adopt the innovation first, then the individual is more likely to adopt it. So although giving people access to computers and mobile devices is an important first step, it is not enough to eliminate the digital inequalities.

A recent study tried to identify what determined people's "Internet connectedness" and found that, even more important than socioeconomic status, ethnicity, or access to home computer were (1) the social environment—that is, whether people have family and friends who also use the Internet and who can help them resolve Internet-related problems and (2) whether they see the Internet as central to important activities (Jung, 2008). This study showed that even though people may be avid video game players, they may still see computer skills as being for others and as irrelevant to their own lives.

Providing access to computers is one way to overcome the digital divide in developing countries.

Another theory—which is similar to the diffusions of innovations theory—is proposed by Dutch sociologist Jan van Dijk (2004) and addresses strategies for reducing digital inequalities. Van Dijk, like researcher Wei (2012), emphasizes that access to computer hardware or mobile devices is only one part of exclusion from the digital world. To survive and thrive in the digitized world people must have access to four levels of access to technocapital: mental, material, skills, and usage. Furthermore, each level builds on the previous one.

Mental access—the first and perhaps most important level of technocapital and perhaps the easiest to overcome—relates to motivation and acceptance of new media as meaningful, and probably most people now believe that digital skills are important. As we noted previously, however, older people and some poor people still do not see the benefit for themselves and more effort needs to be directed to overcoming these mental-access barriers.

The second level of technocapital—material access to digital hardware—is where most public policy currently focuses. For example, one U.S. federal program uses telephone taxes to pay for Internet connections in elementary schools; state and local funds are used to pay for Internet connections at public libraries; and companies donating computer and technical training are given tax incentives. On a more global scale, computer hardware and software developers have been working for years on inexpensive sturdy laptops, for example, the One Laptop per Child project that has provided low-cost laptops in developing countries (although they were never able to produce the $100 version they promised). They now have produced a laptop and a tablet for $200. Of course in the meantime, the developing world has experienced their own mobile computing revolution and there are now a number of manufacturers working on low-cost devices for that market. There's the Intel Classmates PC, for example (with similar hardware, but more expensive software than its OLPC cousin); there's the Worldreader project (it delivers villages a library full of e-books via Kindles); and there's the now-infamous Aakash tablet, which was sold in India for $35 but with problems of reliability and functionality (Watters, 2012). Clearly, without access to hardware and Internet connections, acquiring technocapital can be impossible.

The third level of technocapital—skills access—is also critical. Many non-users view lack of training and lack of user-friendly technology as barriers, and frustration levels can be significant. To facilitate skills access, hardware and software developers must better understand the minds of users, taking into consideration their diverse cultural communication norms and practices. We need "technology that can think like the user" and that can think like users from many cultural backgrounds. Some experts blame the failure of the One Laptop Per Child project partially on the lack of training for teachers and children, "almost as though we believe we can simply parachute technology in to a classroom and expect everyone to just pick it up, understand it, use it and prosper" (Watters, 2012).

Finally, usage access means knowing how to use a variety of computer applications. For example, learning to build a Web site or navigate SNSs or conduct online banking takes more know-how than using the computer to play games or send email. More important, those who are at the high end of multimodality use the computer in ways that are professionally and personally enhancing; for example, they visit sites that provide useful information about national and international news, health and financial information, government services, and product information (Hargittai & Hinnant, 2008). Even if people have computers, their lack of technological proficiency and social resources may frustrate them in high-tech societies (Cheong, 2008). As we noted previously, the notion of multimodality explains a lot of the variation in digital inequalities. Female, older, poorer, and less-educated people use the Internet for limited basic applications, which, experts point out, are also associated with less political communication and participation (Wei, 2012).

6   Ethics and Interactive Media

6   **Identify and describe three ethical challenges involving interactive media use.**

One message we hope you take from this text is that interactive media are not good or bad in themselves, nor better or worse than offline communication. They are simply different. However, these differences can allow for irresponsible, thoughtless, or even unethical communication. How can you become an ethical user of social media? There are at least four areas of ethical consideration: (1) presentation of identity online, (2) privacy issues, (3) posting ethical messages, and (4) building online relationships.

Ethics and Online Identity

As we discussed previously, the issue of identity and ethics online is complex, and one can take various positions on the issue. An extreme position would be that one should never misrepresent oneself. On the other hand, some interactive media (e.g., MMOGs) clearly offer legitimate opportunities to take on a new identity or pseudo-identity, and in some cases, social media users have good reasons to mask their true identity (for example, victims of cyberbullying and victims of domestic abuse or online harassment). It's fairly common to assume a pseudonym/handle on Tumblr or Twitter, that reflects your interests, or because your preferred nickname may be already taken. Perhaps a more challenging issue is deciding when to set up a second Facebook page or another SNS with a pseudo-identity because you don't want all your posts to be seen by all your potential audiences, or you want to post opinions that may be unaccepted by some of your friends/acquaintances. One general principle might be "Do no harm." As described earlier in *It Happened to Me: Jacqueline*, in the example of Jacqueline's online friend, who pretended not to be married, the behavior was clearly deceitful.

Communication, of course, is interactive and reciprocal; it takes two people to engage in any interaction, and both have responsibility. Among the receiver's responsibilities is the duty to harbor a certain amount of skepticism for messages that may be questionable. In the case of interactive media, skepticism should focus on how people present their identity—particularly in certain contexts (e.g., in SNSs, online forums, chat rooms, or other interactive media sites).

Privacy Issues

A second ethical issue concerns online privacy, and the general guideline of doing no harm can also apply here. Specifically, ethical interactive media use includes respecting others' privacy and not snooping around Facebook or text messages that are not intended for you. There is increasing opportunity for privacy violation as we own more mobile devices (tablet, phones, and so on).

Finally, if you accidentally access private information, you should consider carefully the consequences of sharing this information with others—would the owner of the information want this information to be shared? Will others be harmed by sharing the information? Of course, the harm could be mild (sharing news about a friend that she or he would not want shared) to much more drastic consequences (sharing personal identity information that could result in cyberbullying or identity theft).

Posting Ethical Messages

A third ethical issue is the incivility of messages posted on SNSs, blogs, and especially Twitter. When bloggers disclose their feelings and opinions, they become vulnerable to personal attacks via comments left by readers. Women seem to be frequent targets of vulgar or insulting comments—from death threats to manipulated photos (Humphries & Vered, 2014). Some Web site and software developers have suggested that a set of guidelines for conduct be created and implemented to "bring civility to the Web" (Bryson, 2013). Some progress is being made as bloggers control if and when they will allow anonymous comments by strangers, and they often make explicit which behaviors they will (and will not) tolerate. However, an ethical stance is a balanced one. Some bloggers become so obsessed with policing comments that their blogs cease to become anything but an echo chamber because any dissenting comment is labeled as a violation of the rules of the blog. Discussion needs to be civil, but when disagreement of any kind is labeled as offensive trolling, then discussion becomes impossible.

Building Ethical Mediated Relationships

The first step in building ethical relationships is to remember the characteristics of interactive media—the variations in media richness, social presence, opportunities for anonymity, deception, etc. First, present yourself as honestly and truthfully as you can and behave as you would in real life. How you act online may be the most direct way that people—including potential employers as well as love interests—will perceive you. You also need to give recipients of your message enough information to discern the "tone" of your message. For example, you may have to explain in words (or emoticons) the humorous tone that in person you would communicate with facial expressions or gestures.

A second step is to consider which form of communication is appropriate for your message. Here, relevant factors are your relationship with the receiver and the purpose of the message. For example, in a work context, a lean email message can convey essential information. However, personal messages may be better delivered in person, especially if miscommunication is likely and you need immediate feedback to make sure you are understood.

7   Improving Your Mediated Communication Skills

7   **Discuss ways to improve your own mediated communication skills.**

What should you take from this text that can help you be a better communicator? First, you can strive to communicate more politely, following guidelines for interactive media netiquette. Second, you can use social media effectively in job hunting.

Interactive Media Etiquette

Just as we have norms of courtesy for traditional, FtF communication, we also have etiquette for computer-mediated communication. Let's look at several new media forms and the challenges they pose for communicating politely.

EMAIL   Because email is still prevalent in work and school contexts (for example, contacting professors), it is worth considering how to increase its effectiveness. The most important guideline is to think before writing a message and hitting the send button. Remember that what you put in writing can never be unwritten and that others besides the intended recipient may see it. Here are a few specific suggestions:

- Give your email a context. Don't just write "FYI" or "Hi" in the subject field; let the recipient know specifically what you're writing about. This is especially important in work contexts. Because of the status-leveling effects of email, people get many more messages now than they ever did by telephone, so they want to know the subjects of those messages.

- Address the recipient appropriately. If the recipient is your professor, address him or her by title unless you are securely on a first-name basis. It's always better to err on the formal side rather than the informal. Abruptly starting with "Hey!", "Hi there," or "I need to talk with you about my grade" is not respectful.

- Check your spelling carefully. Sending emails full of typos and grammar mistakes, or written like a text message, communicates a lack of respect for yourself and the recipient.

MOBILE PHONES   Research shows that although most users think they have good phone manners, in one study 70 percent said they knew someone with bad phone manners and people report being irritated or annoyed by the use of phones in public places (Don't text on the toilet and get rid of that comedy ringtone, 2014).

Here are some tips for cell phone use:

- **Be safe**. Texting while driving is not worth risking your life. If you must talk on the phone (if its legal in your state), keep calls short, even if you're using your Bluetooth. There's no difference in accident statistics between drivers using hand-held versus hands-free phone devices.

- Texting while walking is almost as dangerous. At best, it's annoying for others to have to move out of the way while you're walking with your head down and your eyes on your phone. If there's no one around, you risk tripping, falling, running into objects, or not being aware of surroundings that can make you vulnerable.

- **Respect your friends**. Put your phone away when you're with friends. They came to be with you, not to watch you talk with others on your phone. Let voice mail do its job. Take your earbuds out. It's hard to tell if you're talking to them, someone on the phone, or an invisible friend. If you absolutely need to take or make a call or text, step away from the group and keep it short.

- **Respect the servers**. Don't use your phone while ordering in a restaurant. One study showed that food takes longer to get to the table now because servers have to wait for diners to finish talking on the phone call/texting before ordering.

Surveys report that loud cell phone conversations in public places are one of the top complaints about bad manners with regard to computer mediated communication.

- **Use your 'inside' voice** when speaking on the phone in public places, and don't use the speakerphone. Turns out that people tend to talk louder on cell phones; we don't know why, but they do. If you must speak, maintain a distance of at least 10 feet from the nearest person.

- **Avoid annoying ring tones**. Not everyone appreciates hearing your favorite song or ringtone when you get phone call. Keep it simple.

- **Take a photo or two** of your food in a restaurant, of performers at a concert, or of yourself on vacation but wait to edit, crop, annotate, and post to social media. If you're with other people—it's annoying.

- **Respect universal quiet zones**. Of course no cell phone use in libraries, museums, churches, theatres, or funerals.

- **Choose wisely about texting or calling**. If it's something you need to decide now, just make a phone call instead of exchanging 50 texts about where you want to go or what you want to do with a friend. If time isn't a factor, send a text.

SOURCES: http://lifehacker.com/5937223/the-most-annoying-things-your-do-with-your-phone-that-you-should-quit-or-at-least-be-aware-of
http://www.texashste.com/documents/curriculum/principles/mobil_manners.pdf.

MICROBLOGGING   As microblogging services such as Twitter have grown in popularity, they pose etiquette challenges of their own. Here are some suggestions:

- Use your real name, especially if you're tweeting for professional or business reasons.

- Don't use punctuation in your username as typing punctuation on mobile devices can be difficult.

- Establish accurate and complete profiles so others know who you are. Include only important information and leave out unnecessary details.

- Be selective in who you follow, especially when you're starting on Twitter; start slowly following people you know and who know you. Then, as you start tweeting regularly, follow more people based on your interests. Don't necessarily expect those you follow to follow you. If you follow too many people, others may think you're a spammer.

- Maintain your dignity and be respectful in language and tone. Remember that those reading your tweets have feelings. Respect your followers as you want to be respected.

- Be judicious in your tweets and retweets. It's annoying to see the same tweets again and again.

- Be careful about sharing too much information. Share only information that you don't mind making public.

- Use good grammar. Bad grammar reduces the effect of your message so take a minute to proof your tweet before sending.

- Make your tweets clear and brief. If your message is too long, send a direct message.

- Be careful about using too many hashtags. Too many makes your tweet hard to read and makes you look like a spammer.

SOURCES: http://mashable.com/2013/10/14/twitter-etiquette
http://www.smedio.com/7-things-not-to-do-on-twitter/
http://www.dummies.com/how-to/content/what-not-to-do-on-twitter.html

As you can see, the overarching principle here is to be considerate of others' time and convenience. Put yourself in the place of the person receiving your message and ask yourself, "Would I appreciate the way this message has been worded and transmitted?" If the answer is yes, you are probably doing all right.

Using Social Media in Job Hunting

Social media are playing an increasingly important role in job searches for both employers and job applicants. How can you use mediated messages effectively in searching for employment?

First of all, network. Get the word out that you're looking (but, of course, be discreet if you don't want your current employer to know). Use as many media forms as possible—Facebook, Twitter, LinkedIn. LinkedIn allows you to search by people, jobs, and companies; you can also join groups related to your industry and participate in job-related discussions. In general, the more visible you are, the more likely you are to make the contacts that will lead to a job while meeting a lot of professionals who share your same career aspirations. And you never know where *the* contact might happen.

Be thoughtful and considerate in contacting and following up with potential employers. After a meeting or interview, it's good to follow up with a short thank-you email. Similarly, be sure to thank anyone who helps you by giving you leads or recommendations. However, don't continue to try to get in touch after that. If you push too hard, you'll look like a stalker rather than an eager applicant.

A final suggestion is to remember to help others. In your job search, you may come across information or contacts that may not be relevant to your search but might be helpful to a friend, colleague, or online acquaintance. What goes around comes around—the person you help today may be in a position to do you a favor next week or next year.

Interactive media are deeply imbedded in the way we do business and research and in the ways we socialize and connect with others. Clearly, we have much to think about as we use these tools in every context to communicate responsibly, ethically, equitably, and with social awareness.

Summary

Interactive media are now a constant reality in our lives and impact our daily activities in multiple ways. This pervasiveness provides the first and primary reason for learning more about this topic. A second reason is that understanding interactive media and having good media skills will help you be more successful personally and professionally.

Interactive media are defined as a collection of mediated communication technologies that are digital and converging and tend to be interactive. In contrast to mass media where messages are generally one to many, new media messages converge, meaning they can be sent one to one, one to many, or many to many. Interactive media include social media, email, and text messaging and present us with many communication choices in our everyday lives. These media are neither good nor bad, but better viewed through a dialectical lens—as having potentially both beneficial and harmful impacts.

Interactive media vary in two ways, in media characteristics and social processes, that yield four communication dimensions that help us understand how the various communication forms impact our choices: media richness, social presence, self-presentation and self-disclosure. Interactive media choices have implications for how we present ourselves online (self-presentation, anonymity, and pseudoanonymity) In addition, interactive media afford access to many more potential relation ships, and these relationships are not bound by time or space. Using a dialectical lens, interactive media can strengthen and weaken interpersonal relationships as they are both durable and fragile. Interactive media also impact work relationships.

Interactive media uses are also affected by societal forces and, especially with respect to digital inequalities—differential access and knowledge about these media, often along income, educational, ethnic/racial, and national lines. Power also comes into play in digital equalities, as it does in other parts of society because the most powerful are the ones who develop and define computer literacy and expertise—sometimes excluding those from less powerful groups. Two theories are proposed to help us understand and reduce these inequalities: diffusion of innovation and four levels of technocapital.

Communicating ethically using interactive media is especially important in presentation of identity online, in respecting others' privacy, in posting messages, and in building online relationships. Suggestions for communicating effectively using new interactive include following appropriate etiquette in using email, Twitter, mobile phones, and using social media effectively when job hunting.

Key Terms

interactive media
digital
social media
Social Networking Sites
   (SNSs)
Massively Multiplayer Online
   Games (MMOGs)
synchronous
asynchronous

media richness theory
social presence
social presence theory
collapsing contexts
spreadability
lurkers
spam
phishing
cyberbullying

pseudoanonymity
avatars
catfishing
cloud storage
digital divide
cultural capital
technocapital
multimodality

Apply What you Know

1. Don't use any interactive media for twenty-four hours and then answer the following questions. To what extent did you miss these forms of communication? What did you miss most and least? What might you conclude about the role interactive media play in *your* everyday life and relationships? How do you view those who have limited access to new communication technologies?

2. Select any personal Web page from the Internet and describe the identity you think the person is trying to project. Describe the elements that contribute to this identity. What kind of information is presented? What information is missing?

Glossary

asynchronous communication in which messages are sent and received at different times

avatars digital alter-egos or versions of oneself, used in MMOGs

catfishing creating an intentionally deceptive social media profile

cloud storage storage of data online on multiple servers, accessible from multiple locations

collapsing contexts in social media, not knowing exactly who is reading one's posts

cultural capital cultural knowledge and cultural competencies that people need to function effectively in society

cyberbullying the deliberate and repeated misuse of communication technology by an individual or group to threaten or harm others

digital information that is transmitted in a numerical format based on only two values (0 and 1)

digital divide inequity of access between the technology "haves" and "have nots"

interactive media a collection of mediated communication technologies that are digital and converging and tend to be mobile

lurkers people who read, observe, but do not actively participate in online communities/sites

Massively Multiplayer Online Games (MMOGs) text-based "virtual reality" games in which participants interact with enrichments, objects, and other participants

media richness theory theory that describes the potential information-carrying capacity of a communication medium

multimodality the range or breadth of Internet activities

phishing the practice of trying fraudulently to get consumer banking and credit card information

pseudoanonymity projecting a false identity

social media group of Internet-based applications that allow the creation and exchange of user-generated content

Social Networking Sites (SNSs) Web-based service where people construct their profiles, identify others with whom they share a connection, and interact with others within the system

social presence degree of psychological closeness or immediacy engendered by various media

social presence theory suggests that face-to-face communication is generally high in this kind of social presence, and that media vary in the amount of social presence they convey

spam unwanted commercial messages and advertisements sent through email

spreadability the ease with which content can be spread on social media

synchronous communication in which messages are sent and received at the same time

technocapital access to technological skills and resources

References

Alzouma, G. (2012). Far away from home … with a mobile phone! Reconnecting and regenerating the extended family in Africa. In P. H. Cheong, J. N. Martin, & L. P. Macfadyen (Eds.), *New media and intercultural communication: Identity, communication and politics* (pp. 193–208). New York: Peter Lang.

Anderson, A. (2014a). The "Nasty Effect": Online incivility and risk perceptions of emerging technologies. *Journal of Computer- Mediated Communication, 19,* 373–387.

Anderson, A. (2014b, January 21). Global digital statistics 2014—the numbers are up. *gettingsmart.com*. Retrieved May 19 2014, from: http://gettingsmart. com/2014/01/global-digital-statistics-2014-numbers/.

Anderson, J., & Rainie, L. (2014, March 11). Digital life in 2012. *Pew Internet & American Life Project*. Retrieved May 16, 2014, from: http://pewinternet.org/ Reports/2011/Disability.aspx.

Ante, S. E., & Weber, L. (2013, October 22). Memo to workers: The boss is watching. *online.wsj.com*. Retrieved May 25, 2014, from: http://online.wsj .com/news/articles/SB100014240527023036724045791514404889119138.

Baker, L. R., & Oswald, D. L. (2010). Shyness and online social networking services. *Journal of Social and Personal Relationships, 27,* 873–889.

Bennhold, K. (2011, June 23). Generation FB. *The New York Times*. Retrieved July 21, 2011, from: http:// www.nytimes.com/2011/06/24/opinion/ global/24iht-June24-ihtmag-bennhold-22.html?_ r=1&scp=11&sq=youth%20social%20media&st=cse.

Boase, J. (2013). Implications of software-based mobile media for social research. *Mobile Media & Communication, 1*(1), 57–62.

Bosker, B. (2014, February 4). The oversharers are over sharing: 10 years on, the Facebook generation is covering up. Huffingtonpost.com. Retrieved May 18, 2014, from: http://www.huffingtonpost.com/bianca-bosker/facebook-10-anniversary_b_4718871.html.

Bourdieu, P. (1986). The forms of capital. In J. G. Richardson (Eds.), *Handbook of theory and research for the sociology of education* (pp. 241–258). Westport, CT: Greenwood.

Boyd, D. (2014). *It's complicated: The social lives of networked teens.* New Haven: Yale University Press.

Boyle, C. (2012, February 23). Trial for Rutgers student accused of cyber-bullying his gay roommate begins Friday. Retrieved May 18, 2014, from: http://www.nydailynews. com/news/rutgers-university-student-accused-cyber-bullying-gay-roommate-committed-suicide-begins-friday-imn-new-jersey-article-1.1027771.

Brandtzæg, P. B. (2012). Social Networking Sites: Their users and social implications—a longitudinal study. *Journal of Computer-Mediated Communication, 17,* 467–488.

Brock, A. (2012). From the Blackhand side: Twitter as a cultural conversation. *Journal of Broadcasting & Electronic Media, 56*(4), 529–549.

Bryson, D. (2013, July 23). What is web civility. *enduranceinternational.com*. Retrieved May 27, 2014, from: http://enduranceinternational.com/our-mission/ web-civility/what-is-web-civility.

Bruns, A., & Stieglitz, S. (2013). Quantitative approaches to comparing communication patterns on Twitter. *Journal of Technology in Human Services, 30*(3–4), 160–185.

Brustein, J. (2013, August 27). Your boss won't stop spying on you (Because it works). *businessweek.com*. Retrieved May 25, 2014, from: http://www.business-week.com/articles/2013-08-27/your-boss-wont-stop-spying-on-you-because-it-works.

Byrne, S., Katz, S. J., Linz, D., & Mcilrath, M., (2014). Peers, predators, and porn: Predicting parental underestimation of children's risky online experiences. *Journal of Computer-Mediated Communication, 19,* 215–231.

Calderon, A. (2013, May 28). 16 reasons you should never add your boss on Facebook. buzzfeed.com. Retrieved May 27, 2014, from: http://www.buzzfeed.com/ ariellecalderon/16-reasons-you-should-never-add-your-boss-on-facebook.

Carr, N. (2008, July/August). Is Google making us stupid? What the Internet is doing to our brains. *The Atlantic, 302*(1), 56–63.

Cheong, P., & Poon, J. (2009). Weaving webs of faith: Examining Internet use and religious communication among Chinese Protestant transmigrants. *Journal of International and Intercultural Communication, 2*(3), 189–207.

Cheong, P. H. (2008). The young and techless? Investigating internet use and problem-solving behaviors of young adults in Singapore. *New Media & Society, 10*(5), 771–791.

Cheong, P. H. (2010). Faith Tweets: Ambient religious communication and microblogging rituals. *M/C Journal: A Journal of Media and Culture*. http://journal. media-culture.org.au/index.php/mcjournal/article/ viewArticle/223.

Cheong, P. H., & Gray, K. (2011). Mediated intercultural dialectics: Identity perceptions and performances in Virtual Worlds. *Journal of International and Intercultural Communication, 4*(4), 265–271.

Cheong, P. H., Halavais, A., & Kwon, K. (2008). The chronicles of me: Understanding blogging as a religious practice. *Journal of Media and Religion, 7,* 107–131.

Chuma, W. (2014). The social meanings of mobile phones among South Africa's 'digital natives': A case study. *Media, Culture & Society, 36*(3), 398–408.

Coyne, S. M., Stockdale, L., Busby, D., Iverson, B., & Grant, D.M. (2011). "I luv u :)!": A descriptive study of the media use of individuals in romantic relationships. *Family Relations, 60,* 150–162.

Daft, R. L., & Lengel, R. H. (1984). Information richness: A new approach to managerial behavior and organization design. *Research in Organizational Behavior, 6*, 191–233.

Daft, R. L., & Lengel, R. H. (1986). A proposed integration among organizational information requirements, media richness, and structural design. *Management Science, 32*(5), 544–571.

Dainton, M. (2013). Relationship maintenance on Facebook: Development of a measure, relationship to general maintenance, and relationship satisfaction. *College Student Journal, 47*(1), 113–121.

D'Costa, K. (2014, April 25). Catfishing: The truth about deception online. *ScientificAmerica.com*. Retrieved June 27, 2014, from: http://blogs.scientificamerican.com/anthropology-in-practice/2014/04/25/catfishing-the-truth-about-deception.

Demographics of Internet users. (2014, January). *Pew Internet & American Life Project*. Retrieved June 26, 2014, from: http://www.pewinternet.org/data-trend/internet-use/latest-stats/.

Don't text on the toilet and get rid of that comedy ringtone. (2014, March 4). Reuters, Dailymail.co.uk. Retrieved May 25, 2014, from: http://www.dailymail.co.uk/sciencetech/article-2572841/Dont-text-toilet-rid-comedy-ringtone-The-ultimate-mobile-phone-etiquette-guide-revealed.html.

Duggan, M., & Smith, A. (2013, December 30). Social media update 2013. *Pew Internet & American Life Project*. Retrieved February 23, 2014, from: http://www.pewinternet.org/2013/12/30/social-media-update-2013/.

Duran, R. L., Kelly, L., & Rotaru, T. (2011). Mobile phones in romantic relationships and the dialectic of autonomy versus connection, *Communication Quarterly, 59*(1), 19–36.

Elphinston, R. A., & Noller, P. (2011). Time to face it! Facebook intrusion and the implications for romantic jealousy and relationship satisfaction. *Cyberpsychology Behavior, and Social Networking, 14*(11), 631–635.

Ferman, R. (2014, April 1). Cyber-bullying: Taking on the tormentors. *huffingtonpost.com*. Retrieved May 18, 2014, from: http://www.huffingtonpost.com/risa-ferman/cyberbullying-taking-on-t_b_5064537.html.

Flacy, M. (2014, January 16). Woman loses $300,000 in Christian Mingle online dating scam. digitaltrends.com. Retrieved May 27, 2014, from: http://www.digitaltrends.com/social-media/woman-loses-300000-christian-mingle-online-dating-scam/#!Q9KZ3.

Florini, S. (2014). Tweets, Tweeps, and signifyin': Communication and cultural performance on "Black Twitter." *Television & New Media, 15*(3), 223–237.

Fox, S. (2011, January 21). Americans with disabilities and their technology use. *Pew Internet & American Life Project*. Retrieved August 29, 2014, from http://pewinternet.org/Reports/2011/Disability.aspx

Fox, S., & Rainie, L. (2014, February 27). The Web at 25 in the U.S. *Pew Internet & American Life Project*.

Retrieved May 19, 2014, from: http://www.pewinternet.org/2014/02/27/the-web-at-25-in-the-u-s/.

Friedman, M. (2011, March 28). How do I love thee? Let me tweet the ways. *Time, 177*(12), 62–65.

Galarneau, L. (2014, January 16). The top 10 gaming trends. bigfishgames.com. Retrieved August 29, 2014, from http://www.bigfishgames.com/blog/2014-global-gaming-stats-whos-playing-what-and-why/

Gershon, I. (2010). Breaking up is hard to to: Media switching and media ideologies. *Journal of Linguistic Anthropology, 20*(2), 389–405.

Global Digital Statistics (2014). Retrieved August 29, 2014, from http://www.slideshare.net/ntdlife/2014-global-digital-overview

Greenwood, D. N. (2013). *Fame, Facebook, and Twitter: How attitudes about fame predict frequency and nature of social media use* (4), 222–236.

Hall, J. A., Park, N., Song, H., & Cody, M. J. (2010). Strategic misrepresentation in online dating: The effects of gender, self-monitoring, and personality traits. *Journal of Social and Personal Relationships, 27*, 117–135.

Hargittai, W., & Hinnant, A. (2008). Digital inequality: Differences in young adults' use of the Internet. *Communication Research, 35*(5), 602–621.

Heino, R. D., Ellison, N. B., & Gibbs, J. L. (2010). Relationshopping: Investigating the market metaphor in online dating. *Journal of Social and Personal Relationships, 27*, 427–447.

Hogan, B. (2012). Pseudonyms and the rise of the real-name Web. In J. Hartley, J. Burgess, & A. Bruns (Eds.), A companion to new media dynamics (pp. 290–308). Chichester, UK: Blackwell Publishing Ltd.

Humphreys, S., & Vered, K. O. (2014). Reflecting on gender and digital networked media. *Television & New Media, 15*(1), 3–13.

Jung, J-Y. (2008). Internet connectedness and its social origins: An ecological approach to postaccess digital divides. *Communication Studies, 59*(4), 322–339.

Kaplan, A. M., & Haenlein, M. (2010). Users of the world, unite! The challenges and opportunities of social media. *Business Horizons, 53*, 59–68.

Kleinman, A. (2014, March 18). There's a new scam to steal your Gmail info, and it's hard to catch. *huffingtonpost.com*. Retrieved May 18, 2014, from: http://www.huffingtonpost.com/2014/03/18/gmail-scam-phishing_n_4986510.html.

Klosowski, T. (2012, Aug. 23) The most annoying things you do with your phone that you should quit (or at least be aware of). *lifehacker. com*. Retrieved November 16, 2014, from: http://lifehacker.com/5937223/the-most-annoying-things-your-do-with-your-phone-that-you-should-quit-or-at-least-be-aware-of

Kross, E., Verduyn, P., Demiralp, E., Park, J., Lee, D. S., et al. (2013). Facebook use predicts declines in subjective well-being in young adults. PLoS ONE 8(8). Retrieved June 28, 2014, from: http://www.plosone.org/article/info%3Adoi%2F10.1371%2Fjournal.pone.0069841.

Larson, S. (2014, February 5). How to remove yourself from the Internet. Readwrite.com. Retrieved June 27, 2014, from: http://readwrite.com/2014/02/05/how-to-remove-yourself-from-the-internet#awesm=~oIv4TuHdblrTeh.

Lenhart, A., & Duggan, M. (2014, February 11). Couples, the Internet and Social Media. *Pew Internet & American Life Project*. Retrieved May 19, 2014, from: http://pewinternet.org/Reports/2014/ Couples-and-the-internet.aspx

Levin, A. L. (2013, October 27). *abcnews.com*. Why Facebook shouldn't show your teens pictures to the world. Retrieved May 28, 2014, from: http://abcnews.go.com/m/story?id=20668712&ref=http%3A%2F%2Fnews.google.com%2F.

Madianou, M., & Miller, D. (2013). Polymedia: Towards a new theory of digital media in interpersonal communication. *International Journal of Cultural Studies, 16*(2), 169–187.

Manjoo, F. (2010, August 10). How Black people use Twitter. *Slate.com*. Retrieved April 20, 2014, from: http://www.slate.com/articles/technology/technology/2010/08/how_black_people_use_ twitter.html.

Marder, J. (2012, April 25). Why the engineering, computer science gender gap persists. *scientificamerican.com*. Retrieved May 19, 2014, from: http://www.scientificamerican.com/article/why-the- engineering-and-science-gender-gap/.

McKenna, K. Y. A., Green, A. S., & Gleason, M. E. J. (2002). Relationship formation on the Internet: What's the big attraction? *Journal of Social Issues, 58*, 9–31.

Merryfield, M. (2003). Like a veil: Cross-cultural experiential learning online. *Contemporary Issues in Technology and Teacher Education, 3*(2), 146–171.

Mihailidis, P. (2014). A tethered generation: Exploring the role of mobile phones in the daily life of young people. *Mobile Media & Communication, 2*(1), 58–72.

Mobile Technology Fact Sheet. (2014) *Pew Internet & American Life Project*. Retrieved May 20, 2014, from http://www.pewinternet.org/fact-sheets/mobile-technology-fact-sheet/.

Nosko, A., Wood, E., & Molema, S. (2010). All about me: Disclosure in online social networking profiles: The case of Facebook. *Computers in Human Behavior, 26*, 406–418.

Osborne, M., & Dredze, M. (2014, July). Facebook, Twitter and Google Plus for breaking news: Is there a winner? Paper presented at the International AAAI (Advancement of Artificial Intelligence) Conference on Weblogs and Social Media, Ann Arbor, Michigan.

Patchin, J. W. (2014, April 9). Summary of our research (2004–2014). Retrieved May 18, 2014, from http://cyberbullying.us/summary-of-our-research/.

Payne, E., & Smith, M. (2013). LGBTQ kids, school safety and missing the big picture: How the dominant bullying discourse prevents school professionals from thinking about systemic marginalization or … why we need to rethink LGBTQ bullying. *QED: A Journal in GLBTQ Worldmaking, Inaugural issue*, 1–36.

Pegoraro, A. (2014). Twitter as disruptive innovation in sport communication. *Communication & Sport, 2*(2), 132–137.

Pettigrew, J. (2010). Text messaging and connectedness within close interpersonal relationships. *Marriage & Family Review, 45*, 697–716,

Ramirez, A., & Zhang, S. (2007). When online meets offline: The effect of modality switching on relational communication. *Communication Monographs, 74*(3), 287–310.

Rettie, R. (2009). Mobile phone communication: Extending Goffman to mediated interaction. *Sociology, 43*(3), 421–438.

Roberto, A. J., & Eden, J. (2010). Cyberbullying: Aggressive communication in the digital age. In T.A. Avtgis & A. S. Rancer (Eds.), *Arguments, aggression, and conflict: New directions in theory and research* (pp. 198–216). New York: Routledge.

Rogers, E. M. (2003). *Diffusion of innovations* (5th ed.). New York: The Free Press.

Routledge, H., & de Freitas, S. (2013). Designing leadership and soft skills in educational games: The e-leadership and soft skills education games design model (ELESS). *The British Journal of Educational Technology, 44*(6), 951–968.

Selwyn, N. (2007). Guy-tech? An exploration of undergraduate students' gendered perceptions of information and communication technologies, *Sex Roles, 56*, 525–536.

Sheer, V. (2011). Teenagers' use of MSN features, discussion topic and online friendship development: The impact of media richness and communication control. *Communication Quarterly, 59*(1), 82–103.

Short, J., Williams, E. & Christie, B. (1976). *The social psychology of telecommunications*. New York: Wiley.

Shpigelman, C-N., & Gill, C. J. (2014). Facebook use by persons with disabilities. *Journal of Computer-Mediated Communication, 19*, 610–624.

Smith, A. (2014a, January 6). African Americans and technology use. *Pew Internet & American Life Project*. Retrieved May 19, 2014, from: http://pewinternet.org/Reports/2014/African-American-Tech-Use.aspx.

Smith, A. (2014b, February 3). 6 new facts about Facebook. Pew Internet & American Life Profject. Retrieved August 29, 2014, from http://www.pewresearch.org/fact-tank/2014/02/03/6-new-facts-about-facebook/.

Smith, A. (2014c, April 3). Older adults and technology use. *Pew Internet & American Life Project*. Retrieved May 16, 2014, from: http://www.pewinternet.org/2014/04/03/older-adults-and-technology-use/.

Taddicken, M. (2014). The "privacy paradox" in the Social Web: The impact of privacy concerns, individual characteristics, and the perceived social relevance on different forms of self-disclosure. *Journal of Computer-Mediated Communication, 19*, 248–273.

Tazghini, S., & Siedlecki, K. L. (2012). A mixed method approach to examining Facebook use and its relationship to self-esteem. *Computers in Human Behavior, 29,* 827–832.

13 best dating apps (2012, December 27). the dailybeast.com. Retrieved May 27, 2014, from: http://www.thedailybeast.com/articles/2012/12/27/13-best-dating-apps-ok-cupid-to-grindr- to-sonar.html.

Thompson, L., & Ku, H-Y. (2005). Chinese graduate students' experiences and attitudes toward online learning. *Educational Media International, 42*(1), 33–47.

Tong, S. T., Van Der Heide, B., Langwell, L., & Walther, J. B. (2008). Too much of a good thing? The relationship between number of friends and interpersonal impressions on Facebook. *Journal of Computer-Mediated Communication, 13,* 531–549.

Tufekci, Z., & Wilson, C. (2012). Social media and the decision to participate in political protest: Observations from Tahrir Square. *Journal of Communication, 62*(2), 363–379.

Turkle, S. (2011). *Alone together: Why we expect more from technology and less from each other.* New York: Basic Books.

Turkle, S. (2012, February). TED talk: Connected, but alone? Retrieved May 25, 2014, from: http://www.ted.com/talks/sherry_turkle_alone_together#t-755215.

van Dijk, J. (2004). Divides in succession: Possession, skills, and use of new media for societal participation. In E. P. Bucy & J. E. Newhagen (Eds.), *Media access: Social and psychological dimensions of new technology use* (pp. 233–254). Mahwah, NJ: Erlbaum.

van Dijck, J. (2013). *The culture of connectivity: A critical history of social media.* New York: Oxford University Press.

Walther, J. B., & Parks, M. R. (2002). Cues filtered out, cues filtered in: Computer-mediated communication and relationships. In M. L. Knapp & J. A. Daly (Eds.), *Handbook of interpersonal communication* (pp. 529–563). Thousand Oaks, CA: Sage.

Watters, A. (2012, April 9). The failure of One Laptop Per Child. Retrieved May 21, 2014, from: http://www.hackeducation.com/ 2012/04/09/the-failure-of-olpc/.

Wei, L. (2012). Number matters: The multimodality of Internet use as an indicator of the digital inequalities. *Journal of Computer-Mediated Communication. 17,* 303–318.

Wei, R. (2013). Mobile media: Coming of age with a big splash. *Mobile Media & Communication, 1*(1), 50–56.

Whitty, M. T. (2007). Revealing the "real" me, searching for the "actual" you: Presentations of self on an Internet dating site. *Computers in Human Behavior, 24,* 1707–1723.

Wiley, A. (2013, November 21). DTE employee fired for posting expletives on her Facebook page. *Fox2 News.* Retrieved May 21, 2014, from: http://www.myfoxdetroit.com/story/24038309/ dte-employee-fired-after-explitive-filled-post-on-facebook#ixzz32SrDYXeM.

Williams, D., Martins, N., Consalvo, M., & Ivory, J. (2009). The virtual census: representations of gender, race, and age in video games. *New Media & Society, 11*(5), 815–834.

Winter, K. (2014, April 16). Daaaaaad! You're soooo embarrassing! MailOnline. Retrieved May 21, 2014, from: http://www.dailymail.co.uk/femail/article-2605290/Daaaaaaad-Youre-sooooo-embarrassing-Almost-children-humiliated-parents-social-media.html#ixzz32OKqzly5.

Wood, A. F., & Smith, M. J. (2005). *Online communication: Linking technology, identity and culture* (2nd ed.). Mahwah, NJ: Erlbaum.

Yammering away at the office: Special report: Social networking. (2010, January 30). *The Economist, 394*(8667), 14.

Yee, N. (2014). *The Proteus Paradox: How online games and virtual worlds change us—and how they don't.* New Haven: Yale University Press.

Zywica, J., & Danowski, J. (2008). The faces of Facebookers: Investigating social enhancement and social compensation hypotheses: Predicting Facebook and offline popularity from sociability and self-esteem, and mapping the meaning of popularity with semantic networks. *Journal of Computer-Mediated Communication, 14,* 1–34.

Zickuhr, K. (2014, September 25). Who's not online and why. *Pew Internet & American Life Project.* Retrieved May 19, 2014, from: http://pewinternet.org/Reports/2013/Non-internet- users.aspx.

Credits

Photo Credits

Credits are listed in order of appearance.

Photo 1: Eric Audras/ONOKY - Photononstop/Alamy

Photo 2: First Class Photos PTY LTD/Shutterstock

Photo 3: Alamy

Photo 4: David L. Moore/Lifestyle/Alamy

Photo 5: King, Jerry /CartoonStock

Photo 6: Andresr/Shutterstock

Photo 7: Andresr/Shutterstock

Photo 8: Realimage/Alamy

Photo 9: Chris Howes/Wild Places Photography/Alamy

Photo 10: Jochen Tack/Zuma Press

Photo 11: VAN CAKENBERGHE TO/SIPA/Newscom

Photo 12: BE&W agencja fotograficzna Sp. z o.o/Alamy

Text and Art Credits

Digital Life in 2025, Pew Report

van Dick, J. (2004). Divides in succession: Possession, skills, and use of new media for societal participation. In E. P. Bucy & J. E. Newhagen (Eds.), Media access: Social and psychological dimensions of new technology use (pp. 233-254). Mahwah, NJ: Erlbaum.

Paul Mihailidis (2014). Exploring Mobile Information Habits of University Students Around the World.

Andreas M. Kaplan, Michael Haenlein. (2010) Users of the world, unite! The challenges and opportunities of Social Media. Kelley School of Business, Indiana University.

Walther, J. B. & Parks, M. R. (2002). Cues filtered out, cues filtered in: Computer-mediated communication and relationships. In M. L. Knapp & J. A. Daly(Eds.), Handbook of interpersonal communication (pp. 529–563). Thousand Oaks, CA: Sage.

TBL 01,, Republished with permission of Elsevier Science and Technology Journals, from Users of the world, unite! The challenges and opportunities of Social Media, Andreas M. Kaplan Michael Haenlein., (C)2009; permission conveyed through Copyright Clearance Center, Inc.

Turkle, S. (2011). Alone together: Why we ex-pect more from technology and less from each other. New York: Basic Books. Turkle, S. (2012, February). TED talk: Connected, but alone? Retrieved May 25, 2014, rom, http://www.ted.com/talks/sherry_turkle_alone_together#t-755215

Turkle, S. (2011). Alone together: Why we expect more from technology and less from each other. New York: Basic Books.

Bianca Bosker. The Oversharers Are Over Sharing: 10 Years On, The Facebook Generation Is Covering Up. The Huffington Post.

Roberto, A. J., & Eden, J. (2010). Cyberpullying: Aggressive communication in the digital age. In T. A. Avtgis & A. S. Rancer (Eds.), Arguments, aggressions, and conflict: New directions in theory and research(pp. 198-216). New York: Routledge.

Hogan, B. (2012). Pseudonyms and the rise of the real-name Web. In J. Hartley, J. Burgess, & A. Bruns (Eds.), A companion to new media dynamics (pp. 290–308). Chichester, UK: Blackwell Publishing Ltd.

Turkle, S. (2011). Alone together: Why we expect more from technology and less from each other. New York: Basic Books.

Bennhold, K. (2011, June 23). Generation FB. The New York Times. Retrieved July 21, 2011, from http://www.nytimes.com/2011/06/24/opinion/global/24iht-june24-ihtmag-bennhoold-22.html?_r=1&scp=11&sq=youth%20social%20media&st=cse

Jacqueline

Heino, R. D., Ellison, N. B., & Gibbs, J. L. (2010). Relationshopping: Investigating the market metaphor in online dating. Journal od Social and Personal Relationships, 27, 427-447.

Cruzita

Mei-Lin

TBL 02, Mobile Technology Fact Sheet. (2014) Pew Internet & American Life Project. Retrieved May 20, 4014, from http://www.pewinternet.org/fact-sheets/mobile-technology-fact-sheet/

Manjoo, F. (2010, August 10). How Black people use Twitter. Slate.com. Retrieved April 20, 2014, from: http://www.slate.com/articles/technology/technology/2010/08/how_black_people_use_twitter.html.

Watters, A. (2012, April 9). The failure of One Laptop Per Child. Retrieved May 21, 2014, from: http://www.hack-education.com/2012/04/09/the-failure-of-olpc/ p. 368, Bryson, D. (2013, July 23). What is web civility. enduranceinternational. com. Retrieved May 27, 2014, from: http://enduranceinternational.com/our-mission/web-civility/what-is-web-civility.

Based on Life Hacker, The Most Annoying Things You Do with Your Phone That You Should Quit (or At Least Be Aware Of), http://lifehacker.com/5937223/the-most-annoying-things-your-do-with-your-phone-that-you-should-quit-or-at-least-be-aware-of; Texas Health Science Technology Education, Mobil Manners, http://www.texashste.com/documents/curriculum/principles/mobil_manners.pdf

http://mashable.com/2013/10/14/twitter-etiquette http://www.smedio.com/7-things-not-to-do-on-twitter/ http://www.dummies.com/how-to/content/wh at-not-to-do-on-twitter.html

dex

4, 47, 55, 75, 86, 209, 236

olutism, 19, 22-23
ent, 92, 101-102, 107-108, 117-118, 164, 209, 218
ulturation, 199-201
uracy, 125, 127, 145-146
on, 4, 21, 53, 79, 104, 124-125, 156, 165, 167,
169, 184, 223, 227
ve listening, 170-171
aptation, 146, 182-183
ptors, 126, 142-143
ice, 162, 202
ection, 75, 125, 133, 140-141, 170, 220
rmation, 165
e, 13-15, 27-29, 31-32, 35-36, 39-40, 46-47, 50,
53-54, 57, 63-64, 66, 70, 72, 74, 78-79, 91,
98, 100, 102, 104, 109, 113, 120, 139, 145,
155, 158-159, 161, 164-166, 169, 171-172,
175, 177-178, 180-181, 186-187, 189, 191,
214-216, 218-219, 223-224, 226, 237-239
e identity, 46, 53-54
enda, 42, 55, 58, 160, 168
gression, 34, 110, 124, 127, 132, 237
gressive, 40, 44, 86, 99, 121, 124-125, 133, 189,
216, 237, 239
en, M., 115
alysis, 17, 38, 41-42, 54-55, 84, 116, 118, 124, 126,
145, 155, 170, 172, 197, 199, 226
of perceptions, 197
onymity, 215-217, 230, 233
pearance, 25, 33-35, 37, 41-42, 45, 57, 64, 84, 86,
107, 112, 117, 122, 126, 134-135, 137-139,
142-143, 146, 163-164, 171, 201, 218, 238
propriateness, 20, 22-23, 127, 135
jentina, 177
jument, 156, 211
juments, 5, 12, 19, 79, 83, 157, 237, 239
stotle, 2
iculation, 128, 144
ifacts, 126, 131, 134-135, 137-138, 142-143
sertive, 99, 116
similation, 194
sumptions, 9, 68, 81, 105, 108, 164, 195, 212
ynchronous communication, 209, 234
ynchronous messages, 209
ack, 50, 110, 114
character, 50
personal, 50, 114
tention, 21, 34, 47, 65-66, 69, 71-72, 76, 81-83, 123,
126-128, 130, 138, 143-144, 152, 155-157,
159, 163-165, 168-169, 171, 178, 192, 213,
217
listening and, 152, 155-157, 159, 163-165,
168-169, 171
selective, 65, 71, 76, 81-83
tention span, 152
titude, 24, 56, 59, 86, 168, 190, 198
cultural, 86, 190, 198
titudes, 14, 18, 34, 49-50, 54, 78, 106-107, 109-110,
120, 122, 135, 141, 143, 155, 167, 169-170,
182, 184, 193, 195, 200, 227, 236, 238
of audience, 167
traction, 63-64, 127-128, 136, 143, 146-147, 237
tractiveness, 34-35, 38, 134, 139, 164, 217
and nonverbal communication, 139
physical, 134, 164, 217
tribution, 69-71, 82-83, 85-86, 106, 135
tribution error, 70, 82-83, 86
tribution theory, 69-70, 82-83, 85
tributional bias, 70, 82-83
idience, 18, 20-21, 99, 106, 155, 167, 194, 205,
207-208, 213-214
analysis of, 155
culture, 194

defined, 20
definition of, 155
diversity of, 194
ethics and, 20
immediate, 167
information about, 155, 214
perceptions, 99
target, 208
Audiences, 131, 194, 206, 211, 213-214, 229
Authentic communication, 23
Authority, 12, 92, 95, 191, 215
Avoidance, 132, 145-147
touch, 132, 145

B

Barriers to listening, 155, 159-160, 168
Behavior, 3-5, 8, 12, 15, 17-21, 23-24, 34-35, 37-38,
48, 51, 54, 66-67, 69-71, 73-74, 77-79,
82-86, 93, 98, 111-112, 117, 119-133,
135-147, 150, 158-159, 163, 165-167, 169,
183, 185-186, 191-192, 196, 207, 215-216,
229, 236-238
Belief, 4, 9-10, 14, 17, 19, 23, 36, 50, 77, 124,
188-190, 198
Beliefs, 4, 8, 14, 17-18, 20, 30, 34, 43, 49-50, 52, 54,
68-69, 71, 76-79, 82, 92, 98, 105, 124, 139,
141, 144, 155, 167, 169, 183, 186, 195, 198,
207
of audience, 167
Berger, C. R., 84
Berko, R., 171
Berry, J. W., 199
Bias, 70-71, 73, 76, 82-85, 106, 146, 190
status quo, 84
Blame, 72, 78, 116, 179, 228
Blogs, 57, 59, 115, 117-118, 137, 139, 155, 206-208,
210-211, 213, 217, 220, 230, 236
body, 35, 38-39, 41, 45, 57-58, 63-64, 73, 82, 85-86,
121, 123-124, 126-127, 132, 134, 136,
139-141, 144-147, 157, 163, 168, 171,
209-210, 220, 224
Body language, 145, 157, 163
Body movement, 144
Body movements, 127
Body type, 134, 220, 224
Bond, Michael, 186
Books, 34, 46, 55-56, 76, 84, 98, 115, 121, 145,
171-172, 201, 206, 212, 228, 238-239
Border dwellers, 174, 181, 183-185, 197-198
Broome, Benjamin, 179
Brown, R., 85
Brownell, J., 170
Burgoon, J. K., 84, 130, 144, 147
Burgoon, Judee, 130
Burrell, Nancy, 99
Business, 16-17, 24-25, 56, 59, 78, 97, 117, 131, 134,
138-139, 142, 145, 162-163, 171, 178, 192,
197, 199-201, 208, 220, 232-233, 236, 239

C

Capitalism, 187
Caplan, S. E., 84
Carbaugh, Donal, 40
Caughlin, John, 111
Cell phones, 22, 111, 216, 220, 231
Changes, 2, 14, 24, 46, 84, 91, 93, 95, 111, 146, 180,
185
Channel, 9-12, 16, 22-23, 46
channel of communication, 9
Channels, 6, 9, 22, 121, 127, 159
Channels of communication, 159
nonverbal, 159
Character, 33, 50, 57, 85
Chomsky, Noam, 94
Chronemics, 129, 135, 142-143
Claim, 2, 42, 99, 104, 124, 131
Claims, 17, 47, 50, 92, 124, 132

Clarity, 126
Cleopatra, 30
Climate, 24, 29
group, 29
organizational, 24
Close relationships, 84, 106, 120, 183
Cognitive complexity, 74, 80-84
Cognitive representation, 66, 82-83
Cohort effect, 79, 82-83, 100, 113-114
Colleagues, 9, 35, 47, 81, 99, 129-130, 162, 164-165,
184, 186, 194, 206, 222
Collectivism, 186-187, 190, 201
Collectivist cultures, 187
Collectivistic orientation, 187, 197-198
commentary, 53, 146
Commitment, 21, 109, 153, 171-172, 187, 198-199
Communicate information, 93, 114, 135
Communication, 1-25, 27-32, 34-40, 42, 44, 46, 48-59,
61, 64, 66-67, 71-76, 78-86, 89-118,
119-147, 149, 151-155, 157-159, 161, 163,
165-172, 173-202, 203-213, 215-222,
224-231, 233-239
and emotion, 86, 129, 145
and feedback, 6, 22
anxiety, 3, 86, 216
assertive, 99, 116
barriers to, 151, 154-155, 159, 168, 170
channel of, 9
channels of, 159
competence, 20, 22-24, 99, 111, 155, 171, 182,
185, 196, 201-202
components of, 1, 6, 10, 90-94, 113, 121-122,
141-142, 180
context, 6-7, 15-16, 19-21, 38, 48-49, 84-85, 92,
96-98, 100, 103, 108, 113, 117, 121,
123-124, 126-127, 135, 141-142, 144,
147, 155, 163, 165, 170, 178, 191-192,
196, 200, 210-211, 215-216, 219, 222,
230-231, 233
defensive, 78, 82-83, 112, 161
defined, 6, 14, 17, 20, 48-49, 53-54, 75, 111, 125,
134, 142, 168-169, 180, 197, 233
definition, 6, 8, 15, 21, 48, 94, 103, 120, 123,
153-155, 171-172, 180, 208
definition of, 6, 94, 103, 123, 154-155, 171-172,
180
definitions of, 4, 139, 182, 201-202
effective, 2-3, 19, 21-22, 49, 53, 91, 111-112, 127,
141-142, 151-155, 157-158, 165, 167,
169-170, 175, 181, 195-197, 209, 222
ethical, 16-22, 27-28, 32, 37, 51-53, 80, 110-113,
119-120, 139-142, 151, 166-167,
169-170, 175, 195, 204-205, 217,
229-230
ethics and, 20, 24-25, 27, 51, 80, 83, 90, 109, 119,
140, 166, 174, 195, 199, 204, 229
explanation of, 83
forms of, 74, 132-133, 208-209, 218, 225, 234-235,
237
formula, 195, 200
foundations of, 85, 115
functions of, 73, 93, 115, 119, 123, 135
good, 2-3, 6, 8-9, 11, 17, 20-23, 35-37, 52, 64, 67,
71, 82-83, 85, 106, 111, 114, 141,
152-154, 159, 161, 165, 175-176, 180,
182, 187-188, 190, 198, 205, 207, 209,
212-213, 216, 229, 231, 233, 238
human, 1-25, 27, 55, 61, 66, 73, 85-86, 89, 92,
105-106, 108, 111, 115-116, 118, 119,
128, 130, 144-147, 149, 153, 170-171,
173, 188, 195, 197-198, 203, 212, 235,
237-238
hurtful, 159
impersonal, 131, 133, 136, 144, 210
in families, 73
in society, 1, 6, 20-21, 24, 27, 30-32, 34-35, 40, 53,
61, 64, 75, 79-80, 89, 105, 117, 119, 128,

241

137, 149, 152-153, 155, 163, 173,
193-194, 197, 203, 225, 234
  influence of context, 155
  influence of culture, 196
  influence of individual and societal forces, 6
  intentional, 25, 113, 123, 126
  interaction and, 12, 129, 196
  intercultural, 24, 28, 40, 53-56, 58, 74, 84, 86,
116-118, 145, 170-171, 174-182,
184-187, 190-193, 195-202, 235
  interpersonal, 24, 57, 66-67, 74, 84-86, 93, 127,
129, 136, 143-145, 151, 155, 170, 205,
207, 227, 233, 237-239
  language and, 44, 95, 104-105, 109, 115-116, 161,
182-183
  leadership and, 237
  linear model of, 11
  listening and, 149, 151-155, 157-159, 161, 163,
165-172
  mass, 25, 180, 205, 207-208, 233
  mediated, 97, 99, 115-116, 145, 166-167, 175,
204-205, 208-209, 217-219, 230-231,
233-235, 237-239
  message creation, 6, 22
  models of, 66, 83-84
  multichanneled, 121
  nonverbal, 6-8, 12-13, 15, 23-24, 85-86, 91, 103,
119-147, 152-153, 155, 157, 159,
169-170, 175, 185-186, 209-210, 218
  on Internet, 219
  people with disabilities, 226
  perception and, 64, 71-72, 79, 81, 86
  persuasive, 10, 75, 84, 127, 136, 157, 169
  physical surroundings of a, 8, 23
  power of, 59, 105, 109, 112-113, 170
  principles of, 17, 24
  public, 2-3, 5, 9, 14-15, 18, 37-38, 46, 50-51, 54,
56, 59, 67, 72, 75, 93, 102, 122, 131-132,
135, 138, 142, 144, 146-147, 167, 188,
199, 207, 211, 222, 228, 231
  public communication, 15
  repertoire of, 22, 145
  self-concept and, 210
  small group, 2, 74, 114
  supportive, 10, 98-99, 106, 157-158, 169-171
  transaction, 11
  types of, 7-8, 14, 21, 23, 34, 46, 52, 66, 71, 73-74,
78, 84, 94, 105, 110, 120, 126-128, 133,
141-142, 154, 167, 178, 181, 185, 209,
213, 215, 217
  unintentional, 113
  verbal, 3, 6-7, 15, 23-24, 36, 89-118, 120-122,
124-126, 128, 132-133, 135, 141-145,
152, 155, 170, 186, 206
Communication context, 211
Communication effectiveness, 52
Communication ethics, 1, 16-17, 19-20, 22-24
  absolutism versus relativism, 19, 22
  developing, 22
  in practice, 20
Communication principles, 14, 20
Communication process, 6, 10-11, 15, 23, 28, 32, 74,
93-94, 151, 153-154
  context in, 15
  elements of, 10
  listening and, 151, 153-154
  message and, 6, 23
  messages in, 6, 15
communication skills, 2-3, 5, 20, 22-23, 90-91, 100,
112-113, 119-120, 141, 152-153, 159, 165,
167, 169, 174, 179, 195, 204, 230
Communication studies, 29, 38, 180, 236
communicator, 1-2, 13, 17, 19-20, 22-23, 65, 91, 121,
125, 135, 171, 175, 195-197, 230
  competent, 1, 20, 22
  elements of, 91
  ethical, 17, 19-20, 22, 175, 195, 230
Communities, 8, 17, 30, 34-35, 39, 49-50, 105, 109,
138, 165-166, 176, 183, 187, 208, 211,
213-214, 216, 219, 224, 234
Comparisons, 27, 31, 34, 36-37, 54, 212
Competence, 20, 22-24, 99, 111, 155, 171, 182, 185,
196, 201-202
Complementarity, 136-137, 146-147
Complementing, 135
Compliance, 85, 96
Compliments, 162
Components of communication, 1, 6, 121-122
  context, 6, 121

  environment, 122
  feedback, 6
  message, 6, 121
comprehensive listening, 152
Compromise, 50
Computer-mediated communication, 97, 99, 115-116,
230, 235, 237-239
  self-disclosure and, 99
Computers, 111, 187, 208, 225-228, 237-238
Confidentiality, 18, 166, 221
Confirming communication, 90, 109, 111, 113-114
Confirming messages, 111
Conflict, 3, 5, 24, 49, 86, 96, 99, 112, 115, 117, 129,
154, 179, 187, 189, 191, 196-197, 199, 210,
237, 239
  and culture, 96, 197, 199
  and power, 179
  content, 239
  conversation in, 115, 191
  culture and, 86, 117
  defined, 49, 197
  ethics and, 24, 199
  gender and, 117
  group, 187, 197
  interpersonal conflict, 24
  issues of, 179
  management of, 115
  online, 5, 189, 196, 210, 237, 239
  principles of, 24
  process of, 49, 154
  relationship, 3, 5, 24, 86, 96, 187, 189, 210, 237
  types of, 154
Confucianism, 190
Connotation, 113
Connotative meaning, 8, 95, 108, 113-114
Connotative meanings, 95, 114
Consciousness raising, 30
Constraints, 13, 24
Construct, 40, 49, 74, 84, 208, 215, 217, 234
Constructive marginal people, 185, 197-198
Constructs, 38, 40, 74, 82-83, 101
Content meaning, 8, 22-23
Context, 6-7, 15-16, 19-21, 38, 43, 48-49, 84-85, 92,
96-98, 100, 103, 108, 113, 117, 121,
123-124, 126-127, 135, 141-142, 144, 147,
155-156, 163, 165, 170, 178, 191-192, 196,
200, 210-211, 214-216, 219, 222, 230-231,
233
  characteristics of, 100, 191, 230
  culture and, 6, 117
  nonverbal cues and, 124
  of communication, 6, 15, 38, 49, 84, 98, 117, 121,
124, 142, 144, 147, 163, 170, 210-211,
216, 230
  of messages, 7, 19, 121, 141, 215, 230
  pragmatic, 97
  words and, 7, 92, 98
Contextual rules, 95, 97, 114
Contradicting, 135, 141-143
Contrast, 34, 38, 41, 46, 50-51, 95, 101, 104, 108,
126, 132, 142, 165, 185, 187-190, 194, 208,
214, 223, 233
Control, 14, 42, 80, 93, 115, 122, 126, 131-133,
135-136, 141-144, 156, 188, 192, 195, 207,
210, 212-214, 221-222, 226-227, 230, 237
Conversation, 8-12, 15, 63, 67-68, 75-76, 97, 99, 110,
113, 115-117, 126, 129-130, 135-136,
139-140, 144, 154, 160-162, 165, 177, 191,
195, 209, 211-212, 216, 218, 224, 235
  culture and, 117, 195
  in conflict, 117
  overlaps in, 97
  turn-taking in, 116
Conversational rules, 95, 97, 114, 159
Conversational turns, 136
Cooperation, 164
Co-rumination, 3
Credibility, 157
Critical listening, 156-158, 169
Critical thinking, 3-4, 17, 22, 24, 154, 156, 167
critical thinking skills, 3-4, 17, 154, 156
Criticism, 38, 76, 96, 159, 161, 184, 190
  listening to, 159, 161
Cross-cultural marriage, 202
Cruise, Tom, 127
Cues, 18, 85, 99, 120-121, 124, 129, 136, 138, 140,
143-145, 155, 163-164, 175, 181, 198,
209-210, 215, 218, 238-239
  speaker, 18, 99, 129, 163-164

  turn-taking, 144
Cultural adaptation, 183
Cultural context, 48, 92, 96-98
Cultural diversity, 177, 193
Cultural values, 174-175, 181-182, 186, 193, 197-198,
227
Culture, 6, 10, 13-16, 22-23, 30, 37-38, 43-47, 50,
54-57, 59, 62-63, 75-77, 79-80, 82, 84-86,
92, 96, 98, 101, 103-104, 116-117, 121,
124-125, 127, 129, 131, 133-134, 139,
142-143, 146, 164, 175, 179-183, 185-202,
206, 212, 226, 235, 238
  and friendship, 200
  and nonverbal communication, 121, 139, 186
  characteristics of, 185, 190-191, 212
  collectivist, 187
  competence and, 185
  conflict and, 129
  conversation and, 75-76
  defined, 6, 14, 47, 54, 75, 125, 134, 142, 180, 197
  dimensions of, 190, 199, 238
  ethnocentric, 77, 197
  feedback and, 55
  feminine, 44
  gender and, 85, 117, 146, 164
  gestures and, 121, 124, 127
  groups and, 180
  language and, 44, 104, 116, 182-183
  listening, 98, 124, 164
  listening and, 164
  masculine, 44, 194
  nonverbal, 6, 13, 15, 23, 47, 85-86, 103, 121,
124-125, 127, 129, 131, 133-134, 139,
142-143, 146, 175, 185-186
  nonverbal behavior and, 121, 125, 139
  organizational, 56, 85, 116
  perception and, 62-63, 79, 86
  physical appearance and, 84
  relationships and, 22, 212
  sensitivity to, 55
  time and, 14, 116, 129, 142
  touch and, 85, 133, 143
  words and, 10, 92, 98, 129
Culture shock, 181-183, 194, 197-199, 202
Cyberbullying, 110-111, 118, 216-217, 229, 233-237

D
Data, 32, 64-65, 82, 85-86, 106, 185, 200, 216, 220,
234, 236
  audience, 106
Dating, 76, 185, 199, 219-220, 236, 238-239
Deafness, 161, 170-172
Deceiving, 16, 140
Deception, 18-19, 24, 81, 140-141, 216-220, 230, 236
  effects of, 18, 236
  in relationships, 24
  reasons for, 216
Decision-making, 14
Decoding, 6, 22-23, 85, 121, 124, 144-147, 153
  nonverbal communication and, 145
Definition, 6, 8, 15, 21, 47-48, 94, 103, 120, 123,
153-155, 171-172, 180, 208
Definitions, 4, 6-7, 17, 139, 153, 182, 201-202
  of communication, 6, 17
  research, 153, 201
Delivery, 129
Demand touching, 133-134, 142-143
democracy, 212
Demographics, 170, 172, 223, 226, 236
Denotative meaning, 8, 94, 109, 113-114
Description, 94-95, 113, 116, 118, 138, 208
Descriptive language, 94
Development of relationships, 210
Dialect, 92, 97-98, 101-103, 107, 113-114, 209
Dialectics, 174, 190-192, 197, 235
Dialogue, 21, 24-25, 144, 171, 193, 199
Disconfirmation, 130, 144, 147
Disconfirming communication, 90, 109-111, 113-114
Discourse, 55, 84, 100, 116, 237
Discrimination, 30-32, 41-42, 48, 55, 64, 71, 79, 85-86,
107-109, 119, 137, 139, 142, 165, 182, 196,
200, 213, 218
Dissatisfaction, 111-113, 120, 212, 220
Distancing, 220
Distractions, 10, 157
Diversity, 45, 56, 85, 101, 177, 193-194, 199-201, 217
  and communication, 193, 199-201
  and friendship, 200
  communication and, 193, 200

cultural, 85, 177, 193-194, 199-201
minance, 124, 131-134, 137, 143, 193
ess, 39, 78, 122, 135, 138-139, 145-147, 183
k, Steve, 4
d, 103
ads, 146

st Asian cultures, 76
ooks, 228
ective communicator, 2, 19, 91, 195
ective listening, 150-155, 157, 160, 162, 165, 170
ects of communication, 130, 144, 147
o-defensive function, 78, 82-83
ail, 2, 9, 15, 22, 91, 156, 158, 205, 208-213, 215,
    218, 221-223, 226, 228, 230-231, 233-234
blems, 126, 142-143
oticons, 91, 210, 230
otion, 73, 86, 120, 127, 129, 143-145, 157, 168
and communication, 86
expression of, 120, 145
otional states, 127
otions, 8-9, 23, 73, 112, 115, 126-127, 143,
    145-146, 154, 157, 161-162
listening to, 154, 157, 161
pathic listening, 170
pathy, 157, 165, 168
feeling, 165
listening and, 157, 165, 168
listening with, 165
phasis, 76, 95, 142, 156, 159, 188, 190, 193
capsulated marginal people, 185, 197-198
coding, 6, 22-23, 155-156, 169
thusiasm, 33
vironment, 10, 15, 28, 48, 50, 109, 122, 160,
    181-183, 188, 193, 226-227
isode, 69
uality, 189, 212
ical communication, 16-19, 53
ical standards, 17, 19
ics, 1, 13, 15-17, 19-25, 27, 51-52, 62, 80, 83, 90,
    109-110, 112, 119, 140-141, 150, 166,
    170-171, 174, 195, 199, 204, 229
and intercultural communication, 174, 195, 199
and media, 17
and perception, 62, 80, 83
and verbal communication, 90, 109
communication and, 15, 19, 51, 119, 174, 229
defined, 17, 20
definition, 15, 21, 171
intercultural communication, 24, 171, 174, 195, 199
interpersonal, 24, 170
listening and, 150, 166, 170-171
of listening, 150, 166, 170-171
organizational, 24, 171
relationship, 15-17, 21-24, 52, 170, 204
nic identity, 28, 43-44, 53-54, 176
hnicity, 13-14, 32, 41, 43, 50, 53, 56, 70, 78, 91, 98,
    102, 109-110, 113, 116-117, 139, 155,
    158-159, 165, 169, 175, 178, 182, 184,
    199-200, 205, 219, 222-223, 227
hnocentrism, 77-78, 82-83, 195
valuating, 4, 20, 141, 151, 153-154, 162, 169, 215
valuation, 35, 86, 112, 139, 162
listening and, 162
ways to improve, 112
vidence, 4, 17, 19, 22, 99, 123, 137, 146, 154,
    157-158, 163, 188, 224, 227
xamples, 5, 16, 19, 27, 31, 35, 40, 47, 51, 70, 79, 90,
    98, 100, 107, 109, 112, 114, 122, 133, 135,
    180, 183, 194, 208
brief, 133
hypothetical, 112
using, 112, 135
xpectancy violation theory, 130
xperiments, 64
xpression, 12, 120, 122-125, 128-129, 136, 138, 142,
    144-145, 168, 170, 188, 196, 210, 218
ethnic, 124-125
facial, 120, 124-125, 128, 136, 138, 142, 144-145,
    210
xtended family, 235
ye behavior, 126-128, 144
ye contact, 128, 156, 159, 163-165, 209
and listening, 163
meaning of, 156

Face, 2, 9, 11, 17, 21, 32-33, 42, 55, 58, 91, 97, 99,
    110, 120-121, 126-127, 131, 134, 151,
    155-156, 166, 183, 196, 199, 207-211, 214,
    218, 220-221, 234, 236
Facebook, 2, 5, 9, 19, 35, 43, 45, 52, 57, 59, 111, 151,
    154-155, 157, 165, 178, 205-211, 213-216,
    219-222, 226-227, 229, 232, 235-239
Face-to-face communication, 42, 210, 234
Facial expression, 124-125, 128, 136, 142, 210
Facial expressions, 39, 120-121, 124, 126-127, 135,
    143-145, 209, 230
Fact, 2-3, 7, 11-13, 31, 35, 38, 49-51, 66-67, 70,
    78-81, 98, 103, 107, 109, 120-122, 124, 127,
    139, 151-152, 157-161, 166, 171-172, 175,
    179, 184, 188, 193, 205-207, 216, 218, 220,
    223, 226-227, 237, 239
facts, 21, 81, 93, 114, 161, 176, 200, 202, 237
using, 81, 93, 161
Familiarity, 76-77, 124, 161
Family, 2, 6, 8-9, 13-15, 17, 28, 32-34, 38-39, 46-49,
    51, 64, 67-68, 76, 79-80, 86, 92, 96, 109,
    114-115, 125, 131, 133, 143-144, 157, 164,
    168, 171, 176, 178, 180, 182-188, 191, 194,
    196, 199-202, 214, 227, 235, 237
and technology, 227, 237
definition of, 6, 171, 180
relationships in, 185
rules of, 17, 92, 185
types of, 8, 14, 34, 46, 133, 178, 185
Faulkner, Shannon, 40
Feedback, 5-6, 10, 22-23, 37, 55, 111, 127, 153, 159,
    169, 230
culture and, 6, 37
interpersonal, 127
listening and, 153, 159, 169
Field of experience, 12-13, 16, 22-23
Fields, 223
Fillers, 129
films, 39, 191, 205-206
Flexibility, 134
Flirting, 128, 178
Flores, Lisa, 185
Focus groups, 185
Followers, 214, 232
Force, 69, 113, 179
Formal language, 91
Formality, 189
Forum, 50, 56, 59, 215
Forums, 213, 219, 229
Foucault, Michel, 45
Frame of reference, 222
Frames, 15, 69, 82
free speech, 110, 115-116
Friendship, 20, 133, 142-143, 184, 191, 199-200, 214,
    218, 222, 237
Friendship touch, 133, 142-143
Friendships, 193, 196, 217-219
Functional touch, 133, 142-144
Fundamental attribution error, 70, 82-83, 86

G
Gaming, 217, 219, 236
Gates, Bill, 78
Gaze, 121-122, 124, 127-128, 135-136, 140, 210
Gender, 13-14, 27-29, 31-32, 36, 39-42, 44-45, 48, 50,
    53-59, 63, 67, 85-86, 91, 95, 98-100, 104,
    106, 113, 115-118, 127-128, 131-132, 142,
    145-147, 155, 158-159, 164-166, 169, 175,
    178, 180, 186, 197, 201, 205, 213, 215-216,
    218, 222-225, 236-238
and conflict, 237
and culture, 50, 56, 104, 127, 180, 197, 238
and language, 28, 180
and nonverbal communication, 145, 186
and touch, 145
culture and, 13-14, 57, 86, 104, 117, 146, 180, 201
definition of, 155, 180
language and, 44, 95, 104, 115-116
leadership, 14, 106, 116, 118, 237
listening and, 155, 158-159, 164-166, 169
nonverbal communication and, 132, 145
relationships and, 218, 236
self-concept, 27, 31-32, 36, 53-54, 85, 213
self-disclosure, 99, 213, 237
self-disclosure and, 99
stereotypes about, 164, 224
terms for, 14
verbal messages and, 142
Gender identity, 28, 32, 39, 41, 44-45, 53-54

Gender roles, 44, 223
Gender roles and expectations, 44
Generalization, 139
Generalized other, 34-35, 53-54
Geographic location, 223
Gesture, 7, 45, 124-126
Gestures, 7-8, 13, 121, 123-127, 129, 137-138,
    142-145, 209-210, 230
Google.com, 237
Grammar, 92, 94, 98, 113-114, 231-232
Group, 2, 14-15, 17, 21, 23, 29, 34-35, 37, 41-43, 51,
    54, 64, 68, 74, 76-79, 82-85, 87, 93,
    100-101, 103, 107-110, 113-114, 120,
    122-123, 126, 132, 134, 138, 159, 169, 177,
    180, 183-184, 186-187, 190, 193-195,
    197-198, 201, 205, 208, 215-216, 219,
    223-224, 227, 231, 234
characteristics of, 83, 100, 114, 190, 208
conflict, 187, 197
definition of, 103, 123, 180
leadership, 14
primary, 21, 29, 132, 187, 205, 227
secondary, 29
size of, 126
think, 14, 17, 23, 29, 35, 37, 41-43, 51, 54, 64, 68,
    74, 76, 82, 93, 100, 107-108, 114, 159,
    169, 180, 186, 190, 194, 197, 205, 216,
    231, 234
Group communication, 74
Groups, 7-8, 13-14, 17, 19, 21, 23-24, 28-30, 35, 37,
    40-41, 43-44, 46, 50, 53, 68, 71, 77-80,
    82-83, 99, 101-103, 105-107, 110, 113,
    124-125, 137-138, 174, 176, 179-189,
    191-195, 197, 224-227, 232-233
focus, 13, 23, 53, 82-83, 180, 185, 192
virtual, 50

H
Hair, 31, 33, 44, 66-67, 125-126, 134, 138-139, 191
Hale, J., 130, 144, 147
Hall, J., 144-146, 236
Haptics, 126, 132, 135, 142, 144
Hate speech, 90, 109-110, 113-116
Hearing, 37, 48-49, 72-73, 84, 87, 98, 107, 128, 151,
    153-155, 157, 159-161, 164, 169-171, 177,
    231
deafness and, 161, 171
Heider, Fritz, 69
Hierarchy, 13, 31, 75-76, 79-80, 82, 105, 116, 118,
    137, 139, 150, 163-164, 189, 193
Hofstede, Geert, 186
Honesty, 19, 166
Houston, M., 115-117, 199
Human communication, 1-25, 27, 61, 85-86, 89,
    115-116, 119, 130, 144, 146-147, 149,
    170-171, 173, 203
Humanism, 25
Humor, 5, 93, 117
Hurricane Katrina, 76, 176, 182
Hussein, Saddam, 37

I
Identification, 29, 41, 43, 48, 54, 64, 85-86, 146, 221
Identity, 2-3, 13-14, 18, 21-22, 27-32, 34-58, 64-65,
    78, 91-92, 98, 106-109, 113, 115-116, 129,
    132, 135, 137-138, 158-159, 165-167, 176,
    179, 185, 192, 196, 198-201, 204-207,
    210-213, 215-217, 229, 233-235, 238
Identity, ethnic, 43
Illustrators, 126, 142, 144
IM, 55, 59
Imaginative language, 93
Immediacy, 126, 130, 142, 144, 147, 170, 210, 234
intimacy and, 130
Impression formation, 84
Impression management, 217
Index, 57-58, 235
Individualism, 13, 186-187, 190, 193, 198, 201
Individualistic orientation, 187, 197-198
Inference, 81
Inferences, 69, 74, 81, 124
Influence, 5-6, 9-10, 12-13, 15, 18-19, 28, 32, 34-36,
    38, 44, 46-48, 52-54, 62-64, 67, 69, 72-75,
    78-80, 83-84, 91-92, 98-105, 111, 113-116,
    119, 121-122, 124, 129, 131, 133-136,
    142-143, 154-155, 159, 161-164, 167, 174,
    186, 192-193, 196-197, 210, 222
Information, 4, 6, 10-13, 17-19, 22-24, 32, 37, 43, 55,

62, 64-69, 71-72, 74, 77-78, 81-83, 85,
  92-94, 96, 106, 114, 121-123, 135, 138,
  142-143, 146, 152, 154-158, 160, 163-164,
  166, 168-170, 195-197, 206-210, 213-219,
  222, 225, 227-230, 232-234, 236-237, 239
  definition of, 6, 94, 123, 154-155
  ignoring, 164
  negative, 37, 65-66, 68-69, 71, 78, 81-83, 92, 114,
    196, 214, 216-218, 222
  power and, 96, 106, 222
  sources of, 160, 197, 207
Informational listening, 156-157, 169
Innovations, 227-228, 237
  diffusion of, 227, 237
Intentional communication, 25
Interaction, 6, 8-12, 14-15, 19-21, 24, 28-30, 32, 34,
  40, 53, 65, 69, 72, 78, 85-86, 96-97, 117,
  119-120, 123-124, 129, 133, 135-137,
  142-145, 147, 151, 153, 158, 160, 162-163,
  180-181, 183, 186, 191-193, 196, 208-212,
  215, 218, 221, 229, 237
Intercultural communication, 24, 28, 53-55, 58, 74,
  116-118, 171, 174-176, 178-181, 186,
  190-193, 195-202, 235
  and self-awareness, 196
  feedback and, 55
  gender and, 28, 117
  increased opportunities for intercultural contact,
    176
  language and, 116
  listening and, 171
  meaning, 24, 179
  nonverbal, 24, 175, 186
  political and historical forces, 191-192
  time and, 116
Intercultural listening, 170
Interdependence, 187
  group, 187
Interest, 74, 123, 126, 128, 136, 139, 156-157,
  168-169, 196, 209, 213, 219-220
Interference, 9-10
International Listening Association, 153, 171-172
Internet, 19, 43, 46, 50, 52, 57, 101, 110, 115, 165,
  205, 208, 213, 215, 219, 221, 223-229,
  234-239
  email, 205, 208, 213, 215, 221, 223, 226, 228, 234
  privacy and, 229
Interpersonal communication, 24, 74, 84, 86, 145, 227,
  237-239
  and emotion, 86, 145
  mediated, 145, 237-239
  principles of, 24
  small group communication, 74
Interpersonal conflict, 24
Interpersonal constructs, 74
Interpersonal relationships, 205, 207, 233, 237
interpretation, 4, 65, 69, 72, 80, 82-83, 120, 136
  explanation of, 69, 83
  perception and, 72
Interpreting, 6, 23, 121-122, 124-125, 136, 142, 154,
  170
Interrupting, 126, 158, 167-168
Interruptions, 9, 99, 116
Intersexuality, 45
Interviewing, 5, 78
Interviews, 28, 39, 131, 182, 185, 192
Intimacy, 8, 17, 93, 130-131, 133, 135-136, 141-143,
  145, 212, 218-220
  expressing and managing, 135-136, 142-143
Intimate distance, 131, 142, 144
Invasion, 132
Involuntary long-term travelers, 181, 197-198
Involuntary short-term travelers, 181, 197-198
Issues, 8, 17, 19, 21-22, 28, 46, 50-52, 57, 75, 79, 84,
  94, 115-116, 118, 120, 129, 139, 151, 162,
  165-166, 179, 181, 183, 204-205, 211, 213,
  215, 217, 221-222, 226, 229, 237

J

Jackson, D. D., 25
Janusik, L. A., 171
Jargon, 103, 113-114, 164
Jealousy, 220, 236
Jewelry, 38, 134, 138
Jokes, 5, 20, 28, 98, 108, 164
Jones, S., 145, 170-171
Journals, 103, 106, 116, 239
Judgment, 55, 95, 112, 130, 139, 165, 214
  listening and, 165

K

Kant, Immanuel, 19
Kinesics, 124, 126, 135, 142, 144, 147
Kluckhohn, Florence, 186
Knapp, M., 85, 145
knowledge, 2-3, 24, 46, 72-73, 77, 93, 114-115, 121,
  127, 141-142, 152, 160, 176, 179, 182-183,
  196-198, 225, 233-234
Kohonen, Susanna, 97

L

Language, 7, 10, 14, 22, 28, 34, 43-44, 51, 53-54,
  90-95, 97-110, 112-118, 128-129, 144-145,
  157, 161, 163, 171, 178-183, 185, 191, 198,
  218, 232
  accurate, 99, 232
  appropriate, 22, 44, 98, 105, 109, 112-113
  appropriate use of, 22, 113
  characteristics of, 100, 114, 185, 191
  components, 10, 22, 90-94, 113, 180
  connotation, 113
  culture and, 14, 104, 117, 180, 185
  dating, 185
  definition of, 94, 103, 171, 180
  descriptive, 94-95
  elements of, 10, 91, 114
  formal, 28, 91, 97, 105
  functions, 51, 90-95, 100, 113, 115, 144
  gender and, 28, 117, 128
  gender-neutral, 106
  generic, 106
  grammar, 92, 94, 98, 113-114, 232
  immediate, 191
  importance of, 10, 28, 90-91, 98, 191, 198
  informal, 54, 114, 129, 157
  jargon, 103, 113-114
  listening and, 157, 161, 163, 171
  meaning, 7, 10, 14, 22, 51, 91, 93-95, 104, 106,
    108-109, 113-115, 129, 144, 179
  meaning in, 94, 104, 114
  of bilingual and multilingual speakers, 92
  offensive, 109, 113
  power and, 44, 106-107
  power of, 105, 109, 112-113
  racist, 28
  role in communication, 92, 104
  semantics, 94-95, 104, 113, 115
  sexist, 28
  slang, 100-101
  sounds, 10, 22, 94, 98, 101, 107, 113-116, 129,
    144, 191
  stereotype, 53-54, 99, 107, 109
  technical, 10, 171
  technology, 28, 91
  voice and, 103, 163
  words, 7, 10, 43-44, 91-92, 94-95, 97-101,
    104-106, 108, 113-116, 128-129,
    144-145, 157, 163, 185, 218
Language use, 22, 28, 93-94, 98, 100-101, 104, 112,
  115-116
Laswell, H. D., 24
Leader, 24, 42, 79, 145, 192
Leaders, 16, 25, 50, 79, 82, 152, 171, 189
Leadership, 14, 24, 106, 116, 118, 152, 217, 237
  communication and, 116
  culture and, 14
  emergent, 24
  ethics and, 24
  group, 14
  in groups, 24
Lengel, R. H., 236
Leveling, 221, 231
Lexical choice, 98, 113-114
Lexicon, 57, 59, 115
Libraries, 228, 231
Lighting, 8
Liking, 84, 93, 130, 137
Linear model of communication, 11
LinkedIn, 206, 210, 226, 232
Links, 214
listeners, 151-152, 154-155, 157-159, 161, 163,
  167-171
  ethical, 151, 167, 169-170
  role of, 151, 163, 170
Listening, 98, 124, 128, 149-172, 213
  active, 156, 170-171
  barriers, 150-151, 154-155, 159-160, 162-163,
    168-170
  barriers to, 150-151, 154-155, 159-160, 168, 170
  barriers to effective, 150-151, 154, 170
  critical, 152, 154, 156-159, 165, 167, 169
  deafness and, 161, 171-172
  defined, 168-169
  definition of, 154-155, 171-172
  effective, 150-155, 157-158, 160, 162, 164-165,
    167, 169-170
  empathic, 170
  empathy and, 165
  ethics and, 150, 166
  ethics of, 170
  evaluating, 151, 153-154, 162, 169
  evaluative, 162
  eye contact and, 128
  feedback and, 159
  gender and, 128, 158, 164
  importance of, 98, 150-151, 153
  improving, 150-151, 167, 171
  informational, 156-158, 169
  intercultural, 170-171
  international listening association, 153, 171-172
  interpreting, 124, 154, 170
  language and, 161
  nonjudgmental, 157, 164
  objective, 162
  offensive, 166
  passive, 151
  process of, 151, 153-154, 159, 168-169
  racist, 166
  receiving and, 155, 169
  styles, 155-156, 158, 165, 170-172
  to others, 151, 154-157, 160, 162, 164, 169-170
  types of, 128, 154, 162, 167, 213
Listening skills, 150-158, 160, 165, 167, 169-171
  ethics and, 150
Listening style, 155-159, 166, 169-171
Long-term versus short-term orientation, 190, 197-19
Looking-glass self, 32, 35, 53-54
Love, 4, 7, 21, 52, 93, 109, 133, 135, 142, 144, 200,
  230, 236
  gender and, 236
  types of, 7, 21, 52, 133, 142
Love-intimate touch, 133, 142, 144
Lying, 5, 16-19, 72, 140-141, 216, 219
  ethics of, 17, 140-141

M

Magazines, 29, 35, 46-47, 98, 134, 139
Main points, 157
  effective, 157
Management, 57, 115, 144, 152, 164, 194, 217, 221,
  236
Mapping, 24, 238
Maps, 66-67, 102
Marriage, 5, 31, 84, 86, 117, 121, 184, 187, 199-200,
  202, 237
Marriages, 184-185
  interracial, 184-185
Mean, 4, 7, 11-12, 46, 50-51, 54, 57, 59, 74, 81, 103,
  106, 108-109, 112, 114, 121, 123-125, 132,
  142, 145, 153-154, 160, 166, 168, 170, 175,
  180, 195, 205, 207, 209, 221, 225
Meaning, 2, 5-8, 10-12, 14-16, 22-24, 29-30, 35, 39,
  46-49, 51, 65-66, 69, 71, 82-83, 86, 91,
  93-96, 104, 106, 108-109, 113-115, 119-127,
  129-130, 135, 141-144, 151, 153-154, 156,
  169, 179, 194, 205, 208, 211, 227, 233, 238
  connotative, 8, 94-95, 108, 113-114
  denotative, 8, 94, 109, 113-114
  multiple, 15, 51, 121, 123, 127, 130, 135, 144, 205
    211, 233
  of touch, 143-144
  of words, 7, 108, 113
Media, 2, 6, 13, 17-18, 34-35, 40, 42, 44, 49-50, 52,
  55-56, 59, 67, 75, 78, 91, 98-99, 102, 107,
  110-111, 116, 134, 139, 151-152, 155,
  160-161, 167, 169-172, 194, 197, 203-239
  and children, 228
  individual and, 6, 40, 50, 98
  interpersonal relationships and, 207
  messages, 2, 6, 17-18, 40, 44, 56, 59, 75, 78, 91,
    107, 110-111, 134, 139, 151, 155, 161,
    167, 169-170, 206-213, 215-219,
    221-222, 229-234
  movies, 34-35, 98, 219
  relationships and, 111, 207, 212, 218, 220, 236
  study of, 2, 116, 206, 219, 235

edia richness theory, 209-210, 233-234
ediated communication, 97, 99, 115-116, 166, 175, 204-205, 208-209, 217, 219, 230-231, 233-235, 237-239
ediated messages, 218, 232
ediated relationships, 230
ediation, 115
ehrabian, Albert, 124
emory, 152
  listening and, 152
en, 13-14, 30-31, 38, 43-44, 46, 48, 51-52, 56, 64, 66, 73, 79, 85, 87, 92, 96, 98-100, 105-106, 109-110, 114, 116-117, 122, 124, 127-128, 131-134, 138-139, 145-147, 158, 161, 185, 194, 206, 219, 223-224
ental access, 228
essage, 2, 4-12, 16, 18, 22-23, 86, 91, 93-94, 111-112, 121, 123-124, 126-127, 129-130, 135, 140-143, 151-152, 154-157, 162-163, 166, 168-170, 205, 207, 209, 211, 215, 218, 220-221, 229-232
  asynchronous, 209
essages, 2, 6-8, 10, 12, 15-19, 22-23, 32, 36, 40, 44, 47-48, 54, 56, 59, 72, 75, 78, 85, 91, 96, 107, 110-111, 113, 119-127, 129-130, 133-136, 138-144, 151, 153-155, 157, 161-163, 165-170, 175, 206-213, 215-219, 221-222, 229-234
  ambiguous, 17, 121, 142
  confirming, 110-111, 113
  content, 8, 22-23, 54, 59, 85, 157, 165, 169, 206-209, 211-212, 215, 232, 234
  context of, 19, 85, 113
  creation, 6, 8, 22, 91, 208, 212, 234
  levels of, 75, 136, 163, 221, 233
  listening and, 151, 153-155, 157, 161-163, 165-170
  nonverbal, 6-8, 12, 15, 23, 47, 85, 91, 119-127, 129-130, 133-136, 138-144, 153, 155, 157, 169-170, 175, 209-210, 218
  relational, 7, 96, 121, 157, 165, 167, 209-210, 217
  relationship, 7-8, 15-18, 22-23, 91, 96, 113, 121, 125, 133, 142-143, 155, 162, 165, 170, 210, 213, 215, 217-219, 221-222, 230
etaphor, 185, 236, 239
indful, 81, 164, 168-169, 196
indfulness, 81, 84, 168
obile phones, 187, 205-206, 225, 231, 233, 235-237
ode, 187-188, 209
odels, 1, 10-12, 35, 66, 82-84
  of communication, 1, 10-11, 66, 84
  psychological, 84
onitors, 220
onochronic time, 193
oods, 9, 120, 143, 210
otivation, 85, 135, 145, 182, 195, 197, 220, 228
ovement, 30, 42, 126, 133, 137, 144-145, 176
  facial, 126, 144-145
ovies, 33-35, 46, 98, 168, 191, 219
ulac, A., 116
ultiracial identity, 42, 53-54
uslim identity, 49
ySpace, 9, 206

N
ame-calling, 140
arrative, 57
ational identity, 28, 30, 43, 53-54, 56-57
ative American cultures, 76, 97
eeds, 3, 33, 42, 52, 91, 121, 123, 142, 155-156, 187, 198, 212, 216, 220, 225, 228, 230
  establishing, 142
egative comments, 222
egativity, 85
etiquette, 207, 230
etworking, 91, 206, 208, 211, 214, 216, 218, 220-221, 223, 226, 233-234
ew media, 35, 50, 55, 59, 167, 208, 220-222, 226-228, 230, 233, 235-236, 238-239
  characteristics of, 208, 230
  defined, 233
ews sources, 18
ewspapers, 106
oise, 6, 8-12, 16, 22-23, 66, 69, 71-72, 160-161
  electronic, 9, 22-23
  emotional, 72, 160-161
  explanation of, 69
  external, 9
  internal, 9, 71
ominalists, 104, 113, 115

Nonverbal behavior, 12, 24, 85, 119-127, 130, 135-147, 185
Nonverbal codes, 119-120, 123, 125-126, 137, 142, 144
Nonverbal communication, 24, 86, 91, 119-147, 186
  adaptors, 126, 142-143
  and culture, 127
  and emotion, 86, 129, 145
  and interpretation of, 136
  appearance and artifacts, 126, 134-135, 137-138, 142
  body movements, 127
  body movements and, 127
  body type, 134
  chronemics, 129, 135, 142-143
  clothing and, 123, 134, 137, 143
  codes of, 137
  color and, 134
  complementing, 135
  cultural influences, 125
  culture, 86, 121, 124-125, 127, 129, 131, 133-134, 139, 142-143, 146, 186
  culture and, 86, 134, 146
  deceiving, 140
  decoding, 121, 124, 144-147
  definition of, 123
  emblems, 126, 142-143
  emotional expressions, 127
  environment, 122
  eye behavior, 126-128, 144
  facial expression, 124-125, 128, 136, 142
  flirting, 128
  function of, 24, 132, 135-136, 144-145
  functions of, 119, 123, 135
  gender and, 128, 146-147
  gestures and, 121, 124, 127
  guidelines for ethical, 119, 140-141
  haptics, 126, 132, 135, 142, 144
  illustrators, 126, 142, 144
  improving, 86, 119-120, 141, 146
  interpreting, 121-122, 124-125, 136, 142
  kinesics, 124, 126, 135, 142, 144, 147
  nature of, 133
  olfactory, 86
  paralinguistics, 126, 128, 135, 142, 144
  proxemics, 129-130, 135, 142, 144
  regulating, 122, 135-136, 142, 144
  regulators, 126, 142, 144
  relationships and, 130, 136-137, 144
  repeating, 135
  silence, 141
  space, 126, 129-132, 135, 142-144, 146
  substituting, 135
  subtle nonverbal behaviors, 122
  territoriality, 129, 131-132, 144
  time, 121, 125-126, 128-130, 134-135, 142-144, 146
  time and, 126, 129, 142
  touch, 91, 132-134, 136, 141-145
  touch and, 133, 143
  touch as, 136, 145
  types of, 120, 126-128, 133, 141-142
  vocal behavior, 128
Nonverbal cues, 120-121, 124, 138, 140, 155, 175, 209-210, 218
  and self-disclosure, 210
Nonverbal messages, 6, 15, 23, 119-121, 123-124, 126-127, 135-136, 138-143, 153, 169
Nonverbal reciprocity, 136-137
Norms, 2-3, 14, 20, 23, 34, 54, 76-77, 79, 84, 92, 105-106, 109, 142-143, 158-159, 163-164, 185, 193, 197, 222, 228, 230
  group, 2, 14, 23, 34, 54, 76-77, 79, 84, 109, 159, 193, 197
Notes, 45, 50, 72, 96, 102, 138, 167, 199
Nuclear family, 186

O
Obama, Barack, 13, 42, 47, 128, 193
Olsen twins, 31
Online identity, 213, 217, 229
Online relationships, 52, 217-220, 229, 233
Openness, 155, 164, 167
Organization, 65-66, 72-73, 80, 82-83, 85, 117, 128, 138, 153, 161, 171-172, 176, 194, 201-202, 236
  characteristics of, 83
  culture and, 117, 201
  definition of, 171-172

  explanation of, 83
  of perception, 65, 85
Organizational communication, 24
  ethics, 24
Others, 3-5, 8, 10, 13-23, 27-42, 46-54, 63-65, 67-83, 92-93, 95, 97-99, 101, 103, 105, 107-115, 120-131, 133-134, 136-144, 151-157, 159-160, 162-166, 168-170, 179, 186-187, 191-197, 200, 205-208, 210-220, 223, 225, 227, 229, 231-234
  listening to, 151, 154-155, 157, 159-160, 163-164, 166, 168-170
  perceptions of, 63-64, 67, 74-75, 79, 81, 83, 99, 113-114, 200, 215
  self-image and, 37
Outing, 114
Outlines, 66
Overlaps, 97, 116

P
Pace, 111, 122, 212
Palin, Sarah, 67
Panel, 194, 200, 202
Panels, 64
Paradox, 214, 237-238
Paralinguistics, 126, 128, 135, 142, 144
Paraphrase, 156
Paraphrasing, 157
Pauses, 97
Peers, 91-92, 100, 133, 163, 227, 235
Perception, 46, 54, 62-65, 68, 71-77, 79-86, 90-91, 104-105, 115, 137, 145, 147
  analysis of, 145
  and personality characteristics, 72
  and social roles, 63, 80, 82
  attribution error, 82-83, 86
  awareness, 79, 81
  checking, 81
  cognitive complexity, 74, 80-84
  communication, 46, 54, 64, 71-76, 79-86, 90-91, 104-105, 115, 137, 145, 147
  cultural background, 76, 81
  culture and, 77, 86, 104
  defined, 54, 75
  ethics and, 62, 80, 83, 90
  formation, 84
  gender, 54, 63, 85-86, 91, 104, 115, 145, 147
  improving, 62, 80, 86, 90
  internet, 46, 115
  interpretation, 65, 72, 80, 82-83
  interpretation of, 72
  media, 75, 91
  nature of, 46
  organization, 65, 72-73, 80, 82-83, 85
  person, 46, 54, 64-65, 68, 71-76, 79, 81-83, 137
  processes, 62, 65, 71-72, 75, 80-83, 85
  processes of, 65, 85
  selection, 65, 72, 80, 82-83, 85, 145
  stereotyping, 68, 82, 84
  understanding of, 46, 54, 74, 145
Perception checking, 81
Perception process, 62-63, 80, 83
Perceptions, 14, 23, 36, 63-64, 66-67, 69, 71, 73-77, 79-83, 92, 99, 113-114, 132, 146, 158, 180, 196-198, 200, 215, 223, 235, 237
  explanation of, 69, 83
  family and, 180
  listening and, 158
  of others, 63-64, 67, 71, 74-75, 79-81, 83, 114, 197
  stereotyping and, 196, 215
Performance of identity, 38-39, 53-54
Personal attacks, 79, 230
Personal constructs, 74
Personal distance, 131, 142, 144
Personal identity, 29, 38, 50, 53-54, 210, 212, 229
Personal language, 93, 113, 115
Personal space, 132, 146
Personality, 13, 33, 55, 57, 69-72, 82, 84-85, 93, 115-116, 124, 131, 134, 137, 144-147, 164, 171, 185, 187, 197-198, 219, 236
Personification, 73
Perspective, 17, 19, 55, 84, 104-105, 115, 123, 175, 195-196, 199, 202, 212
  definition of, 123
  psychological, 84, 115, 199
Persuasion, 5, 219
  on Internet, 219
Persuasive speaking, 156-157, 169
  evaluating, 169

Phat, 100
Phishing, 215-216, 233-234
Phoneme, 94
Phonemes, 94
Phonology, 94-95, 104, 113, 115
Physical appearance, 84, 163-164
Physical attractiveness, 164
Physical setting, 8
Pinker, Steven, 105
Plato, 2, 19
Play, 32-33, 35, 44, 49, 64, 75, 92, 145, 152, 168-169,
    174, 177, 185, 192, 197, 205, 207, 209, 212,
    214, 223, 228, 233-234
Politeness, 81, 97
    negative, 81
Polytheistic religions, 190
Population, 32, 48, 56, 176-178, 200-202, 224-225
Position, 9, 19, 22, 30, 75-76, 79-84, 105, 112, 122,
    137, 151, 166, 179, 195, 213, 229, 233
Posture, 121, 124, 126, 136, 141, 144, 210
Power, 14, 32, 42, 44, 55-56, 58-59, 62, 71, 75, 79-80,
    82, 90-91, 96-97, 99-100, 104-109, 112-114,
    116, 124, 131, 133-134, 137-138, 142-143,
    145-147, 163, 170, 174, 179-180, 189-190,
    192-193, 197-198, 200, 204, 222, 225, 233
    and accent, 107
    and organizations, 189, 198, 200
    and words, 106
    culture and, 14, 104, 134, 146, 180
    expert, 163
    information, 32, 55, 62, 71, 82, 96, 106, 114, 138,
        142-143, 146, 163, 170, 197, 222, 225,
        233
    language and, 44, 104-105, 109, 116
    legitimate, 80
    sources of, 116, 197
    types of, 14, 71, 105, 133, 142
Power distance, 189-190, 193, 197-198
Power distances, 189
PowerPoint, 76
PowerPoint slides, 76
Practicing, 21, 24-25, 84
Pragmatics, 25, 84, 94-95, 97-98, 104, 113, 115-116
    definition of, 94
Preferred personality, 187, 197-198
Prejudice, 77-79, 82-84, 119, 137, 139-140, 142,
    164-165, 215, 218
Prejudices, 165, 196
Presentation, 5, 38, 53-54, 141, 209-211, 213-214,
    229, 233
    ending, 214
    facial expression, 210
    gestures, 209-210
Presentations, 238
Pressure, 73, 153, 185
Presumption, 31
Primary identities, 29, 53
Primary territories, 132
Problem-solving, 235
Production, 188, 200
Professional touch, 133, 142, 144
Pronunciation, 92, 98, 101, 113-114
Proof, 212, 232
Prototypes, 66-67
Proxemics, 129-130, 135, 142, 144
Proximity, 8, 143, 181, 217
Psychology, 2, 24-25, 55-57, 64, 83-85, 87, 92, 103,
    106, 116, 121, 124, 137-138, 144-147, 170,
    199-200, 237
Public communication, 15
    ethics, 15
Public distance, 131, 142, 144
Public space, 135
Public speaking, 5, 167
    listening and, 167
Public sphere, 199
Public territories, 132
Punctuality, 129-130
Purpose, 74, 190, 230
    identifying, 190
    of communication, 74, 230
    specific, 74

Q
questionnaire, 64, 84, 86, 155, 190
Questionnaires, 182
Questions, 2, 21, 23, 28, 69, 76, 81, 96-97, 99-100,
    114, 153, 156, 158-161, 163, 166, 197, 234
    responding to, 153, 156

survey, 153

R
Race, 13, 28-29, 31-32, 36, 40-44, 48, 50, 53, 55-56,
    58, 76, 86, 91, 98, 101-102, 110, 113, 139,
    165, 175, 178, 182, 184-185, 191, 193-194,
    199, 201, 205, 215, 218-219, 222-224, 238
Racial identity, 41-43, 53-54
Racism, 182, 188, 193, 200, 215
Radio, 5, 9, 39, 182, 200, 205, 221
Reality TV, 79, 194, 200, 202
Reasoning, 36, 56, 123
Receiver, 10-12, 16, 22, 96, 110, 112, 114, 135, 211,
    229-230
Receivers, 121, 133
Receiving, 6, 23, 45, 65, 82, 122, 153, 155, 169, 183,
    232
Reciprocity, 131, 136-137
Reentry shock, 182, 197-198
Reference groups, 35, 37
References, 24, 54, 84, 115, 144, 170, 198, 235
Reflected appraisals, 27, 31-38, 53-54
Reframing, 86
Regional differences, 187
Regulating interaction, 135, 142, 144
Regulators, 126, 142, 144
Relational communication, 237
Relational development, 217
Relational listening, 165
Relational maintenance, 115, 200
Relational messages, 209
Relationship meaning, 8, 22-23
Relationships, 2-9, 12, 15, 17-18, 20-24, 30, 38, 52,
    71, 75, 84, 86, 90-93, 96, 104, 106, 109, 111,
    113-114, 116-117, 120, 129-131, 133,
    136-137, 142, 144-145, 152-153, 162,
    165-167, 169-170, 179, 183-185, 187,
    191-194, 196-197, 199-200, 205-207,
    209-210, 212-213, 217-222, 229-230,
    233-239
    breadth of, 234
    computer-mediated communication and, 238-239
    culture and, 6, 30, 86, 104, 117, 185
    definition of, 6
    development of, 84, 86, 104, 144, 199, 210, 236
    ethical, 17-18, 20-22, 52, 111, 113, 120, 142,
        166-167, 169-170, 205, 217, 229-230
    family and, 187, 194
    gender and, 117, 236
    love and, 7
    media and, 205, 207, 212-213, 220, 233, 235, 238
    messages in, 6, 15, 144
    nonverbal messages and, 120, 136
    online, 5, 52, 116, 196, 206, 210, 213, 217-222,
        229-230, 233-239
    primary, 6, 21, 131, 187, 205, 233
    self-disclosure and, 219
    small group, 2, 114
    stages of, 133, 153, 218, 220
    types of, 7-8, 21, 23, 52, 71, 84, 120, 133, 142,
        162, 167, 185, 209, 213, 217
    workplace, 116, 136, 152, 165, 170, 193, 200, 207,
        217, 221-222
Relativism, 19, 22-23
Relativists, 19, 104, 113, 115
Relaxation, 126, 142, 144
Reliability, 170-171, 228
Religion, 14-15, 28, 31, 40, 49-50, 53, 55-56, 59, 101,
    110, 175, 178, 180, 191, 219, 235
Religious identity, 49-51, 53-54
Remembering, 142
Repeating, 135
Repetition, 210
Reporting, 116
Representations, 66-67, 82, 99, 238
Reproduction, 56, 59
Research, 55-56, 63-64, 66, 73, 76, 79, 84-86, 92, 96,
    98-100, 115-116, 124, 127-128, 130-132,
    144-147, 151-153, 156, 158, 168, 170-171,
    186, 190, 196, 199-201, 216, 227, 231, 233,
    235-237, 239
    accuracy of, 146
    books, 55-56, 76, 84, 98, 115, 145, 171, 201, 239
    documents, 239
    examples, 79, 98, 100
    interviews, 131
    museums, 231
    online, 55-56, 116, 151, 196, 216, 227, 233,
        235-237, 239

patterns in, 146
    statistics, 56, 170-171, 231, 235-236
    strategy for, 216
    topic, 73, 158, 233, 237
Research methods, 63
Responding, 3-4, 22, 80, 98, 121, 132, 149-172, 186,
    199, 213
    empathic, 170
Response, 4-5, 10, 19, 23, 68, 81, 85, 111, 130, 132,
    143, 154, 171, 175, 190, 209, 214, 222, 224
    listening and, 154, 171
Résumé, 225
Reverse culture shock, 182, 197-198
Rhetoric, 57, 74, 117, 199
Rhythm, 104, 128-129, 144
Rice, C., 200
Rich media, 210
Ring tones, 231
Roberts, Julia, 127
Robots, 92, 180, 212
Role expectations, 39, 53-54
Roles, 6, 10, 23, 34, 38-39, 44, 51, 54, 57, 63, 79-80,
    82, 93, 115, 117, 144, 174, 192, 223, 237
    individual, 6, 10, 23, 34, 38, 51, 54, 63, 79-80, 82,
        115, 174, 192, 237
    maintenance, 115
    research, 63, 79, 115, 144, 237
    task, 144
Romantic love, 7
Romantic relationship, 145, 200
    communication in, 145, 200
Rules, 17, 20, 23, 34, 54, 70, 92, 94-95, 97-98, 101,
    103, 105, 113-115, 124-125, 138, 142, 144,
    146, 159, 185-186, 193, 197, 207, 230
    cultural, 23, 54, 92, 97-98, 103, 125, 142, 159,
        185-186, 193, 197
Rumor, 166

S
Sapir-Whorf hypothesis, 104-105, 113, 115-116, 118
Sarcasm, 141
Sartre, Jean-Paul, 19
Satisfaction, 71, 115, 117, 120-121, 145-146, 152-153,
    220, 236
Scripts, 38-39, 54, 66-67
Second Life, 208, 211, 217
Secondary identities, 29, 53
Secrecy, 18-19
Seinfeld, Jerry, 131
Selective attention, 65, 71, 81-83
Selective exposure, 207
Self, 3, 5, 24, 27, 31-32, 34-38, 42, 46-47, 49, 52-58,
    64, 69-70, 76, 78, 82-83, 85-86, 91-92, 99,
    106, 110-111, 114-117, 132, 146-147, 158,
    161, 167-168, 179-180, 187, 196-197, 201,
    209-211, 213-214, 216, 219, 233, 236-238
    blind, 46
    looking-glass, 32, 35, 53-54
    material, 187, 214
    open, 36, 38, 64, 167, 197, 214, 216
    social, 3, 24, 27, 31-32, 34-38, 42, 46-47, 52-58,
        76, 78, 82, 85-86, 91, 99, 110-111, 114,
        116-117, 132, 146-147, 161, 168, 179,
        197, 209-211, 213-214, 216, 219, 233,
        236-238
    spiritual, 49, 54
Self-awareness, 179, 196-197
Self-concept, 27, 31-32, 36-38, 53-54, 85, 210, 213
    communication and, 53
    culture and, 37
    defined, 53-54
    development of, 210
    gender and, 85
    self-fulfilling prophecy, 38, 53-54
    self-image and, 37
    sex and, 36
    understanding of, 31, 36, 54
Self-disclosure, 99, 210-211, 213, 219, 237
    self-presentation, 210-211, 213
Self-esteem, 5, 35, 37, 53-55, 58, 91-92, 132,
    146-147, 214, 216, 238
    improving, 146
Self-evaluation, 35
Self-fulfilling prophecies, 27, 31-32, 36, 52-53
Self-fulfilling prophecy, 35, 38, 52-54
Self-image, 32, 37, 54, 64, 110-111, 114
Self-knowledge, 179, 196
Self-labels, 116
Self-monitoring, 236

246

lf-perception, 46, 54
lf-presentation, 38, 53-54, 210-211, 213-214, 233
lf-respect, 37, 53-54, 57
lf-serving bias, 70, 82-83
lf-worth, 78, 83, 161
mantics, 84, 94-95, 104, 113, 115
nsory model, 76
paration, 15, 183
quence, 57, 67, 83
rvice-task function, 136
x, 7, 13, 15, 31-32, 36, 44, 55, 57-58, 64, 70, 72, 80, 85, 87, 98, 115, 117, 125, 128, 133, 144, 146-147, 185, 217, 237
x roles, 57, 115, 117, 144, 237
xting, 46
xual orientation, 13, 113, 122, 146, 165, 175, 178, 213
arpening, 63
ort-term orientation, 190, 197-198
yness, 235
olings, 34, 99, 159
gnificant others, 34
gns, 124, 132, 138, 145-146
ence, 84, 117, 141, 151, 209
    culture and, 117
    ethics of, 141
milarity, 84
mulation, 217
ills access, 228
ang, 100-101
des, 76
nall group communication, 74
    communication, 74
nall groups, 179
    understanding in, 179
nall talk, 129
niling, 7, 85, 120, 123, 125, 138, 140-141, 209-210
nith, A., 56, 236-237
ocial categorization, 77
ocial class, 27-29, 31, 40, 47-48, 50, 53-55, 138
ocial class identity, 47-48, 53-54
ocial comparison, 32, 34-35, 38, 77, 79
ocial comparisons, 27, 31, 34, 36-37, 54
ocial distance, 131, 142, 144
ocial identity, 29-30, 47, 54, 56, 58, 116, 198
ocial movement, 30
ocial networking, 91, 206, 208, 211, 214, 216, 218, 220-221, 223, 233-238
ocial networking sites, 91, 208, 211, 214, 216, 218, 221, 223, 233-235
ocial presence, 209-211, 230, 233-234
ocial roles, 63, 79-80, 82
ocial support, 183
ocial-polite touch, 133, 142, 144
ociology, 85, 103, 235, 237
ocrates, 2
ource, 3, 11, 21, 33, 35, 41, 45, 49, 52, 58, 96, 111, 115, 124, 132, 147, 153, 155, 161-162, 171, 177-178, 182, 194, 211, 223
ources, 18, 40, 42, 64, 73, 95, 107, 116, 155-156, 160-161, 176, 197, 207, 212, 232
pace, 39, 55, 116, 126, 129-132, 135, 142-144, 146, 155, 157, 199, 217, 233
    personal, 131-132, 142, 144, 146, 155, 157, 217
    power and, 131
    proxemics, 129-130, 135, 142, 144
    territoriality, 129, 131-132, 144
peaker, 18, 20, 94, 97, 99, 104, 112-113, 115-116, 129, 135, 156-157, 159-165, 167-168
peakers, 3, 7, 9, 18, 20-21, 80, 92-95, 97-98, 102-105, 112-113, 121, 128-129, 137, 157, 168
peaking, 5-6, 11, 13, 34, 44, 56, 92, 97-98, 101-103, 107-108, 110, 117-118, 126, 135, 140, 151-152, 155-157, 159-161, 167, 169, 180, 185-186, 188, 211, 227, 231
peech, 21, 24, 47, 81, 85, 90, 95-97, 100-101, 103, 105-107, 109-110, 113-117, 126, 129, 140, 144-145, 156-158, 160, 163, 170, 199, 215
    culture and, 117
    hate, 90, 109-110, 113-116
    paralinguistic aspects of, 129
    racist, 140, 215
    sexist, 81, 140
peech act, 95-96, 113, 115, 117
peech act theory, 95, 113, 115
peeches, 75
    persuasive, 75
pelling, 231

Spitzberg, B., 24, 85
Stalking, 212
Star, 31, 58, 201
statements, 16, 99, 112-113, 215, 222
Statistics, 41, 45, 56, 161, 170-172, 202, 225, 231, 235-236
    use of, 161, 225, 231, 235-236
    using, 161, 170, 231
Status, 9, 29, 32, 36, 47, 51, 53, 55, 84, 96, 99-100, 106, 133-135, 137-138, 145-146, 163-164, 180, 193, 209-210, 219-221, 226-227, 231
Stereotype, 36, 49, 53-57, 68, 77-78, 80, 99, 107, 109, 190, 196, 224
Stereotypes, 14, 36, 53, 57, 68, 77-78, 80, 82, 84-86, 99, 106-108, 116, 118, 139, 158, 164, 185, 196, 200-202, 218, 223-224
Stereotyping, 68, 78, 82, 84, 109, 116, 186, 190, 196-197, 215
Stimuli, 9
Stories, 57, 76, 93, 153, 170, 177, 207
Stress, 30, 103, 128-129, 144, 157, 160, 170, 181, 183, 190, 198, 201, 221
Strodtbeck, Fred, 186
Style, 13, 38, 68, 75, 98-100, 102-104, 106, 109, 128, 132-134, 137, 139, 155-159, 166, 169-171, 194-196, 201, 223
    defined, 75, 134, 169
    language and, 104, 109
    level of, 104
Substituting, 135
Summarizing, 156
Superiority, 38
Support, 3-4, 50, 85, 106, 116, 125, 138, 170, 183, 200-201, 213
Surprise, 127, 212
Surveillance, 111, 207, 212, 221
Surveys, 184, 186, 231
Symbol, 6-7, 22-24
Symbolic communication, 24
Symbolic interactionism, 31, 55
Symbols, 7-8, 10, 65, 67, 92, 124-125, 132, 144
Sympathy, 182
Symposium, 84
Synchronous communication, 209-210, 234
Synesthesia, 72-73, 84, 87
Syntax, 94-95, 102-104, 113, 115
System, 7, 17, 46, 50, 55, 84, 97, 110, 115, 126, 137, 145, 182, 188, 208, 234

T
tables, 106
Taboo, 79
Taboos, 144
Tannen, Deborah, 165
Tattoos, 39, 57-58, 138, 146
Team, 30, 38, 43, 98, 109, 138, 178, 188, 196, 219
Technical language, 10
Technology, 9, 28, 50, 72, 91, 111, 130, 204-206, 209, 212, 216, 222-228, 234-239
    communication and, 28, 91, 111, 209, 235-236, 238-239
    nonverbal, 91, 130, 209
    organizational, 28, 236
Telephone, 9, 128, 143, 209-210, 228, 231
Television, 2, 9, 15, 21, 29, 33-34, 39-40, 42, 46, 98, 122, 134, 143, 160, 184, 194, 205, 208, 236
Temperature, 8, 65
Tension, 15, 28, 47, 50, 126, 144, 175
Territorial behavior, 131
Territoriality, 129, 131-132, 144
Territory, 35-36, 132, 144
Test, 21, 35-37, 42, 57-58, 64, 66, 72, 81, 85, 91, 110, 141, 162
Testimony, 31
Text messaging, 2, 9, 22, 175, 205, 207-211, 218, 220, 233, 237
Texting, 9, 91, 101, 157, 210, 212, 220, 231-232
Thesis, 57
Thought, 5-7, 12, 29, 38, 42, 46, 63, 81, 85-86, 92, 105-107, 111, 116, 121, 132, 153, 160, 164, 180, 182, 190
Time, 2, 5, 7-8, 10-11, 14, 17, 19-20, 22-23, 30, 32-34, 36-37, 40-42, 52, 55, 58, 62, 64-65, 69, 74-76, 78-80, 83, 92-93, 96-97, 100-103, 107, 109, 112, 114-116, 121, 125-126, 128-130, 134-135, 142-144, 146, 151-154, 157-158, 160, 162-163, 165, 167, 169-171, 176-177, 180-183, 185, 187-188, 191, 193-194, 196, 198, 200, 202, 206, 209,

213-214, 217-218, 220-221, 224, 232-234, 236
Time of day, 8
Time-oriented listener, 167
Topic, 10, 18, 22, 48, 73-74, 91, 108, 138-139, 158-159, 166, 205, 208, 211-212, 224, 233, 237
    choosing, 10, 166
Topics, 1, 4, 27, 31, 62, 73-74, 79, 90, 97, 100, 102, 119, 124, 150, 156, 174, 204, 224
Touch, 52, 63, 65, 73, 85, 91, 132-134, 136, 141-145, 205, 212, 233
    social-polite, 133, 142, 144
Transaction, 11
Transitions, 25, 40
Trevino, L. K., 24
Trolling, 215, 230
Trust, 17, 24, 71, 76, 220, 222
Truthfulness, 17-18, 22
Turn-allocation system, 97
Twitter, 2, 9, 91, 151, 155, 206-208, 213-215, 224, 226-227, 229-230, 232-233, 235-237, 239

U
Uncertainty, 222
Understanding, 2-3, 6, 8, 12, 15, 20, 22, 24, 28-29, 31, 34, 36, 40, 46, 49, 54-55, 59, 61-87, 93, 95-97, 101, 107-108, 114, 117, 121, 129, 145-146, 153-154, 156-157, 169-171, 176, 179-180, 186, 196-199, 201, 204-205, 207-209, 233, 235
    barriers to, 154, 170
    listening and, 153-154, 156-157, 169-171
Unethical communication, 5, 16, 51, 229
United States, 6-7, 13, 15-16, 28-32, 41, 43-44, 46-49, 51, 63, 75-79, 81, 86, 98, 101-102, 105, 107-108, 110, 114, 124-125, 127-131, 133-135, 137, 139, 143-144, 159-161, 175-177, 179, 181-184, 186-195, 199-201, 207, 225-226
    dialects, 98, 101-102
    social classes in, 47
Usage access, 228

V
Validity, 42, 171
Value-expressive function, 79, 82, 84
Values, 8-9, 13-14, 17, 20, 23-24, 28-29, 34, 48, 50-51, 65, 76-77, 79, 84, 92, 106, 153, 174-175, 180-183, 185-186, 190, 193-199, 201, 208, 227, 234
Variety, 2-3, 5-6, 10, 17, 20, 44, 47, 64-65, 71-72, 79-80, 93, 103, 112, 121, 123-124, 127, 129, 135, 151, 156, 158, 161, 169, 208, 220, 223, 228
Verbal communication, 89-118, 125, 133
    components of language, 90-94, 113
    Malaysians, 97
    role of language, 93
Verbal messages, 113, 126, 135, 141-144
Verbs, 94
Video, 41, 99, 128, 177, 207, 209, 213, 216, 221, 224, 226-227, 238
videos, 122, 155, 206, 211, 214
View of human nature, 188, 197-198
Violation, 37, 39, 130, 132, 221, 229-230
Violence, 40, 57, 71, 110, 132, 175, 179, 183, 201, 217
Vocal behavior, 128
Vocal cues, 129, 163-164
Vocal qualities, 128, 142-143
Vocal variety, 44
Vocalizations, 128-129, 142, 144, 159
Voice, 75, 100, 103-104, 115, 121, 124, 128-129, 142, 144, 151, 163-165, 209-210, 216, 231
    volume of, 129
Voice qualities, 121, 128, 142, 144
Volume, 104, 128-129, 136, 144, 160
Voluntary long-term travelers, 181, 197-198
Voluntary short-term travelers, 181, 197-198
Voting rights, 193

W
Watzlawick, P., 25
Websites, 111
Wikipedia, 211
Willingness to communicate, 86
Withdrawing, 112

Withholding information, 17-18, 22
Wolvin, A., 171
Women, 3, 9, 14, 30-31, 35, 43-45, 48, 51-52, 54-55,
        57-58, 64, 66-68, 71, 73, 79-80, 85, 87, 92,
        98-100, 106, 109, 114-118, 124-125,
        127-128, 131-134, 139, 145-147, 158, 161,
        165, 185, 194, 199, 201-202, 219, 223, 230
    patterns of touch, 133
Word choice, 7, 100, 102, 114
Words, 7, 9-10, 38, 43-44, 47, 63, 65, 67, 73, 77, 82,
        84, 87, 91-92, 94-101, 104-106, 108,
        113-116, 120, 122, 124, 128-130, 140, 142,
        144-145, 154, 156-157, 159-160, 162-163,
        166, 185, 200, 209-210, 218, 230
    and culture, 10, 96, 101, 104
    and relationships, 38, 129
    characteristics of, 100, 114, 185, 230
    connotative meaning of, 95
    function of, 144-145
    power of, 105, 113
Workplace, 28, 51, 98-99, 116, 136, 141, 152, 165,
        170, 193, 200, 207, 217, 221-222
    relationships in, 217, 221
World Wide Web, 208

Y
Yahoo!, 201
YouTube, 41, 208, 211, 215, 226